W0106585

Virtual Environments '95

Selected papers of the Eurographics Workshops
in Barcelona, Spain, 1993,
and Monte Carlo, Monaco, 1995

M. Göbel (ed.)

SpringerWienNewYork

Dr. Martin Göbel
Fraunhofer-Institut für Graphische Datenverarbeitung
Darmstadt, Federal Republic of Germany

Typesetting: Camera ready by authors

Graphic design: Ecke Bonk

Printed on acid-free and chlorine-free bleached paper

With 134 partly coloured Figures

ISSN 0946-2767
ISBN-13:978-3-211-82737-6   e-ISBN-13:978-3-7091-9433-1
DOI: 10.1007/978-3-7091-9433-1

Preface

Virtual Environments - (VE) the new dimension in man-machine-communication - have been developed and experienced in Europe since 1990. In early 1993 the Eurographics Association decided to establish a working group on Virtual Environments with the aim to communicate advances in this fascinating area on a scientific and technical level. In September 1993 the first workshop on VEs was held in Barcelona, Spain, in conjunction with the annual Eurographics conference. The workshop brought together about 35 researchers from Europe and the US. The second workshop was held together with Imagina '95 in Monte Carlo, Monaco. This time, around 40 researchers from Europe, the US, but also from Asia met for a 2-day exchange of experience.

Needless to say - as in all Eurographics workshops - we found the atmosphere very open and refreshing.

The workshops were sponsored by ONR (Office of Naval Research), UK; US Army Research Institute, UK; University of Catalonia, Spain; EDF France; CAE France, INA France and IGD Germany and locally organized by Daniele Tost and Jaques David.

While in the first workshop in 1993 many concepts in VE were presented, the '95 workshop showed up various applications in different areas and demonstrated quite clearly that Virtual Environments are now used in interactive applications.

This book contains 22 reviewed papers that have been presented in Barcelona and Monte Carlo and revised for this book. The areas which are discussed in the papers cover visual presentation aspects, gesture but also speech interaction issues, applications and VR systems. The papers demonstrate very clearly the emphasis and the results of various research activities in VE. Basic research and applied industrial experiments, both can be found today within the same VE project.

Martin Göbel
Darmstadt, July 1995

Contents

Is VR Better than a Workstation?

A Report on Human Performance Experiments in Progress

David Mizell
Stephen Jones
Research & Technology Organization
Boeing Information and Support Services

Paul Jackson
Texas A&M University

Dasal Pickett
Morris Brown College

Abstract. This paper is a preliminary report on a set of experiments designed to compare an immersive, head-tracked VR system to a typical graphics workstation display screen, with respect to whether VR makes it easier for a user to comprehend complex, 3-D objects. Experimental subjects were asked to build a physical replica of a three-dimensional "wire sculpture" which they viewed either physically, on a workstation screen, or in a stereoscopic "boom" VR display. Preliminary results show less speed but slightly fewer errors with the VR display. The slower speed is probably explainable by the overhead involved in moving to and grasping the boom display.

1.0 Introduction

The overall goal of the virtual reality research project at Boeing Information and Support Services is to enable a capability to visualize and interact with 3-D aircraft CAD geometry in an immersive virtual environment. Accordingly, for the past three years we have been focused on algorithmic issues such as rendering complex CAD geometry at VR speeds, and computing collisions in real time to enable more realistic interactions between users and virtual objects.

This is not to say that we believe that every aircraft engineer needs to have a VR system in his/her office. If an aircraft hydraulics engineer has to design a single 2-ft. section of hydraulic tubing, then a CAD workstation is perfectly adequate. She/he can enter and modify the tube design, view it from any angle, and so on. If, however, the designer wants to view this tube in its installed location among the complex tangle of hydraulics and other systems inside the main landing gear wheel well, the view on the workstation screen intuitively does not seem to be as useful as a view of the same geometry within a virtual environment.

Perhaps the ultimate payoff for VR is in the potential for interaction. Our hydraulics engineer could conceivably move tubes around and change their shape, all in first person, accomplishing a design task with much more speed and understanding of the consequences of each design decision than on a workstation. We hypothesized, however, that even if we limited ourselves to visualization, without any sort of manipulation capability, that VR still might outperform a workstation. The basic notion is that, because of the way the brain correlates information from the visual system and the proprioceptive sense, plus motion parallax, plus the advantage of stereo vision, that VR might give a user a more accurate understanding of complex assemblages of 3-D geometry than a workstation view.

We had the following sort of anecdotal evidence: a Boeing engineer assigned to the Space Station project, who had been thoroughly involved in the CAD design of space station components, when viewing the CAD geometry of the Lab Module in our VR system for the first time, exclaimed "Wow! It's so big!" He had looked at the same geometry on his workstation for more than a year, but it had always looked small on his screen. Then he was suddenly placed in a position that appeared to him as if he were a few feet from the entrance to the lab module, and he discovered that he had to bend his neck from very high to very low to look from the top of the design to the bottom.

Thus it seemed to us that it would be worthwhile to try to experimentally assess and quantify, if possible, a difference in a user's being able to comprehend a complex three-dimensional scene between viewing it in 2-D on a workstation screen and viewing the scene via an immersive VR system, with a stereoscopic display, a fairly wide field of view, and a head tracking system.

2. Previous Work

Most of the human performance experiments in VR have focused on measuring the effectiveness or degree of presence imparted by a virtual environment [3, 6, 8, 10, 11], or comparing the relative effectiveness of different picking and placing metaphors used within the same virtual environment [2, 12]. Only a few have tried to compare VR with a more "conventional" computer graphics system [1, 7]. This is probably because throughout most of the brief history of VR research, the perception was fairly universal that there was no point in trying to experimentally compare VR systems to graphics workstations. The VR hardware simply wasn't good enough to meaningfully be compared. The displays were abysmally low-resolution, the gloves too inaccurate, the head trackers too slow or noise-sensitive, and the rendering performance was inadequate for any but cartoon-like virtual worlds. Whatever the intrinsic merits of the technology might be, a 1990-vintage VR system would have lost every time in a head-to-head competition with a 1280x1024-pixel color graphics workstation screen.

The vendors have steadily been improving the quality of VR hardware and software, however. We can now get color HMDs with 640x480 resolution, there is a new generation of faster head trackers, we can obtain ever-faster graphics rendering hardware, and so on. By now, it is reasonable to consider comparing VR to other visualization technologies. The experiments reported here were inspired by this perception about improving VR hardware and by the experimental work done by Randy Pausch and his colleagues at the University of Virginia, in which they compared head-coupled to non-head-coupled searching of a virtual space [7].

3. The Experiment Design

We debated many different approaches to experiments that might shed light on this hypothesis. Some placed the user inside a virtual space with virtual objects possibly on all sides around the user. Others showed the user a set of objects of relatively small size, all viewable by the user at once. We referred to these two paradigms as "inside the box" versus "outside the box." Ware and Osborne made a similar distinction in [11], using the terms "eyeball in hand" versus "scene in hand." We settled on an "outside the box" experiment, not because we believed that this class of application were likely to yield the highest leverage for VR (most of us believed the opposite), but because we considered it the simplest experiment for us to get started with.

We created some three-dimensional puzzles. The base of each puzzle was a sheet of pegboard, 18 inches by 16 inches. We obtained some aluminum rods of .25 in. diameter, which fitted snugly into the holes in the pegboard. We bent the rods into a variety of shapes and painted them different colors. Selecting from four to eight of the rods, we would insert them into a pegboard, creating a sort of three-dimensional "wire sculpture." We bent and painted pairs of the rods identically, so that we could construct two instances of each puzzle we designed. Using the CAD package MultiGen, we also created 3-D solid models of each of the puzzles we designed.

The task each of our volunteer experimental subjects were given was to build a duplicate copy of a puzzle. He or she would be given an empty pegboard base and a randomly-arranged set of bent rods. This set would include all the rods needed to build a replica of the puzzle in question and a few extra ones. The key variable in the experiment was the way the subject would be shown what the completed sculpture, which they were to duplicate, looked like. They would either be shown (1) an actual physical pegboard with the rods inserted in the correct positions, (2) a CAD model of the completed puzzle on a workstation screen, or (3) a CAD model of the completed puzzle, viewed in a stereo VR display: a Fakespace boom. In each case, the representation of the solved puzzle was placed close to the table where the subject was constructing the duplicate, so he/she could refer to the solution as often has he/she wished, from whatever point of view he/she wished. In order to minimize the influence of user interface issues, the workstation was equipped with a Polhemus tracker mounted on a small wooden plaque. If the subject moved or rotated the wooden plaque, the view of the completed puzzle on the workstation screen would move or rotate correspondingly. Using the completed physical puzzle as a reference for constructing a duplicate was our experimental control. We wanted to compare the performance difference between the workstation and the VR references.

We (subjectively) selected four levels of difficulty among the puzzles. Each subject would go through a coached training session with the simplest puzzle, and then undergo four timed and scored trials. We devised a scoring system for grading the accuracy of the replication of the puzzle. It was based on whether the subject used the correct rod, whether the rod was in the correct hole in the pegboard, and how near the rod was to the correct rotational orientation.

We ran some "calibration" experiments which indicated that if we used about 15 subjects per interface there would be a 90% chance of detecting if two interfaces differed by 40% in time to complete a puzzle. We enrolled subjects by putting an announcement in a Boeing Computer Services internal information bulletin. Volunteers were selected on a first-come basis and randomly assigned to an interface in a manner that balanced for gender, so that there were 12 man and 9 women assigned to each of the interfaces.

The ideal way to structure this experiment would have been to have several puzzles somehow known to be of the same difficulty to replicate, and then have each subject use each interface, thereby mitigating the problem of inherent differences in each subject's abilities to work with 3-D geometry. This wasn't practically feasible, however, so instead we had each subject complete each of the three puzzles with only one of the display interfaces.

We used what is called a cross-over design of the experiment [4, 5, 9] by structuring the test so that each subject completed each of the three puzzles in some order. Each subject was randomly assigned to one of the six permutations of the orderings of the puzzles by difficulty. In a fourth trial, each subject repeated the first puzzle. This was done in order to be able to factor out the amount of learning that took place during the test.

4. Results

The values for mean completion times, adjusted for gender and learning effects, are given in Table 1. The boom is faster on average than the workstation screen for the simplest puzzle tested, but slower for the other two, although none of the differences in completion times between boom and workstation were statistically significant. It isn't hard to guess why the boom had slower times. With the physical model or with the workstation, a subject could quickly glance back and forth between the completed puzzle and his/her duplicate. There was no quick glancing with the boom. The subject had to move a greater distance, grasp the boom handles and place his/her face against the display. This may explain why the boom was faster than the workstation screen only in the case of the simplest puzzle. It may be that this puzzle was easy enough to comprehend that the subjects only had to look back at it a few times, and the enhanced comprehension afforded by the VR interface was not dominated by the inefficiencies in looking back and forth. This aspect of the experiment made us wish we had a "hybrid" HMD that could switch under software control between occlusive and transparent. That way, when a subject looked toward the virtual representation of the completed puzzle, the display would show the graphical object, but when the subject looked back at his/her physical replica, the display would turn transparent. Such a display would make glancing back and forth between the solution and the replica as easy as in the physical case.

Complexity	Physical	Workstation	Boom
Easy	47.3	141.9	130.2
Medium	90.4	280.3	330.3
Difficult	179.8	425.1	482.4

Table 1. Mean completion times in seconds

Table 2 shows the average error scores (larger number means more errors) for each of the three interfaces. The boom shows fewer errors than the workstation screen, but a standard analysis of variance (ANOVA) on the scored data indicates that only the difference between the physical model scores and the workstation scores is statistically significant.

Physical	Workstation	Boom
.36	.67	.53

Table 2. Mean error scores

5. Future Work

This is definitely "work in progress." Our results are inconclusive. We still believe, however, that some variant of this approach is capable of yielding solid results. There are many more experiments of this sort we could do. We plan to repeat these experiments as described above later this year, using a hybrid see-through/occlusive HMD being prototyped for us by Virtual IO, Inc. Next, we want to look at experiments using virtual environments that surround the subject, i.e., those which put the user "inside the box." Intuition says that the workstation would be at a considerable disadvantage in that case.

There are many open issues with respect to experimentally comparing VR with other human-computer interfaces:

• Are we testing the right hypotheses, with the right experiments?

6

- How do we factor out accidental influences, such as unfamiliar or intimidating user interfaces? Some subjects were very uncomfortable using the boom, for example.
- How should we train subjects with the tools prior to an experiment?
- How should we measure and adjust for differences in experience with 3-D visualization? Some of our subjects had no such experience; others had years of professional experience using 3-D CAD systems.

Of these, the most critical is the design of meaningful experiments. There is room for many more players in this game.

6. References

1. Chung, J. "A Comparison of Head-tracked and Non-head-tracked Steering Modes in Targeting of Radiotherapy Treatment Beams." In *Proceedings, 1992 Symposium on Interactive 3D Graphics*, April 1992, pp. 193-196.

2. Arthur, K., Booth, K., Ware, C. "Evaluating 3D Task Performance for Fish Tank Virtual Worlds." *ACM Transactions on Information Systems* Vol. 11 no. 3, July 1993, pp. 239-265.

3. Henry, D., Furness, T. "Spatial Perception in Virtual Environments: Evaluating an Architectural Application." *Proceedings, IEEE Virtual Reality Annual International Symposium*, September 1993, pp. 33-40.

4. Johnson, N., Kotz, S. *Encyclopedia of Statistical Sciences*, Wiley, New York, 1989.

5. Jones, B., Kenward, M.G. *Design and Analysis of Cross-Over Trials*, Chapman and Hall, New York, 1989.

6. Mowafy, L., Russo, T., Miller, L. "Is Presence a Training Issue?" *Proceedings, IEEE Symposium on Research Frontiers in Virtual Reality*, 1993, pp. 124-125.

7. Pausch, R., Schelford, M., Proffitt, D.A. "A User Study Comparing Head-Mounted and Stationary Displays." *IEEE Symposium on Research Frontiers in Virtual Reality*, 1993, pp. 41-45.

8. Piantanida, T., Boman, D., Gille, J. "Human Perceptual Issues and Virtual Reality." *Virtual Reality Systems*, Vol. 1, no. 1, March 1993.

9. Ratkowsky, D.A., Evans, M.A., Alldredge, J.R. *Cross-Over Experiments*, Marcel Dekker, 1993.

10. Slater, M., Usoh, M. "Presence in Immersive Virtual Environments." *Proceedings, IEEE Virtual Reality Annual International Symposium*, September

1993, pp. 90-96.

11. Ware, C., Osborne, S. "Exploration and Virtual Camera Control in Virtual Three Dimensional Environments." *Computer Graphics* Vol. 24 no. 2, March 1990, pp. 175-183.

12. Zahi, S., Milgram, P. "Human Performance Evaluation of Manipulation Schemes in Virtual Environments." *Proceedings, IEEE Virtual Reality Annual International Symposium*, September 1993, pp. 155-161.

The Influence of Dynamic Shadows on Presence in Immersive Virtual Environments

Mel Slater, Martin Usoh, Yiorgos Chrysanthou[1],
Department of Computer Science, and
London Parallel Applications Centre,
QMW University of London,
Mile End Road,
London E1 4NS, UK.

Abstract. This paper describes an experiment where the effect of dynamic shadows in an immersive virtual environment is measured with respect to spatial perception and presence. Eight subjects were given tasks to do in a virtual environment. Each subject carried out five experimental trials, and the extent of dynamic shadow phenomena varied between the trials. Two measurements of presence were used - a subjective one based on a questionnaire, and a more objective behavioural measure. The experiment was inconclusive with respect to the effect of shadows on depth perception. However, the experiment suggests that for visually dominant subjects, the greater the extent of shadow phenomena in the virtual environment, the greater the sense of presence.

Keywords. Virtual environment, virtual reality, presence, shadows, depth perception.

1. Introduction

We describe an experiment to examine the effect of shadows on two different aspects of the experience of immersion in a virtual environment (VE): depth perception and presence. It is well-known that shadows can significantly enhance depth perception in everyday reality [1,5,7]. Shadows provide alternative views of objects, and provide direct information about their spatial relationships with surrounding surfaces. VR systems typically do not support shadows, and yet potential applications, especially in the training sphere, will require participants to make judgements about such relationships. Even the simple task of moving to an object and picking it up can be problematic when observers cannot easily determine their own distance from the object, or its distance from surrounding objects. We introduce dynamic shadows to examine whether such task performance can be enhanced.

We have argued elsewhere [8] that presence is the key to the science of immersive virtual environments (virtual reality). We distinguish, however, between immersion and presence. Immersion includes the extent to which the computer displays are

---

[1] emails: mel, bigfoot, yiorgos @ dcs.qmw.ac.uk. URL: http://www.dcs.qmw.ac.uk/

extensive, surrounding, inclusive, vivid and matching. The displays are more extensive the more sensory systems that they accommodate. They are surrounding to the extent that information can arrive at the person's sense organs from any (virtual) direction. They are inclusive to the extent that all external sensory data (from physical reality) is shut out. Their vividness is a function of the variety and richness of the sensory information they can generate [11]. In the context of visual displays, for example, colour displays are more vivid than monochrome, and displays depicting shadows are more vivid than those that do not. Vividness is concerned with the richness, information content, resolution and quality of the displays. Finally, immersion requires that there is match between the participant's proprioceptive feedback about body movements, and the information generated on the displays. A turn of the head should result in a corresponding change to the visual display, and, for example, to the auditory displays so that sound direction is invariant to the orientation of the head. Matching requires body tracking, at least head tracking, but generally the greater the degree of body mapping, the greater the extent to which the movements of the body can be accurately reproduced.

Immersion also requires a self-representation in the VE - a Virtual Body (VB). The VB is both part of the perceived environment, and represents the being that is doing the perceiving. Perception in the VE is centred on the position in virtual space of the VB - e.g., visual perception from the viewpoint of the eyes in the head of the VB.

Immersion is an objective description of what any particular system does provide. Presence is a state of consciousness, the (psychological) sense of being in the virtual environment. Participants who are highly present should experience the VE as more the engaging reality than the surrounding world, and consider the environment specified by the displays as places visited rather than as images seen. Behaviours in the VE should be consistent with behaviours that would have occurred in everyday reality in similar circumstances.

Presence requires that the participant identify with the VB - that its movements are his/her movements, and that the VB comes to "be" the body of that person in the VE. We speculate that the additional information provided by shadows about the movements of the VB in relationship to the surfaces of the VE can enhance this degree of association, and hence the degree of presence. However, we were unable to test this in the current experiment. We do, however, consider the proposition that shadows, increasing the degree of vividness of the visual displays, will enhance the sense of presence.

2. Experiment

2.1 Scenario

The experimental scenario consisted of a virtual room, the elevation of which is shown in Figure 1. Five red spears are near a wall, but behind a small screen. Another green spear is at position G. The subject begins the experiment by moving to the red square (X), and facing the spears. The instruction is to choose the spear nearest the wall, observing from position X. Having chosen that spear, the subject moves towards it, picks it up and returns to X. There the subject turns to the left, facing a target on the far wall. The subject must orient the spear to point approximately towards the target, fire and guide it towards the target by hand movements. The instructions were that the spear must be shot at the target, and that it must be stopped the instant that its point hit the target. Finally, the subject must bring the green spear to position X. This was repeated six times for each subject.

Prior to the start of the experiment each subject was given a sheet explaining these procedures, and the first run was for practice, the experimenter talking the subject through the entire scenario. Runs 1 through 5 were carried out by the subject without intervention by the experimenter. Between each run the subject was advised to relax with closed eyes, either with or without the head-mounted display (HMD, see below), although all but one continued to wear it during the two minutes that it took to load the program for the subsequent run. Each of the five runs were the same apart from the distances of the red spears from the wall. Also, some runs displayed dynamic shadows of the spears and the small screen, while others did not.

Eight subjects were selected by the experimenters asking people throughout the QMW campus (in canteens, bars, laboratories, offices) whether they wished to take part in a study of "virtual reality". People from our own Department were not included.

Table 1
Runs of the Experiment for Each Subject
1,2,3,4 denotes the four point-light positions of Figure 1
0 denotes no shadows

Subject	No. shadow scenes / 5	Run 1	Run 2	Run 3	Run 4	Run 5
1	1	0	0	2	0	0
2	1	0	0	2	0	0
3	2	0	0	2	3	0
4	2	0	0	2	3	0
5	3	0	1	2	3	0
6	3	0	1	2	3	0
7	4	0	1	2	3	4
8	4	0	1	2	3	4

The design is shown in Table 1, which indicates the positions of the point-light source for those runs that included shadows. Note that of the 40 runs, 20 included shadows.

2.2 Spatial Variables and Hypotheses

The variables measured in order to assess the effects of shadows on spatial judgement were as follows:

Spear Selected. S: the spear selected from observation position X. The spears ranged from 50 cm to 90 cm from the wall, positioned with 10 cm variations. The small screen in front of the spears obscured the positions where they touched the floor, for any subject standing at position X. Also, because their distances from the wall varied only slightly, their heights, as judged from position X would look the same. It was therefore very difficult to judge which spear was nearest the wall. Variable S was the rank order of the spear chosen, where 1 would be the nearest to the wall, and 5 the furthest.

The hypothesis was that subjects would be able to use the shadows of spears on the walls to aid their judgement about the closeness to the walls, so that those runs that included shadows would result in a greater number of correct spears being chosen.

Distances from Target. C: this is the distance of the point of the spear from the centre of the target at the position that it was stopped in flight by the subject.

The hypothesis was that the subjects would be able to use the shadow of the spear in flight, especially its shadow on the target wall, to help guide the spear towards the target. Therefore, the mean distance should be less for the shadow runs than for the non-shadow runs.

D: this is the distance that the point of the spear was behind or in front of the target at the position that it was stopped by the subject.

The hypothesis is as for C, except that here we would expect a greater shadow effect since the action required to stop the spear in flight (releasing a button on the hand-held 3D mouse) is simpler than that involved in guiding the spear to the bulls eye. Moreover, at the moment the spear point touched the target wall, it would also meet its shadow.

2.3 Presence Variables and Hypotheses

In previous studies we have used subjective reported levels of "presence" based on a questionnaire. In this method subjective presence was assessed in three ways: the sense of "being there" in the VE, the extent to which there were times that the virtual world seemed more the presenting reality than the real world, and the sense of visiting somewhere rather than just seeing images. In the present study these three basic determinants were elaborated into six questions, each measured on a 7-point scale, where lowest presence is 1, and highest is 7 (see Appendix A). The overall presence score (P) was conservatively taken as the number of high (6 or 7) ratings amongst the six questions, so that $0 \leq P \leq 6$.

Although we have obtained good results with such subjective measures before, in the shadow experiment we introduced in addition a more "objective" measurement of presence. This was achieved by having one particular object (a radio) in both the real world of the laboratory in which the experiment took place and the virtual world of the room with spears.

Just before the practice run the subjects were shown a radio on the floor against a large screen in the laboratory. They were told that they would see "the radio" in the virtual world, and that occasionally it would switch itself on. Whenever they heard the sound they should point towards "the radio", and press a button on the hand-held mouse. This would act as an "infra-red" device to switch the radio off. Before they entered into the VE the radio was momentarily switched on, deliberately not tuned to any particular channel therefore causing it to play an audible but meaningless tone. Each time that the subject entered into the VE, i.e., at the start of each run they were told: "Orient yourself by looking for the red square on the floor and the radio". The radio was placed in the VE at the same position relative to the red square as the real radio was to the position of the subject just before entering the VE.

At four moments during the experiment, always while the subject was (virtually) on the red square, the real radio was moved to one of four different positions. These were 1m apart from each other, on a line coincident (in the real world) with the small screen by which the radio was located (in the virtual world). The ordering was selected randomly before the start of the experiment. The virtual radio was always in the same place. Therefore the subject would hear the sound coming from a different location compared to the visible position of the radio. The idea is that (other things being equal), a high degree of presence would lead to the subject pointing towards the virtual radio rather than the real one. Hence we tried to cause and use the conflict between virtual and real information as an assessment of presence. Those (two) subjects who did ask about the contradiction were told "Just point at where you think the radio is". Throughout, both the real radio and the virtual radio were referred to as "the radio", deliberately allowing for a confusion in the minds of the subjects.

It is important to note that we mean "presence" in a strong behavioural sense with respect to this measurement. The questionnaire attempts to elicit the subject's state of mind. The radio method though is concerned only with their behaviour. If they pointed to the virtual radio because of a need to obey the experimenter, or because it was a matter of "playing the game", then so be it. Provided that they act in accordance with the conditions of the VE, this is behavioural presence.

Let R be the angle between the subject's real pointing direction and the direction to the real radio. Let V be the angle between the subject's virtual pointing direction and the direction to the virtual radio. Small V therefore occurs when the subject points towards the virtual radio. We use $P_a = R/V$ as the measurement of the extent to which the subject tends towards the virtual radio - a small V in comparison to R would result in large P_a. Therefore larger values of P_a indicate greater tendency towards the virtual.

There were two hypotheses relating to P_a: First, that it would correlate positively with P, and second that the greater exposure of the subject to shadows, the greater the value of P_a. Of course, we would also expect that the greater the exposure to shadows, the greater the value of P.

2.4 Representation System Dominance

A clear objection to this procedure is that it could be measuring the extent of visual or auditory dominance rather than presence. Faced with conflicting information from two senses, the resulting action is likely to depend on which sensory system is "dominant". In previous work [9,10] we have explored the relationship between dominant representation systems and the extent of subjective presence, and have always found a very strong relationship. This is based on the idea that people differ in the extent to which they require visual, auditory or kinesthetic/tactile information in order to construct their world models, and that each person may have a general tendency to prefer one type of representation (say visual) over another (say auditory). We found that in experiments where the virtual reality system presented almost exclusively visual information, the greater the degree of visual dominance the higher the sense of presence, whereas the greater degree of auditory dominance, the lower the sense of presence.

In this shadow experiment therefore we employed an updated version of the questionnaire we used in [10] which is given to the subjects before attending the experimental session. This questionnaire attempts to elicit their preferences regarding visual, auditory and kinesthetic modes of thinking. It presents 10 situations, each one having three responses (one visual, one auditory, and one kinesthetic response). Subjects are asked to rank their most likely response as 1, next most likely as 2, and least likely as 3. From this a V score is constructed as the total number of V=1 scores out of 10, and similarly for A and K. Alternatively the sums of the responses may be used. These V and A variables can therefore be used to statistically factor out the possible influence of visual or auditory dominance on the radio angles.

The hypothesis with respect to V, A and K would be that V and K would be positively correlated with presence (however it is measured) whereas A would be negatively correlated, in line with our previous findings. Note that by construction, there are only 2 degrees of freedom amongst V, A and K.

3. Apparatus

3.1 Equipment

The experiments described in this paper were implemented on a DIVISION ProVision system, a parallel architecture for implementing virtual environments running under the dVS (v0.3) operating environment. The ProVision system is based on a distributed memory architecture in which a number of autonomous processing modules are dedicated to a part of the virtual environment simulation. These processing modules or Transputer Modules (TRAMs) are small self-contained parallel processing building blocks complete with their own local memory and contain at least one Inmos Transputer which may control other specialised peripheral hardware such as digital to analog converters (DAC). Several modules exist. These include:

- the module to act as the module manager.
- the DAC module for audio output.
- polygon modules for z-buffering and Gouraud shading.
- application specific modules for the user applications.

The dVS operating environment (Grimsdale, 1991) is based on distributed Client/Server principles. Each TRAM or processing cluster is controlled by an independent parallel process known as an Actor. Each provides a set of services relating to the elements of the environment which it oversees. Such elements presently consist of lights, objects, cameras, controls (i.e. input devices), and collisions between objects. Thus, an Actor provides a service such as scene rendering (visualisation actor). Another Actor may be responsible for determining when objects have collided (collision actor) and yet another for hand tracking and input device scanning. All these Actors are co-ordinated by a special Actor called the Director. Communication between the different Actors can only be made via the Director. The Director also ensures consistency in the environment by maintaining elements of the environment which are shared by the different Actors.

The ProVision system includes a DIVISION 3D mouse, and a Virtual Research Flight Helmet as the head mounted display (HMD). Polhemus sensors are used for position tracking of the head and the mouse. The displays are colour LCDs with a 360×240 resolution and the HMD provides a horizontal field of view of about 75 degrees.

All subjects saw a VB as self representation. They would see a representation of their right hand, and their thumb and first finger activation of the 3D pointer buttons would be reflected in movements of their corresponding virtual finger and thumb. An example is shown in Plates 1 and 2. The hand was attached to an arm, that could be bent and twisted in response to similar movements of the real arm and wrist. The arm was connected to an entire but simple block-like body representation, complete with legs and left arm. Forward movement was accompanied by walking motions of the virtual legs. If the subjects turned their real head around by more than 60 degrees, then the virtual body would be reoriented accordingly. So for example, if they turned their real body around and then looked down at their virtual feet, their orientation would line up with their real body. However, turning only the head around by more than 60 degrees and looking down (an infrequent occurrence), would result in the real body being out of alignment with the virtual body.

The 3D mouse is shaped something like a gun. There is a button in the position of the hammer, which is depressed by the thumb. This causes forward motion in the direction of pointing. There is a button on each side of this central thumb button, each activated by the thumb. The left one was used to fire the spears - while this button was depressed the spear would move in a direction determined by hand orientation. The spear would stop on release of this button, and could not be activated again, thus giving the subject one chance per spear. The right thumb button was used as the "infra-red" radio switch. Corresponding to the trigger is a button for the forefinger.

This is used to pick objects - squeezing this finger button while the virtual hand intersects an object results in the object attaching to the hand. Subjects were able to master these controls very quickly.

3.2 Shadow Algorithm and Frame Rates

The shadow algorithm is described in detail elsewhere [3]. It is based on a dynamic Shadow Volume BSP tree [2], constructed from polygons in arbitrary order, that is without the necessity of a separate scene BSP tree. Shadows are created as polygons in object space. Creation of new shadows and changes to shadows are communicated dynamically to the renderer via the Director.

For reasons described below, the entire scene was small, consisting of 413 triangles, of which only 52 would be likely to influence shadow creation. The frame rate achieved without shadows was 9Hz. The frame rate with shadows, 6 to 8Hz, was not very satisfactory, but due to the particular version of the dVS software architecture in use on this machine at the time of the experiment.

Without rendering the shadow algorithm runs on this machine at a frequency of between 19 and 21Hz depending on the complexity of the view at any moment. The renderer does not however run at this frequency during dynamic changes of a virtual object, due to update problems associated with the extant implementation of the dVS dynamic geometry object. Therefore, when rendering and the associated communication time is included, the frame rate is 6 to 8Hz. (A new version of dVS is intended to solve this problem).

dVS v0.3 maintains the concept of a "dynamic geometry object". This is a vertex-face structure representing a (possibly empty) set of polygons. The actual polygons belonging to this object can be created or modified at run time. When such a change is made to a dynamic object, there is an "update" generated that sends the object to the Director for distribution to the Visualisation Actor and then onto to the renderer.

Upon any change of a virtual object the shadow algorithm recomputes the shadow scene outputting any modified shadow polygons, i.e. any polygons that have been deleted and any that have been created. This information is transmitted to the shadow generation module which will mark deleted polygons as invisible to be re-used later by new shadow polygons. The module uses a linked list structure of dynamic objects - the shadow object. Each element in the list is a dynamic object consisting of 32 shadow polygons. This linked list structure is necessary in order to break down the entire list of potential shadow polygons into smaller chunks, rather than have one dynamic geometry object for all possible shadows, since the dynamic geometry implementation can only send updates of an entire dynamic object to the Visualisation Actor. Note that a change in one single shadow polygon will result in the communication of a complete 32-polygon dynamic object. If, unfortunately, 33 shadow polygons change, then two dynamic objects consisting of 64 polygons are communicated, and so on.

There is one important implication of this for the spatial judgement component of the experiment - obviously the spear travels more slowly when there are shadows. Without shadows the mean velocity is 92 cm/sec, and with shadows 47 cm/sec. Therefore it can be argued that differences in targeting performance might result from the velocity rather than the use of shadows. However, the effect of this can be examined statistically. With regard to the influence on presence we would argue that the slower frame rate in the case of shadows would tend to have a negative effect on presence.

4. Results

4.1 Spatial Variables

Spear Selected. Shadows made no difference at all to the selection of the "correct" spear (the one closest to the wall).

Distances from Target. Consider first C the distance of the point of the spear from the centre of the target. A regression analysis was used to examine the effect of velocity, showing that velocity within each of the shadow/ no-shadow groups was did not have a statistically significant effect. The mean distance without shadows is 152cm and 115cm with shadows. However, the difference between these two is not statistically significant.

Consider next D, the perpendicular distance of the point of the spear from the wall of the target. This could be positive (spear stops in front of the target) or negative, the spear stops behind). Carrying out a within-group regression analysis to examine the effect of velocity again shows that velocity is not statistically significant. The means are -39.9cm without shadows, and 3.3cm with shadows. The standard errors are 3.6 and 3.5 respectively and the difference is significant at 5%. The medians of the shadow and non-shadow D values are -3cm and -38cm respectively.

Although the within-group velocity appeared not to be statistically significant in each case, there is still some doubt about whether the inference about better performance in the case of shadows is safe. The variation of velocity within groups was not very great (the minimum and maximum velocities were 81.6 to 99.0 for the non-shadow group, and 36.0 to 60.4 for the shadow group). Subsequent experiments should attempt to produce a greater similarity in performance between the two groups.

4.2 Presence

Subjective Presence. P is the number of "high" questionnaire scores, as a count out of 6. We therefore treated P as a binomially distributed dependent variable, and used logistic regression.

In logistic regression [4], the dependent variable is binomially distributed, with expected value related by the logistic function to a linear predictor. Let the independent and explanatory variables be denoted by $x_1, x_2, ..., x_k$. Then the linear predictor is an expression of the form:

$$\eta_i = \beta_0 + \sum_{j=1}^{k} \beta_j x_{ij} \quad (i = 1, 2, ..., N)$$

....(1)

where N (=8) is the number of observations. The logistic regression model links the expected value $E(P_i)$ to the linear predictor as:

$$E(P_i) = \frac{n}{1 + \exp(-\eta_i)}$$

....(2)

where n (=6) is the number of binomial trials per observation.

Maximum likelihood estimation is used to obtain estimates of the β coefficients. The deviance (minus twice the log-likelihood ratio of two models) may be used as a goodness of fit significance test, comparing the null model ($\beta_j = 0$, j = 1,...k) with any given model. The change in deviance for adding or deleting groups of variables may also be used to test for their significance. The (change in) deviance has an approximate χ^2 distribution with degrees of freedom dependent on the number of parameters (added or deleted).

Table 2
Logistic Regression Equations
$\hat{\eta}$ = fitted values for the presence scale
A = Auditory Sum, NS = number of shadows
Standard Errors shown in brackets

Model
$\hat{\eta}$ = 15.0 + 0.7*NS - 9.5*A
(3.7) (0.4)

Overall Deviance =3.454, d.f. = 5
χ^2 at 5% on 10 d.f. = 11.070

Deletion of Model Term	Change in Deviance	Change in d.f.	χ^2 at 5% level
NS	4.123	1	3.841
A	9.088	1	3.841

Table 3

Normal Regression Equations

$\hat{P}_a$ = fitted values for the angular discrepancy

NS = number of shadows

Group	Model
Visually dominant	$\hat{P}_a$ = -13.6 + 10.6*NS (3.7)
Auditory dominant	$\hat{P}_a$ = 9.427 + 0.08*NS (3.7)

Multiple Correlation Coefficient, R^2 =0.29, d.f. = 36

Table 2 shows the result of the fit with P as the dependent variable, and the number of shadow runs (NS) and the auditory sum score (A) as the explanatory variables, across the 8 subjects. These were the only statistically significant variables found, and this supports the hypothesis that subjective presence is positively related with the shadow effect. As we have found previously, given this exclusively visual VE, the greater auditory dominance, as measured by the sum of A responses to the pre-questionnaire, the less the reported subjective presence.

Angular Discrepancy. Here we take P_a as the dependent variable and carry out a Normal regression with number of shadows (NS) and the representation system scores as the explanatory variables. NS proved once again to be significant and positively related to P_a. However, the V, A and K variables were not significant. Nevertheless it seemed important to try to rule out the possibility that the result with the angular discrepancy was simply due to visual or auditory dominance. Therefore a new factor was constructed, "sensory dominance" which has the value 1 if V>A otherwise 2. Hence this directly refers to visual or auditory dominance. The result of the regression analysis including this was interesting: for those who were visually dominant, there is a significant positive relationship between P_a and NS, whereas there is no significant relationship for those who were dominant on the auditory score. This is shown in Table 3. (It so happened that 4 of the subjects were visually dominant).

5. Conclusions

There are three main issues : First, the point of this paper is not that we have an algorithm that can generate shadow umbrae rapidly in dynamically changing scenes. Even in this very small scene the rendering frame rate was no where near adequate on this particular architecutre, though its performance is excellent on standard workstations running under X11[3]. There is clearly a lot of work to do in the location of this algorithm in the dVS system architecture, in order to obtain maximum performance by minimising communication bottlenecks.

Second, although we have considered depth and spatial perception problems in the experiment, again, this is not the major point. It is more or less obvious, from everyday reality, and from perceptual studies that shadows do indeed enhance depth perception. Moreover, our experimental design in this regard was not ideal, since we did not control a factor (velocity) that potentially has an impact on the results.

Third, the real point of the experiment was the examination of the relationship between dynamic shadows and the sense of presence. This result is not obvious, and was motivated by the idea that presence is (amongst other things) a function of immersion, and immersion requires vividness. We used two independent measures - one subjective from the post-experiment questionnaire, and the other objective, as a ratio of angles of real to virtual pointing directions. Each method gave similar results, and the two measures were significantly correlated. Moreover, we found that for those people who were more visually dominant their (angular ratio) presence increased with exposure to shadows but that this did not hold for those who were dominant on the auditory scale. Increase in the subjective presence scale was also associated with an increase in shadow exposure, but with a decrease in the auditory scale. These results also support our earlier findings regarding the importance of the sensory system preferences in explaining presence.

We suspect that much stronger results on presence would have been obtained had we been able to allow the virtual body to cast shadows. However, this was not practical given the communication bottleneck problems discussed in §3.2.

If an application does not require presence, there is little point in using a virtual reality system. If a virtual reality system is used for an application, then there is little point to this unless it can be shown that a sense of presence is induced for most of the potential participants. Should the results of our shadow experiment be confirmed by later studies then it will have been shown that the great computational expense of shadow generation is worth-while for those applications where the participants are likely to be "visually dominant".

Acknowledgements

This work is funded by the U.K. Engineering and Physical Sciences Research Council (EPSRC), the Department of Trade and Industry, and DIVISION Ltd, through grant CTA/2 of the London Parallel Applications Centre. Thanks to David Sweeting of Aeronautical Engineering Department of QMW, for helping to find subjects for the experiment.

References

1. Cavanagh, P., Leclerc, Yvan G. (1989) Shape from shadows. Journal of Experimental Psychology: Human Perception & Performance, 15 (1), 3-27.

2. Chin, N., Feiner, S. (1989) Near Real-Time Shadow Generation Using BSP Trees, Computer Graphics 23(3), 99-106.

3. Chrysanthou, Y., Slater, M. (1995) Shadow Volume BSP Trees for Computation of Shadows in Dynamic Scene, ACM SIGGRAPH Symposium on Interactive 3D Graphics (April, 1995).

4. Cox, D.R. 1970. *Analysis of Binary Data*, London: Menthuen.

5. Gregory, R.L. (1990) Eye and Brain: The Psychology of Seeing, Fourth Edition, Weidenfield and Nicholson, 182-187.

6. Grimsdale, C. (1991). dVS - Distributed Virtual environment System, Proceedings of Computer Graphics 91 Conference, London.

7. Puerta, A.M. (1989) The power of shadows: shadow stereopsis. Journal of the Optical Society of America, 6, 309 - 311.

8. Slater, M. A. Steed and M. Usoh (1994) Steps and Ladders in Virtual Reality, ACM Virtual Reality Science and Technology (VRST), eds G. Singh and D. Thalmann, World Scientific, 45-54.

9. Slater, M. and M. Usoh, Representation Systems, Perceptual Position and Presence in Virtual Environments, Presence: Teleoperators and Virtual Environments, 2.3 MIT Press, 221-234.

10. Slater, M., M. Usoh, A. Steed, Depth of Presence in Virtual Environments, Presence: Teleoperators and Virtual Environments, 3.2 (in press).

11. Steuer, J. (1992) Defining Virtual Reality: Dimensions Determining Telepresence, Journal of Communication 42(4), 73-93.

Appendix A: Presence Questions

All questions were answered on a 1 to 7 scale, not reproduced here for space reasons.

1. Please rate *your sense of being there* in the virtual reality.

2. To what extent were there times during the experience when the virtual reality became the "reality" for you, and you almost forgot about the "real world" of the laboratory in which the whole experience was really taking place?

3. When you think back about your experience, do you think of the virtual reality more as *images that you saw*, or more as *somewhere that you visited* ?

4. During the course of the experience, which was strongest on the whole, your sense of being in the virtual reality, or of being in the real world of the laboratory?

5. When you think about the virtual reality, to what extent is the way that you are thinking about this similar to the way that you are thinking about the various places that you've been today?

6. During the course of the virtual reality experience, did you often think to yourself that you were actually just standing in a laboratory wearing a helmet, or did the virtual reality overwhelm you?

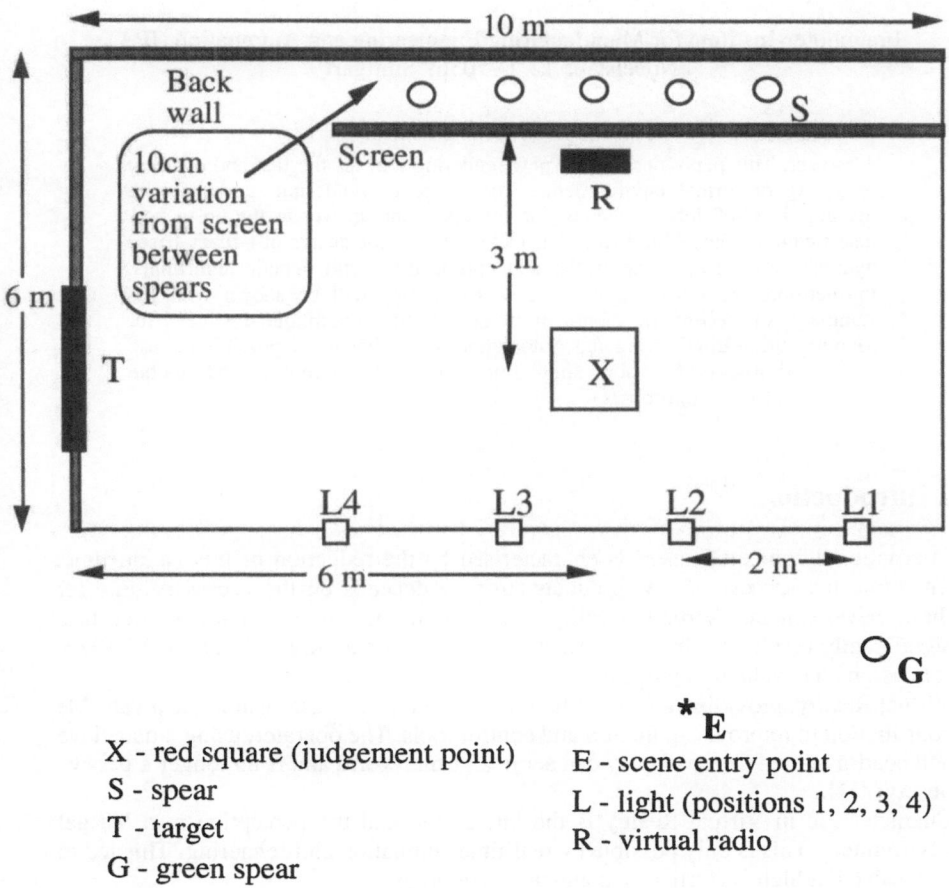

X - red square (judgement point)   E - scene entry point
S - spear   L - light (positions 1, 2, 3, 4)
T - target   R - virtual radio
G - green spear

Figure 1
Plan View of the Virtual Environment

Editor's Note: see Appendix, p. 293 for coloured figures of this paper

A Fuzzy Controlled Rendering System for Virtual Reality Systems Optimised by Genetic Algorithms

Prof. Dr. R. D. Schraft, J. Neugebauer, T. Flaig and R. Däinghaus

Fraunhofer-Institute for Manufacturing Engineering and Automation (IPA),
Nobelstaße 12, D-70569 Stuttgart

Abstract. This paper describes a new rendering tool for the fast and efficient rendering of virtual environments. The usage of rendering modules with dynamic level-of-detail technology is the upcoming answer to the up to now insufficient graphical hardware. The paper outlines the design of a fuzzy-based dynamic level-of-detail controller and optimisation with genetic algorithms. Furthermore the potential of this new technology will be shown with the summary of recent development work at the Fraunhofer-Institute for Manufacturing Engineering and Automation, which has made possible the use of Virtual Reality for robot simulation, off-line programming and remote operation of industrial robots

1 Introduction

International competetiveness is characterised by the reduction of innovation time. Therefore the success of new products strongly depends on the necessary time for their development. Virtual Reality, as a new 3D human-computer interface significantly accelerates the processes of creating and handling 3D data in 3D space for design and evaluation purposes.

Virtual Reality, providing advanced human-computer-interfaces can make a valuable contribution to improve simulation and control tools. The operator, using a dataglove and head-mounted stereo display can act in a virtual world and is no longer a passive observer [1].

Characteristic in Virtual Realtiy is the interaction and the perception in a Virtual environment. This is only possible by real-time simulation and rendering. This led to expensive but high performance computer technology.

The Fraunhofer-Institutes carrying out applied research for small and medium-sized enterprises (SME) is familiar with industrial demands. For establishing VR simulation technologies in industry it is necessary to develop fast rendering algorithms to be able to use relatively cheap hardware for real time rendering tasks.

This paper outlines a new dynamic level-of-detail algorithm which is based on a fuzzy-controller with parameters which are optimized by genetic algorithms.

2 Requirements for Visualisation Tools

All graphical systems have limited capabilities that affect the number of geometric primitives that can be displayed per frame at a specific frame rate. The general requirement is a maximum frame rate including optimal quality of the displayed scene. These two goals are in contradiction to each other. The driving force behind IPA development is to find the best compromise between quality of the scene and frame rate.

Because of the existing limitations, maximising visual output quality while minimising the polygon count, level-of-detail processing is one of the most promising tools available for managing scene complexity for the purpose of improving display performance.

To reduce rendering time, objects that are visually less important in a frame can be rendered with less detail or in a lower degree of abstraction. The level-of-detail approach to optimising the display of complex objects is to construct a number of progressively simpler versions of an object and to select one of them for display for example as a function of range.

This method requires the creation of multiple representations of an object with varying levels of detail or levels of abstraction. Rules must be given to determine the best representation of the object to be displayed [2].

The requirement must be met, that enough representations of an object with different quality levels exists. Only on a comprehensive list of graphical representations a satisfactory work of a graphical output controlled rendering is guaranteed.

To use extended level-of-detail-technology, a large set of graphical representations must be designed. Several methods are known. The easiest method is to design repesentations in different degrees of abstraction by hand. Also semi automatic or automatic methods are possible. The objective is to get representations with different numbers of polygons. The rendering of any single polygon is the most important criterion for the graphical performance of the computer. One very simple representation of an object is the bounding box, build up with six polygons, another one is a minimal convex hull. This representation looks like a rubber balloon stretched over the described object. Often it is enough to use this representation in a very complex scene or in case of background scenery.

Other automatically created level-of-detail representations can be generated by defining tolerance measures around the surface of the described object. If neighboring vertices are inside of this predefined tolerance measure, all polygons belonging to these vertices are merged. With this method different level-of-detail representations can be designed by graduated tolerances. This procedure is very efficient to design large landscapes, Figure 1.

If the virtual world is designed by polygonal representations of analytical surfaces like cylindrical, torus or cone surfaces, each surface can be directly created in different representations. These must be fine-tuned, because non-fitting adjacent surfacees could result. A broomstick for example could be shown by a cylinder with a rounded end built of a spherical surface. The usage of different levels of detail will create a confusing look. There is the possibility of holes appearing and edges might not fit anymore, Figure 2.

Assuming that enough different representations of any object are designed, the algorithm deciding the current representation is the most important part of the rendering modul.

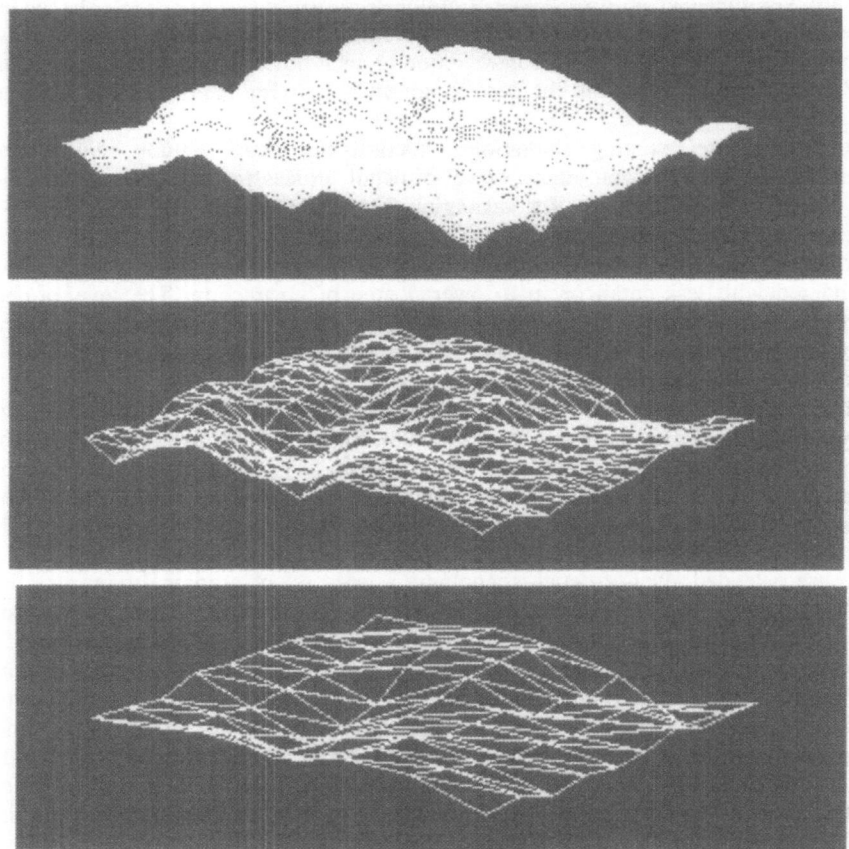

Fig. 1. Three landscape representations

Rules have to be defined to change the level of detail. The governing influencing factors are the following [3]:

- Distance from the viewer to the concerned object
  The distance is an important parameter. The nearer an object is, the more important it is for the whole scene.
- Size of the object
  Of the same importance is the size of an object. Both parameters together define the size of the considered object on the screen.
- Position in relation to the center of the display
  The user wearing a Head Mounted Display will usually look in the center of the viewed scene. Objects on the edge of the visible frustrum are therefore assumed to be less important then objects in the middle of the screen.

- Complexity of the object
  The complexity of an object is expressed by the number of polygons used to display the object.
- Special interest of the object
  Some objects have a predefined special interest. In a robotic workcell the gripper of the robot e.g. would be more interesting than many other objects.
- Velocity of the object
  Using velocity of objects as a parameter the importance of fast objects can be reduced as these can't be seen correctly, like for example the propeller of a plane.

A continuous change of the representations of different objects may result from free navigation of the user in the virtual world. This change can be a visual problem, because of the resulting tremendous flickering of the whole scene. As the human eye especially perceives motion a continuous change of object representations disturbs the impression of the viewed scene.

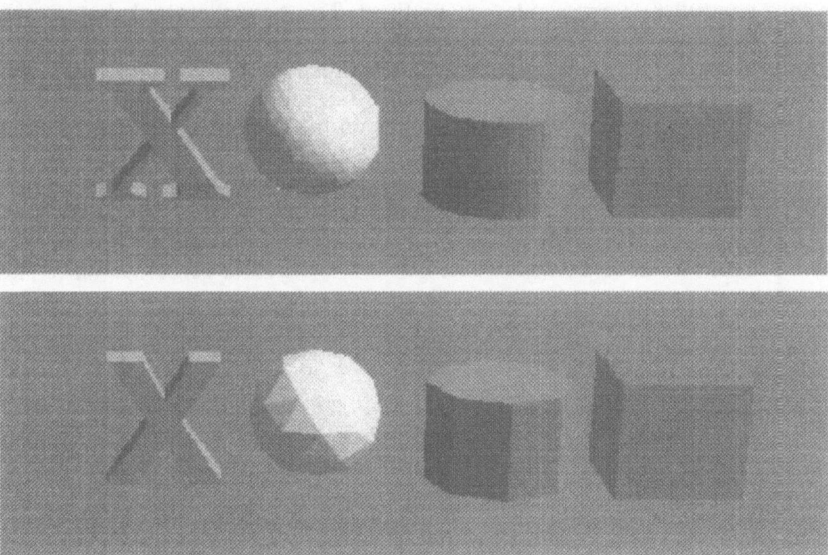

Fig. 2. Arrangement of geo primitives

The problem in adjusting the rendering modul are the many parameters in the abstraction algorithms. The question is how to reach the optimum between high frame rate and high level of detail. One condition is that the visual output is done for a subjectivly deciding human being. Another is the contradiction because of opposite goals of the criteria. For example an object at a far distance is not very important, although the same object has a higher importance possibly because of a definition as an object of interest. The arising contradiction can be balanced by using fuzzy logic algorithms.

3 A dynamic adjustable Rendering System

The dynamic control of the graphical level-of-detail has various advantages and has become state of the art with the introduction of the Silicon Graphics rendering package Performer. The philosophy is to use graphical abstractions for some scene objects in a stress situation of the graphical output. But the only benefit of the SGI Performer is to decide either to give the best (normal) quality or to simplify the scene by leaving out some details of the scene. Different representations of objects are possible, but very complicate to model.

Performer is layed out for peaks of stress situations. The disappearance of objects in these situations cannot be accepted in most applications. A controller has to be layed out to control the scene permanently, because stress situations must be expected anytime. A permanent abstraction of the scene has to be possible.

This can be reached best by using a fuzzy logic controlled rendering modul. With the use of a controller, a frame rate can be fixed. The controllers task is to reach the desired frequency of frames per second by selecting one of the different representations of the single objects. It is the user's job to give the system the best compromise between the fastest display frame rate and the best quality of the output to tolerate. This adjustment strongly depends on the subjective quality perception of the viewer.

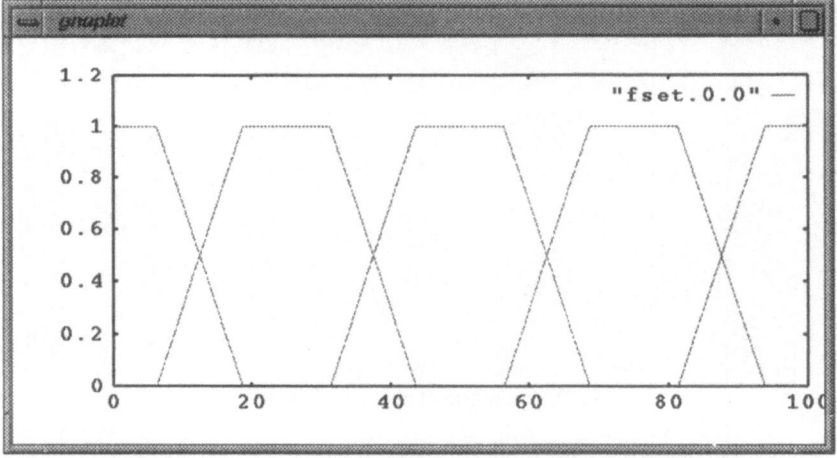

Fig. 3. The membership function of the deciding parameters

The successful aproach controlling principle in discrete environments is the philosophy of fuzzy logic. All incoming values can simply be rated. All factors of the output decision can be considered carefully. The fuzzy logic controller gives a soft and easy to control switching of the representations of graphical objects. The fuzzy logic controler gives the best way in rating the complexity of the current scene and offers a soft deviation of the desired frequency. The problem of the disturbing flickering from the oscillation in conventional controllers can be minimised.

The benefit of a fuzzy logic controller is the very easy usage of input values by using linguistic variables. These variables - also called membership functions - describe the state of every influencing parameter in form of a natural language. The distance to an object of the scene for example can be descibed in words like *very near, near, middle, far* or *very far*. Every condition is represented by a fuzzy set. They define the memberships of the conditions to an interval of discrete values. If e.g. the current distance is detected by the system, the fuzzy algorithm could recognize the fuzzy set *far* to 80 percent and *very far* to 40 percent. All other parameters like size, complexity etc. are evaluated similar.

All decisions of any parameter are brought together by rules. In these rules the connections between the different parameters (distance, size and complexity of objects etc.) of the scene description are evaluated like:

> if distance is far and size is big
> then give a better representation

> if complexity is low and size is small
> then give a more abstract representation

Any combinations of these rules are possible. The valid output of the rules can have opposite evaluations, but the important advantage of fuzzy logic controllers is the possibility to compensate all opposites and to find an optimal average in evaluating the input values.

The evaluation of the complete set of rules via defuzzyfication returns a discrete value, that the rendering modul uses to decide which representation is the current best choice. The more rules are used and the more variables are interpreted, the better is the stability of the controller. This stability is achieved by decreasing the controllers oscillation and the minimising of the withcoming flickering of the graphical output.

So far it is easy to define a controller to decide the representations of single objects. But the task is not to optimise the output of the objects in a scene, but the impression of the scene itself. The controller must be optimised to give the best subjective scene impression to the user.

The missing link to an improved controlled rendering modul is the evaluation of the complete scene. How can a complex scene be evaluated? The limited output ressources determine the decisions of the controller of every single object in the current scene. The evaluation of objects have to be seen in relation to the output of the whole scene. This means that the controllers decisions are depending not only on static parameters but on the connection of the scene building objects.

The fuzzy logic controller must be optimised by a training in well known virtual worlds. The decision base of the controller are the membership functions and the rule base. The rule base cannot be changed softly, all connections are fix. Size and the form of the fuzzy sets in the membership functions can be manipulated though.. The sets are defined as trapeziod shaped memberships, built up by a quadrupel The four coordinates defining the sets can be manipulated to get a modified characteristic of the controller.

28

How can the controller be adjusted to detect the best decision of object representatives with a minimum of oscillating but holding a fixed frame rate and an optimal subjective scene display? With the modification of all defining points of fuzzy sets in the five incoming membership functions 36 parameters can be found to modify. The best output depends on an optimum rating of these parameters.

4 Optimisation by Genetic Algorithms

Genetic algorithms (GA) have some properties that make them interesting as a technique for selecting high-performance membership functions for fuzzy logic controllers. Due to these properties, GAs differ fundamentally from more conventional search techniques. They consider a population of points and not a single one, they use non-deterministic probabilistic rules to guide their search. GAs consider many points from the search space simultaneously and therefore they have a reduced chance of converting to a local optima [4].

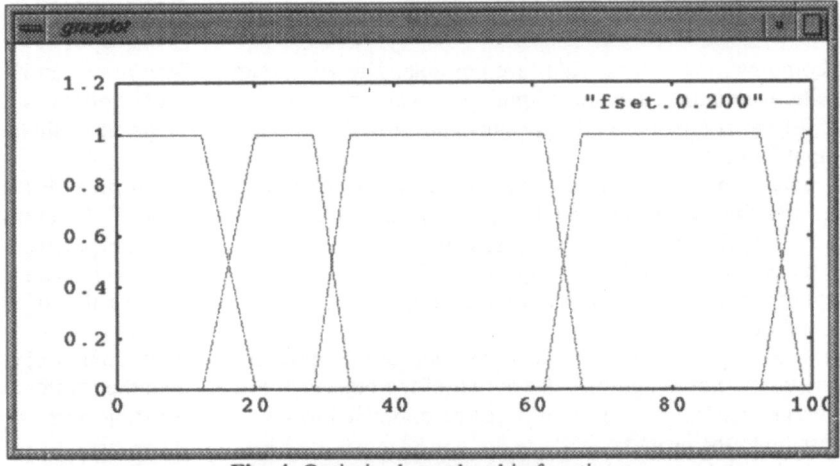

Fig. 4. Optimised membership function

GAs work on the basis of the evolutionary theory [5]. The parameter set defining the problem to optimise - in the special case the defining points of the membership functions - are seen as a DNA of an biological individual.

The result of the search procedure is the definition of the optimal parameter set. This set can be found by starting the evolution with a large number of individuals with an identical parameter set (DNA). The DNA of individuals can be inherited. During the inheritage the DNA of the individuals is modified by crossing or mutation. Crossing means the changing of random parts of the parameter set between two individuals, mutation is a mechanism that exchanges single parameters within the set of an individual. The descendants generated by these algorithms build up the new population.

The generated new individuals are tested iteration by iteration. The biological rule of the survival of the fittest is applied. Every new individual (parameter set for the solution of the optimisation problem) is rated in a typical environment.The duration of these tests is to long to calculate thousands of iterations. Instead of this a average function of typical rendering outputs was created. This function simulates the typical characteristic of the rendering system, the rating of the single individuals can be calculated without graphical output. If the test has a positive result the current parameter set is a good solution for the membership functions. The individual is strong enough and keeps alife, otherwise the individual dies.

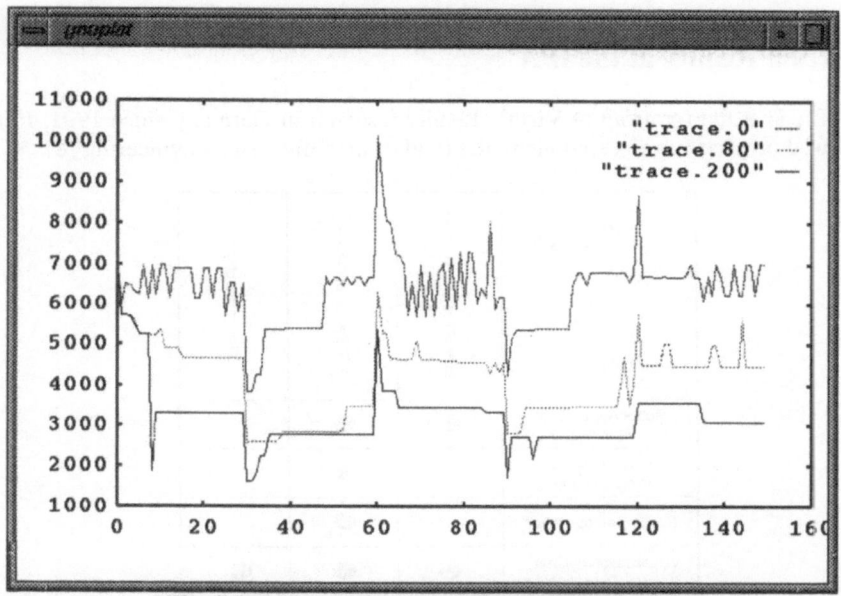

Fig. 5. Frame rate of the controlled rendering modul

The best parameter sets for the membership functions can be found by following only the fittest individuals. Like in the evolution only the fittest individuals inherit their DNA. After a while the fittest individuals are selected and every parameter set will deliver a good definition of the considered membership function.

Genetic algorithms are not random walks through the search space. They use random choice efficiently in their exploitation of prior knowledge to locate near-optimal solutions rapidly. An example of the successful work of the manipulation of the membership functions can be seen in Figure 3 and Figure 4.

The membership function for the distance to the current object is defined as fuzzy sets with the conditions very near, near, middle, far and very far. The predefined membership function are_defined symetrically to give the best assumption for the optimising genetic algorithm. The result of the optimisation can be seen in Figure 4.

The defined fuzzy sets still exists, the difference to the predefined membership function is the modified placement and shape of the single sets related to the complete function.

The rating algorithm is a simulated walk through a virtual world. A nonstatic change of visible objects is simulated by a step function response of the controller. In Figure 5 can be seen that the automatically optimised controller delivers a minimum oscillation and a very fast adjusting to the desired frame rate.

The rating algorithms are so fast that a learning on the fly can be reached. A permanent optimising in running simulations is possible. In every new virtual world the membership functions can be optimised. An individual controller parameter definition of the controller for every new scene can be designed [6,7].

5 Virtual Reality at the IPA

The IPA is at the forefront of Virtual Reality research in Germany since 1991. First industrial projects have been done in the field of manufacturing engineering [8].

Application Areas / Applications	Industrial Projects at the IPA	VR System at the IPA	VR System others
Robot Application Planning	●	●	
Robot Off-line Programming		●	
Robot Teleoperation		●	
Visualisation of CAD-Data	●	●	●
Presentation of Product Ideas		●	●
Presentation of Product Proposals	●	●	
Rapid Prototyping		○	○
Manufacturing Planning		○	
Handling- and Assembly Planning		○	
Operator Systems for Machines		○	
Interactive Learning Systems		○	○

○ concepts   ● applications

Fig. 6. Virtual Reality Applications at the IPA

Figure 6 shows an overview of the use of Virtual Reality system at the IPA. There are industrial projects in the planning of robot work cells, visualisation of CAD-data and presentation of product ideas.

Further applications have been realised like off-line programming and teleoperation. Rapid Prototyping, manufacturing planning, assembly planning, operator systems and training systems are areas for further development.

6 The Demonstration Centre Virtual Reality at the IPA

The high interest from the public and the industrial side was accorded to further Fraunhofer-Institutes which deal with this innovative technology.
The Fraunhofer-Society has faced the challenge of this new technology and is now active in making this potential accessible to industry. The project is to be efficiently supported by the Demonstration Centre for Virtual Reality. In January 1993 this institution has taken up its work for the period of five years [9].
The establishment of the Fraunhofer-Institute Demonstration Centre for Virtual Reality is to present smaller and middle-sized companies new techniques of Virtual Reality, to reduce fear of contact between industrial practice and Virtual Reality research and to demonstrate prototypes of Virtual Reality applications in a practical and vivid way.
The following services are available in teh Demonstration Centre for Virtual Reality at the IPA in Stuttgart:
• Dispersion of availabel knowledge on Virtual Reality,
• Training of personnel from interested companies,
• Presentation of demonstration appliances and processes,
• Consultancy for companies,
• Application and test of new and already available applications and
• Development and demonstration of exemplary applications.

7 Conclusion

Virtual Reality technology makes a valuable contribution to improve simulation and control tools. The operator, using a dataglove and a head-mounted stereo display can act in a virtual world and is no longer a passive observer.
To get the best response from the Virtual Reality system, the graphical output must be efficiently high. Best usage of advanced rendering functionality (possible to combine with commercial products like Performer (SGI) or other high performance rendering systems) are reached by new developed control moduls.
As high performance can now be achived even with inexpensive hardware advanced rendering tools for VR systems can now be used for industrial applications.

References

1. Flaig, T. "Echtzeitorientierte interaktive Simulation mit VR4RobotS am Beispiel eines Industrieprojektes", Tagungsunterlagen des 2. VR-Forum ´94, Anwendungen und Trends, Februar 1994, Stuttgart, Deutschland.
2. N.N.: "IRIS Performer Programming Guide",1994

32

3. Däinghaus,R. "Dynamische Geometriedatenhaltung für schnelles Rendern in effizienten Virtual Reality-Systemen", Tagungsunterlagen des 2. VR-Forum ´94, Anwendungen und Trends, Februar 1994, Stuttgart, Deutschland.

4. Goldberg, D.E.:"Genetic Algorithms in Search, Optimization and Machine Learning", Addison Wesley, 1989

5. Holland, J.:"Adaption in Natural and Artifical Systems", The University of Michigan Press, Ann Arbor, 1975

6. Zadeh, L.A.:"The Concept of a Linguistic Variable and its Application to Approximate Reasoning", New York, 1973

7. Karr, C. "Genetic Algorithms for Fuzzy Controllers", AI Expert, P26-33, February 1991

8. Neugebauer. J-G., Flaig,T. "IPA - Trendsetter der Produktionstechnik, Richtungsweisende Beispiele für wirtschaftliche Produktion und Automatisierung", MI Moderne Industrie, September 1993, Stuttgart.

9. Neugebauer, J.-G. "Virtual Reality - The Demonstration Centre", Meckler Conference - Virtual Reality International ´93, April 1993, London, Great Britain.

Generating Multiple Levels of Detail from Polygonal Geometry Models

G. Schaufler and W. Stürzlinger
GUP Linz
Johannes Kepler University Linz
Altenbergerstrasse 69, A-4040 Linz, Austria/Europe
[schaufler I stuerzlinger]@gup.uni-linz.ac.at
Tel.: +43 732 2468 9228

Abstract. This paper presents a new method for solving the following problem: Given a polygonal model of some geometric object generate several more and more approximative representations of this object containing less and less polygons. The idea behind the method is that small detail in the model is represented by many spatially close points. A hierarchical clustering algorithm is used to generate a hierarchy of clusters from the vertices of the object's polygons. The coarser the approximation the more points are found to lie within one cluster of points. Each cluster is replaced by one representative point and polygons are reconstructed from these points. A static detail elision algorithm was implemented to prove the practicability of the method. This paper shows examples of approximations generated from different geometry models, pictures of scenes rendered by a detail elision algorithm and timings of the method at work.

1 Introduction

In several papers on recent developments in computer graphics the presented algorithms rely on the availability of several approximations of decreasing complexity to the polygonal representation of one geometric object (referred to as levels of detail - LODs - throughout this paper). Primarily for performance reasons these algorithms choose one of the approximative representations of the objects in the course of their work thereby trading quality for speed. Examples are the visualization of complex virtual environments [2], 3D graphics toolkits [5] or indirect illumination calculations [7]. In visualization of virtual environments LODs allow to retain a constant frame rate during the navigation through the environment by adapting the detail of the visible objects to the complexity of the visible part of the scene and the graphics performance of the used hardware. Indirect illumination calculations attain performance gains through substituting different LODs while calculating the energy exchange between two objects.

The authors of these papers do not mention how to automatically obtain the different LODs. Either they use very coarse approximations such as bounding volumes or they model each LOD by hand thereby multiplying the effort for generating the geometry database.

In the field of surface reconstruction from laser range device data algorithms have been developed which allow to decimate the number of triangles used to represent the original surface. However, these algorithms are very costly as far as computational complexity is concerned and are less suitable for geometry models of CAD software [3]. Other methods filter large triangle or polygon meshes with the aim to retain the detail of the digitizing process but do not generate several LODs (see e.g. [1],[9],[10]). The presented method fills the gap between the computationally and algorithmically complex surface reconstruction from laser range data by a user selectable number of triangles and the generation of models of varying complexity by hand. It automatically generates different LODs from CAD geometry models. The original model is referred to as the level 0. Coarser LODs are referred to as level 1, level 2 and so on.

The goal in designing the method was execution speed while keeping a close resemblance to the original model. In coarser LODs the number of polygons must decrease significantly. Small details of the model can be left out but the overall structure of the object should stay the same with as little polygons as possible. It is important to keep the silhouette of the object to minimize annoying artifacts during blending between different LODs and to keep the error low which is introduced into the algorithm making use of the LODs.

The method uses a hierarchical clustering algorithm to perform the task of removing the detail from the models and generating coarser approximations to the models. In the first stage the clustering algorithm generates a hierarchy of clusters from the points in the model. Different algorithms exist to generate such a hierarchy - the "centroid" or "unweighted group pair" method [8] is used in the current implementation. Depending on the desired degree of approximation the method traverses the calculated cluster tree to a specific depth and either keeps the geometry model or replaces parts by coarser approximations.

The current implementation of the proposed method is suitable to calculate LODs from polygonal objects containing several 1000 data points. In an interactive viewer the generated LODs are used to render environments of geometric objects at interactive frame rates. The viewer chooses a LOD for each visible object depending on the size of its on screen projection without introducing highly noticeable artifacts into the rendered views. The program allows navigation through the environment as well as a close inspection of the objects' LODs generated by the method.

2 Previous work

Hoppe et al. [3] have presented a method to solve the following problem: Starting from a set of three dimensional data points and an initial triangular mesh they produce a mesh of the same topology which fits the data well and has a smaller number of vertices. They achieve this by minimizing an energy function which explicitly models the competing desires of conciseness of representation and fidelity to the data by using three basic mesh transformations to vary the structure of the triangle mesh in an outer optimization loop. For each triangle mesh found they optimize the energy function by slight changes to the vertex positions of the triangle mesh. The method is fairly complex and demanding as far as computational and implementational efforts are concerned.

DeHaemer et al. [1] have presented two methods for approximating or simplifying meshes of quadrilaterals topologically equivalent to regular grids. The first method applies adaptive subdivision to trial polygons which are recursively divided into smaller polygons until some fitting criterion is met. The second method starts from one of the polygons in the mesh and tries to grow it by combining it with one of its neighbours into one bigger polygon. Growing the polygon stops when the fitting criterion is violated. These methods work well for large regular meshes and achieves reductions in polygon numbers down to 10% for sufficiently smooth surfaces.

Turk's re-tiling method [9] is best suited for polygonal meshes which represent curved surfaces. It generates an immediate model containing both the vertices from the original model and new points which are to become the vertices of the re-tiled surface. The new model is created by removing each original vertex and locally re-triangulating the surface in a way which matches the local connectivity of the initial surface. It is worth mentioning that models containing nested levels of vertex densities can be generated and that smooth interpolation between these levels is possible.

Schroeder et al. [10] deal with decimation of triangle meshes in the following way: In multiple passes over an existing triangle mesh local geometry and topology is used to remove vertices which pass a distance or angle criterion. The holes left by the vertex removal are patched using a local triangulation process. Using their approach Schroeder et al. successfully decimate triangle meshes generated with the marching cube algorithm down to 10%.

All these approaches have in common that they start out from polygon meshes which contain a lot of redundancy: they exploit the fact that in most areas of the surfaces curvature is low and vertices or triangles can be left out or combined without losing features of the surface. Vertices in such areas fullfil the preconditions under which simplifications to the mesh are made. However, such preconditions for simplification are rarely met in human modelled CAD objects where flat surfaces are constructed from large polygons. They cannot be further simplified with these strategies. Moreover the approaches are quite complex to implement and computationally intensive as they all involve re-triangulation and multiple passes over the polygon mesh.

It has been pointed out by a reviewer that the proposed method is similar to the method introduced by Rossignac et al. [6]. Rossignac uses a regular grid to find points in close proximity which is disadvantageous in the case of greatly differing object sizes. The method proposed in this paper uses a hierarchical object-adaptive clustering scheme instead which can deal with such differences and does not introduce any grid size into the generated models. The method does not require the polygon mesh to contain a lot of redundancy nor does it require the mesh to be of any predetermined type or topology. In fact it is well suited to continue from where the above algorithms finish. It works on polygonal objects of several 1000 vertices as in hand modelled CAD objects and explicitly generates several LODs from these objects in one pass over the object's geometry while retaining the overall shape and size of the objects. It is designed to be fast and efficient on such models and is well suited to generate the LODs while the object database is loaded into memory.

3 Overview of the Approach

This approach implements a reasonable fast method to generate several LODs from polygonal object models. This papers terminology refers to the original model as level 0. The algorithm was not required to exactly keep the topology of the geometry as did the algorithms mentioned in the former section. Nevertheless the generated LODs resemble the original model closely though with less and less polygons. The coarsest LOD should not contain more than a few dozen polygons for an original object consisting of several 1000 polygons.

The algorithm can be described as follows:

- Apply a hierarchical clustering algorithm to the vertices of the object model to produce a tree of clusters.

- For each LOD generate a new (less complex) object model using cluster representatives instead of original polygon vertices.

- Remove multiply occurring, redundant primitives from each LOD.

In the second stage a layer in the cluster tree is determined which describes the way the LOD approximates the original model. Using the clusters of this layer, each polygon has its vertices replaced by the representative of the cluster it belongs to. This may leave the number of vertices unchanged (if all points fall into different clusters), the number of vertices may be reduced, the polygon may collapse into a linestroke or its new representation may be a single point. In this way formerly unconnected parts of the model may eventually become connected when separated points of different polygons fall into one cluster and are, therefore, mapped onto one cluster representative. However, as the clustering algorithm only clusters spatially close points the overall appearance of the object remains the same depending on the degree of approximation desired in the current LOD. In particular polygons become bigger if their points are moved apart through clustering. Therefore, the surface of the object will never be torn apart.

4 Hierarchical Clustering

Clustering algorithms work on a set of objects with associated description vectors, i.e. a set of points in multidimensional space. A dissimilarity measure is defined on these which is a positive semidefinite symmetric mapping of pairs of points and/or clusters of points onto the real numbers (i.e. $d(i,j) \geq 0$ and $d(i,j) = d(j,i)$ for points or clusters i and j). Often (as in this case) the stronger distance is used, where in addition the triangular inequality is satisfied (i.e. $d(i,j) \leq d(i,k) + d(k,j)$) as in the Euclidean distance. The general algorithm for hierarchical clustering may be described as follows (although very different algorithms exist for the same hierarchical clustering method [4]):

Step 1   Examine all inter-point dissimilarities, and form a cluster from the two closest points.

Step 2   Replace the two points clustered by a representative point.

Step 3   Return to Step 1 treating constructed clusters the same as remaining points until only one cluster remains.

Prior to Step 1 each point forms a cluster of its own and serves as the representative for itself. The aim of the algorithm is to build a hierarchical tree of clusters where the initial points form the leaves of the tree. The root of the tree is the cluster containing all points.

Whenever two points (or clusters) are joined into a new cluster in Step 2, a new node is created in the cluster tree having the two clusters i and j as the two subtrees. For the new cluster a representative is chosen and a dissimilarity measure is calculated describing the dissimilarity of the points in the cluster. The representative g of the new cluster is calculated from

$$g = \frac{|i| \, g_i + |j| \, g_j}{|i| + |j|} . \qquad |i| = \text{number of points in cluster i.}$$

The dissimilarity measure d equals the distance of the two joined clusters i and j:

$$d = d(i,j) = \|g_i - g_j\| .$$

The run-time complexity of this approach can be analyzed as follows: Step 1 is the most complex in the above algorithm ($O(N^2)$ in a naive approach). The time required to search the closest pair of points can be decreased by storing the nearest neighbours for each point or cluster. Therefore, a BSP-tree is built from the points at the cost of $O(N\log N)$ to facilitate the initialization of the nearest neighbour pairs (at the equal cost of $O(N\log N)$).

Each time Step 2 is performed the nearest neighbour data is updated at the cost of $O(N)$ on the average yielding a total complexity of the algorithm of $O(N^2)$. As stated in the paper of Murtagh [4] hierarchical clustering can be implemented with a complexity of less than $O(N^2)$, so a future implementation should incorporate such optimizations or one of those clustering algorithms to make the method suitable for dealing with more complex geometry models.

5 Finding the Approximative Polygonal Model

The tree of clusters generated by the hierarchical clustering algorithm is used as the input to the next stage of the method - the automatic generation of several LODs. Starting from the highest LOD (coarse approximation) the algorithm proceeds towards level 0 (the original model). For each level to generate a size of object detail is determined which can be ignored in this level. The found size will be used to choose nodes in the cluster tree which have dissimilarity measures (i.e. cluster distances) of similar magnitude. 1/8th of the room diagonal of the object's bounding box works well in most cases for the coarsest approximation.

Next a descend into the cluster tree is made starting from the root until a node is found the dissimilarity measure of which is smaller than the neglectable detail size of the current LOD. For each such cluster a representative is calculated and all the points in the cluster are replaced by this representative. The point which is furthest away from the object's centre is taken as the cluster representative. Although other methods are possible (see section 8) this one delivered the most satisfying results. It keeps the overall shape and size of the objects and has the additional advantage that no new vertices need to be introduced into the object's model. Using the cluster average might result in better looking shapes of the LOD but tends to produce LODs which are increasingly smaller compared to the original object and results in annoying effects during rendering.

From the found layer of clusters in the cluster tree a new geometric object with the same amount of (possibly degenerate) polygons is calculated, only the point coordinates of some of the polygons vertices change. Now each polygon is examined to find out whether it is still a valid polygon or if it has collapsed into a line stroke or a point. Moreover, polygons with more than 3 vertices might need to be triangulated as their vertices are not plane in general. Polygon normals are calculated anew for each LOD. In models of tessellated curved surfaces the normals may be interpolated at the vertices if desired.

6 Cleaning up the New Model

As polygons may collapse into line strokes and points, care must be taken not to incorporate unnecessary primitives into the LODs. For example lines or points which appear as an edge or vertex of a polygon in the current LOD can be discarded. Even certain polygons can be left out.

In a second pass over the new approximated geometry those primitives in the LODs are identified which can be removed without changing the look of the LOD. All points which occur as a vertex of a valid polygon or of a valid line are flagged and all lines which occur as an edge of a valid polygon, too. Assuming that the models are composed of closed polyhedra (as is usually the case) - all pairs of polygons which contain the same vertices in reversed sequence and all polygons which contain the vertices of another valid polygon in the same orientation can be flagged as well.

For the sake of speed these flagged primitives can be removed from the LOD geometry. However, if it is required to retain the relationship between the primitives in the LODs and the original geometry model, the flagged primitives can be retained and need not be processed.

The next (finer) LOD is generated in the same way, only the size of neglectable object details is decreased by a certain factor (in the current implementation the factor is 2, which proved to work well). Therefore, a lower layer is chosen in the cluster tree where clusters are smaller and represent smaller features. As a result less detail of the original model is left out because less points fall into one cluster.

Different LODs generated by the method are shown in Fig. 1 (see Appendix). Top left shows the original model, the other three groups of pictures show higher LODs of the object in a close-up (big pictures) and magnified versions of both the original model (small left) and the LOD (small right) from a distance for which this LOD is appropriate.

7 A Viewing System Based on Levels of Detail

A viewing system using the LODs was implemented both to visually control the results of the method and to demonstrate the usability of the LODs in rendering of complex virtual environments. Generally speaking the incorporation of LODs into the viewer resulted in sufficient speedup for near interactive frame rates (5-10 Hz) on a graphics system with a peak performance of 25K polygons per second: Fig. 2 (see Appendix).

Prior to drawing the scene the system determines the visible objects by classifying their bounding boxes to the viewing frustum. For the potentially visible objects the length of the projection of the bounding box diagonal is calculated to give a measure at which LOD the object should be rendered. Then all the polygons facing the viewer are rendered using the Z-buffer algorithm.

8 Results and Timings

The proposed method for the automatic generation of LODs works well for polygonal object models of some 1000 vertices. Models can contain any kind of polygons (convex, concave, general) as long as the triangulation algorithm for approximated polygons can handle them. However, convex polygons are preferable for high rendering speed. Lines and points are legal primitives as well. The objects' meshes should be closed although a violation of this requirement does not prevent the algorithm from being used on the model.

It is possible to vary the method in several ways to better match the requirements of the application for which the LODs are generated. First the number of LODs generated for each object can be adapted by changing the factor by which the dissimilarity measure is updated from level to level. Second the selection of the representative for each cluster can be chosen from a variety of possibilities (cluster average, point in cluster closest to cluster average, point in cluster furthest from object centre, random point in cluster...). Third the primitives generated by the method can be made to include points, lines or polygons or any combination. Fourth the degenerated polygons can be left within the LODs to keep the relationship between the primitives in the original model and the LODs. This is useful for transferring information from the primitives of one LOD to the other (e.g. color, texture, ...).

The method was applied to a wide variety of objects achieving acceptable results as far as speed and quality of the approximation are concerned. The resulting LODs are not easily distinguished from the original models when viewed from increasing distances but contain far less polygons than the original models.

Fig. 3 (see Appendix) shows some more examples of objects and their LODs from a close as well as from a suitable viewpoint, i.e. an appropriate distance for the use of the respective LOD. The statistics of the algorithm are summarized in Table 1 for the objects in Fig. 1 (see Appendix) and Fig. 3 (see Appendix). They were obtained on a Mips R3000 CPU.

40

Table 1: Statistics for the new method

Model	Level 0 Polys/Points	Level 1 (polygons)	Level 2 (polygons)	Level 3 (polygons)	Level 4 (polygons)	Time (sec) Total for 4 LOD
Lamp	790 / 3084	492 (62%)	210 (27%)	63 (8%)	37 (5%)	2.9
Shelf	1783 / 6628	740 (42%)	472 (26%)	454 (25%)	231 (13%)	3.0
Plant	6064 / 25926	3674 (61%)	1225 (20%)	339 (6%)	57 (1%)	57.0

9 Future Work

As already mentioned briefly we are investigating at two areas of further research. First we want to further speed up the hierarchical clustering algorithm by making best use of the optimizations described by Murtagh [4]. This work will decrease the order of complexity of the clustering algorithm below $O(n^2)$ allowing to deal with more complex object models in less time.

Second we want to build a new mode into our viewer which guarantees a constant frame rate through the method described by Funkhouser et al. [2]. We hope to outdo their results in variations in the frame rate as our object models are well structured and probably allow faster and better estimation of the rendering complexity of the visible objects.

Further research is needed to increase the flexibility of our method and to further improve the overall look of the LODs. Moreover, we are investigating the applicability of LODs to other application areas.

References

1. Simplification of Objects Rendered - Polygonal Approximations. *Michael J. DeHaemer, Jr. and Michael J. Zyda*. Computers & Graphics Vol. 15, No.2 pp 175 - 184, 1991.
2. Adaptive Display Algorithm for Interactive Frame Rates During Visualization of Complex Virtual Environments. *Thomas A. Funkhouser, Carlo H. Séquin*. SIGGRAPH 93, Computer Graphics Proceedings, pp 247-254, 1993.
3. Piecewise Smooth Surface Reconstruction. *Hugues Hoppe, Tony DeRose, Tom Duchamp, Mark Halstead, Hubert Jun, Jon McDonald, Jean Schweitzer, Werner Stuetzle*. SIGGRAPH 94, Computer Graphics Proceedings, pp 295-302, 1994.
4. A Survey of Recent Advances in Hierarchical Clustering Algorithms. *F. Murtagh*.The Computer Journal, Vol. 26, No. 4, 1983.
5. IRIS Performer: A High Performance Multiprocessing Toolkit for Real-Time 3D Graphics. *John Rohlf, James Helman*. SIGGRAPH 94, Computer Graphics Proceedings, pp 381-394, 1994.
6. Multi-Resolution 3D Approximations for Rendering Complex Scenes. *J. R. Rossignac, P. Borrel*. Computer Science, IBM T.J. Watson Research Center, Yorktown Heights, NY 10598, 2 1992.

7. Geometric Simplification for Indirect Illumination Calculations. *Holly Rushmeier, Charles Patterson, Aravindan Veerasamy*. Proceedings of Graphics Interface '93, 1993.
8. Numerical Taxonomy; The Principles and Practice of Numerical Classification. *Peter H. A. Sneath, Robert R. Sokal*. Publisher W. H. Freeman, San Francisco, 1973.
9. Re-Tiling Polygonal Surfaces. *Greg Turk*. SIGGRAPH 92, Computer Graphics Proceedings, pp 55-64, 1992.
10. Decimation of Triangle Meshes. *William J. Schroeder, Jonathan A. Zarge, William E. Lorensen*. SIGGRAPH 92, Computer Graphics Proceedings, pp 65-70, 1992.

Editor's Note: see Appendix, p. 294f. for coloured figures of this paper

Fine Object Manipulation in Virtual Environment

Ryugo KIJIMA, Michitaka HIROSE
JSPS Research Fellow
Department of Mechano-Informatics,
Faculty of Engineering, University of Tokyo
7-3-1 Hongo, Bunkyo-ku, Tokyo, 113, Japan
E-mail: kijima@ihl.t.u-tokyo.ac.jp

Abstract: We have developped two calculation method for the manipulation in virtual environments. Impetus Method is based on only one phenomena, collision between the fingertip and the object. We start with the simple manipulation to push the object with one degrees of freedom and expand it to treat with more complicated phenomena. RSPM realizes the detailed manipulation. By using this, the object can be grasped, manipulated by 3 fingertips.

1: Introduction

Natural and realistic object manipulations in virtual environments (VE) are important because the true application necessarily contains the object manipulation[8]. Moreover, the operator can recognize the law that dominates the behavior through the act of manipulation (active presence) in addition to the (passive) presence through the visual sense (Figure 1). Untill now, the realized manipulations have been generally based on gestures, and these manitulations seem to be very simple, symbolic, and not realistic.

The manipulation is realized by calculating the behavior of the object driven by a virtual hand. The behavior of the virtual object is an artifact. We can define any behavior. It appears that we can easily generate the behavior similar to that in the real world by

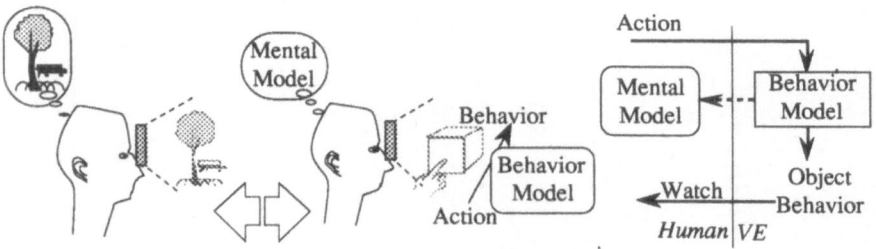

Visual (passive) Presence   (Active) Presence via Interaction

Fig. 1. Realistic Manipulation Causes Active Presence

calculations based on physical laws. There are, however, cases in which physical laws cannot be applied, especially in VE without force-feedback.

There have been many attempts and inventions for easier manipulation. Although some of them work well and effectively, there is a difficulty to combine different manipulation algorithms according to the various situations where the object locates in. What seems to be lacking is to explore the nature of difficulties in such calculations, and to systematize the methodology.

The goal of this study is to develop effective manipulation algorithms, and to make clear how we should manage different manipulation calculations. Although this paper does not fully acheive this goal, two example manipulation calculations with fingertips in VE without force feedback, are developed, and several discussions are shown based on this development to generalize the behavior calculation.

First, authors discuss the calculation for object manipulation generally.

Secondary, the "Impetus method" is described. It is based on a simple phenomenon, the collision between fingertip and object surface. We start with simple movements with 1 degree of freedom. This is naturally expanded to represent movement with 2/3 degrees of freedom, static and dynamic friction, stiffness, rotational moment, and restriction on a surface. This method belongs to the category of semi-dynamics.

Third, a "representative spherical plane method" for grasping and manipulating object by 3 fingertips, is described. It is based on the restricted interaction among three fingertips and a sphere that represent the object. This method enables detailed, fine manipulation by 3 fingertips. This belongs to the region of kinematics.

At last, the discussion of the above methods and future work is described.

2: Generation of Object Behavior

The calculation of the interaction or of the object's behavior in VE has different characteristics from those in popular Graphical Usr Interface (GUI) such as drag, pull-down, etc,. In the case of VE, it is more complicated. Generally, it has 3 degrees of freedom, and utilizes multiple contact point (fingertips, etc.). The number of states of the manipulated object are larger in VE than in GUI's. The largest difference is the detection to which model the behavior of the object belongs. In the case of VE, it should be based on geometrical information while those in GUI's are mainly based on symbol information such as a mouse click.

Symbol information simplifies the detection in exchange for giving up some detailed behavior. For example, in a VE, if the gesture of a hand (symbol information) mainly

44

decides whether the hand grasps the object or not, the object is grasped without considering the geometrical relation between the fingertips and the surface of the object. These calculations based on symbol information are not suitable to generate detailed behavior.

2.1 Problem and Assumptions

In the case of VE without force feedback, the position/orientation of the hand or fingertip are monitored by sensor(s), and this data forms a virtual hand that interacts with the object. Namely, the hand's position as input is used to drives the object, and there is no output to the real hand. The data flow between the real hand and the virtual object is basically only one way.

In the case of VE with force feedback, most general method is, to sense the position of the hand, to calculate the interaction based on the position, and to display the impedance, force or the relation between position, velocity and force. Nevertheless, the data flow between the real hand and the virtual object is two way (Figure. 2.1).

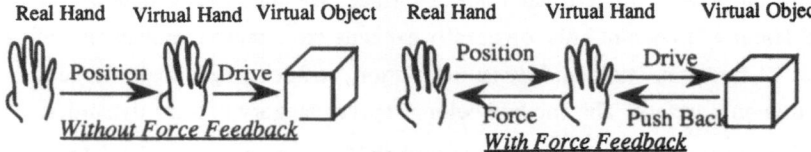

Fig. 2.1. Dataflow

1: Only the position is obtained as input from the real world

This means we cannot include the term of force in the calculation. If we introduce some assumption that defines the relationship between the force and the situation (position, velocity and the other term that has been obtained), the force can be achieved. Because the assumption dominates the all of the calculations which are to follow, it should be chosen very carefully [6].

2: There is no output from the virtual world to the real hand

This means the movement of the real hand cannot be restricted, or cannot be modified by the reaction force from the virtual object.

Therefore, the position of the real hand could easily become different from that of the virtual hand. This is a serious problem because the calculation based on the position data implicitly assumes that it is based on the actual position of the real hand. To solve this problem, an assumption that defines the relationship between the real hand and virtual hand is needed. Also this assumption should be chosen very carefully [6].

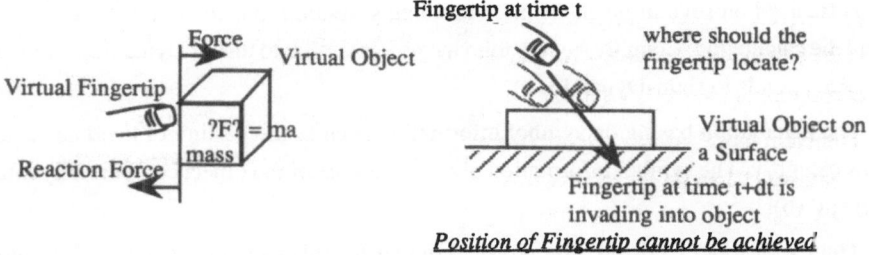

Fig. 2.2 Calculation Problems in VE without Force Feedback

2.2 Kinematics, Dynamics

As an example, let us think about the case where a solid object is grasped by three fingers. This activity can be divided into three phases (Figure 2.3).

(a): Free

No finger comes into contact with the surface of the object. The behavior of the object can be calculated based on physical laws such as Newtonian Physics. If the world contains gravity, the object will fall freely. If the world contains viscous resistance, the velocity of the object will decrease gradually. Because the term of force appearing in the calculation is not the force between finger and object, there is no problem. This belongs to the category of dynamics.

(b): Restrictive

If the fingers grasp the object tightly, the position and orientation of the object have a strong relation to the positions of the fingertips. This can be calculated based on Kinematics. Kinematics as part of Mechanics, can deal with restrictive phenomena, such as, a pair of gears that engage each other, a set of arms that are connected with links, etc. The behavior of a grasped object is similar to such phenomena. Kinematics does not utilize the term of force. Therefore this belongs to the category of Kinematics-like methods. Section 4 corresponds to this region. Kinematics-like methods simplify the phenomena, avoiding the term of force, the need of wider bandwidth (higher calculation and sensing cycle)[5][7].

(c): Boundary

When some of the fingers are very close to the surface of the object, Kinematics is not suitable because the relation between the fingertips and the object will change rapidly. Also Dynamics as a part of Physics is not suitable because there is a force between the fingertip and the object, and because it suits for uniform or "flat" phenomena. Dynamics as part of Mechanics deals with the term of force explicitly, but it is focused on several mechanisms, introducing assumptions to simplify the theory and the calculation. Roughly saying, this category is similar to that of Dynamics. Section 3 corresponds to semi-Dynamics.

The calculation basing on symbol information such as the gesture of hand neglects this category. The symbol information divides the state of the object compulsorily into (a) and (b).

Thus with force feedback, the physical model for this category is not perfect. For object manipulations by robot-manipulator, there are several hypotheses and theories.

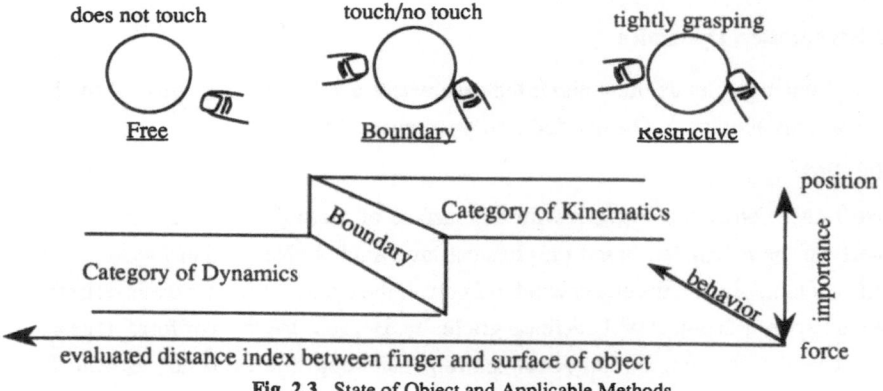

Fig. 2.3. State of Object and Applicable Methods

2.3 State Transition

The term "situation" can be defined as a set of parameters that describes both the state of the object and the state of the surrounding environment. For example, let us suppose that the virtual world consists of a virtual hand and a virtual object. The state of the object is a set of parameters such as the position of the object, the size, the velocity, etc. Because there is only the hand besides the object, the state of the surrounding environment is a set of parameters such as the position of the hand, gesture, etc,. The term means the combination of them. All the parameters form a configuration space that is used in computational kinematics [4]. One situation is a point in configuration space.

The object changes its behavior over these categories, and one category contains multiple regions of situation. One region corresponds to one calculation model of behavior.

When a calculation model is defined, the applicable region in the configuration space is restricted. Therefore the detection of which region the object belongs to, or which is a suitable calculation model for the object, is important to manage the over all calculations [3].

The fragmentary inventions of calculation that are not systematized, easily declined to error. The minor error in one model of behavior sometimes causes unreasonable state transition and changes the overall behavior largely.

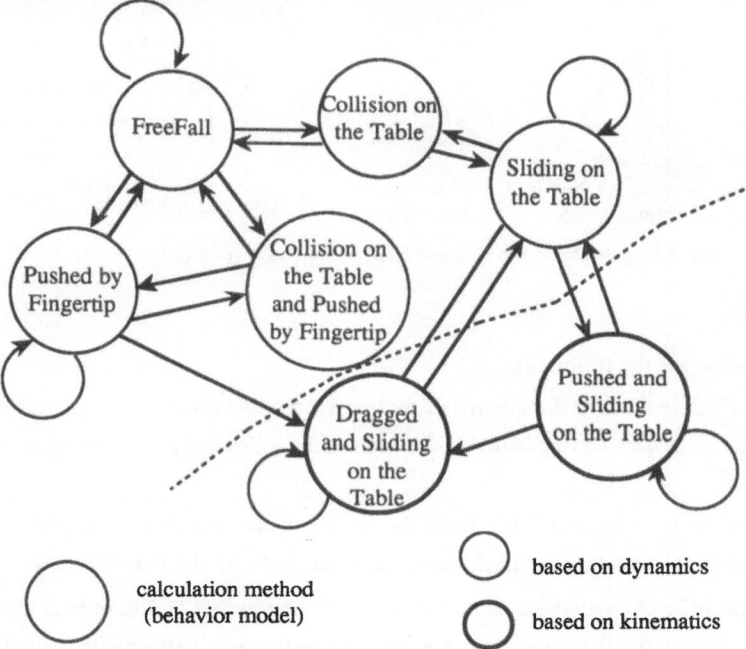

Fig. 2.4 An Example of a Set of Behavioral Laws and State Transition

3: Impetus Method

3.1 Basic Concept

This method aims to calculate the behavior of solid objects, manipulated with fingertip(s). Applicable manipulations and neighboring regions are pushing an object with finger(s) as shown in (Figure 3.1).

We start with defining clearly the set of axioms including the fundamental quantity that causes the movement of the object. The second step involuves detecting the applicable region from the axioms. The third step is to expand this to more complicated phenomena systematically.

In other words, the third step is the purpose, which is dependent on the second. The second step connects the state transitions and models correctly, which need to be clearly defined.

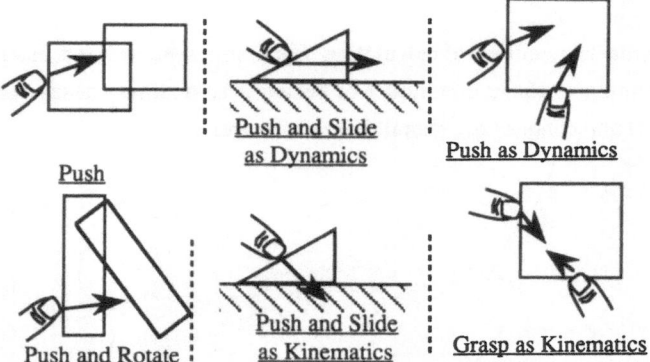

Fig. 3.1 Applicable Phenomena and Neighboring Region of Impetus method

3.2 Axioms

The axioms are the following:

Law 1: "The reason for the change of motion is impulse force, which is defined as the invasion vector of the fingertip"[1]. This needs the following assumptions to enable calculation:

Assumption 1: "Reaction force from the object to the finger is negligible". This requires several secondary assumptions such as the mass of object is zero, etc.

Assumption 2: "Any element cannot invade into the object"[2]. Not only at the time of the calculation point on the time axis, but also at the time between the calculation point, finger, other objects cannot invade into the inside of the object being manipulated.

3.3 The calculation and the detection of the boundary of applicable region

Figure 3.2 shows a basic calculation where one fingertip is pushing the surface of an object. Here, all the movements have only one degree of freedom.

At the time-index = n, the position of the fingertip is outside the object. At the next time segment of calculation, the fingertip position (gotten from sensor) invades into the object. Between time n and n+1, a collision occurrs. Using linear interpolation, the correct collision time and the trajectory of the fingertip and the object are calculated. Namely, the object position at n+1 is calculated from the fingertip position at n, n+1, object position and velocity at n, using simple interpolation.

$$Po'[n+1] = Po[n] + Vo[n] * dt$$
$$I = Po'[n+1] - Pf[n+1]$$
$$Po[n+1] = Po'[n+1] + I$$

As the invasion vector increases/decreases, the distance from fingertip to the surface of the object increases/decreases respectively. The invasion vector acts similarly as an impetus or impulse force.

The impulse from the fingertip is modified systematically by attributes such as collision factor, mass/rotational inertia ratio, dynamic friction coefficient, static friction limit, restriction on the surface, etc. It must be noticed that these (virtual) attributes are not the same attributes as in physics, but cause similar effects as those in Physics. Hence, we can control the properties of the phenomena easily.

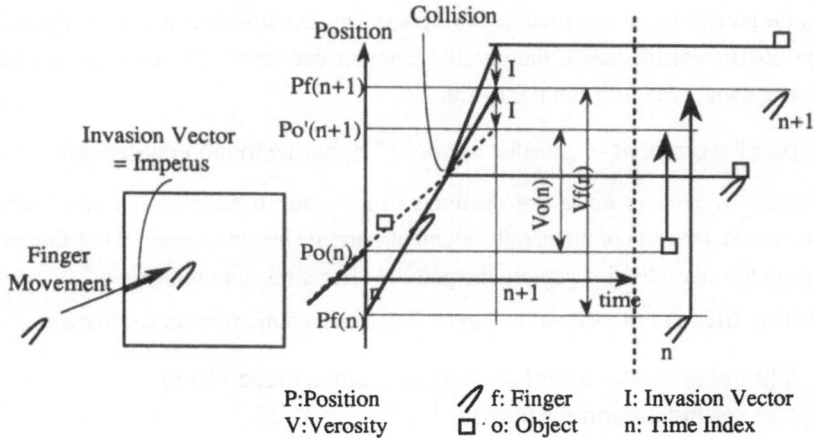

P:Position   f: Finger   I: Invasion Vector
V:Verosity   o: Object   n: Time Index

Fig. 3.2. Calculation Based on Invasion Vector

(Collision factor)

The Impetus I in the equation (1) is modified by collision factor "e", which should range from 0.0 to 1.0.

$$Po[n+1] = Po'[n+1] + e * I$$

(Damping)

Next, a damping coefficient d is introduced. This represents phenomena such as the friction between objects being manipulated and their surrounding environment. As damping increase, the movement of object decreases. Impetus I in the equation (1) is modified in the following manner by introducing damping factor "d", which should range from 0.0 to 1.0.

$$Po[n+1] = Po'[n+1] + e * d * I;$$

(3D movement)

This is naturally expanded into movement with 3 degrees of freedom.

(Friction)

Static and the dynamic friction between the finger and the surface of the object are introduced. Until now, only the magnitude of the Impetus is modified by 2 factors. Here, the Impetus is divided into the normal element that is orthogonal to the object surface, and the parallel element that is parallel to it.

Only the parallel element is modified to represent the dynamic friction. As the dynamic friction coefficient increases, the parallel element decreases. The dynamic friction coefficient should ranges from 0.0 to 1.0.

parallel element -> parallel element * dynamic friction coefficient

To detect whether or not a state belongs to the static friction region or dynamic friction region, the ratio of the parallel element/normal element is used. If the situation belongs to the static friction region, the parallel element is not modified.

The static friction limit should be larger than the dynamic friction coefficient.

if (parallel element/normal element > static friction limit)
      state = dynamic friction
else   state = static friction

(Rotational Movement)

This is expanded into rotational movement by introducing a rotational Inertia ratio "r". The inertia ratio is similar to the ratio of rotational inertia by mass. This indicates the relative easiness of rotation to that of parallel movement. In the case that the mass of the object concentrates around the gravity center, it can easily be rotated compared with the ease of parallel movement. In the case that the mass exists mainly on the surface of object, it is relatively difficult to rotate.

Here, the Impetus is divided into two components. One is the parallel component that is parallel with a vector from the fingertip to the center of the object. Another is the rotational component that is the rest of the Impetus. This should cause the rotational movement.

rotational Impetus = rotational component * r * distance from the center of the object to the fingertip.

The rotational impetus is used to cause rotation. In our experimental system, this is directly converted to rotation for one time (from time n to n+1), continuous rotation is not supported.

(Restrictive movement on a plane)

The restriction of movement on a plane is introduced. This is achieved by simply eliminating the component that meets at right angle to the restriction plane.

3.3 Region detection

The applicable region of this method is detected by investigating whether or not the result of calculation satisfies assumption 2 or not. The problem is that "the result satisfies assumption 2" does not necessarily mean "the values used in the calculation satisfy assumption 2". In order to solve this problem, we introduce a restriction to the calculation as follows: "If the object satisfies assumption 2 in the region of time [t1 .. t2), it satisfies the assumption 2 at t2."

3.4 Experiment System

Figure 3.3 shows the system for experiments. The computation of the behavior and the generation of graphics are performed on IRIS VGX-210 workstation. Polhemus IsoTrak and DataGlove is used to sense the fingertip point. All the program is written on VisAge that is an toolkit to generate virtual environment. VisAge is developed by the first author of this paper, and is consist of libraries and tools to develop the virtual reality application. It contains a simple management structure for behavior calculations. Objects are maintained in a form of a tree. Each object is defined as a set of attribute and a pointer to a function that defines the behavior. The function is called automatically by the management structure referring the tree. As a programming style, it is recommended to divide the function into two parts, the detection of applicable region

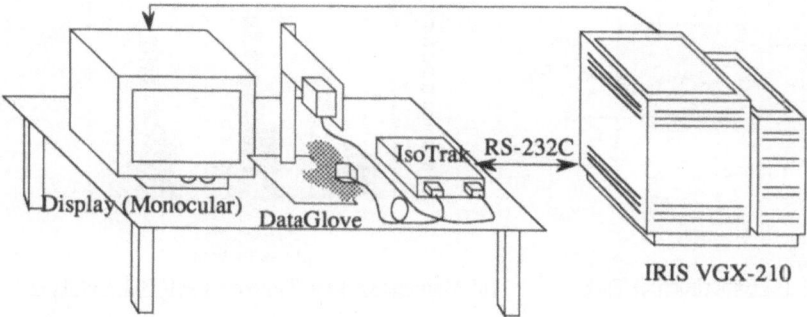

Fig. 3.3. System for Experiment

52

and the behavior calculation itself. The state transition is implemented by changing which function the pointer indicates.

The experiment in section 4 is performed on the same system.

3.5: Experimental Result

The experimental task was to place an object in the indicated region by pushing the object with one finger. Case 1 has 3 degrees of freedom parallel movement in free space. Case 2 has 2 degrees of freedom parallel movement and 1 degrees of freedom rotation on a plane. In both cases, the result shows that this manipulation is easier as compared to general symbolic manipulation.

Especially in case 1, the user used 2 states of friction properly according to the phase of task. This contributes to the improvement of performance. (Figure 3.3, 3.4)

Also the results showed that the user could "feel" the (virtual) attribute (friction ratio). In the real world, physical quantities are receipt as stimulus, cause the senses. Virtual attributes cause sense through the recognition of relations between the motion of the hand and the behavior of the object.

4:   Representative Spherical Plane Method

4.1   Basic Concept

In this section, RSPM (Representative Spherical Plane Method) is detailed. This is for grasping and manipulating an object with 3 fingertips.

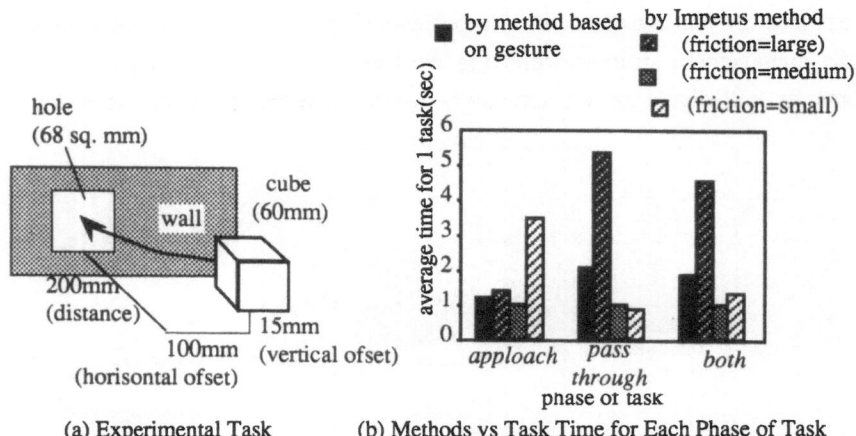

Fig. 3.4. Experiment 1

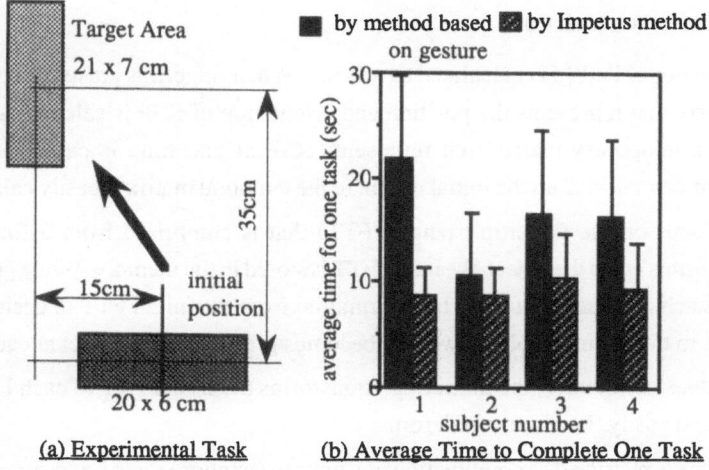

(a) Experimental Task   (b) Average Time to Complete One Task

Fig. 3.5. Experiment 2

To begin with, let us introduce a sphere (RSP) with radius r that represents an object. The fingertips manipulate this sphere, and the object behaves similarly as this sphere. RSP moves according to the position of 3 fingertips, therefore, 3 fingertips only slide on the RSP while it is grasping the object. This movement of RSP is defined as the behavior of the object.

The merits of this method are as follows:

- Fine Manipulation with fingertips

The freedom of a finger is larger than that of the back of the hand, and a finger is more accurate. A finger is a "fine" part of the hand. In conventional gesture based manipulation methods, the position and orientation of grasped objects are gotten from the back of hand, and not from the finger. Fingers are utilized only for gesture detection. On the contrary, via RSPM, user can drive objects by their fingertips. This means the user could manipulate objects with more accuracy.

- Uniformity of Manipulation;

　　The user can manipulate any object with the same feel of manipulation.

- Uniformity of Calculation;

　　Any object can be manipulated based on the same algorithm.

RSPM begins with the condition that all 3 fingers are involved in the object, and that 3 fingers can grasp RSP. The second condition is checked by calculating the radius of circum circle of the triangle whose vertices are 3 fingertips. The second condition is equivalent to that the radius of circum circle is smaller than that of RSP.

54

4.2   Behavior Calculation

The behavior of RSPM is calculated as follows. When fingertips grasp the object, an initial matrix that represents the position and orientation of RSP is calculated. While grasping, a temporary matrix that represents RSP at that time is calculated. The transformation matrix from the initial matrix to the temporal matrix is easily calculated.

Let us focus on the fingertip triangle (FTT) that is comprised from 3 fingertips. When fingertips grasp the object, the initial FTT is stored in the memory. While grasping, the FTT is achievd each time. The transformation from the initial FTT to each FTT is equivalent to that from the object when it becomes grasped to the object at each time.

If FTT does not deform, the matrix that transforms the initial FTT to each FTT can be calculated easily. But in fact it deforms.

The matrix is restricted as combination of a unitary (rotation) matrix and a translation matrix. To avoid deformation, the following calculation is used;

(1): To move initial FTT such that the gravity center locates at that of each FTT.

(2): To rotate it around the gravity center such that the normal vector becomes equal to that of each FTT.

(3): To rotate around the normal vector such that the vertexes become closest to corresponding vertexes of each FTT. As the performance criterion, authors adopted the summing of absolute angle between the vectors that is from gravity center to vertex.

The result is calculated directly in analytical way, not in repetitive way. The system cycle was 60Hz, which include retrieval of data from sensor, calculation, graphics generation on IRIS VGX-210 workstation.

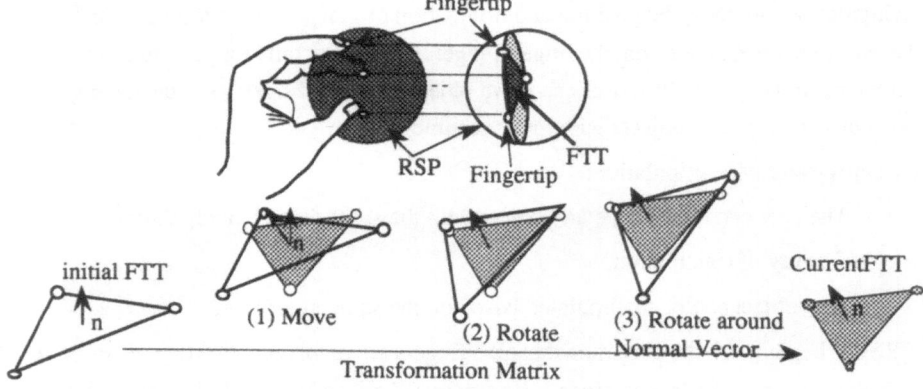

Fig. 4.1 Representative Spherical Plane Method

4.3 Experiment

A simple experiment was performed. A target cube and another cube were displayed. Each surface was painted in different colors. The task was to manipulate the cube so that whose orientation matches with that of the target cube. Two methods was utilized. One was RSPM, another was general method based on gesture such that "if the gesture is FIST and the hand is near to the object then grasp" and that "the movement is the same as that of the back of hand".

The subjects performed 10 times per method. The average time to complete the task was measured. Users grasped object several times because the range of rotation was limited. They repeated grasping, rotating, releasing. Also the time of grasping was counted.

Figure 4.2 shows the result.

The average time for RSPM was shorter than that of method based on gesture. Also the number of re-grasp was smaller in the case of RSPM. This indicates the range of rotation increased in RSPM and RSPM was easier method than the conventional gesture based method.

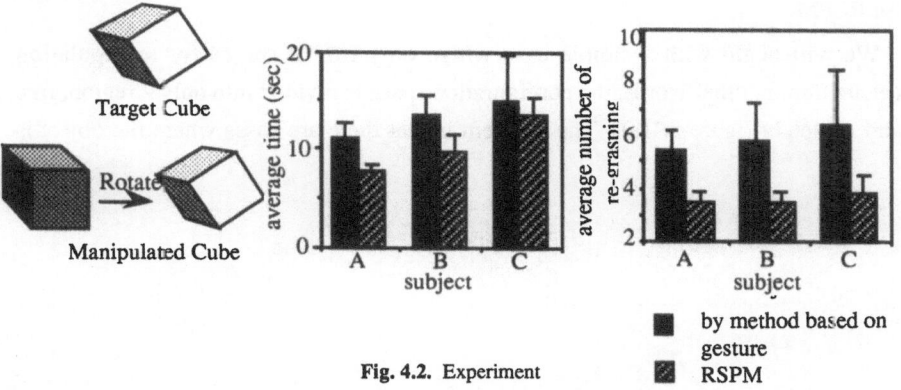

Fig. 4.2. Experiment

5 Discussion and Future Work

5.1 Extending Impetus Method into Multi-finger Manipulation

Currently the Impetus Method deals the interaction between one fingertip and the object. The authors are testing an algorithm for the manipulation by two fingertips. Two impetuses from two fingertips are simply added and the result moves the object. This is partly generates the correct behavior. When one fingertip is invading into the object, the object is moved by one impetus. There is the case where the moved object contains another fingertip. This breaks the assumption 2 and causes the incorrect behavior. The authors are testing several algorithms to merge multiple impetuses and several detection algorithms. Although some of them work well in some cases, the suitable combination for any case has not been found.

Under some successful situations, the sequence as follows is achieved:

1: one finger continuously pushes the object.

2: two fingers pushed the object alternatively

3: two finger pushes the object at once

4: the object becomes not to satisfy the assumption 2, state is changed into the region of kinematics, the object is picked up by two fingers.

5.2 Discussion on Region Detection for RSPM

Although the experimental result shows the improvement of manipulation performance from the conventional manipulation method, RSPM leaves room for improvement. Much still remains to be done about the condition when RSPM begins (grasp object) and ends (release object), namely, the detection of the applicable region for RSPM.

We will begin with a simple case where only RSPM serves for manipulation calculation. In other words, the configuration space is divided into only 2 region, free and grasped (Figure 5.1(a)). The problem is that there are cases where the object is

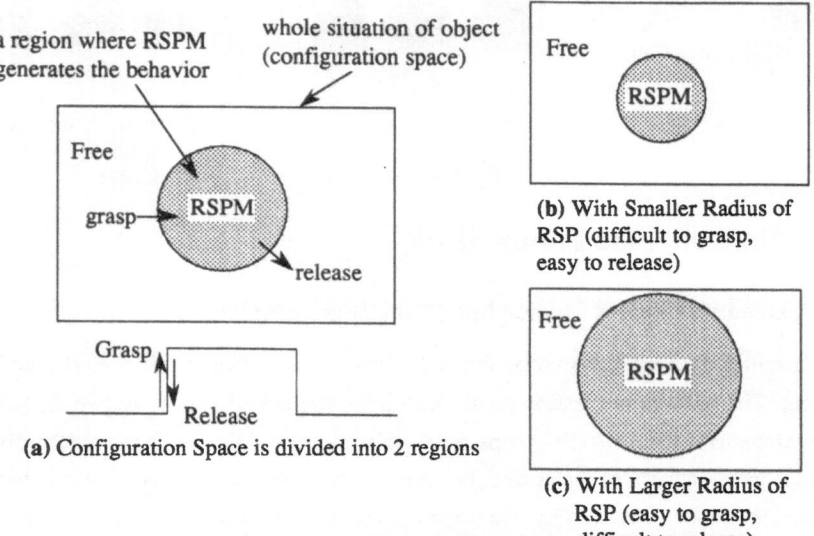

(a) Configuration Space is divided into 2 regions

(b) With Smaller Radius of RSP (difficult to grasp, easy to release)

(c) With Larger Radius of RSP (easy to grasp, difficult to release)

Fig. 5.1. Applicable region of RSPM

released while the user does not intend to release it, and the object is still grasped while the user intends to release it. The programmer can control the easiness to grasp and to release by the radius of RSP. As the radius increases, the region of RSPM widens, the object becomes easier to grasp and more difficult to release (Figure 5.1(c)). This parameter is not enough because it cannot increase/decrease both the easiness to grasp and release at once. To say as analogy, the control of the size of the region is not enough while it is useful to control the nature of manipulation.

To solve this problem, authors introduced the hysteresis (Figure 5.2). Before grasping (when the object is free), the radius of RSP is set to r1, and When the object is grasped, it is set to r2. When we give r1 a smaller value and r2 a larger value, it becomes more difficult to grasp and it becomes more difficult to release. This does not seem to improve the feel of manipulation. To say by analogy, we need to find the suitable shape of the boundary line of the region.

The discussion above is the region of RSPM itself. We may note briefly the further problem on the relation among different manipulation methods. Each method has an applicable region. As the discussion above shows, it is not easy to design the region solely. If there are several methods, it is needed to think about the overlapped region, about the void space of 2 regions.

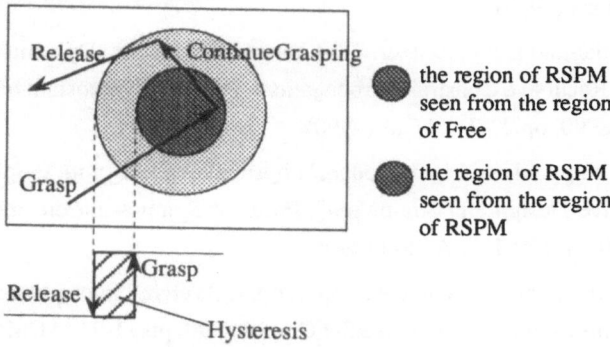

the region of RSPM seen from the region of Free

the region of RSPM seen from the region of RSPM

Fig. 5.2. Introducing Hysteresis

6 Conclusion

First, the calculation for object manipulation was generalized.

Authors pointed out that calculation of object behavior was defined as a set of pairs of the calculation model and the applicable region, the region detection. The type of region was classified into 3 categories, Dynamics, Kinematics and the boudary category of them.

Second, Impetus Method as Dynamics-like method was described for the behavior calculation of the boundary category. It was based on a simple phenomenon, the collision between fingertip and object surface. Experimental result showed superiority to the conventional method.

Third, RSPM for grasping and manipulating object by 3 finger tips, was described as Kinematics-like method. Experimental result showed superiority to the conventional method

At last, the expansion of Impetus Method into the manipulation by multiple fingertips was discussed. Also the applicable region of RSPM method was discussed.

References

[1] David Baraff, "Fast Contact Force Computation for Nonpenetrating Rigid Bodies", Procs of SigGraph '94, pp.23-34, ACM (1994)

[2] David Baraff and Andrew Witkin. "Dynamic Simulation of Non-penetrating Flexible Bodies", Procs of SigGraph '92, pp.303-308, ACM (1992)

[3] Michael Gleicher. "Integrating Contraints and Direct Manipulation", Procs of Symposium on Interactive 3D Graphics '92, pp.171-174, ACM (1992)

[4] "Qualitative Reasoning", Section 8: Computational Kinematics, Toyoaki Nishida, Asakura Books (1993)

[5] Peter Schroder and David Zeltzer. "The Virtual Elector Set: Dynamic Simulation with Linear Recursive Constraint Propagation", Procs of Symposium on Interactive 3D Graphics '90, pp.23-31, ACM (1990)

[6] Jeffrey A. Thingvold and Elaine Cohen, "Physical Modeling with B-spline Surface for Interactive Design and Animation", Procs of Symposium on Interactive 3D Graphics '90, pp.129-137, ACM (1990)

[7] Andrew Wilkin, Michael Gleicher and William Welch, "Interactive Dynamics", Procs of Symposium on Interactive 3D Graphics '90, pp.11-21, ACM (1990)

[8] David Zeltzer, "Autonomy, Interaction, and Presence", PRESENCE, Vol.1, No. 1, pp.128-132, MIT Press (1992)

Fast algorithms
for drawing Nonuniform B-spline surfaces:
a practical application in Virtual Environment

M. Bergamasco

PERCRO

Simultaneous Presence, Telepresence and Virtual Presence

Scuola Superiore S. Anna

Via Carducci, 40, 56127 Pisa, Italy

e-mail: bergamasco@sssup1.sssup.it

D. Bucciarelli, P. Degl'Innocenti

Humanware s.r.l

Via XXIV Maggio 62, 56127 Pisa, Italy

Tel/Fax +39-50-554108

Abstract: The paper we intend to present deals with the problem of drawing parametric surfaces in real-time. A new fast sequential and parallel algorithm for approximate parametric surfaces with polygons is described. Its application on a single and multi-processor system is presented by emphasizing the constraints imposed by real-time applications for Virtual Reality. In particular a practical utilization of parametric surfaces for the modeling of a virtual hand-arm complex is described.

1   Introduction

The requirements of real-time performances can be considered one of the irremissible aspects to be taken into account when the control of a direct interaction with Virtual Environments must be obtained. This fact assumes even greater importance for those applications tied with manipulative procedures, in which the human operator is asked to touch, explore and grasp virtual objects according to a realistic behaviour [7] [8].

The constraint of achieving a high degree of realism in the performance of such operations involves all afferent sensory modal pathways of the interface systems. In particular, as far as the visual component is concerned, the intense utilization of high level rendering techniques for the graphical representation of the objects and human body parts belonging to the Virtual Environment must be considered. In this paper we address the problem of achieving an adequate real-time graphical representation of human body parts by exploiting a new algorithm based on Nonuniform B-spline surface descriptions.

As a theoretical introduction to the problem is given in the following by means of a brief description of the definition of nonuniform B-splines. For a complete introduction to the theory of parametric surfaces representation refer to [1][2][3][5][4].

If np is the number of control points and k is the order of nonuniform B-splines, the nonperiodic knot vector, for a curve or surface with the end points coincident with the end control points, is:

$$T = (t_0, \cdots, t_{np+k}) = (\underbrace{0, \cdots, 0}_{k}, t_k, \cdots, t_{np}, \underbrace{1, \cdots, 1}_{k})$$

Remember that we have to define only one knot vector with a curve, while, in the case of a surface, we have to define two knot vectors, one for each component. The blending functions are:

$$N_{i,1}(u) = \begin{cases} 1 & \text{if } t_i \leq u \leq t_{i+1} \\ 0 & \text{otherwise} \end{cases} \tag{1}$$

$$N_{i,k}(u) = \frac{(u - t_i)N_{i,k-1}(u)}{t_{i+k-1} - t_i} + \frac{(t_{i+k} - u)N_{i+1,k-1}(u)}{t_{i+k} - t_{i+1}} \tag{2}$$

The general formula for evaluating a parametric surface, of n per m control points, in a point (u, v), is:

$$\boxed{Q(u, v) = \sum_{i=0}^{n} \sum_{j=0}^{m} p_{i,j} N_{i,k_u}(u) N_{j,k_v}(v)} \tag{3}$$

where k_u and k_v are the order in u and v of the surfaces.
For evaluating the efficiency of each alghoritms, we define:

$$Cost_Q(n, m, k) = nm Cost_N(k) \tag{4}$$

where

$$Cost_N(k) = \begin{cases} 1 & \text{if } k = 0 \\ 4 + 2Cost_N(k - 1) & \text{otherwise} \end{cases}$$

as the number of multiplications for evaluating the parametric surface in (u_{index}, v_{index}) with the function Q.

2   The algorithm

If we fix a set S of ns sample points:

$$S = \{(u_0, v_0)_0, \cdots, (u_{ns-1}, v_{ns-1})_{ns-1}\} \tag{5}$$

we can define a new function:

$$NN_{i,j}(index) = N_{i,k_u}(u_{index})N_{j,k_v}(v_{index}) \tag{6}$$

We can now define the matrix $NT_{n\times m\times ns}$ (N Table) with $NT_{i,j,index} = NN_{i,j}(S_{index})$; for example the 2D matrix $NT_{i,j,1}$ is equal to:

$$\left\{ \begin{array}{cccc} NN_{0,0}(S_1) & NN_{0,1}(S_1) & \cdots & NN_{0,m-1}(S_1) \\ NN_{1,0}(S_1) & NN_{1,1}(S_1) & \cdots & NN_{1,m-1}(S_1) \\ \cdots\cdots\cdots\cdots\cdots\cdots\cdots\cdots\cdots\cdots\cdots\cdots\cdots\cdots\cdots\cdots \\ NN_{n-1,0}(S_1) & NN_{n-1,1}(S_1) & \cdots & NN_{n-1,m-1}(S_1) \end{array} \right\}$$

The function (3) becomes:

$$Q(u, v) = Q_S(index)$$

where:

$$\boxed{Q_S(index) = \sum_{i=0}^{n}\sum_{j=0}^{m} p_{i,j} NT_{i,j,index}} \tag{7}$$

At this point we can easily precalculate NT and evaluate the parametric surface in (u_{index}, v_{index}) with only nm multiplications. As for (4) we can define

$$Cost_{Q_S}(n, m, k) = nm \tag{8}$$

The function $N_{i,j}$ (and the value of $NT_{i,j}(index)$ which is function of N) is equal to zero for many values of i and j. For (1) and (2) the function $N_{i,k}(u)$ (and for (6), the function $NN_{i,j}(index)$) is zero $\forall u \notin [t_i, t_{i+k}]$ and $\forall v \notin [t_j, t_{j+k}]$. This suggests another improvement for the algorithm. We can define the matrix $RIT_{ns\times 2}$ (Row Index Table) with $RIT_{index,0}$ equal to:

$$Min\{0 \leq i < n \quad | \quad \forall \quad 0 \leq j \leq m, NT_{i,j,index} \neq 0\}$$

and $RIT_{index,1}$ equal to:

$$Max\{0 \leq i < n \quad | \quad \forall \quad 0 \leq j \leq m, NT_{i,j,index} \neq 0\}$$

and the matrix $CIT_{ns\times n\times 2}$ (Column Index Table) with $CIT_{index,i,0}$:

$$Min\{0 \leq j < m \quad | \quad NT_{i,j,index} \neq 0\}$$

and $CIT_{index,i,1}$:

$$Max\{0 \leq j < m \quad | \quad NT_{i,j,index} \neq 0\}$$

CIT is defined only for $RIT_{index,0} < i < RIT_{index,1}$. The function (7) becomes:

$$FQ_S(index) = \sum_{i=RIT_{index,0}}^{RIT_{index,1}} \sum_{j=CIT_{index,1,0}}^{CIT_{index,i,1}} p_{i,j} NT i, j, index \qquad (9)$$

The evaluation of the parametric surface in (u_{index}, v_{index}) now it costs:

$$(RIT_{index,1} - RIT_{index,0})(CIT_{index,i,1} CIT_{index,i,0}) \qquad (10)$$

multiplications. The value of (10) is a function of the knot vectors (the function $N_{i,k}(u)$ is zero outside the range $[t_i, t_{i+k}]$) and it is not easy to estimate the value of $Cost_{FQ_S}$. For simplicity we can use this definition:

$$Cost_{FQ_S}(n, m, k) = \alpha n m \qquad \text{where} \quad 0 < \alpha < 1 \qquad (11)$$

with α as a function of knot vectors of the Nonuniform B-spline. Normally α is mainly a function of the order of the parametric surfaces. We can now evaluate the relative efficiency of our new algorithm with respect to classic algorithm:

$$E = \frac{Cost_Q(n, m, k)}{Cost_{FQ_S}(n, m, k)} = \frac{Cost_N(k)}{\alpha} \gg 1$$

In a practical case E is greater than 180-200.

3 The multi-processor evolution of the algorithm

The algorithm described in Section 2 is sequential but can be easily extended for direct use on a parallel machine. There is the theoretical possibility of implementing the algorithm on a massive SIMD parallel computer and on a MIMD parallel machine with local memory, but we will describe only a theoretical and practical method for using parametric surfaces on a symmetric multi-processor system with shared memory and with a small number of processors, because this type of computer is the more diffuse and available kind of parallel machine. On a symmetric multi-processor system with shared memory and a small number of processors, the cost of communication and synchronization suggests to calculate more parametric surfaces in parallel than to calculate a single surface on multiple CPU. For writing a library with a C-like language in order to calculate nonuniform B-spline in parallel, we suppose to have the following function:

- a function *name of semaphore*=InitSem(*Initial value of the semaphore*);

- a function V(*name of semaphore*) for doing a signal on a semaphore;

- a function P(*name of semaphore*) for doing a wait on a semaphore;

Figure 1: A B-Splines based virtual Hand/Arm used for force feedback experiments at Scuola Superiore S.Anna.

- a function SProc(*name of a function*), a variant of the UNIX function fork, for creating a new process that is a clone of the process that called SProc and that shares the virtual address space of the parent process.

The shared dates of the library are:

```
#define MAX_BUF_SIZE 40

semaphore ProdSem,CalcedSem,MutexSem;

float ****NTable;
int ***RIT,****CIT;

ParamSurfacePtr PSurface[MAX_BUF_SIZE];
PolygonGridPtr SurfBuffer[MAX_BUF_SIZE];
NormalGridPtr SurfNormalBuffer[MAX_BUF_SIZE];

short SurfaceInBuffer,
   SurfaceCalced,NumSubdiv[2];
```

where *NTable* is a table of values defined by the (6). Please note that in a practical implementation, the set S, defined in (5), is a regular grid of values between $(0,0)$ and $(1,1)$:

$$NTable[i][j][k][t] = N_{i,k_u}\left(\frac{k}{NumSubd_u - 1}\right)$$
$$N_{j,k_v}\left(\frac{t}{NumSubd_v - 1}\right)$$

where $NumSubd_u$ and $NumSubd_v$ are the numbers of subdivision of the interval $[0 \cdots 1]$ in u and v. In the library, NumSubdiv[0] will be equal to $NumSubd_u$ and NumSubdiv[1] to $NumSubd_v$. The set S defined in (5) now becomes:

$$S_{k,t} = \left\{\begin{array}{ccc}
(0,0) & \cdots & (0,1) \\
\left(\frac{1}{NumSubd_u-1},0\right) & \cdots & \left(\frac{1}{NumSubd_u-1},1\right) \\
\cdots\cdots\cdots\cdots\cdots\cdots\cdots\cdots\cdots\cdots\cdots \\
(1,0) & \cdots & (1,1)
\end{array}\right\}$$

RIT and *CIT* will be initialized according to the definitions given in Section 2. The meaning of *ProdSem, CalcedSem, MutexSem, SurfaceInBuffer, SurfaceCalced* will be explained below. The initialization function, that is called only at the startup of the program, is:

```
void InitBSpline(short NumCtrlPnt[2],
  float *KnotVectorU,short NumKVU,
  float *KnotVectorV,short NumKVV,
  short NumSubd[2],short NumProc)
{
  int i;

  NumSubdiv[0]=NumSubd[0];
  NumSubdiv[1]=NumSubd[1];

  NTable=AllocAndInitNTable(NumSubd,
    KnotVectorU,NumKVU,
    KnotVectorV,NumKVV,NumCtrlPnt);

  RIT=AllocAndInitRIT(NumCtrlPnt,
    NumSubd,NTable);
  CIT=AllocAndInitCIT(NumCtrlPnt,
    NumSubd,NTable);

  ProdSem=InitSem(0);
  CalcedSem=InitSem(0);
  MutexSem=InitSem(1);

  SurfaceInBuffer=SurfaceCalced=0;
```

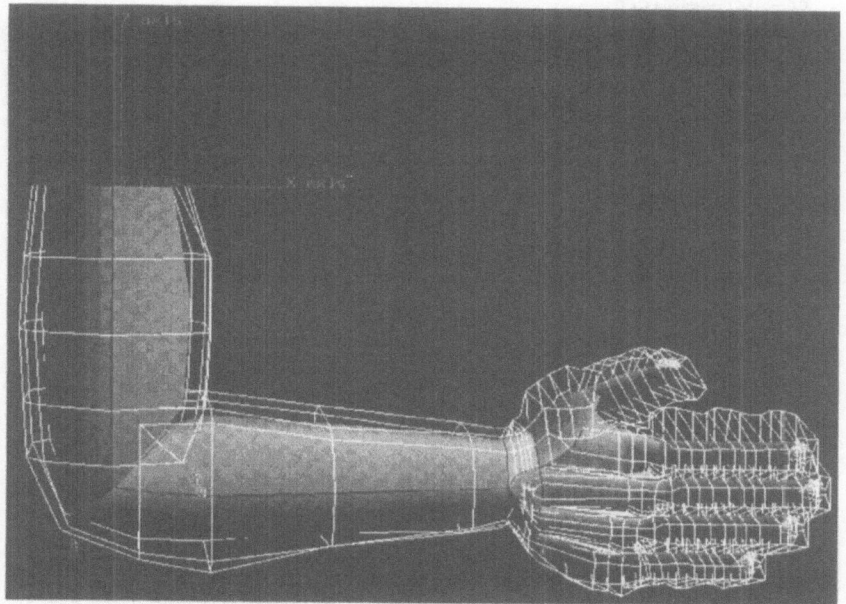

Figure 2: The virtual Hand/Arm and the grids of control points of the parametric surfaces.

```
  for(i=0;i<NumProc;i++)
    SProc(SurfProc);
}
```

In this function we precalculate *NTable*, *CIT* and *RIT* as described in Section 2. The semaphore *ProdSem* is created and initialized to 0; on this semaphore the parent will signal to the children processes, generated by the function *SProc*, when a new nonuniform B-spline is present in the buffer *PSurface*. The semaphore *CalcedSem* is created and initialized to 0; on this semaphore the children processes will signal when they finished the calculus of the transformation between parametric surface and the grid of polygons. The semaphore *MutexSem* is used for mutual exclusion by the children processes. *SurfaceInBuffer* is the index of the first free cell in *PSurface* and it is equal to the number of surfaces in the buffer. *SurfaceCalced* is the index of the first parametric surface in the buffer *SurfaceInBuffer* to be calculated. The code of the library is:

```
void SurfProc(void)
{
  int x,y,cn;

  for(;;) {
    P(ProdSem);
    P(MutexSem);
```

```
      cn=SurfaceCalced;
      SurfaceCalced++;
      V(MutexSem);

      for(x=0;x<NumSubdiv[0];x++)
        for(y=0;y<NumSubdiv[1];y++)
          FastEvalP(PSurface[cn],
            x,y,SurfBuffer[cn][x][y]);

      CalcSurfaceNormal(SurfBuffer[cn],
        SurfNormalBuffer[cn]);

      P(CalcedSem);
  }
}

void CalcSurfacePoint(PSurfacePtr cp,
  PolygonGridPt pg,NormalGridPtr ng)
{
  PSurface[SurfaceInBuffer]=cp;
  SurfBuffer[SurfaceInBuffer]=pg;
  SurfNormalBuffer[SurfaceInBuffer]=ng;
  SurfaceInBuffer++;

  V(ProdSem);
}

void WaitCalcSurface(void)
{
  int i;

  for(i=0;i<SurfaceInBuffer;i++)
    P(CalcedSem);

  SurfaceCalced=SurfaceInBuffer=0;
}
```

The function *FastEvalP()* is the implementation of the formula (11).

In *SurfProc()* we call the function *CalcSurfaceNormal()* for calculating the normals to the surface *SurfBuffer[cn]*. A typical use of the functions in the library is the following:

```
main()
{
  ...
  PSurfacePtr cp[NS];
  ...
  InitBSpline(...);
  ...
  for(;;) {
```

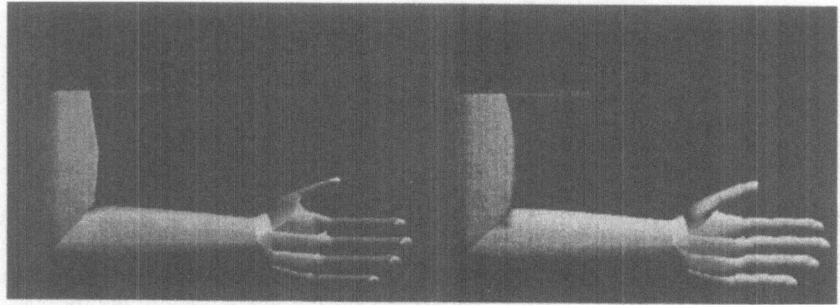

Figure 3: The parametric surfaces approximated with 4x4 polygons (left) and 8x8 polygons (right).

```
    CalcSurfacePoint(cp[0],...);
      ...
    CalcSurfacePoint(cp[NS-1],...);
      ...
    /* Do everything you want. */
      ...
    WaitCalcSurface();
    DrawSurfaces(cp,NS);
  }
}
```

4 Modeling a virtual hand and arm by parametric surfaces

A set of 40 nonuniform B-splines was used to design a virtual arm and hand. We successfully use our mono and multi-processor alghoritm for converting parametric surfaces in polygons meshes for a practical application. We conduct experiments using an *Arm Exoskeleton System* (see [6]) and a *Hand Exoskeleton System* developed at Scuola Superiore S. Anna [9].

The exoskeletons are capable of recording all arm and hand movements and to replicate forces on the arm and the hand. By moving the control points (see Fig. 2 for the grids of control points) of parametric surfaces according to the data coming from the exoskeletons, we are able to draw a virtual hand and arm that replicates and follows the position and the shape (empirically representing the deformation of the skin) of the real hand and arm.

Also we developed a physically based simulation of the virtual environment for replicating by means of the exoskeletons, on the real arm and hand, forces generates by virtual objects (see [7] [8]).

We obtained 12-15 frames per second with the mono-processor version of the alghoritm on a Silicon Graphics Personal Iris 4D/35TG with some very simply objects and a virtual arm/hand drawn with 40 nonuniform B-splines approxi-

Indigo R4000 100MHz	frame/sec
GL	5.4
New Algorithm	28.9

Table 1: Comparison between GL and our new algorithm.

mated by 4x4 polygons meshes (see Fig. 3 for 4x4 and 8x8 approximations) for a total of 640 polygons.

With a very complex environment like that showed in Fig. 1 and 40 nonuniform B-splines approximated by 4x4 polygons meshes for a total of 640 polygons we obtained 16-20 frames per second with the multi-precessor version of the alghoritm running on a Silicon Graphics Powers 440VGX (a multi-processor with four MIPS R3000 processors and a fast graphic subsystem).

On the same machine we obtained more than 32 frames per second, by transforming from parametric representation to polygons meshes more than 1300 parametric surfaces per second, for an application requiring a simple virtual scenario.

During the development of the research we make a compared test between our single processor algorithm described in (7) and *nurbssurface()* of SGI Graphics Library. For the test of drawing a B-spline modelled virtual hand on an Indigo R4000 100MHz, we obtained the results described in the table 4.

The GL function achieves a better visual apparency, probably because it uses an adaptative approximation of the parametric surfaces, but our preliminary version of the algorithm is about 6 times faster than the GL equivalent function. With the final version of the algorithm and a multi-processor system, you can achieve an increment of performances of more than one order of magnitude. This is a crucial point with the constraints imposed by a real time application as Virtual Reality.

5   Conclusions

The article we have presented describes a new approach to the design of virtual hand and arm in a Virtual Environment. A complete description of a new mono and multi-processor alghoritm has been presented. Experimental results on a high performance real-time practical application has been described.

Acknowledgments

The research activity described in this article has been developed under the project EP5363 GLAD-IN-ART and Esprit Basic Research 6358 SCATIS.

References

[1] Michael E.Monterson, *"Geometric Modeling,"* John Wiley & Sons, 1985.

[2] Faux, I.D. and Pratt, M.J., *"Computational Geometry for Design and Manufacture"*, Ellis Horwood, Chichester UK, 1979.

[3] Farin, G., *"Curves and Surfaces for Computer Aided Design"*, 2nd edn, Academic Press, Boston, 1990.

[4] David F.Rogers, J.Alan Adams, *"Mathematical Elements for Computer Graphics,"* Mc Graw Hill, 1990.

[5] Alan Watt, Mark Watt, *"Advanced Animation and Rendering Techniques"*, Addison-Wesley, 1992.

[6] M. Bergamasco, B. Allotta, L. Bosio, L. Ferretti, G. Parrini, G.M. Prisco, F. Salsedo, G. Sartini, "An Arm Exoskeleton System for Teleoperation and Virtual Environments Applications," *IEEE International Conference on Robotics and Automation*, San Diego, CA, May 1994.

[7] M. Bergamasco, P. Degl' Innocenti, D. Bucciarelli, G. Rigucci, "Grasping and Moving Objects in Virtual Environments: a preliminary approach towards a relistic behaviour," *IEEE International Workshop on Robot and Human Communication*, ROMAN'94, Nagoya, Japan, July 1994.

[8] M. Bergamasco, P. Degl' Innocenti, D. Bucciarelli, "A Realistic Approach for Grasping and Moving Virtual Objects," *IEEE/RSJ/GI International Conference on Intelligent Robots and Systems 1994*, IROS'94, Monaco, September 1994

[9] M. Bergamasco, F. Salsedo, L. Ferretti, A. Scoglio, G. Piperno, *"Force Feedback Interfaces for Virtual Environments Applications,"* submitted to *MONTPELLIER'95*, Montpellier, France, June 1995.

Virtual molecules, rendering speed, and image quality

Helmut Haase, Johannes Strassner, Fan Dai

Fraunhofer Institute for Computer Graphics (Fraunhofer IGD),
Wilhelminenstr. 7, D-64283 Darmstadt, Germany*

Abstract

In this paper we present a system for investigating molecule data by means of Virtual Reality techniques. This allows new insights into the structure of individual molecules as well as into the interaction between multiple molecules. Scientific Visualization, especially when performed in Virtual Environments, must consider two opposing demands: Maximum image quality at sufficient frame rates. With this in mind we discuss a general scheme for determining the quality of (3D) graphical computer systems. For this scheme, we are focusing on the user's perception of the system. Therefore, we do not include factors like memory size or processor speed directly, even though they may influence other features which we consider crucial for Graphics System Quality (GSQ), e.g., rendering speed. We identify three components of Graphics System Quality: Data quality, image quality, and interaction quality. We show that our system for immersive investigation of molecule data is unique in its advanced combination of image quality and interaction quality.

Keywords: Molecular Modeling, Virtual Reality, Scientific Visualization, Realtime Interaction, Graphics System Quality

1 Graphics System Quality

As hardware and software for Virtual Reality[2] improve rapidly, it becomes feasible to apply these new technologies to one of the major fields of computer graphics: Scientific Visualization[9].

There are already a number of applications utilizing this synergy (virtual windtunnel[6], VR in dataflow systems[25], the CAVE environment with several visualizations[8], and material testing, 3D weather visualization, medical training, and visualization of room accoustics, all in [14]). Whenever VR is to be used for Scientific Visualization, the opposing demands of image quality and rendering speed have to be met in a certain way [7].

---

*Email: {haase, strassne, dai}@igd.fhg.de — http://www.igd.fhg.de

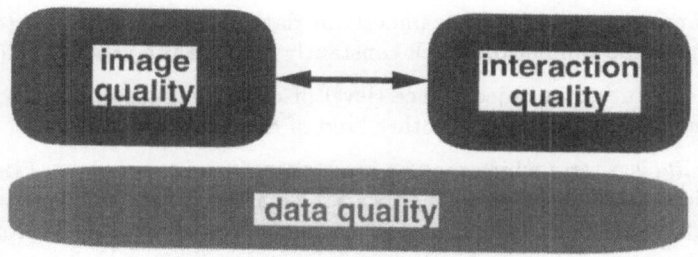

Figure 1: Main factors influencing Graphics System Quality.

Starting from this observation, we developed a general scheme for determining the quality of a (**3D**) graphical system. This scheme is a revised and elaborated version based on previous suggestions[10][14]. The scheme does not explicitely comprise "hidden" features like memory size or processor speed, even though they may influence factors which we consider important for Graphics System Quality (GSQ), e.g., rendering speed. Rather, the scheme comprises features which are visible to the user directly.

The scheme consists of three main components (see fig. 1): Data quality, image quality, and interaction quality. The details of these main components are summarized in Table 1.

Data Quality	Image Quality	Interaction Quality
1. Only geometric or image data	• Object space resolution	• Rendering speed (static,sequence,realtime)
2. Static semantics (precomputed)	• Image space resolution	• Degree of interaction (none, interactive, VR)
3. Dynamic semant. (online vis.)	• Color space resolution	• Number of users (none, one, multiple)
	• Rendering/shading (wireframe, flat, gouraud, phong)	

Table 1: Components of Graphics System Quality.

In the following, we will explain the components of the GSQ scheme in more detail.

Data quality stands for the semantics of graphic objects. Possible data qualities are:

1. no semantics, i.e., no other data represented by graphic objects;

2. static semantics, i.e., each graphic object represents static data which may be accessed by the system (e.g., an arrow in a visualization system may represent a velocity vector);

3. dynamic semantics, i.e., the underlying data changes within time (e.g., due to an online simulation which constantly changes the velocity field).

Note that resolution in object space (level of detail) is subsumed under image quality, but that it actually is another kind of data quality.

Image quality is a term which may be used with different meanings. First of all, its definition may depend on the application area, e.g., text, technical drawings, video. For the sake of this paper, we are mainly interested in (sequences of) raster images of scientific 3D data. Furthermore, image quality can be investigated on a very basic level (spatial resolution of pixels, dynamic range, etc.), on higher levels (geometric distortion, feature distortion, etc.), or even on a very high conceptual level (style, redundancy, etc.). For an overview of the state-of-the-art of definition and measurement of image quality, see [12].

Image quality is an assembly of several factors, all influencing the amount of information which is accessible from a single image. For our purposes, the following characteristics seem most important for the definition of image quality:

- Resolution in object space: number of polygons of a geometric object (in VR known as level of detail) or size of voxel dataset.

- Resolution in image space: number of pixels in x and y direction, i.e., resolution in 'dots per inch' times width or height of image.

- Resolution in color space: number of colors in the image; often depending on the number of bitplanes in the graphics hardware of the computer which is being used.

- Rendering/shading method: e.g., wireframe rendering, flat shading of polygons, gouraud or phong shading.

Finally, *interaction quality* is an important component of the GSQ scheme. It comprises:

- Rendering speed: measured in frames per second (fps); roughly we may identify three classes of rendering speed: single frames (< 0.1 fps), frame sequences (0.1 fps to 10 fps), and realtime rendering (> 10 fps).

- Degree of interaction: this item depends on the devices which are being used and on the interaction techniques. We distinguish three classes of interaction: no interaction (batch mode); interactive (usual interaction by means of keyboard or mouse, display on computer screen); and immersive (feeling of being surrounded by a 'world' which is actually computer generated; often achieved by means of special input and output devices like data glove or head mounted display as well as by special interaction techniques such as direct manipulation of 3D objects).

- Number of users: to be more precise, this means the number of users which are able to interact with the system simultaneously during its operation. Again there are three classes: no user (batch mode); one user (single user system); and multiple users (e.g., computer supported cooperative work).

Up to now, the scheme presented here is still preliminary. Work is under way to further elaborate this scheme, to develop a quantitative measure for Graphics System Quality, and to apply the scheme to different samples of scientific visualization. In this process we will also perform psychological tests.

The remaining part of this paper will be focused on a system we developed for immersive investigation of molecule data. Even though the system only offers the most basic data quality (geometry without semantics), both image quality and interaction quality have reached a high level which allows for new ways of investigation.

2   Computer Supported Molecular Modeling

In general, data must be interpreted in order to become useful information. Often, biochemical data are best interpreted by the use of 3D representations. In the past, wooden or plastic models were used in order to investigate the three-dimensional structure of molecules. In the mid-1960s, computers became powerful enough for first small applications in interactive computer graphics. Research on computer systems to understand and model molecular structures was reported by MIT in 1966 [20]. Other early works – all of them utilizing vector graphics hardware – were reported in [16] and in [18].

Later, research on computer systems for molecular modeling has also been reported in [26], [23], [21], [30], [27], [29], and [3]. In order to examine interaction between two molecules, explicit van der Waals energy and/or Coulombic energy can be computed. Algorithmic approaches to examine docking of guest molecules to host stuctures has been investigated in many papers, examples are [11] and [13]. Most techniques have been incorporated in commercially available systems, e.g., by BIOSYM Technologies, Inc. [4].

Nevertheless, 3D presentation techniques and interaction methods using a "conventional" (mouse-menu driven) user interface still have some disadvantages: spatial relationships are often difficult to recognize and no direct navigation or handling of graphic objects is possible.

Robert Langridge, who began to apply interactive 3D computer graphics to molecules in 1964, just recently observed that "a system which provides real time, interactive three dimensional ray traced images of arbitrary objects is not here yet", and therefore, in visualizing molecules "it is often convenient to switch between the real-time (usually vector) interactive display and the shaded 'realistic' display"[19].

Lately, Virtual Environment (VE), or Virtual Reality techniques offer new possibilities of presentation and investigation of multidimensional data interactively at high quality. From its very beginning, handling of 3D graphics and interaction with 3D objects strived to be as intuitive as possible. Immersion offers the highest degree of intuitive interaction. Especially Scientific Visualization can benefit from the possibility of immersion. VR techniques have been utilized for visualization of molecular data as reported in [22], [5], and in [28].

Plastic models of molecules are still in use sometimes, but today, computer graphics allows to view molecules in 3D in a much more flexible way without the tedious process of assembling small parts by hand, allowing for display of additional information as well as for computation of constraints in the manipulation of molecules which were hard to imagine just 30 years ago.

In chemistry, several different models for molecules are known which help in understanding 3D structure and properties of a molecule. Each of these models stresses certain properties and is more or less appropriate for certain tasks.

Ball-and-stick-models represent atoms by spheres and bondings by sticks (see color plate 4, Appendix). Types of atoms are distinguished by characteristic colors (e.g., red for oxygen). The distance between atoms and the angle of bondings becomes apparent.

Surface models allow to project properties like the electrostatic potential onto the shell by means of a color coding scheme (see color plate 1, Appendix).

Enzyme-substratum-complexes play an important role in biochemical processes. Enzymes are catalysts of chemical reactions within cells. If they are present, the activation energy of a reaction is lowered. The enzyme reacts with its substratum, which is a certain chemical substance. It is important to note that the substratum fits to the enzyme like a key to its lock. By means of the enzyme-substratum-complex, the substratum is induced to participate in a specific chemical reaction.

Some enzymes can be deactivated by inhibitors which modify the surface of the enzyme in a way which makes it impossible for it to form an enzyme-substratum-complex.

In the following we will present the details of a VE system which allows interactive investigation of molecules and of the relationships between enzyme, substratum, and inhibitor.

3 VRMol - A System for the Immersive Investigation of Molecule Data

The aim of the system *VRMol* which was designed at Fraunhofer-IGD in Darmstadt is to investigate properties of individual and relationship of multiple complex molecules interactively within a highly immersive environment.

Therefore, several Virtual Reality and Scientific Visualization techniques have been implemented within this system.

A *level of detail* technique with several levels of detail is used to achieve fast rendering while still showing as many details as possible due to resolution.

Ball-and-stick representations of molecules contain a large number of spheres depicting atoms. In our system, these spheres are not rendered as ordinary polygonal objects. Instead, a fast, specialized *algorithm for rendering spheres* is being utilized for higher performance.

Another way to speed up rendering which is suggested here and which was implemented successfully is *utilization of several rendering pipelines*. On a multi-processor multi-pipeline machine, individual processes running on individual processors and using individual rendering pipelines can be used to render the two images for a stereo display in parallel, accessing common data structures in shared memory.

The 'surface' of a molecule can be displayed transparently with surface colors depicting electrostatic potential, hydrophobic potential, etc. In order to gain the frame rates mandatory for interactive handling of larger molecules, surface triangles are organized to form triangle strips (a special form of polygon meshes). Fast rendering of *transparent triangle strip surfaces* is supported by graphics hardware, but the transparent strips need to be sorted in viewing direction to avoid artifacts.

In order to allow simultaneous movement of viewer and a molecule, *two different multidimensional input devices* are supported: a data glove for viewing and a space mouse for rotating and translating a molecule.

Virtual menus allow selection of the molecules to be displayed as well as of their parameters: ball-and-stick representation with or without simultaneous surface model, etc.

Finally, *fast shadows* have been implemented in order to give the viewer an impression of shape, size, and position of each molecule in addition to the stereo display. Shadows have been realized by computing projections from several standard rotations and by displaying the appropriate one as a texture on the synthetic floor of the scene.

All the techniques which were realized in this system contribute in one way or another to the final goal of investigating molecules in high quality at interactive frame rates. They may also be used in other applications like assembly tasks, virtual material testing, medical training, 3D weather forecast, etc.

4   Implementation

The concepts which are outlines in this paper were implemented on a Silicon Graphics workstation with three RealityEngineII graphics pipelines, and with space mouse, data glove, and large screen projection as external devices.

VRMol was realized by extending an existing Virtual Environment system (Virtual Design [1]). Therefore it belongs to category 2 according to our characterization of Immersive Scientific Visualization systems in [15].

Molecule data can be imported in form of the common pdb file format (Brookhaven Protein Data Bank). Since this file does not contain the bondings directly, they must be inferred from the data available. This makes it neccessary to include a complete table of all possible bonding atoms for each amino-acid.

The corresponding surface model has been computed outside of VRMol in a preprocessing step [29]; it is read into the system from an external file. Several molecules can be loaded into the system in order to compare them or to combine them at will.

5 Image Generation

The molecules are displayed in any combination of ball-and-stick and surface model. Atoms are represented by colored spheres, bondings by approximated "cylinders" with strips consisting of ten triangles (i.e., 5 faces). Smooth appearence of these "cylinders" is achieved by Gouraud shading.

Several levels of detail are used to represent atoms, bondings, and surfaces. Depending on the distance between viewer and object, a geometric representation is chosen for the object which posesses as few polygons as possible while still looking realistically (see next section). These geometric models were automatically generated with an inhouse reduction algorithm [24].

The surface model may be rendered transparently in order to see the interior ball-and-stick model or opaquely in order to gain a better perception of surface colors. These colors depict properties of the shell. In a preprocessing step, all surface triangles are organized to form triangle strips for faster hardware rendering. The transparent surface polyons are sorted in viewing direction in order to avoid artifacts. Thus, for each surface we precompute a number of objects sorted according to different viewing directions. Since transparent sufraces do not allow a precise perception of colors or small surface details, we use a reduced geometry in the case of transparent surface models in order to speed up the rendering process. During real time operation the system selects the object which gives best results according to the current viewing angle. Strip generation and the sorting process for transparency are explained in more detail in separate sections.

Size and position of a molecule can be perceived due to a shadow [31] which is cast onto a "floor" (see color plate 4, Appendix). For several standard orientations of the molecule, exact shadows have been precomputed. One of them is shown under the molecule. If the molecule is rotated about an axis other than the vertical one, the precomputed shadow is replaced by another one if a certain angle is reached. Even though this 'flipping' is hard to perceive, smooth transition from one precomputed shadow to the next is desired. Some ideas exist to solve this problem (e.g., interpolation between two images, etc.), but no satisfactory solution has been implemented yet.

In order to be able to estimate accurately surface colors (and thus surface properties), the molecule under investigation always must be properly lit. Increasing the ambient light would lead to a brighter image, but colors would look less intense and perception of differences in shell properties would be more difficult. Therefore, a point light source slightly above the eye point is used which results in deep colors even in surface pockets that normally would be in the shade.

The numerical value associated with a color can be interesting in order to decide if a substratum fits to an enzyme. This information could be shown in a legend at the left border of the screen. Data probing (e.g., with the index finger of the data glove) would also help in this task but is not yet implemented.

Each time a complex molecule is displayed in ball-and-stick representation, a huge number of spheres has to be rendered. Therefore, it makes sense to treat spheres as rendering primitives within our system. This drastically reduces rendering time as well as the time required to load the molecule description upon initialization of the system. The rendering of the spheres is based on a special library from Silicon Graphics. One can choose between 30 different resolutions for a sphere. Before rendering a sphere, a number of parameters like resolution, center point, radius, color, and material must be specified. Because of a special caching for this primitive the spheres must be sorted depending on these parameters.

All atoms of one molecule should be organized in one large special object in order to calculate the transformation matix only once.

Backface culling speeds up the rendering process and makes it easier to navigate in a molecule, because one can fly inside a sphere and still see what lies behind it.

A further speedup was achieved by utilizing two rendering pipelines on our triple pipe machine for stereo rendering. We implemented three UNIX processes accessing a common shared memory. The application process initially writes all the graphics data structures into shared memory. It also handles all input devices and updates transformation matrices, visibility flags, etc. Two rendering processes access the shared memory to read all graphics data structures and to render one image of the stereo pair each. In order to decouple application process and rendering processes, all graphics data structures are helt in memory twice: one copy may be manipulated by the application while the other (stable) one is being used for rendering. In order to activate changes, the rendering processes are told to access the graphics data structures which have been changed by the application while the application now will access the data structures which formerly were used for rendering. All communication between the processes is performed by means of the shared memory.

6 Level of Detail

A detailed surface and smooth rendering of spheres are important for the visualization of molecules but also expensive regarding performance. The desired realism could be achieved by employing very complex models. But, the number of polygons which can be rendered in real time is limited. Therefore, a technique called "level of detail" is used in order to get a compromise between realistic appearance and scene complexity.

The farther away an object is from the observer, the fewer details can be distinguished. This is due to perspective shrinking of an object and limited screen resolution.

Therefore, the complexity of an object can be reduced according to its distance from the observer without loss of realism. If an object occupies the full field of view at a distance d_0, then it will occupy $\frac{1}{i^2}$ of the field of view at distance $d_i = i * d_0$. The following figure shows how the apparent size of an object is decreasing with increasing distance from the observer.

Since the apparent size of an object decreases dramatically up to a distance

78

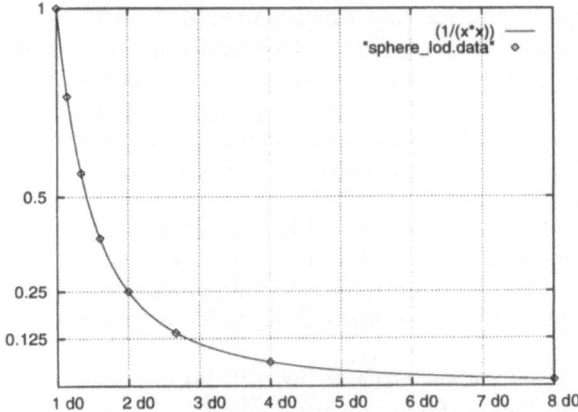

Figure 2: Level of Detail: Distance of an object and associated apparent size. Schematic view (left) and exact values (right).

of $4d_0$, it is recommended to supply most levels of detail for this interval. This results in a relatively high frame rate in spite of complex objects. The marks in the figure present a suggestion for assigning 8 levels of detail to distances.

In order to generate reduced models which resemble the high resolution model as good as possible, automatic reduction algorithms have been developed [24].

Level of detail is a technique which is used whenever smooth interaction at high frame rates is more important than precise representation of an object. For example, during movement of an object representing a complex data set, it can be useful to choose a reduced model complexity. Thus, the system will adopt to the speed of the user and not vice versa.

If object hierarchies are used, each level of detail is represented by a subtree. Several subtrees are stored for each object and at rendering time, the subtree with appropriate complexity is chosen according to observer's distance, movement criteria, or the like.

In the case of rendering complex molecules, many spheres of the same color and with the same level of detail have to be rendered for each frame (e.g., carbon atoms at a medium distance from the viewer). If spheres are rendering primitives of the graphics system, rendering a huge number of identical spheres is much faster than rendering each sphere individually. In general it can be noted that each change of material (e.g., of color) costs time. Therefore, it does make sense to sort atoms according to color and to level of detail and to render all identical atoms consecutively without setting the material each time.

The level of detail technique brings a good gain in performance if a large number of rendering objects are so far away from the viewer that their complexity is reduced considerabely. Unfortunately, in scenes like the one shown in color plate 3 (see Appendix), this technique is not sufficient since many atoms are relatively close to the observer. Here, viewing culling should be used in addition, i.e., all objects which lie outside the viewing frustum will not be considered for rendering. This technique is useless in scenes like the one in color plate 1 (see appendix) where all objects are visible, but it is very effective each time the viewer is somewhere among the objects.

7 Triangle Strips

One possibilty to describe a surface model is the declaration of points which are connected by edges and where a number of edges form a polygon. A more efficient description is the use of triangle strips. With this technique a number of triangles is specified by a list of points. Three points specify a triangle. Every next point forms a new triangle together with the two previous points. Rendering speed is proportional to the average length of all triangle strips, i.e., for maximum performance one has to generate triangle strips with maximum length.

The following algorithm computes long triangle strips while taking into account the ordering constraints due to z-buffer artefacts when rendering transparent objects:
First the object must be traingulated.
Next, a reduction can be performed in order to reduce the complexity of the object without loosing too much details of the shape.
The starting triangle for the first strip is the one which has maximum distance from the observer. The second triangle for the strip is any of the three which are neighbours to the first triangle. The third triangle can be any of the four neighbours of the two previous triangles. To continue a triangle strip with more than three polygons there are only two possibilities (i.e., the two 'ends' of the strip).
In order to avoid artefacts during transparent z-buffer rendering, for every new triangle it must be checked that there is no yet unused polygon which would be covered by the new one.
This process is repeated until the triangle strip cannot be computed any more. If there are still unused triangles after this strip is completed, a new strip is started with the one unused triangle which has maximum distance from the observer.

Triangle strips from opaque surface models can be generated in a similar way. Because of the higher average lenght of these strips we have precomputed objects for both cases in our system.
We observed a speedup of approximately the factor two due to the usage of triangle strips.

8 Z-Buffer and Transparency

One of the most commonly used algorithms in computer graphics is the z-buffer algorithm for hidden surface removal. Graphics workstations normally have this algorithm implemented in hardware. It is very well suited for rendering opaque objects.

For the rendering of surface models together with ball-and-stick representation as well as for shadows we need transparency. Unfortunately, in the case of transparent objects the z-buffer algorithm introduces errors depending on the order of rendering of the polygons (color plate 5, see Appendix).

In the case of transparent polygons, the z-buffer algorithm compares the z-value of each pixel of a polygon after scan conversion with the corresponding entry in the z-buffer. If the new value is less than the value in the z-buffer, then you have to blend the color value of this entry with the new color value according to the transmission coefficient of the polygon.

We see that all opaque objects must be rendered before all transparent objects. Furthermore, all transparent polygons must be sorted according to distance from the viewer before rendering them back to front.

Molecular surfaces have no intersecting polygons and generally they are more or less convex. Thus, for each surface we precompute a number of graphical objects sorted according to different viewing directions.

The following algorithm assumes that small rotations ($< 90^0$) or changes of the viewing direction do not introduce strong artefacts. Therefore, we need only six instances of each surface: For each of the three coordinate axes one increasing and one decreasing version. See the following figure for naming conventions.

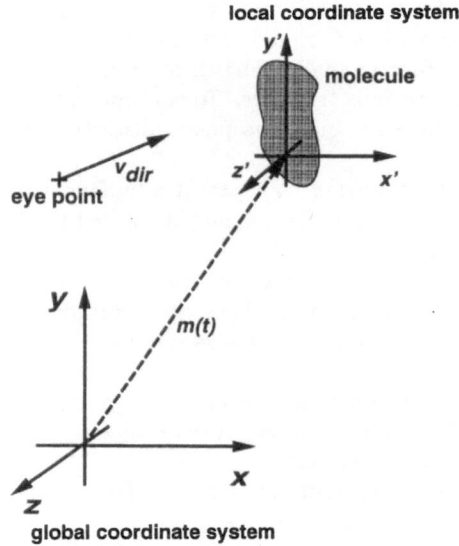

Figure 3: Naming conventions for determining the correctly sorted object for transparent z-buffer rendering.

For each molecular surface model there is a local coordinate system. The origin of this system is in the middle of the molecule. One can compute this point by dividing the sum of the atom coordinates by the number of atoms. During translation of the molecule this middle point $m(t)$ must be updated (with t = time).

A rotation of the surface model by a 3x3 rotation matrix $R(t)$ results in the following relation between the axes of the local and of the global coordinate system:

$$x' = R(t) * x - M'$$
$$y' = R(t) * y - M'$$
$$z' = R(t) * z - M'$$

where $M' = R(t) * m(t)$.

The viewing vector v_{dir} is the difference between the center of interest and the eyepoint.

Now we compute the scalar products of the transformed axes of the local coordinate system and the viewing vector:

$$scp_{x'} = x' * v_{dir}$$
$$scp_{y'} = y' * v_{dir}$$
$$scp_{z'} = z' * v_{dir}$$

The maximum of these scalar products gives us the main direction from which we are looking at the object:

$$scp_R = maximum(|scp_{x'}|, |scp_{y'}|, |scp_{z'}|),$$
$$R \in x, y, z$$

Now we choose the object which is sorted in direction R if $scp_R \geq 0$. Otherwise, the object which is sorted in the opposite direction is chosen.

By means of this algorithm, the correct objects of molecular surface models are selected which can be rendered transparently without artefacts. The algorithm can easily be augmented to choose the correct object from a lager number of orientations.

9   User Interface

Since the properties of the molecule as indicated by the surface model are of major importance for assessment of a molecule, a large screen stereo projection is used instead of a head mounted display. A head mounted display would allow much more intuitive navigation, but the low resolution of the device available for this project as well as its weight make the projection superior to the head mounted display.

A data glove is used for navigation, i.e., to change the position of the observer. An additional space mouse is used to rotate and to translate the molecule. Translation of the space mouse can be switched off in order to ensure that the molecule only rotates at a fixed position. We observed that even an unexperienced VE user can easily view a molecule by means of the space mouse.

Due to these two input devices it is also possible to rotate the molecule while changing the point of view simultaneously.

Control of the VE system is done mainly via certain data glove gestures. They were selected with special consideration of intuitive handling, e.g., the center of interest can be changed by moving the index finger.

For the assessment of molecules, viewing from several directions as well as fast switching between different representations for each of them is needed.

A virtual 3D menu floating in space is provided for selecting different representations which can be switched on or off (see color plate 2, Appendix). It offers a choice of all molecules currently available. Furthermore, ball-and-stick or surface model can be toggled independently. A toggle between opaque and transparent appearance is also avaiable. Of course, if the surface is rendered opaquely and the molecule is seen from a distance, the ball-and-stick-model is not visible and can be automatically disabled for rendering to save time.

In order to increase interactivity of the system, larger molecules are not rendered while the menu is active.

In addition to this main menu, individual menus could be offered for each currently displayed molecule to set properties of this molecule.

Visual examination of the surface structure of molecules can be used to find out which substratum and which inhibitor fit a certain enzyme.

A molecule is moved by means of a space mouse. Selection of a molecule can be performed by pressing a key of the space mouse. This has the disadvantage of being limited to up to eight molecules due to the number of keys on a space mouse.

Instead of moving the molecule with the space mouse, it could be grabbed with the data glove and moved arbitrarily. The echo of the glove is scaled in order to allow navigation within a molecule. Thus, a molecule can only be grabbed directly when the observer is close to it. Often, one wants to see the whole scene while moving a molecule. This can be achieved by means of a "ray" which is controlled by the hand. If this ray points to a molecule, any gesture done with the hand will be applied to the molecule. Thus, a molecule may be moved or a menu may be opened for it from a distance.

10   Conclusion and Future Work

The system presented here serves for analyzing individual molecules as well as for investigating pairs of molecules. It is a prototype which is being used to evaluate techniques for Immersive Scientific Visualization. It also demonstrates the importance of combining high image quality (transparent, colored surfaces of molecules casting shadows on the virtual 'floor', large numbers of shaded spheres) and high interaction quality (high frame rates, immersive devices and interaction techniques) in one system.

A useful extension would be data probing in order to determine properties on the shell of a molecule exactly. Billboards showing available molecules could be used instead of the virtual menu for selecting molecules. This would show to the user where a molecule will appear after it is selected. Collision detection [17] is necessary in order to achieve a more realistic handling of scenes containing more than one molecule and in order to investigate the fitting of molecules. Accoustic feedback should be given if a collision is detected. Force feedback devices could eventually be used for the fitting process once they become available [5]. They could also give a feeling of the stiffness of molecules and of the degrees of freedom in bending them. Furthermore, docking behaviour of molecules should be investigated by a combination of interactive techniques as discussed here together with algorithmic approaches [11][13].

By means of this particular application we wanted to motivate that Scientific Visualization will benefit from new developments in user interface technology which are commonly described by the term Virtual Environments. Immersive Scientific Visualization, i.e., Scientific Visualization giving the user the impression of being within a highly realistic but actually computer generated environment, will supplement traditional, keyboard-and-mouse based Scientific Visualization.

We are only at the beginning of Immersive Scientific Visualization which will give a new quality to traditional Scientific Visualization, leading to a large number of new applications in such fields as industry (e.g., assembly simulation), physics (e.g., deforming FE data sets), chemistry (e.g., fitting of enzyme and inhibitor), and medicine (e.g., operation planning and training).

Future research will focus on how to combine Virtual Environement and Scientific Visualization technologies best. We will find that many applications will benefit or just become possible due to these new approaches. Still, research needs to be done on many fields, e.g., force feedback, fast collision check, physically-based modelling, etc.

Also, there is need for further investigation and classification of rendering methods and other factors influencing Graphics System Quality. Only a quantitative metrics of Graphics System Quality will allow us to build systems which can automatically select the best combination of image quality and interaction quality on a given hardware configuration for each specific set of data and for each individual user.

11 Acknowledgements

We thank Dr. Heiden from the Department of Chemistry at the Technical University of Darmstadt for providing all chemical data. Furthermore we thank all the colleagues and students at our lab who contributed to the software which served as a basis for the system presented in this paper (particularly Bernd Krause), and Prof. Encarnação for creating the environment which made this

84

work possible.

References

[1] Astheimer, P., Felger, W., Müller, S.: *Virtual Design: A Generic VR System for Industrial Applications*, Computers & Graphics, Vol. 17, N0. 6, pp. 671-677, 1993

[2] Astheimer, P., Dai, F., Göbel, M., Kruse, R., Müller, S., Zachmann, G.: *Realism in Virtual Reality*, In: Thalmann, N., Thalmann, D. (Eds.): Artificial Life and Virtual Reality, John Wiley & Sons, 1994, pp. 189-210

[3] Bergman, L.D., Richardson, J.S., Richardson, D.C., Brooks, F.P.: *VIEW - An Exploratory Molecular Visualization System with User-Definable Interaction Sequences*, Computer Graphics Proceedings, SIGGRAPH 1993, pp. 117-126

[4] BIOSYM Technologies, Inc., 9685 Scranton Road, San Diego, CA 92121-3752, USA

[5] Brooks, F.P.: *Project GROPE - Haptic Displays for Scientific Visualization*, Computer Graphics 24(4), pp. 177–185, 1990

[6] Bryson, S., Levit, C.: *The Virtual Windtunnel*, IEEE Computer Graphics and Applications, 12, 4, pp. 25-34, 1992

[7] Bryson, S., Levit, C.: *Lessons learned while implementing the virtual windtunnel project*, Visualization '92, Tutorial # 2, 4.1–4.7, 1992

[8] Cruz-Neira, C., Leight, J., Papka, M., Barnes, C., Cohen, S.M., Das, S., Engelmann, R., Hudson, R., Roy, T., Siegel, L., Vasilakis, C., DeFanti, T.A., Sandin, D.J.: *Scientists in Wonderland: A Report on Visualization Applications in the CAVE Virtual Reality Environment*, Proc. IEEE Symposium on Research Frontiers in VR, San Jose, pp. 59–66, October 1993

[9] Earnshaw, R.A., Wiseman, N.: *An Introductory Guide to Scientific Visualization* Springer Verlag, 1992

[10] Encarnação, J.L., Astheimer, P., Felger, W., Frühauf, Th., Göbel, M., Müller, S.: *Graphics & Visualization: The Essential Features for the Classification of Systems.*, In: Proc. International Conference on Computer Graphics ICCG'93, Bombay, India, February 1993

[11] Freeman, C.M., Catlow, C.R.A., Thomas, J.M., Brode, S.: Chem. Phys. Lett., Vol. 186, p. 137, 1991

[12] Gerfelder, N., Müller, W.: *Quality Aspects of Computer Based Video Services*, in: Proc. of the 1994 European SMPTE Conference, Cologne, Germany, pp. 44–67, Sept. 1994

[13] Goodford, P.: *A Computational Procedure for Determining Energetically Favourable Binding Sites on Biologically Important Macromolecules*, Journal of Medical Chemistry, Vo.. 28, p. 849, 1985

[14] Haase, H., Göbel, M., Astheimer, P., Karlsson, K., Schröder, F., Frühauf, Th., Ziegler, R.: *How Scientific Visualization can benefit from Virtual Environments*, CWI Quarterly, The Netherlands, 1994

[15] Haase, H., Dai, F., Strassner, J., Göbel, M.: *Immersive Investigation of Scientific Data*, to appear in: Nielson, G., et al. (Eds.), CS Press, 1995

[16] Jones, T.A.: *A Graphics Model Building and Refinement System for Macromolecules*, Journal of Appl. Cryst., Vol. 11, pp. 268–272, 1978

[17] Kamat, V.V.: *A Survey of Techniques for Simulation of Dynamic Collision Detection and Response*, Computers & Graphics. Vol. 17, No. 4, pp. 379–385, 1993

[18] Langridge, R., Ferrin, T.E., Kuntz, I.D., Connolly, M.L.: *Real-Time Color Graphics in Studies of Molecular Interactions*, Science, Vol. 211, No. 4483, pp. 661–666, 1981

[19] Langridge, R.: *The Role of Visualization in Molecular Biology*, in: Gershon, N.: "Is Visualization REALLY Necessary? The Role of Visualization in Science, Engineering, and Medicine", in: Proc. Visualization '93, San Jose, p. 344, October 1993

[20] Levinthal, C.: *Molecular Model-Building by Computer*, Scientific American 124(6), pp. 42–52, 1966

[21] Max, N., Getzoff, E.D.: Spherical Harmonic Molecular Surfaces, IEEE Computer Graphics and Applications, pp. 42–50, July 1988

[22] Ouh-Young, M., Beard, D.V., Brooks, F.P.: *Force Display Performs Better than Visual Dispaly in a Simple 6-D Docking Task*, Proc. IEEE Int. Conf. Rob. Autom., pp. 1462–1466, 1989

[23] Roch, M., Weber, J.: *Computer graphics in chemical education and research*, Computers and Graphics 1/1987, pp. 55–60

[24] Schröder, F., Roßbach, P.: *Managing the Complexity of Digital Terrain Models*, Computers & Graphics, Vol. 18, No. 6, pp. 775–783, 1994

[25] Sherman, W.R.: *Integrating Virtual Environments into the Dataflow Paradigm*, Fourth Eurographics Workshop on Visualization in Scientific Computing, Abingdon, UK, April 1993

[26] Stewart, S.D.: *Computer Generated Molecular Modeling*, Simulation, July 1986, pp. 18–23

[27] Surles, M.C.: *An algorithm with linear complexity for interactive, physically-based modeling of large proteins*, Computer Graphics (SIG-GRAPH '92 Proceedings), 1992, pp. 221–230

[28] Taylor, R.M., Robinett, W., Chi, V.L., Brooks, F.P., Wright, W.V., Williams, R.S., Snyder, E.J.: *The Nanomanipulator: A Virtual-Reality Interface for a Scanning Tunneling Microscope*, Computer Graphics, Proc. SIGGRAPH, Anaheim, pp. 127–134, August 1993

[29] Waldherr-Teschner, M., Goetze, T., Heiden, W., Knoblauch, M., Vollhardt, H., Brickmann, J.: *MOLCAD - Computer Aided Visualization and Manipulation of Models in Molecular Science*, In: Post, F.H., Hin, A.J.S. (Eds.): Advances in Scientific Visualization, Springer-Verlag, pp. 58–67, 1992

[30] Weber, J., Fluekiger, P., Field, M.J.: *Computer-animated chemical models*, In: Computer Animation '90 (Second workshop on Computer Animation), Magnenat-Thalmann, N., Thalmann, D. (eds.), Springer-Verlag, pp. 21–29, 1990

[31] Woo, A., Poulin, P., Founier, A.: *A Survey of Shadow Algorithms*, IEEE Computer Graphics & Applications, pp. 13–32, November 1990

Editor's Note: see Appendix, p. 296 ff. for coloured figures of this paper

Searching for Facial Expression by Genetic Algorithm

Heedong Ko[+]   Jeong-Hwan Kim[*]   Jaihie Kim[*]
ko@kistmail.kist.re.kr   frog@wagner.kist.re.kr   jhkim@bubble.yonsei.ac.kr

[+] Korea Institute of Science and Technology (KIST), CAD/CAM Laboratory
[*] Yonsei University, Department of Electronics

Abstract. FACS(Facial Action Coding System) was proposed by the psychologists, Paul Ekman and Wallace V. Friesen, to describe a facial expression in terms of 46 muscular movements, called AUs (Action Units). Here, a mesh model of a human face is defined and each action unit deforms the mesh model according to the corresponding movements specified in the FACS system. The mesh model is deformed to create a facial expression by activating several action units with their intensity values. In this paper, we propose a method using GA (Genetic Algorithm), known widely as a function optimizer, to extract the components of an arbitrary facial expression automatically where the expression may be input by a 3D measuring device or a 2D image. By using these components, we can construct more realistic facial expressions tailored to individual characteristics.

1. Introduction

Many meanings can be transmitted by the look of a facial expression of a person, reflecting the emotion of the person such as happiness, anger, sadness and many other delicate nuances. Likewise, if the computer displays its internal state to us through the look of a human face, we may construct a more familiar computer interface. The machine having a human face ! The virtual environment for us to communicate with machines as if they were our friends ! This is a human-computer interface we are pursuing as a part of the virtual reality (VR) research at Korea Institute of Science and Technology (KIST).

As a part of VR research, we are investigating how an artificial agent inhabiting a virtual world may communicate its internal state to us in the external world by the human facial expression. The purpose of this paper is to present an experimental result in finding out the components of a facial expression automatically from 3D contour or 2D image of the facial expression using a genetic algorithm (GA). Each component specifies what part of a face changes and to what extent. A component is defined by an action unit according to the facial action coding system (FACS) [1]. Using these components, we aim at reconstructing a facial expression that is closer to the characteristics of an individual facial expression.

1.1 Facial action coding system (FACS)

FACS was suggested by the psychologists, Paul Ekman and Wallace V. Friesen, in order to describe human facial expressions in the 1970's. According to FACS, there are

46 primitive muscular movements in a human face called action units (AUs), and a facial expression can be synthesized by the combination of these action units. For example, the expression describing happiness is composed of the muscular movements which raise the inner eyebrows, pull the corners of lips, and drop a jaw. Fig. 1. shows appearance changes due to the combination of action units and their relative strengths (or intensities). Table 1. describes the kinds of action units and their functions.

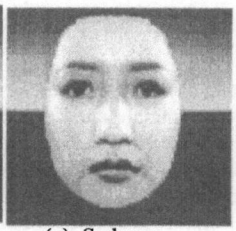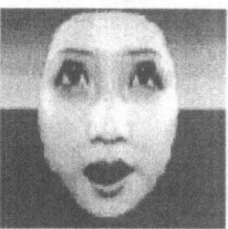

(a) Expressionless face   (b) Happiness   (c) Sadness   (d) Surprise

(b) AU combination : 1(0.4) +12(0.4) +26(0.4)
(c) AU combination : 1(0.3) +4(0.6) + 15(0.4)
(d) AU combination : 1(0.7) + 2(0.7) + 5(0.7) + 26(0.7)

Fig. 1. Appearance changes due to AU combinations

Table 1. Action Units

AU No.	Function	AU No.	Function
1	Inner brow raiser	24	Lip presser
2	Outer brow raiser	25	Lips parts
4	Brow lowerer	26	Jaw drop
5	Upper lid raiser	27	Mouth stretcher
6	Cheek raiser	28	Lips suck
7	Lid tightener	29	Jaw thrust
8	Lips toward	30	Jaw sideways
9	Nose wrinker	31	Jaw clencher
10	Upper lip raiser	32	Bite
11	Nasolabial furrow deepener	33	Blow
12	Lip, corner puller	34	Puff
13	Sharp lip puller	35	Cheek suck
14	Dimpler	36	Tongue bulge
15	Lip corner depressor	37	Lip wipe
17	Chin raiser	38	Nostril compressor
18	Lip pucker	39	Nostril dilator
19	Tongue show	41	Lip droop
20	Lip stretcher	42	Slit
21	Neck tightener	43	Eyes closed
22	Lip funneler	44	Squint
23	Lip tightener	45	Blink
		46	Wink

The action units are defined with respect to a 3D triangular mesh model of an human face. An action unit may modify the coordinates of the corresponding mesh points according to the intensities of the action units. Currently, our AU system is based on Choi's [2]. One can create all facial expressions at his will if he knows the composing elements of a facial expression.

1.2 Previous Work

Many researchers have been working in the field of the face analysis and synthesis. Terzopoulos and Waters developed a method for tracking facial features and reproducing facial expression through images [3]. Choi proposed a system which analyzes and synthesizes the facial features assuming that any facial image is a weighted sum of facial image bases [2]. Mase [4] introduced a method to track facial action units using optical flow and Essa developed the system further [5]. Takeuchi and Franks concentrated on modeling of a facial expression and developed an environment for rapid face construction [6]. However, because their works are based on 2D facial images, their reconstructed facial expressions may suffer difficulties in reflecting 3D information correctly and most of them treated a facial analysis and tracking of prototypical facial expressions rather than the synthesis of a facial expression specific to an individual. Here, we concentrate on reconstructing a facial expression revealing 3D characteristics of each person's facial expression. So it is necessary to measure the accurate 3D contour of a face.

At Expo'93, held in Taejon, Korea, KIST demonstrated a face sculpturing robot system that obtains the 3D contour of a person's face using a projection type multislit beam topography [7]. All the facial features are defined a priori for the model face. By matching the model face with the contour of the measured face, the contour regions belonging to different facial features are recognized. Then, the recognized face data is affine transformed at the feature level to show different facial expressions. Each transformation was defined a priori in terms of action units and their relative strengths by a knowledgeable person about FACS. From the transformed data, a robot program sculpturing the person's face is automatically generated with different cutting conditions for each facial features.

The measured contour has a irregularly spaced grid points as shown in Fig. 2 (a). From the contour data, a Z map data is constructed by generating the z values of the crossing points from the regularly spaced parallel lines along the x and y axes as shown in Fig. 2 (b). After the model mesh data for a face is approximately matched with a Z-map data, additional vertices are added to make the surface of a face smooth and the expressions look more natural as shown in Fig. 3 (b). Using the facial mesh data obtained from the 3D contour measurement of a person and rules of FACS, an expression specific to the individual can be constructed. However, modeling of a human expression was very time consuming and the result was an approximation of the person's individual characteristics. So a facial expression composer was developed to input various action unit combinations and their intensities conveniently by a musical chord. This is achieved by mapping each key in the MIDI keyboard to an action unit.

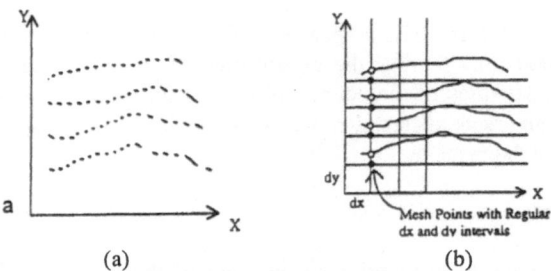

(a)   (b)

Fig. 2. Conversion of measured data into regular mesh data

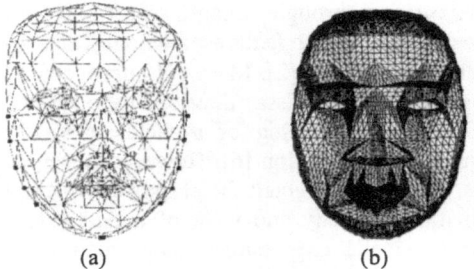

(a)   (b)

Fig. 3. Model face with characteristic and mesh model of an expressionless face

Using the facial expression composer, a MIDI keyboard player can generate an arbitrary facial expression by playing a musical chord. Unfortunately, this method may create an expression with no corresponding human facial expression. The facial expression composer later extended to animating the change of a facial expression according to a musical passage [8]. A facial expression represents the listener's emotion when listening to a music and changes according to the musical passage. This is achieved by mapping the emotion of the musical passage to the expression. First, the musical attributes like harmony, tempos, and pitches are mapped to human emotions which are in turn mapped to facial expressions. The system had only nine facial expression types where each type has several minor variations. It was very time consuming to extend this library of facial expressions.

1.3 Problem statement

A person may display his / her emotional state through a facial expression and according to FACS, the expression can be represented by a combination of the AUs and their intensities as muscular movements of the face. In a facial animation and synthesis phase, however, it is up to us to model the combination for each facial expressions. Since the modeling process is very time consuming, the number of facial expression we could construct is limited. Unfortunately, the number of facial expressions is numerous according to various emotional states of a person as well as individual's characteristic look. We open our eyes and mouths wide to make others notice that we are surprised, but these actions are different from one person to the other and we cannot define a canonical facial expression for any kind of emotion. So the number of facial expressions we can imagine is enormous and it is almost impossible to analyze each individual and search for the right combination of the AUs and their intensities, one by one. For example, if each action unit has 10 intensities, we have to search for the facial expression among 10^{46} combinations at the worst case.

Because the search space of the problem we are to solve is very large, we need the heuristic optimal search technique. Besides, it is a multi-modal function and may be discontinuous [9]. That is, it has so many local peaks in its search region, which makes it difficult to apply a simple hill-climbing method based on the calculus-based search technique which finds the global minimum or maximum only in convex continuous spaces, to locate the global peak. Another widely used method in optimization is the simulated annealing method [10, 11], which offers a way to overcome this major drawback of the calculus-based method, but the price to pay is a huge computation time and the searching process is basically sequential in nature. To avoid converging into the local maxima as well as to improve the converging time by searching in parallel, we apply GA (Genetic Algorithm) in finding the right combination of action units toward a target facial expression.

GA known widely as function optimizer was suggested first by Holland in 1970's [12]. GA is an adaptive method which may be used to solve the search and the optimization problems. The method is based on the genetic processes of biological organisms. Over many generations, natural populations evolve according to the principles of natural selection and survival of the fittest. The power of the GAs comes from the fact that the technique is robust, and can deal successfully with problem area with discontinuous and non convex problem space. GAs are not guaranteed to find global optimum solution to a problem, but they are generally good at finding *acceptably* good solutions quickly [13, 14]. The major part of problem modeling is the chromosome representation and the evaluation function which assigns a reward to each coded solution. During the run, parents must be selected for reproduction, and recombined to generate off-springs. The next section explains how we encoded searching for the target facial expression in terms of AUs using GA.

2. Searching for facial expression by Genetic Algorithm

We explain the search procedure in finding the right combination of action units and their intensities from the contour of a person's expressionless face toward a facial expression when the expression is given by its Z map measurement. The measuring data of this experiment, which captures 3D contour of an expressionless face, is obtained by using a projection type multislit beam topography. Because an action unit acts only on the coordinates of mesh vertices of a face model, these measuring data must be converted to the model mesh format. By using the characteristic points that are identified on the measuring data as anchors, the model mesh is transformed to fit the measurement data.

Unfortunately, the projection type multislit beam topography technique is not suitable for measuring objects with discontinuous pattern. As a result, the 3D contour of a facial expression is not input from the measuring device. Instead, the target facial expression was input by simulation: we apply the action units to the expressionless face but hide which action units were applied to the search procedure. If the mesh data of a target face are replaced by the real 3D measured data of an arbitrary facial expression, we can obtain the information of muscular movements for arbitrary realistic expressions.

Then, the goal of the searching process is to find the parameters (AUs and their intensities) causing the global minimum evaluation by the evaluation function of the GA procedure searches. That is, the evaluation procedure is a function of the difference of the vertex coordinates with a target face. So by using GA, we can reduce our problem, synthesizing facial expressions and making the canonical set of facial expressions more realistic, to cost-minimizing heuristic search.

The GA procedure was implemented in two different ways. In nature, the GA is based on a string structure, which represents the chromosome of an object being evolved. The first method models a chromosome with a bit string while the second one implements the combination of action units with an integer array. The first implementation using the binary bit strings is a typical modeling case of the genetic algorithm which matches Holland's schema theorem best. However, we also apply another method, an integer model, which reduces the problem domain size.

2.1 Approach 1 : Binary bit string model

Modeling. In the binary bit string model, a chromosome consists of the intensity information of 35 AUs out of 46 possible AUs - only 35 AUs have been implemented - and four bits are assigned to each AU so that 16 intensities can appear. Each bit string is implemented by a gray code not to make a critical disturbance by a bit mutation [15]. In Fig. 4, the intensities of AU1 and AU4 are 7 and 4 respectively.

0100	1001	0010	0110............0110	0101	0001	0101
AU1	AU2	AU3	AU4 AU32	AU33	AU34	AU35

Fig. 4. Chromosome model using binary bit string

Evolutionary process. The GA procedure approximately is divided into four parts, evaluation, selection, crossover and mutation.

Evaluation function. The evaluation process measures the difference between the vertex coordinates of the face caused by the combination of AUs represented by the chromosome string and those of the target face. At the evaluation stage, the scaling of the parameters is necessary for the continual convergence toward the global minimum. That is, the fitness scale is regulated so that the dominant individual's with high fitness values may appear in latter stages rather than in early stage. If some dominant individuals appear in early stages, the law of natural selection will prevent others from evolving and few dominant individuals will survive. This means the population loses the diversity and the possibility of the searching process pre-converging to a local minima (or maxima) increases. On the other hand, if the diversity increases too much, most of all individuals have similar fitness values, the evolutionary process will be excessively time-consuming and the possibility of oscillation will increase. Therefore, the harmony between two contrary aspects, *diversity* and *convergence*, must be maintained. In our experiment, the fitness value of an individual is set to the square of a raw fitness and 0.01 is added to an exponent at every generation to enlarge the differences of the fitness values among individuals in a population as shown in Fig. 5.

Selection, Crossover and mutation. The process of reproduction can be divided into selection and crossover. The selection process applies the mixture of the method that always makes the fittest remain in the next generation and fills the population of the next generation with the members of the previous generation according to their expected values of the selection and a roulette wheel scheme. We take the multiple point crossover scheme because single point crossover produces insufficient changes for the chromosomes, which has no fewer than 144 bits as its genes.

Crossover reveals two aspects. It makes two crossover chromosomes exchange each good nature genes and improves their characters and in the other view point, it gives diversity to the chromosomes by modifying the genes which are the borders during the exchange process of the genes. For our chromosomes, if we apply single crossover scheme, only one among 35 AUs is affected. After many generations , the evaluation converges gradually to some point, but in many times it is trapped to a local minimum or local maximum. In GA, to avoid this situation we must provide the diversity to the population which is supplied, in most cases, by mutation. In our experiment, we have the crossover playing the role actively by modifying the number of the points of the crossover dynamically as the distribution of the average fitness of the population is gradually concentrated on some small restricted region. This implementation is opposite to De Jong's opinion [16] - an increased number of crossover points is likely to result in a random shuffle and fewer important schemata can be preserved. However, the experiment showed it could help to the improvement of a performance, which is shown in Fig. 6., for the increased points of crossover operations were used for increasing *diversity* when a population was pre-converging to a local optima.

A mutation rate is adapted to the distribution of the population at each generation. As the normalized average fitness of the population increases, the mutation rate will increase. However, increasing diversity may aggravate the converging process, by causing the evaluation function to oscillate. In such a case, the algorithm will be similar to a random search and makes no sense. It is important to harmonize those two aspects of the total process, *diversity* and *stability*, to make the evaluation function converge into the global minimum or maximum. In our experiment, the search space is very large and the evaluation function is multi-modal, so it is highly likely to be trapped to a local optima, so the diversity is emphasized.

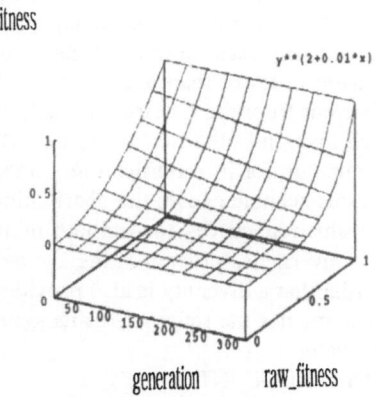

Fig. 5. Fitness scaling

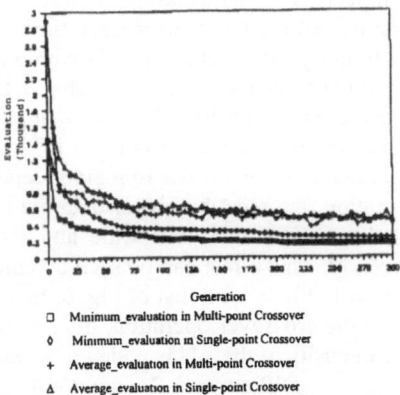

Fig. 6. multi-point vs. single point crossover

94

Convergence : experimental result

The individuals' fitness values of a population gradually approach to an adjacent region in a search space when the convergence is reached after many generations. Fig. 7. shows the convergence process when the size of a population is 300, the crossover probability is 0.7, a mutation rate is the cube of a normalized fitness, and a selection schedule is the mixture of the roulette wheel method and expectation value of each individual.

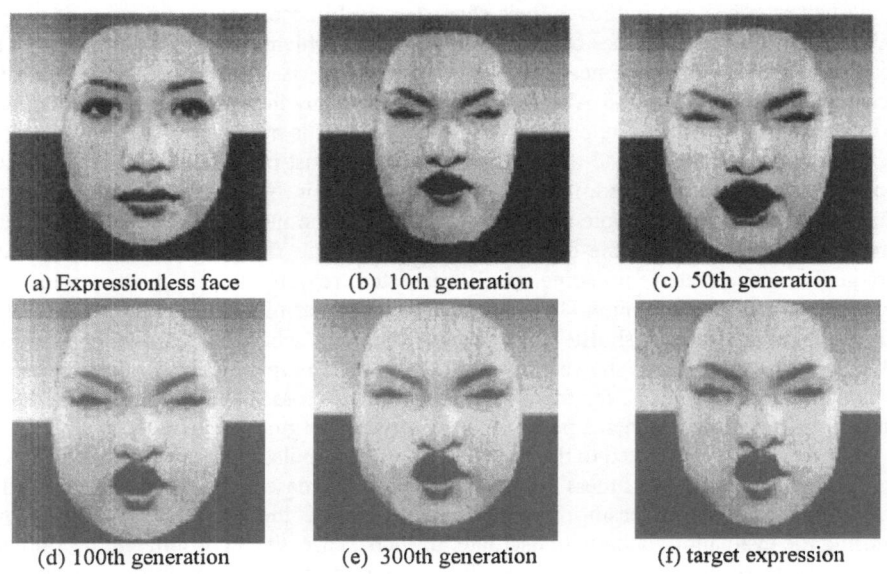

| (a) Expressionless face | (b) 10th generation | (c) 50th generation |
| (d) 100th generation | (e) 300th generation | (f) target expression |

Fig. 7. Convergence process of binary bit string model

2.2 Approach 2 : Chromosome modeling using an integer array

Our second implementation, an integer array model, has a result similar to that of the first except the fast convergence time. This is due to the reduction of the search space by limiting the number of AUs within a chromosome to 15 because in most instances the number of the AUs composing a facial expression is fewer than ten - the search space are reduced from 2^{144} to $_{35}P_{15} \times 10^{15}$. Different from the bit string model, its crossover points are the borders of the AUs, which gives no modification to the AU parameters so that it has to mainly depend on the mutation for its modification. So the mutation rate must be higher than the former's, but this scheme causes the distribution of the evaluation values wide and the average evaluation curves to oscillate more severely. This effect can be seen by comparing the convergence process of the average fitness in Fig. 8 with that of Fig. 6. In addition, in order that a diversity is also provided from the crossover operation, in case that a chromosome has the same AU as its gene, the intensity of the AU is added or subtracted by the value:

$$\text{Difference} * \text{Random(MAX\_INTENSITY)} / \text{MAX\_INTENSITY}$$

with the probability of 0.5. Fig. 8 and 9 show the convergence process of integer array

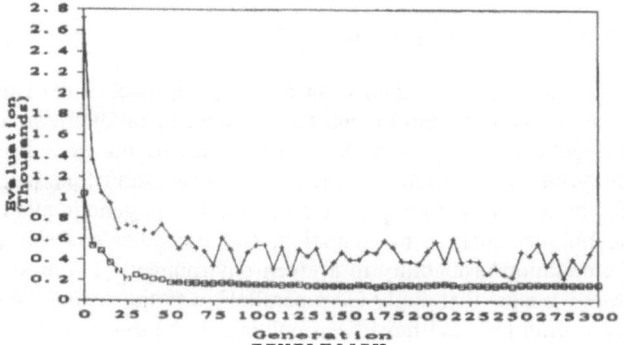

□ Minimum_evaluation
+ Average_evaluation

Fig. 8. Evolutionary process

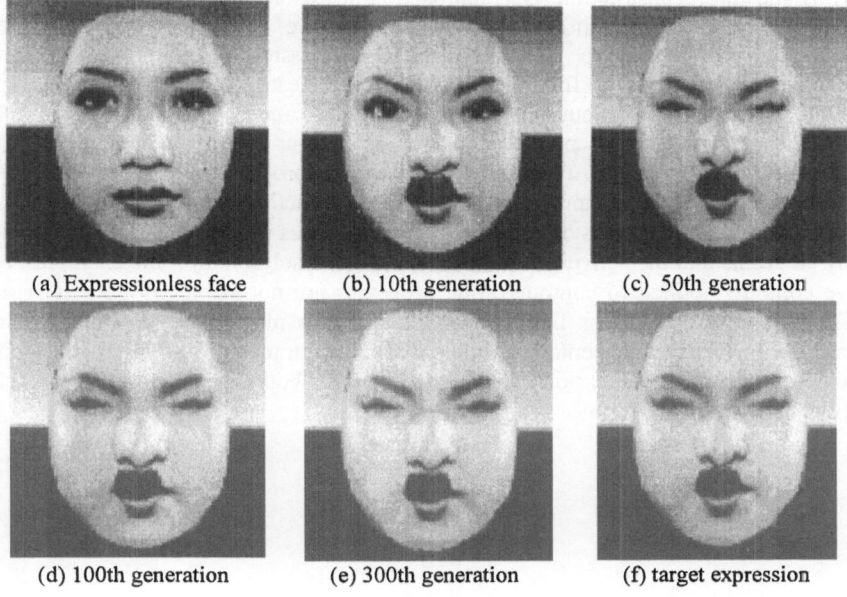

(a) Expressionless face   (b) 10th generation   (c) 50th generation

(d) 100th generation   (e) 300th generation   (f) target expression

Fig. 9. Appearance changes through generations

model when the probability of the chromosome mutation is 0.3, AU mutation probability is 0.1, the probability of an intensity mutation is 0.2 and other parameters are the same with the former method.

2.3 Difficulties in convergence process

The numerical evaluation of the data from our two approaches does not completely converge into the global optimum though the resultant facial expression is almost the same with the target expression when we inspect them with our eyes. It is guessed that the fact is mainly due to the multi-modality of the evaluation function. To solve the problem, it may be useful to apply a hybrid method of the genetic algorithm with the local search techniques such as hill-climbing, and use other strategies, for example adaptation of a mutation probability to a given environment [14] or sequential niche method [9]. Many papers that apply GA's parallelism to the sequential methods such as simulated annealing [10, 11] have been published and those concepts will also be helpful to the oscillation problem.

3. Future work

So far, we described the method of finding components of a facial expression for the analysis and the reconstruction. Our approach is based on real 3D measurement data which provide a precise information of the structure of an expressionless face. However, it is difficult to measure a facial expression. Furthermore, the data acquisition and analysis of finding facial features takes several seconds to several minutes. Therefore, the input phase must be significantly extended for real time applications. So we have been extending the 3D contour capturing process using 2D image based facial analysis. First, as a model fitting process, we revised the model mesh in accordance to an input face image using interactive feature finding process. The contour fitting processes of a face in many researches use an active contour model [3, 6]. It seems that the active contour model is a good solution in some examples, but active contours applied to contour fitting processes are not stable yet and it is still challenging to use them for finding facial features in movement. We are working toward adding automatic contour fitting process and tracking system to use active contours to our facial expression generation system for both on-line and off-line facial analysis and synthesis system.

4. Conclusions

It is necessary to find out the combination of AUs, the components of a facial expression, and their intensities for each expression to build natural looks. This paper presents a search method for the parameters of the composing elements of a facial expression automatically. The facial expressions are reflections of human emotion and one's thought. Therefore, finding out their components means constructing a basis for creating a medium possessing the human feeling which connects man with a machine.

Especially in VR application, constructing a realistic facial expression is an indispensable part of building an artificial agent inhabiting a virtual world and this increases the realism of a medium which links a real world with a virtual one. It makes the environment of the man-machine interface more familiar to man. For instance, if the facial expressions are used as means of communication between the guide machine and the users, it can eliminate the user's feeling of rejection which often arises when we face the machine. As a facial expression is an effective tool for a man to communicate with the other humans, the artificially generated facial expression can be used to represent an inner state of a computer whose operational state is difficult to estimate and understand at a single glance by a human user.

In addition, when it is necessary to transfer facial expressions, if all their vertex data or the differences of the coordinates of the vertices between them are to be transmitted, there will be a large amount of data and this may cause congestion in the communication channel even with advanced image compression methods like MPEG 2. So if we can transfer only control parameters of the action units and change the facial expressions with one basic expression at each end, we can expect a large data compression.

Moreover, our system can be used to analyze the psychological state of a man. If the data of a facial expression are given, we can extract the components of an expression and infer the emotional state of the expression. With this purposes in mind, this research focuses on generating facial expressions at our will by implementing AUs which describes more individualized characteristic facial expressions.

References

1. Paul Ekman and Wallace V. F. : Facial Action Coding System. Consulting Psychologists Press Inc. (1978)

2. C. S. Choi, H. Harashima and T. Takebe : Analysis and synthesis of facial expressions in knowledge-based coding of facial image sequences. IEEE Int. Conf. Acoust., Speech Signal Process. (ICASSP-91) , 29M9.7 May (1991)

3. D. Terzopoulos, K. Waters : Analysis and synthesis of facial image sequences using physical and anatomical models. IEEE trans. on PAMI, vol. 15, No. 6, June (1993)

4. Kenji Mase : Recognition of facial expressions for optical flow. IEICE transactions, Special Issue on Computer Vision and its Applications, E74(10) (1991)

5. Irfan A. Essa, Trevor Darrell and A. Pentland : Tracking facial motion. Proceedings of the IEEE workshop on nonrigid and articulate motion, Austin, Texas, April (1994)

6. Akikazu Takeuchi and Steven Franks : A Rapid Face Construction Lab. SCSL-TR-92-010, May 7 (1992)

7. Heedong Ko, Moon-Sang Kim, Hyun-Goo Park and Seung-Woo Kim : Face sculpturing robot with recognition capability. CAD Vol. 26, NO. 11, pp 814-821, (1994)

8. Hee-Dong Ko, Sook-Jae Shin and Seung-Ah Chang : Changes of Facial Expression According to Musical Passage, Journal of the Korea Computer Graphics Society,

Vol. 1, No. 1, pp. 80-85, March (1995)

9. D. Beasley, D. R. Bull, Martin, R. R. : Sequential Niche Technique for Multimodel Function Optimization. Evolutionary Computation 1(2), pp101-125, (1993) MIT PRESS

10. R. A. Rutenbar : Simulated annealing algorithms : An Overview. IEEE Circuits and Devices Magazine, pp.19-26, January (1989)

11. S. Kirkpatrick, C. D. Gelatt, and M. P. Vecchi : Optimization by Simulated annealing, Science, vol.220, no.4598, pp.671-680,May (1983)

12. J. H. Holland : Adaptation in Natural and Artificial Systems. MIT Press (1975)

13. D. Beasley, D. R. Bull, Martin, R. R. : An Overview of Genetic Algorithms University Computing, 15 (2), pp. 58-69 (1993)

14. D. Whitley : A Genetic Algorithm Tutorial. Technical Report CS-93-103. Nov 10 (1993)

15. D. E. Goldberg : Genetic Algorithms in search, optimization & Machine Learning. Addison-Wesley (1989)

16. De Jong, K. A. : An analysis of the behavior of a class of genetic adaptive systems. Dissertation abstracts International 36(10), 5140B. (University Microfilms No.76-9381)

Coordinating Vocal and Visual Parameters for 3D Virtual Agents

Catherine Pelachaud
Dept. of Computer Science and Systems
University of Rome "La Sapienza"
pelachau@graphics.cis.upenn.edu

Scott Prevost
Dept. of Computer and Information Science
University of Pennsylvania
prevost@linc.cis.upenn.edu

Abstract

This paper presents an implemented system for automatically producing prosodically appropriate speech and corresponding facial expressions for animated, three-dimensional agents that respond to simple database queries in a 3D virtual environment. Unlike previous text-to-facial animation approaches, the system described here produces synthesized speech and facial animations entirely from scratch, starting with semantic representations of the message to be conveyed, which are based in turn on a discourse model and a small database of facts about the modeled world.

1 Introduction

As research on the simulation of autonomous virtual human agents progresses, two major issues in human-machine interaction must be addressed. First, proper intonation is necessary for conveying the information structure of utterances with respect to the underlying discourse structure, expressing important distinctions of contrast and focus ([27, 24, 25]). Realistic facial expressions and lip movements help in providing relevant information about discourse structure, turn-taking protocols and speaker attitudes ([8, 9, 18]). Moreover, in a face-to-face conversation, facial displays play an important communicative role.

Simulating this communicative role for animation requires symbolic specification of the semantics and pragmatics of movements. Faces change expressions continuously, and many of these changes are synchronized with what is going on in concurrent conversation. Facial expressions are linked to the content of speech (scrunching one's nose when talking about something unpleasant) as well as affect (smiling when remembering a happy event). They can replace sequences of words (e.g. "the food was [wrinkle nose, stick out tongue]") as well as accompany them [9], and they can serve to help disambiguate what is being said when the acoustic signal is degraded. They do not occur randomly but rather are synchronized to one's own speech, or to the speech of others [6, 15]. It is therefore important that the specification of facial expressions takes many different levels of organization into account. We propose that integrating models for generating proper intonation and facial expressions will improve the intelligibility and naturalness of utterances produced by meaning-to-speech systems as well as by more elaborate systems involving virtual animated human agents (e.g. [3]).

The intonation generation model is based on Combinatory Categorial Grammar (CCG – cf. [27]), a formalism which easily integrates the notions of syntactic constituency, prosodic phrasing and information structure. Based on the CCG grammar, a simple discourse model and a small knowledge base represented in Prolog, the system produces spoken responses to database queries with appropriate intonation. Given the precise timings for phonemes and intonational phenomena in the speech wave, we produce precise specifications for generating the lip movements and facial expressions for a graphical model of a human head. Results from our current implementation demonstrate the system's ability to generate a variety of intonational possibilities and facial animations for a given sentence depending on the discourse context.

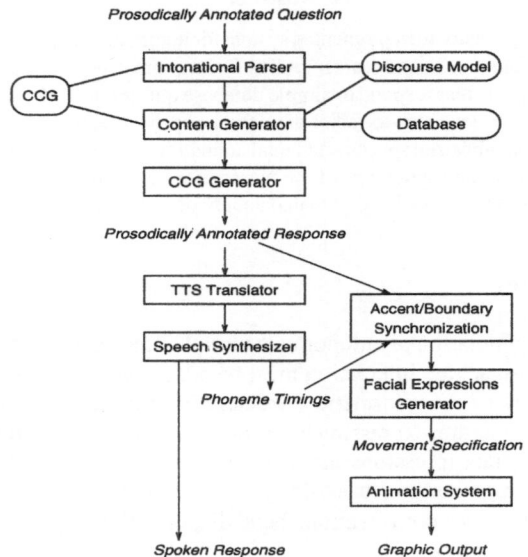

Figure 1: Architecture

Previous work in the area of intonation generation includes studies by Terken ([29]), Houghton and Pearson ([13]), Isard and Pearson ([14]), Davis and Hirschberg (cf. [7, 12]), and Zacharski et al. ([31]). Benoit et al. ([1]), Brooke ([2]), Cohen et al. ([4]), Hill et al. ([11]), Lewis et al. ([16]) and Terzopoulos et al. ([30]) have worked on synchronizing lip movements with speech, producing quite striking results. Takeuchi et al. ([28]) implemented a user-interface in which a 3D facial model responds to queries posed by a user. In this system, the generation of the facial expressions accompanying the answer depends on an analysis of the conversational situation and the selection of facial expressions from a database of facial displays.

The system described here expands the work of the aforementioned researchers by linking contextually appropriate intonation with the corresponding facial expressions, and generating the 3D facial animations automatically from semantic, information structural and discourse structural representations [21].

2 The Implementation

Using the CCG theory of prosody outlined in [27, 24, 25], the implemented system undertakes the task of specifying contextually appropriate intonation and facial animation for spoken responses to database queries. The process, which is illustrated in figure 1, begins with a fully segmented and prosodically annotated representation of a spoken query, as shown in example (1), which involves a simple database of facts about stereo components. The notational system representing the intonation contour in example (1) is an adaptation of the widely used system developed by Pierrehumbert ([23]).[1] For simplicity, we show accented words in capital letters without regard for the different possible types of accents. A simple CCG parser determines the semantics of the question, dividing it into its *theme*, which identifies what the sentence is about, and its *rheme*, which identifies what is important or salient about the theme. We refer to this division of the utterance into theme and rheme as its *information structure*. Certain elements of the theme and rheme may be particularly salient because they are new to the discourse or serve to distinguish among entities or propositions that are already firmly established in the discourse. We say such items are in *focus*, and mark them with the * operator, as shown in examples (2).[2]

(1) I know which components produce MUDDY bass,
   but WHICH components produce CLEAN bass?
   $\quad$ L+H* $\qquad$ LH% $\qquad$ H* $\quad$ LL$

(2) Proposition:
   $s : \lambda x.component(x)\&produce(x, *clean(bass))$
   Theme:
   $s : \lambda x.component(x)\&produce(x, *clean(bass))/$
   $\quad (s : produce(x, *clean(bass))\backslash np : x)$
   Rheme:
   $s : produce(x, *clean(bass))\backslash np : x$

The content generation module has the task of determining the semantics and information structure of the response, marking focused items based on the contrastive stress algorithm described in [25]. For the question given in (1), the strategic generator produces the representation for the response shown in example (3), where the appropriate theme can be paraphrased as "what produces clean bass", the appropriate rheme as "amplifiers", and where the context includes alternative components and audio qualities.

(3) Proposition:
   $s : produce(*amplifiers, *clean(bass))$
   Theme:
   $s : produce(x, *clean(bass))\backslash np : x$
   Rheme:
   $np : *amplifiers$

---

[1] The L+H* and H* markings represent different types of pitch accents in the fundamental frequency contour. The LH% and LL$ markings represent prosodic boundaries. For a brief explanation of the Pierrehumbert-style markings, see [26].

[2] A full explanation of the semantic and syntactic representation in (2) is beyond the scope of this paper. The interested reader should refer to [27, 26].

Using the output of the content generator, the CCG generation module (described in [24]) produces a string of words and Pierrehumbert-style markings representing the response, as shown in example (4).

(4) AMPLIFIERS produce CLEAN bass.
     H*   L   L+H* LH$

The final aspect of speech generation involves translating such a string into a form usable by a suitable speech synthesizer. The current implementation uses the Bell Laboratories TTS system [17] as a post-processor to synthesize the speech wave and produce precise timing specifications for phonemes. The duration specifications are then automatically annotated with pitch accent peaks and intonational boundaries in preparation for processing by the facial expression rules (see also [3]).

Most facial animation systems use the Facial Action Coding System (*FACS*), developed by Ekman and Friesen [10], to annotate facial action. The system describes the visible muscular action based on anatomical studies, using basic elements called action units (*AU*), which refer to the contraction of one muscle or a group of related muscles. A facial expression is described as a set of *AUs*.

Certain facial expressions, which serve *informational structural* functions, accompany the flow of speech and are synchronized at the verbal level. Facial movements (such as raising the eyebrows or blinking while saying "AMPLIFIERS produce CLEAN bass") can appear during accented syllables or pauses. These function are based on the following determinants: conversational signals, punctuators and manipulators. *Conversational signals* correspond to movement occurring on accented or emphatic items to clarify or support what is being said. These can be eyebrow movements (the most commonly used facial expression), head nods, or blinks. *Punctuators* are movements which occur on pauses, reducing the ambiguity of the speech by grouping or separating sequences of words into discrete unit phrases [5]. Slow head movement, blinks, or a smile can accompany a pause. *Manipulators* correspond to biologically necessary functions like blinking to wet the eyes.

As we have seen, a facial expression can have a variety of different meanings (e.g. accentuating an element, punctuating a pause). We propose a high level programming language to describe them, amounting to a formal notation for the different clusterings of facial expressions. Indeed, rather than using a set of *AUs* to specify facial expressions in terms of intonational features in speech, it is more convenient to express them at a higher level, directly denoting their function. These operations are then mapped onto sequences of *AUs* so that we are able to model different facial "styles", in the sense that people differ in their way of emphasizing a word and in the number of facial displays they use. For example, Ekman [9] found that most people use raised eyebrows to accompany an accent while the actor Woody Allen uses eyebrow positions (inner and downward) which generally imply sadness.

Our algorithms incorporate synchrony ([6]), create coarticulation effects, emotional signals, and eye and head movements ([19, 20]). The facial animation system scans the input utterances and computes the associated movements for the lips, the conversational signals and the punctuators. Conversational signals start and end with the accented word. For instance, on *amplifier*, the brow starts raising on 'a', remains raised until the end of the word, and ends raising on 'r'. On the other hand, the punctuator signals, such as smiling, coincide with pauses. Blinking is synchronized at the phoneme level, due to biological necessity, accentuation or pausing. On *amplifier*, for example, the eyes start closing on 'a', remain closed on 'm' and start opening on 'p'.

The computation of the lip shape is done in three passes. First, phonemes, which are characterized by their degree of deformability, are processed one segment at a time using the look-ahead model to search for the proximal deformable segments whose associated lip shapes influence the current segment. For example, in *amplifier* the 'l' receives the same lip shape as the following vowel 'i'—that is, the movement of the 'i' begins before the onset of its sound. Second, the spatial properties of muscle contractions are taken into account by adjusting the sequence of contracting muscles when antagonistic movements succeed one another (i.e. movements involving very different lip positions, such as pucker movements versus the extension of the lips). And finally, the temporal properties of muscle contractions are considered by determining whether a muscle has enough time to contract before (or relax after) the surrounding lip shape.

The tongue, although not highly visible, is an important element of distinction between phonemic elements, especially when these elements are not differentiated by their lip shapes. The tongue is composed of 2 parallel surfaces, each of them made of 10 triangles. A tongue shape is defined by varying the tongue parameters, including the length of the edges of the triangles and the angles between each of the edges. Modifying the length of the edges allows for the narrowing, flattening, stretching and/or compression of the tongue, while changing the value of the angles between edges allows the tongue to bend, curve and/or twist. This model is a simplification of [22].

3 Examples

In the examples shown below, the speaker manifests different behaviors depending on whether s/he is asking a question, making a statement, accenting a word or pausing. When asking a question, the speaker raises the eyebrows and looks up slightly to mark the end of the question. When replying, or when turning over the floor to the other person, the speaker turns the head toward the listener. To emphasize a particular word, s/he raises the eyebrows and/or blinks. During the brief pauses at the end of statements and within statements, the speaker blinks and smiles.

(5) I know which amplifier produces clean BASS,

but which amplifier produces clean TREBLE?
  L+H*   LH%   H* LL$

The BRITISH amplifier produces clean TREBLE.
  H*   L   L+H* LH$

(6) I know which British component produces MUDDY treble,

    but which British component produces CLEAN treble?
      L+H*   LH%   H*   LL$

    The British AMPLIFIER produces CLEAN treble.
           H*   L   L+H* LH$

In utterance (5), the word *British* is accented and accompanied by a raised eyebrow, which indicates a conversational signal denoting contrast. In utterance (6), on the other hand, the word *amplifier* is accented and marked by the action of the eyebrows and a blink (see figure 2 in Appendix). The same argument differentiates the appearance of the movement on the word *treble* in (5) and the word *clean* in (6). Moreover, a punctuating blink marks the end of (6), starting on the pause after the word *treble*. In (5) a blink coincides with the accented word *treble* (as a conversational signal) and with the pause marking the end of the utterance (as a punctuator), resulting in two blinks emitted in succession at the end of the utterance. In both examples, the pause between the two intonational phrases '*the British amplifier*' and '*produces clean treble*', is accompanied by movement of the eyebrows.

4 Conclusions

The system described above produces quite sharp and natural-sounding distinctions of intonation contour, as well as visually distinct facial animations, for minimal pairs of queries and responses generated automatically from a discourse model and a simple knowledge base. The examples in the previous section (and others presented at the workshop) illustrate the system's capabilities and provide a sound basis for exploring the role of intonation and facial expressions in a 3D virtual environment. Future areas of research include evaluating results and exploring the relevance of our current system to large scale animation systems involving autonomous virtual human agents (cf. [3]).

5 Acknowledgments

We would like to thank particularly Dr. Norman I. Badler and Dr. Mark Steedman for their very useful comments. We are grateful to AT&T Bell Laboratories for allowing us access to the TTS speech synthesizer, and to Mark Beutnagel, Julia Hirschberg, and Richard Sproat for patient advice on its use. The usual disclaimers apply. The research was supported in part by NSF grant nos. IRI90-18513, IRI90-16592, IRI91-17110 and CISE IIP-CDA-88-22719, DARPA grant no. N00014-90-J-1863, and ARO grant no. DAAL03-89-C0031.

6 References

[1] C. Benoit: Why synthesize talking faces? In: Proceedings of the ESCA Workshop on Speech Synthesis, pages 253–256, Autrans, 1990.

[2] N.M. Brooke: Computer graphics synthesis of talking faces. In: Proceedings of the ESCA Workshop on Speech Synthesis, Autrans, 1990.

[3] J. Cassell, C. Pelachaud, N. Badler, M. Steedman, B. Achorn, T. Becket, B. Douville, S. Prevost, and M. Stone: Animated conversation: Rule based generation of facial expression, gesture and spoken intonation for multiple conversational agents. In: SIGGRAPH'94, 1994.

[4] M. M. Cohen and D. W. Massaro: Modeling coarticulation in synthetic visual speech. In: D. Thalmann N. Magnenat-Thalmann (eds.): Computer Animation '93. Springer-Verlag, 1993.

[5] G. Collier: Emotional expression. Lawrence Erlbaum Associates, 1985.

[6] W.S. Condon and W.D. Osgton: Speech and body motion synchrony of the speaker-hearer. In: D.H. Horton and J.J. Jenkins (eds.): The perception of Language, pages 150–184. Academic Press, 1971.

[7] J. Davis and J. Hirschberg: Assigning intonational features in synthesized spoken discourse. In: Proceedings of the 26th Annual Meeting of the Association for Computational Linguistics, pages 187–193, Buffalo, 1988.

[8] S. Duncan: Some signals and rules for taking speaking turns in conversations. In Weitz (ed.): Nonverbal Communication. Oxford University Press, 1974.

[9] P. Ekman: About brows: emotional and conversational signals. In M. von Cranach, K. Foppa, W. Lepenies, and D. Ploog (eds.): Human ethology: claims and limits of a new discipline: contributions to the Colloquium, pages 169–248. Cambridge University Press, Cambridge, England; New-York, 1979.

[10] P. Ekman and W. Friesen: Facial action coding system. Consulting Psychologists Press, 1978.

[11] D.R. Hill, A. Pearce, and B. Wyvill: Animating speech: an automated approach using speech synthesised by rules. The Visual Computer, 3:277–289, 1988.

[12] J. Hirschberg: Accent and discourse context: Assigning pitch accent in synthetic speech. In: Proceedings of AAAI: 1990, pages 952–957, 1990.

[13] G. Houghton and M. Pearson: The production of spoken dialogue. In: M. Zock and G. Sabah (eds.): Advances in Natural Language Generation: An Interdisciplinary Perspective, Vol. 1. Pinter Publishers, London, 1988.

[14] S. Isard and M. Pearson: A repertoire of British English intonation contours for synthetic speech. In: Proceeding of Speech '88, 7th FASE Symposium, pages 1223–1240, Edinburgh, 1988.

[15] A. Kendon: Some relationships between body motion and Speech. In: A.W. Siegman and B. Pope (eds.): Studies in Dyadic Communication, pages 177–210, 1972.

[16] J.P. Lewis and F.I. Parke: Automated lip-synch and speech synthesis for character animation. CHI + GI, pages 143–147, 1987.

[17] M. Liberman and A. L. Buchsbaum: Structure and usage of current Bell Labs text to speech programs. Technical Memorandum TM 11225-850731-11, AT&T Bell Laboratories, 1985.

[18] D.W. Massaro: Speech perception by ear and eye: a paradigm for psychological inquiry. Cambridge University Press, 1989.

[19] C. Pelachaud, N.I. Badler, and M. Steedman: Linguistic issues in facial animation. In: N. Magnenat-Thalmann and D. Thalmann (eds.): Computer Animation '91, pages 15–30. Springer-Verlag, 1991.

[20] C. Pelachaud, M.L. Viaud, and H. Yahia: Rule-structured facial animation system. In: IJCAI 93, 1993.

[21] C. Pelachaud and S. Prevost: Sight and sound: generating facial expressions and spoken intonation from context. In: Proceedings of the Second ESCA Workshop on Speech Synthesis, New Paltz, NY, 1994.

[22] C. Pelachaud, C.W.A.M van Overveld and C. Seah: Modeling and animating the human tongue during speech production. In: Computer Animation '94, Geneva, May, 1994.

[23] J. Pierrehumbert: The phonology and phonetics of English intonation. PhD Dissertation, MIT (Dist. by Indiana University Linguistics Club, Bloomington, IN), 1980.

[24] S. Prevost and M. Steedman: Generating contextually appropriate intonation. In: Proceedings of the 6th Conference of the European Chapter of the Association for Computational Linguistics, pages 332–340, Utrecht, 1993.

[25] S. Prevost and M. Steedman: Using context to specify intonation in speech synthesis. In: Proceedings of the 3rd European Conference of Speech Communication and Technology (EUROSPEECH), pages 2103–2106, Berlin, 1993.

[26] S. Prevost and M. Steedman: Specifying intonation from context for speech synthesis. Speech Communication, 15(1-2), pages 139–153, 1994.

[27] M. Steedman: Structure and intonation. Language, pages 260–296, 1991.

[28] A. Takeuchi and K. Nagao: Communicative facial displays as a new conversational modality. In: ACM/IFIP INTERCHI '93, Amsterdam, 1993.

[29] J. Terken: The distribution of accents in instructions as a function of discourse structure. Language and Structure, 27:269–289, 1984.

[30] D. Terzopoulos and K. Waters: Techniques for realistic facial modelling and animation. In: N. Magnenat-Thalmann and D. Thalmann (eds.): Computer Animation '91, pages 45–58. Springer-Verlag, 1991.

[31] R. Zacharski, A.I.C. Monaghan, D.R. Ladd, and J. Delin: BRIDGE: Basic research on intonation in dialogue generation. Technical report, HCRC: University of Edinburgh, 1993. Unpublished manuscript.

Editor's Note: see Appendix, p. 298 for coloured figure of this paper

Consistent Grasping in Virtual Environments based on the Interactive Grasping Automata

Serge Rezzonico1, Ronan Boulic1, Zhiyong Huang1
Nadia Magnenat Thalmann2, Daniel Thalmann1

1) LIG - Computer Graphics Lab, Swiss Federal Institute of Technology
Lausanne, CH-1015 Switzerland
fax: +41-21-693-5328
email: {rezzoni; boulic; huang; thalmann}@lig.di.epfl.ch

2) MIRALab-CUI, University of Geneva, 24 rue du Général Dufour
Geneva, CH -1211 Switzerland
fax: +41-22-320-2927
email: thalmann@cui.unige.ch

Abstract - This paper proposes a general framework to enhance grasping interactions of an operator wearing a digital glove. We focus on a consistent interpretation of the posture information acquired with the glove in order to reflect the grasp of virtual artifacts. This allows higher skill manipulations in virtual environments and also improves interactions with virtual human models. A handshake case-study highlights the application range of this methodology.

key words: grasping, virtual human, data glove

1   Introduction

With the advents of synthetic actors in computer animation, the study of human grasping has become a key issue in this field. The common used method is a knowledge based approach for grasp selection and motion planning [RG91]. It can be completed with a proximity sensor model [EB85] or a sensor-actuator model [vdPF93] for the precise position control of the fingers around the object [MT94]. This method results in an automatic grasping procedure. Moreover, due to the 3D interactive tools widely available today, we decided to study interactive grasping of virtual objects while wearing a digital glove device. Such an approach is also interesting for Virtual Reality where more elaborated hand interaction is now possible with recent generation of digital glove. In this context, we map the real posture of the digital glove on a sensor-based virtual hand in order to ensure a consistent collision-free grasping of virtual objects and to provide a consistent visual feedback. In a second stage, this process can drive the grasp behavior of a virtual human model with a classical inverse kinematics control applied to the arm, or a larger fraction of the body [PB90]. More elaborated control approaches of the arm have been proposed but this is beyond the scope of this paper (see [L93], [HBMTT95]). Both automatic and interactive grasping are integrated within the TRACK system [HBMTT95] hence allowing such grasping interaction as a handshake of an operator with a virtual human model.

We first recall the principle of the multiple virtual sensor grasping and then develop the consistent virtual grasping with the digital glove. The framework of interactively driving the grasp behavior of a virtual human model is then outlined and a case study is presented. A discussion summarizes the performances, the interest and the limitations of the current state of the system. A short section presents the implementation details followed by the general conclusion.

2 Automatic Grasping with Multiple Virtual Sensors

This section briefly recalls the interest of automatic grasping based on virtual sensors (without digital glove). Our approach is adapted from the use of proximity sensors in Robotics [EB85] and the sensor-actuator networks [vdPF93]. More precisely, we use multiple spherical sensors for the evaluation of both touch and distance characteristics as proposed in [MT94]. This was found very efficient for synthetic actor grasping problem. Basically, a set of sensors is attached to the articulated figure. Each sphere sensor is fitted to its associated joint shape, with different radii. The touch property of any sensor is activated whenever colliding with other sensors or objects (except the hand components). This is especially easy to compute with spherical sensors (Figure 1).

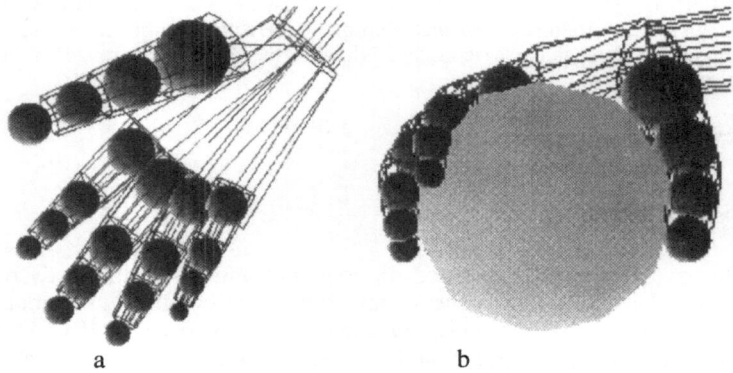

a   b

Figure 1. The virtual hand model with sphere sensors (a); while grasping a sphere (b)

The sensor configuration is important in our method because, when the touch property of a sensor is activated in a finger, only the proximal joints are locked while distal joints can still move. In such a way, all the fingers are finally wrapped around the object, as shown in Figure 1b. When grasping a free form surface object, the sphere sensors are detecting collision with the object. We do not discuss more on collision detection which is beyond the scope of this paper (see [MT94], [K93]).

The automatic grasping methodology is the following [MT94]: first a strategy is selected according to the type and the size of the object to grasp. A target location and orientation is determined for the hand frame and it is realized with the well known inverse kinematics approach. The next stage is to close the fingers according to the selected strategy (e.g. pinch, wrap, lateral, etc.) while sensor-object and sensor-sensor collisions are detected. Any touch detection locks the joints on the proximal side of the associated sensor. The grasping is completed when all the joints are locked or reaching their upper or lower limit.

3 Interactive Grasping with a Digital Glove

When an operator is wearing a digital glove the joint values acquired with the device are normally used to update the visualization of the hand posture. Such approach is pertinent as long as the device is used to specify commands through posture recognition [SZF89]. Among these commands there usually is a symbolic grasp of virtual objects where the relative position and orientation of the object is maintained fixed in the hand coordinate system as long as the grasp posture is recognized. Such approach is suitable for pick-and-place tasks of rigid objects and it is not our purpose to change it.

However, as the virtual environment is becoming more and more complex, especially with the advent of virtual humans, hand-based interactions also evolve in complexity. The limitation of the current approach mostly comes from the rough relative positioning of the hand and the object which does not convey a clear understanding of the action to perform with the object. As everybody has experienced him/herself, we adopt different grasping postures of a same object according to the function we intend to exert with that object because different degrees of mobility are involved for these different tasks (e.g. giving or using a screwdriver). Moreover, the immersion and the interaction in a virtual environment may not only reduce to a matter of pick and place but also imply abilities requiring a greater skill. In such a case the hand associated with the digital glove device provides a high dimensional space not only as a posture space (for command recognition) but also as a goal-oriented space (for precise manipulation or modification of virtual objects with additional tools). For example, interaction with non-manufactured deformable entities (articulated or continuously deformable objects) is best performed with direct hand interaction as it is our most elaborated tool to translate our design intention into action. In such context we need to evaluate precisely their mutual contact location.

3.1 Interactive Grasping Automata

Within this extended application context of the digital glove, it becomes crucial to display a posture of the hand consistent with the on-going manipulation of the virtual object. For this reason, we propose now a new approach for the interactive and consistent grasping of virtual entities with the interactive grasping automata (Figure 2).

110

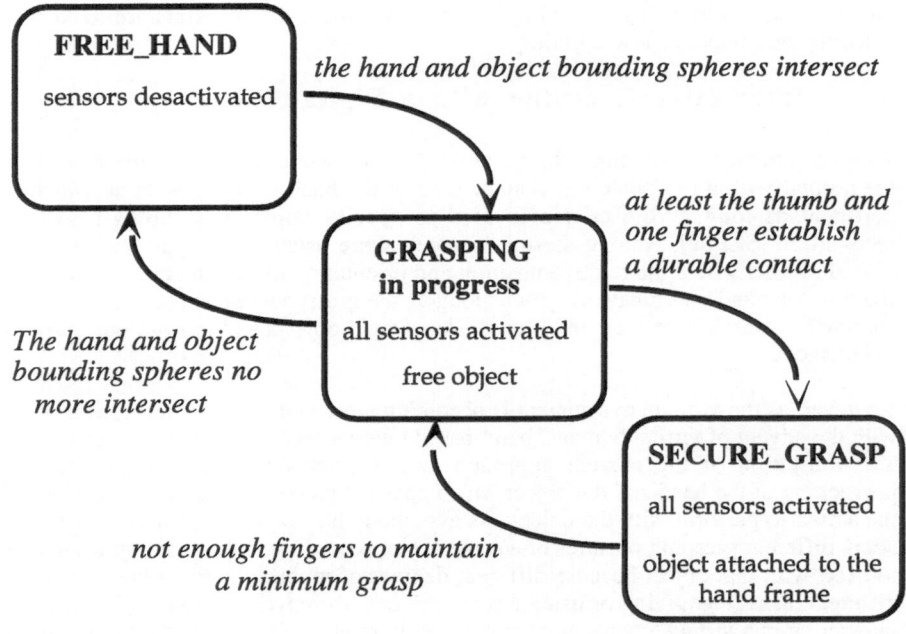

Figure 2 : The interactive grasping automata

In our method we consider three different states of interactive grasping :

FREE_HAND
the hand is freely moving in space without holding any object. The hand posture is displayed as measured with the device. Whenever the hand bounding sphere intersects the object bounding sphere, we enter in the "GRASPING in progress" state.

GRASPING in progress
the touch property of the sensors is continuously evaluated to adjust the posture of colliding fingers with the object to grasp (*the object is fixed or moving in a world coordinate system*). Whenever the hand bounding sphere no more intersects the object bounding sphere, we return to the "FREE_HAND" state. On the other hand, if our simplified grasp condition is established, i.e. at least the thumb and one finger are maintaining a durable contact with the object, we enter the "SECURE_GRASP" state.

SECURE_GRASP
the touch property of the sensors is still used to continuously adjust the posture of colliding fingers with the grasped object (*the object position is fixed in the hand coordinate system*). As soon as the simplified grasp condition vanishes, we return to the "GRASPING in progress" state.

3.2　　Hand Posture Correction

Unlike the automatic grasping procedure, the interactive grasping procedure adjusts the hand posture by opening it rather than closing it. Even with the recent generation of digital glove it is difficult to adjust the grasp precisely so that the fingers establish a permanent contact without penetrating into the virtual object. This is due to the fact that we only a have a visual feedback without any force or touch feedback. However, it would be misleading to conclude that the automatic grasping procedure should also apply in this context. Basically, interactive grasping implies to ensure the highest autonomy of the operator and to provide means of correction rather than removing degrees of freedom.

It is more comfortable for the operator to freely move and close the hand according to the visual feedback of the virtual environment. So our working hypothesis is to rely on the operator to permanently close the grasping fingers slightly more than theoretically necessary. In such a way, the opening correction approach establishes a durable contact which overcomes the unavoidable small variations of hand posture and position (Fig. 3). An optional mode of *Assisted Folding* is also provided to guide the operator in searching the proper grasp posture. In this mode, any sensor initially situated between the first colliding sensor and the finger tip is brought to be tangent to the object. If the sensor is intersecting the object then the associated joint is opened otherwise it is closed. In such a way, the distal part of a colliding finger consistently wraps around the object (Figure 4). The correction algorithm is characterized by an opening-wrapping adjustment loop with eventual Assisted Folding for each colliding finger. So, for each time step, we have :

```
For each colliding finger

        For each sensor distal to the colliding one closest
        to the base (from base side to tip side of the
        finger)

                If the sensor is currently colliding

                        Unfold the closest proximal joint
                          (wrist side)
                          until the sensor is tangent to the
                          object or the joint reaches its limit
                Else
                If in Assisted Folding Mode

                        Fold the closest proximal joint
                          (wrist side)
                          until the sensor is tangent to
                          the object or the joint reaches
                          its limit
                EndIf
        EndIf
    EndFor
EndFor
```

112

Figure 3 details all the stages of the opening-wrapping algorithm for one colliding finger with an elliptic shape (in 2D for clarity). In the example, the joints are all successively opened because the distal sensors (on the finger tip side) are still colliding even after the correction of the proximal ones (on the wrist side). The algorithm begins by unfolding the finger base joint to release the first colliding sensor (fig. 3a,b). Then it unfolds the next joint to remove the following sensor (Fig 3b,c) and the same occurs for the last joint (Fig. 3c,d). In this case the final finger posture consistently wraps around the object.

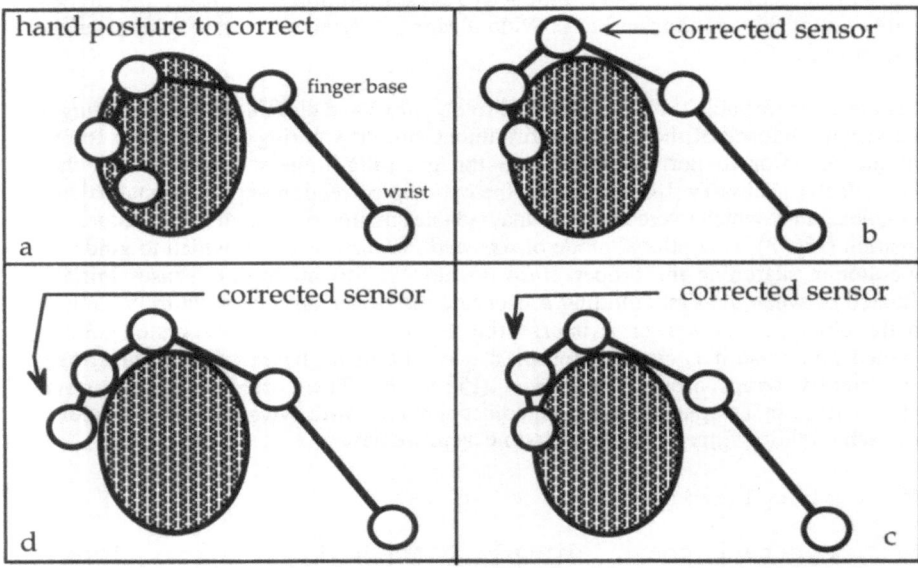

Figure 3 : an example of the opening-wrapping adjustment loop for interactive grasping

The Assisted Folding mode is especially interesting whenever the tip side of the finger is not in the operator field of view (Figure 4). This happens for a large class of grasping postures and objects to grasp. In such a way the operator is given a hint about the full grasp posture of the colliding fingers. Then, from that continuous visual feedback he/she can adjust the hand position, orientation and posture in order to perform a desired grasp. In figure 4 example, the first corrected sensor relies on opening the associated joint while the next two distal sensors are brought to be tangent to the rectangle shape by closing their associated joint.

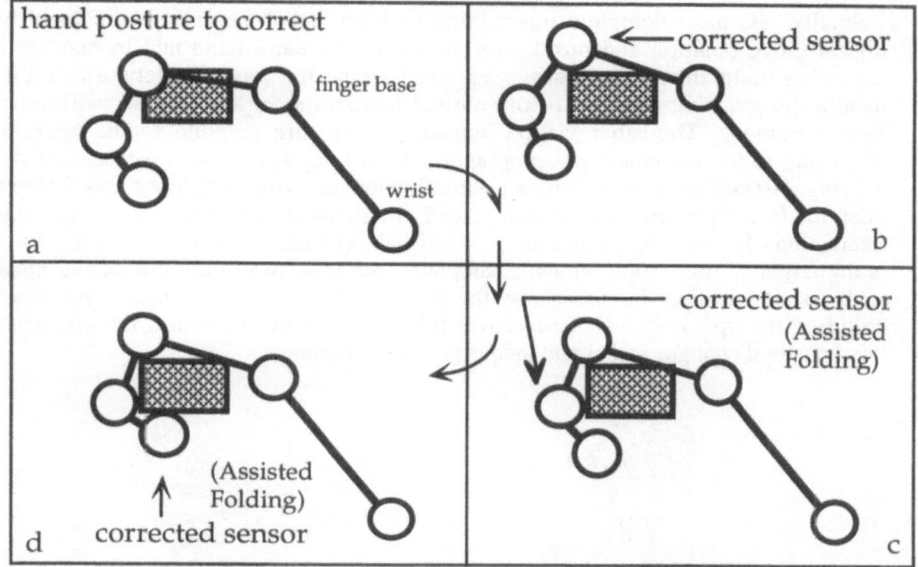

Figure 4 : an example of the opening-wrapping adjustment with assisted folding

4   Integration within the TRACK system

The TRACK animation system is dedicated to human animation design [BHMTT94]. More recently we have begun to evaluate the potential of virtual environments through 3D interaction with virtual humans. As such, both grasping approaches, automatic and interactive, are key features to integrate within the TRACK system. We now present the current state of this integration and outline the progressive intermixing of both techniques in order to allow complex grasping interaction.

- Automatic grasping of static volume primitives and polygonal surfaces has been defined for both one and two hands grasping for the virtual human (Figure 1) [HBMTT95], [MT94]. So it is already possible to exchange handshake between virtual humans by activating their hand motion and automatic grasp in sequence rather than simultaneously (figure 5).

- Autonomous interactive grasping is already performed on volume primitives of the virtual environment and is to be extended on polygonal surface.

- Guiding one virtual human's hand with a 6D device as the Spaceball or a digital glove is an alternate approach to the knowledge-based selection of the grasp posture and positioning relatively to the object. The Automatic grasping closure is then performed to establish a wrapping grasp based on the sensor collision detection while closing the fingers. In such a context, the device must stay in the reachable area of the virtual human's hand otherwise the virtual human has to be globally displaced.

114

- Finally, the most complete intermixing of both techniques is to fully map the digital glove position and posture on the virtual human's hand and to manage it according to the interactive grasping approach. In such a way the operator can fully handle the grasping function of one virtual human model and interact with other virtual humans. The other virtual humans can in turn respond to the operator according to the automatic grasping approach as long as the grasping target is not moving. As an example, we show a virtual actor receiving a floating ball from an operator (see Appendix, the virtual actor is rendered in wireframe for a real-time interaction). For moving objects as in a handshake context, the operator's virtual hand is the target of the virtual human's hand and both have to use the interactive grasp with assisted folding. In such a way the virtual human closes its fingers only when colliding the operator's hand. Moreover this requirement overcomes the operator's hand postural changes and simultaneous position variations.

Figure 5: handshake between virtual actors

5   Results

Three interactive grasping experiments are presented here. They deal with the grasping of regular volume primitives as spheres and cylinders. First figure 6 exhibits the hand model (as provided with the digital glove library from Virtual Technologies). We limit the size of the virtual objects to grasp in order to permit single hand grasping. Figure 7 shows simultaneous view of the real hand posture as acquired with the digital glove (on the right) and the one displayed as the result of the interactive grasping approach (on the left). The sensors are displayed as cubes to reduce the amount of polygons. Figure 8 shows the grasping of a cylinder. (see Appendix for more pictures)

Figure 6 : hand model provided with the CyberGlove from Virtual Technologies

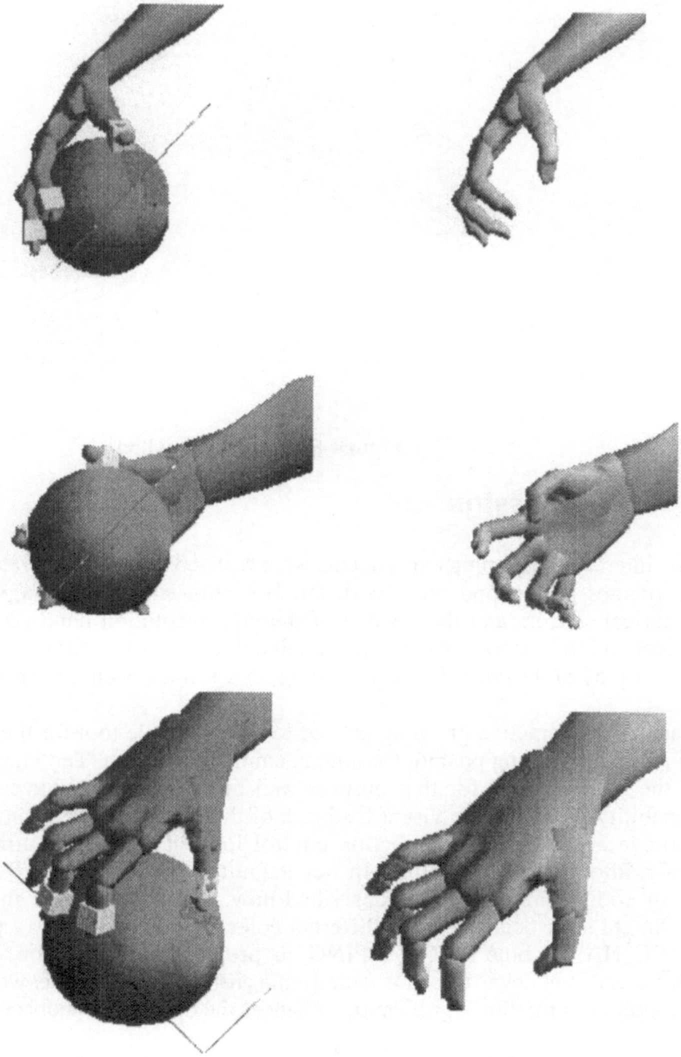

Figure 7 : the corrected (left) and the real (right) hand posture for various viewing angles, hand postures and object sizes (sphere primitives)

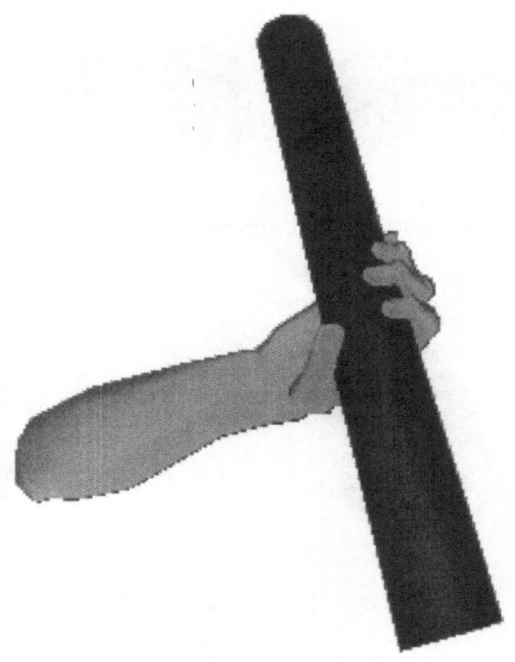

Figure 8: grasping a cylinder

6   Discussion

The interactive grasping experiments were realized at interactive rate of approximately 12 images per second on a workstation screen with the management of up to 20 spherical sensors and the display of the high resolution hand (2600 polygons), the object and the sensors. Although a small delay was perceptible between performance and display of the corrected hand posture, is was not a decisive aspect.

Basically, interactive grasping proved to be a valuable tool for the interactive design of realistic grasping posture for human animation system. The interactive refresh rate is the main criteria for that purpose and our experiments have demonstrated this capability. So, from the visual feedback of the corrected grasp, an operator is able to achieve a good perception-action control loop in order to continuously adjust the grasp into a realistic posture. In our default setting the display is completed with color coding information as described now. Each state of the interactive grasping automata is associated with a different color of the whole hand : pale skin color for FREE_HAND, blue for GRASPING_in_progress and green for SECURE_GRASP. Moreover, whenever a sensor is colliding, its color changes as well. This additional symbolic information significantly enhances the operator's feedback.

Regarding Virtual Environments applications the realism of the grasping posture may not be an essential factor in favor of our approach. In such a context it is often not the point to behave exactly as in the real world. A VE operator is more concerned with a greater manipulation skill rather than a more realistic posture. In that aspect our approach also improves the manipulation of objects by comparison with the well known symbolic grasp. In the symbolic context, the operator has to perform well defined hand postures (at least two distinct ones) so that the recognition system separates properly the grasp from the release commands (not to mention that the object should be selected first). So, whenever the operator wishes to precisely modify the relative position and orientation of the object with respect to the hand (this is the proper definition of a manipulation), he/she has to grasp it, reorient the hand-object system, release the reoriented object and move the hand freely to a new relative orientation. In our approach the reorientation is still performed in that way but the grasp is established in a much simpler way, just by touching the object with the thumb and another finger. Such procedure is much easier and faster that the one based on posture recognition.

As mentioned just before the finger manipulation skill is limited to set the begin and the end of the grasp. Modifying the relative orientation of the object with respect to the hand coordinate system is managed in the same way as symbolic grasping (see above). This procedure is tractable as long as we perform a light grasp involving a small number of fingers. Otherwise, the operator has to repeatedly close and open the hand which can be rapidly uncomfortable.

7 Implementation

We can either use the DataGlove from VPL or the CyberGlove from Virtual Technologies. This latter has been retained for the performance evaluation all along the present experiments. The hand polygonal model provided by Virtual Technologies comes from the 3-D Dataset of Viewpoint DataLabs. The position and orientation of the CyberGlove was acquired with one bird sensor from the "Flock of bird" device from Ascension Technologies. The interactive grasping was performed on a Silicon Graphics Indigo II Extreme. The virtual human and interactive grasping software are written in C language.

8 Conclusion

We have studied interactive grasping of virtual objects to improve the goal-oriented interactions of an operator wearing a digital glove device. The interactive grasping approach with the opening-wrapping algorithm ensures a consistent collision-free grasping of virtual objects which proves to be a valuable visual feedback for the operator hence allowing to manage tasks involving a higher skill than before. Encouraging performances on a standard graphic workstation open the way for integration in fully immersive systems.

Interesting applications of this techniques appear as virtual human models also begin to invade virtual environments or as the digital glove begin to invest animation systems dedicated to human animation design. For example, our approach can drive the grasp behavior of a virtual human model in order to simplify all the grasping studies for production. Both automatic and interactive grasping are integrated within our TRACK animation system.

9   Acknowledgments

We wish to thank our colleague Tom Molet for the implementation of the virtual human model in the framework of the ESPRIT project HUMANOID, Ramon Mas who has developed the first version of the automatic grasping approach, and Manuel Bouvier for the implementation of the cylinder primitive. The research was supported by the Swiss National Science Research Foundation and the Federal   Office for Education and Science.

10   References

[BHMTT94] Boulic R., Huang Z., Magnenat-Thalmann N., Thalmann D. (1994) Goal-Oriented Design and Correction of Articulated Figure Motion with the TRACK System , Computer. & Graphics, Vol. 18, No. 4, pp. 443-452.

[EB85] Espiau B., Boulic R. (1985) Collision avoidance for redundant robots with proximity sensors, Proc. of Third International Symposium of Robotics Research, Gouvieux, October.

[HBMTT95] Huang Z., Boulic R., Magnenat-Thalmann N., Thalmann D "A Multi-sensor Approach for Grasping and 3D Interaction" , Proc. of CGI 95, Leeds

[K93] Kamat V.V. (1993) A Survey of Techniques for Simulation of Dynamic Collision Detection and Response, Computers & Graphics, Vol 17(4)

[L93] Lee P.L.Y. (1993) Modeling Articulated Figure Motion with Physically- and Physiologically-based Constraints, Ph.D. Dissertation in Mechanical Engineering and Applied Mechanics, University of Pennsylvania.

[MT94] Mas R., Thalmann D. (1994) A Hand Control and Automatic Grasping System for Synthetic Actors, Proceedings of Eurographic'94, pp.167-178.

[PB90] Philips C. B., Zhao J., Badler N. I. (1990) Interactive Real-Time Articulated Figure Manipulation Using Multiple Kinematic Constraints, Computer Graphics 24 (2), pp.245-250.

[RG91] Rijpkema H and Girard M. (1991) Computer animation of knowledge-based human grasping, Proceedings of Siggraph'91, pp.339-348.

[SZF89] Sturman D.J., Zeltzer D., Feiner S.(1989) Hands-on Interaction with Virtual Environments, Proc. of ACM SIGGRAPH Symposium on User Interface Software and Technologies, pp 19-24

[vdPF93] van de Panne M., Fiume E. (1993) Sensor-Actuator Network, Computer Graphics, Annual Conference Series, 1993, pp.335-342.

Editor's Note: see Appendix, p. 299 f. for coloured figures of this paper

Hand-Gesture Recognition as a 3-D Input Technique

Ulrich Bröckl-Fox

Universität Karlsruhe
Institut für Betriebs- und Dialogsysteme
Lehrstuhl Prof. Dr. A. Schmitt
Postfach 6980; 76128 Karlsruhe, Germany
EMAIL: ub@ira.uka.de

Abstract. 3-D input techniques based on vision systems are presented: human extremities (hands and head) are observed by a video camera. Certain 2-D parameters of the depicted extremities are used as input parameters for 3-D metaphors.

The 2-D parameters needed and the real-time, contour-based computation of these on standard hardware is presented. Among these parameters, stable hand-shape classification is the key to simple and robust 3-D metaphors. A filter algorithm to separate hand and forearm is described. Different mappings of these parameters into 3-D movements and their metaphorical meanings behind these mappings are shown.

To evaluate these approaches a network-distributed *Virtual Squash* game was implemented, and the effectiveness of the video-based metaphors was compared directly to that of the space-ball. The results reveal that the precision of translations is slightly worse, the number of hits and the velocity of the Virtual squash-racket is slightly better, but the precision of rotations is supreme for video-based hand-gesture input.

1 Introduction

When designing a widget set for interactive user interfaces manipulating 3-D data one has to incorporate easy to grasp metaphors enabling the user to manipulate 3-D objects in a simple way. For 3-D metaphors the following problem arises: a standard workstation neither has a 3-D input medium that can be mapped directly into the 3-D object space nor does it have a 3-D output device. Therefore a special-purpose 3-D input device should be incorporated as an additional input medium into the widget set. A large variety of these devices exists on the market, among these the data-glove rules the virtual-reality market and the space-ball the desktop market. The latter was shown in [10] to be nearly as efficient as the data-glove, both are stated to be up to two times more effective than mouse-driven metaphors such as those described in [7].

On the other hand, vision systems are becoming more and more a standard equipment for current workstations used mainly for tele-conferencing. Towards the data glove using these systems for 3-D interaction offers the advantage of keeping both hands free for typing, mouse selections etc.. According to [24] only 14% of desktop applications currently developed use 3-D graphics. Of these nearly none is pure 3-D. At least some choices, menu selections or options have to be entered by mouse or keyboard.

Most applications constantly swap between 3-D object space and the 2-D space of the graphical user interface. For such applications a data-glove is more likely to be a handicap than an advantage. Towards the space-ball device vision offers at the first sight the advantage of being available without extra cost. As it will be shown by direct comparison in the *Evaluation* section, the video-based 3-D interaction technique is even more efficient than the space-ball device.

The idea to use video input as an input device for human computer-interaction is not new: [18] made the proposal to extend his camera-based system, used to record finger and hand movements in 2-D, into a 3-D system using multiple cameras. The paper presents a technique that implements this idea, but using several cameras is avoided in order to keep costs and computational efforts low.

There exist several other video-based approaches for 3-D interaction: [2] constructed an optical tracker with a scalable work area whereas [21, 22] proposes monocular approaches for desktop applications. [27] presents a hand-gesture taxonomy, the image-flow-based system is still under development. [1] describe their system to control the view on 3-D geometries by observation of the user's head. The same group developed a hand-gesture recognition system [9], introduced the usage of extended Kalman filters for structure and motion estimation of video-based systems in [11] and currently works on full-body interaction as described in [20]. [28] try to detect 27 degrees of freedom using a video-based approach, they obtained 3 degrees of freedom. Prior work in this field of the team in which the author works is summarized in [6].

The new contributions of this paper can be summarized by the following hypotheses that will be underpinned in the rest of the paper:

1. There is almost no need to provide six degrees of freedom at once with an input device: users, especially when untrained, tend to divide a manipulation task requiring both translation and rotation into several single-operation phases.

2. In order to switch between these phases a stable hand-shape recognition system is needed. Only then a change in hand-shape can be used as an event that triggers switching to a different operation.

3. Provided that we are able to implement such a system, it is easy to find three 2-D parameters in the depicted hand that can be used as input parameters for a 3-D metaphor. All these 2-D parameters can be won by integration, not by differentiation operators on the image, which makes the system less sensitive to noise.

4. In applying these simple 3-D metaphors for three extremities (hands and head) instead of one (the hand or head only) in parallel, a simultaneous but intuitive specification of six degrees of freedom is possible again: one hand translates the tool, the other rotates the object while the head's movements manipulate the view on the object and the tool. Through motion parallax the user gets — even if no special 3-D output device such as a shutter stereoscopic is available — a good estimation of the tool's and object's 3-D relation. For using hands in parallel similar findings are reported for the usage of two data-gloves in [3].

2   2-D Parameters

This section gives an overview of the few 2-D parameters needed for a video-based 3-D interaction system, and their efficient calculation.

Contours are computed from the given grey-scale images by a compass-mask algorithm. The integer-valued contours are transformed into real-valued ones by moving the contour points along the grey-scale gradient that is calculated by Sobel operators. The description of these steps can be found in [25]. Finally the real-valued contours are transformed into cubic B-spline curves which acts as a low-pass filter [13]. From this point on we only work with real-valued contours or cubic B-spline curves.

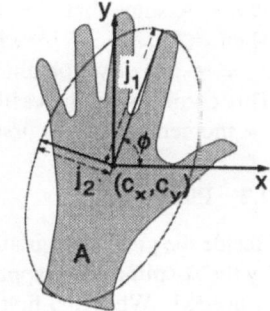

Fig. 1. Needed parameters of the hand.

From the cubic B-spline curves the moments $m_{i,j}$ up to the second order are calculated. From these the area $A = m_{0,0}$, the length of the contour l, the center of gravity $c = (c_x, c_y) = (m_{1,0}, m_{0,1})/m_{0,0}$ and the main moments of inertia j_1, j_2 of the hand[1] are computed as described in [17].

The hand's 2-D orientation ϕ is won as a byproduct of the hand-shape classification described below.

2.1   Computation of 2-D Parameters

To determine the k-th order moments of the hand efficiently several authors proposed to calculate these from the hand's contour using triangulations [19] or run-length encodings [8, 29]. The remainder of this section presents a generalization for polynomials of the approach described in [16] that is based on Greene's integral-theorem.

Theorem 1 *Greene's integral-theorem* (proof see e.g. [15]): *If $B \in R^2$ is a region and ∂B is the positively oriented boundary of B and P and Q have continuous partial derivatives on B then*

$$\int_B \left(\frac{\partial Q}{\partial x} - \frac{\partial P}{\partial y} \right) d(x, y) = \int_{\partial B} P\, dx + Q\, dy.$$

By means of this theorem we are able to compute the moments from contours that are bounded by polynomial curves:

Corollary 2 *Let be B bounded by n cubic polynomial segments*
$\gamma_1, \ldots, \gamma_n : R \rightarrow R^2$,

$$\gamma_i(t) = \begin{pmatrix} \gamma_{i,x}(t) \\ \gamma_{i,y}(t) \end{pmatrix}, \; t \in [0, 1]$$

$$(e.g.) = \begin{pmatrix} c_{i,x,0} + c_{i,x,1} t + c_{i,x,2} t^2 + c_{i,x,3} t^3 \\ c_{i,y,0} + c_{i,y,1} t + c_{i,y,2} t^2 + c_{i,y,3} t^3 \end{pmatrix}.$$

---

[1]The techniques described in this section apply to the face in the same way.

Then

$$m_{p,q}(B) = \sum_{i=1}^{n} \left(\int_0^1 \frac{\gamma_{i,x}^{p+1}(t)}{p+1} \, \gamma_{i,y}^{q}(t) \, \dot{\gamma}_{i,y}(t) \, dt \right).$$

Proof: Assume that $P = 0$ in theorem 1. Further let be $Q = \gamma_{i,y}^{q}(t) \, \gamma_{i,x}^{p+1}(t)/(p+1)$. Then $\partial Q/\partial x = x^p \, y^q$ what is equal to the definition of moments. If we finally set $dy = \dot{\gamma}_{i,y}(t) \, dt$ we obtain the corollary.

This corollary can be easily formulated in a computer algebra system, in the appendix the moments up to the first order are stated in table 1.

2.2 Filters

Beside the grey-scale gradient filter mentioned before and the low-pass filtering induced by the B-spline curve approximation, a third somewhat more hand-gesture related filter is needed. While the first two filters are mainly needed to reduce camera and motion noise the aim of the third filter is to avoid the effects of the forearm entering and leaving the picture. Especially when the observed camera volume is big the parameters of the hand are falsified or even dominated by the forearm's parameters. For desktop applications the following algorithm offers a simple method to eliminate the forearm segments of the hand contour.

The principle of the recursive algo-rithm is depicted in figure 2. In each recursion step the segments lying in a $45°$ sector left and right to the negative major inertia axis (which can be deter-mined from moments up to the second order, see above and [6, 17]) are re-placed by a helical arc. Only in this sector forearm segments can be found due to camera/desktop relation. The

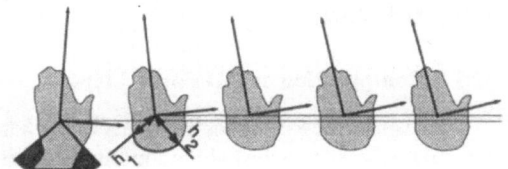

Fig. 2. Some recursions of the forearm-filter. Recursion was repeated 4 times for documentation purpose, $j_1/j_2 < 2$ became true after the first recursion.

recursion is stopped as soon as the quotient j_1/j_2 of the major and minor moments of inertia is less than a constant $k > 1$, normally $k = 2$.

Algorithm 3 (Replacing forearm segments of the hand contour):

Input: Contour $K \in (\mathbf{R} \times \mathbf{R})^n$, $n \in \mathbf{N}$, a periodic sequence of positive-oriented 2-D points, the center of gravity (c_x, c_y), the orientation ϕ of the negative major-inertia axis. The first point of a contour segmented s is denoted by $s.p_0$, the second by $s.p_1$.

Output: Contour K', with the forearm segments replaced by helical segments.

PROCEDURE forearm_filter(VAR K: Contour, VAR c: 2D_Point, VAR ϕ: Angle);
VAR p,c_{new}: 2D_Point; i,n: INTEGER; j_1, j_2: REAL;
BEGIN
    Determine segments s_i, s_j, intersecting with the $\phi \pm 45°$-rotated X-axis
    and the number n of segments lying in between.

```
{ Determine radii of the helix: }
```
$$h_0 := \sqrt{(s_i.p_1.x - c_x)^2 + (s_i.p_1.y - c_y)^2};$$
$$h_1 := \sqrt{(s_j.p_0.x - c_x)^2 + (s_i.p_0.y - c_y)^2};$$
```
FORALL p ∈ {s_i.p_1, ..., s_j.p_0} DO BEGIN
```
    { Replace contour points by helical points: }
$$p.x := c_x + (i/n\,(h_1 - h_0) + h_0)\,\cos(\phi - 45° + i/n\,90°);$$
$$p.y := c_y + (i/n\,(h_1 - h_0) + h_0)\,\sin(\phi - 45° + i/n\,90°);\ i := i + 1;$$
```
END;
```
Determine_Center_of_Gravity_and_Moments_of_Inertia_and_Orientation

$$(K, c_{new}, j_1, j_2, \phi);$$

```
IF j_1/j_2 ≥ 2 THEN   forearm_filter(K, c_new, φ);
END;
```

Theorem 4 *If the width/height quotient q of the depicted arm is always $q < 20$ the algorithm stops after at most 6 recursions.*

Proof: In order to estimate the number of recursion steps we consider figure 3. Here hand and forearm are modeled by a rectangle. Without loss of generality the rectangle is parallel to the X-axis and its height K_0 is 1. This is a worst-case estimation since due to the extension of the wrist and palm the depicted hand is always 'thicker' in Y-direction compared to the forearm. Therefore the rectangle segments replaced by helical segments cause a greater

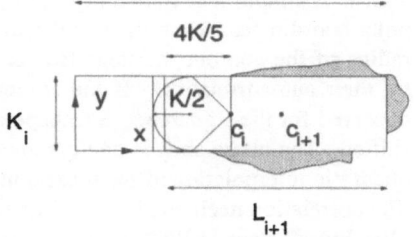

Fig. 3. Identifiers for proof of theorem 4.

quotient j_1/j_2 than the replaced forearm segments and thus a slower convergence. A further upper bound estimation is replacing the helical arc by a rectangle of the width $4K/5$ and height K (see [5] for details on that estimation).

Now we are able to determine the length L_i of the i-th recursion step by the following recurrence relation:

$$L_i = \begin{cases} L_0 & \text{if } i = 0, \\ L_{i-1}/2 + 4/5 & \text{if } i > 0. \end{cases} \tag{1}$$

This recurrence yields — easily to be proven by induction — the following solution:

$$L_n = \frac{8}{5} + \left(L_0 - \frac{8}{5}\right) 2^{-n}. \tag{2}$$

Therefore the recursion stops after at most n steps, with n as follows:

$$n > \log_2 \left(\frac{5\,L_0}{2} - 4\right). \tag{3}$$

Setting $L_0 := q = 20$ (remember $K = 1$ for all steps in the estimation) we obtain $n > 5.52$; that is, $n = 6$ is a upper bound.

124

 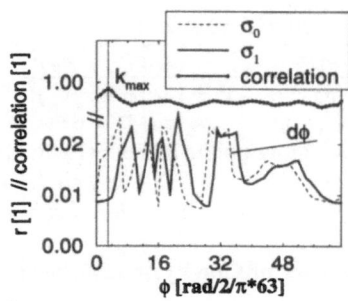

Fig. 4. Using signatures to determine 2-D orientation of the hand, and the class of the hand-shape.

2.3 Stable Classification of Hand-Shapes

In order to determine the class to which a given hand-shape belongs, the hand's contour is transformed into a discrete, one-dimensional function, a so-called *signature*, as depicted above. A simple way to obtain a signature is to transform the centralized contour into polar coordinates. Then the angular axis is split into n intervals and the length of the radius of the contour is integrated for each interval. The signatures are normalized by their autocorrelation. If the contour is rotated as in figure 4 two things can be observed for the signatures: the shape of the signature remains similar, but it is phase-shifted. The phase shift is one parameter we are searching for. It is calculated as the quadratic interpolation of the maximum k_{max} of the correlation of the two signatures. The correlation itself can be calculated efficiently applying the convolution theorem in $O(n \log n)$ steps [12].

To use the correlation of signatures as a means to classify hand-shapes, we use pre-learned signatures of sample-signs and correlate these with a given hand-shape of an unknown class. The correlation's maximum i) determines the class the hand-shape belongs to and ii) gives a measurement for the fidelity of the classification process. It can be shown, that this approach is (2-D) rotation-, translation and scaling-invariant und thus quite user-invariant. It should be noted here that the phase shift $d\phi$ i.e. the 2-D orientation calculated is much more robust towards noise and 3-D rotations of the hand than moment-based approaches. Figure 5 shows the invariance of this simple algorithm towards different users and different orientations of the hand-shape. The columns show the correlation's results for three shape samples, each row stands for a hand sign given from different users in different 2-D orientations.

2.4 Experiments with the Classificator

To evaluate this method it was used to classify dynamic hand-gestures such as hello- and bye-waving and pointing-gestures in the same arrangement as described in [9]. At a recognition speed of 14 Hz a recognition rate of 97.4 % was obtained on an *Intel 486* processor at a clock speed of 50 MHz. No false classifications occurred during the experiments. These results were obtained even though the training gestures were taken from *one* individual, whereas 19 different persons used the hand-gesture recognizer. Even better recognition rates can be obtained if several differently defined signatures

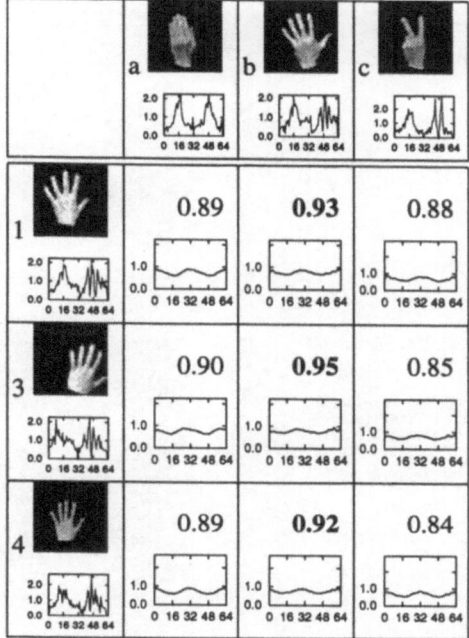

Fig. 5. Examples of hand-shape classifications.

(e.g. the slope density function from [26] instead of radius versus angle) are used to feed a classification algorithm based on [30]. Here for eight different hand-shapes a recognition rate of 98.0 % was achieved. If we skip the user invariance, that is if we use the training-shapes individually, even 99.2 % can be achieved. Details can be found in [5].

3   3-D Metaphors

To ease the description for the following metaphors, only three different hand-shapes, the ones depicted in figure 5, are used. Nonetheless in our 3-D widget-set (cf. [4]) we use more hand-shape-classes as shown in figure 6. The possibility to steer the dialog flow by different hand-shapes is not the *only* means to trigger events, the traditional WIMP[2] interaction paradigm is left to the user. By doing so, we have a simple means of introducing and depicting the possibilities the hand gesture recognizer offers to the user. Possible modes in 3-D interaction are *"Camera in hand"*, *"Scene in hand"* and *"Fly through scene"* with the same functionality as the metaphors described in [31]. The *"Nodo"* operation has the same meaning as lifting the mouse in 2-D graphical user interfaces, i.e., it enables the user to change the hand's position without performing any graphical actions and thus "walk" long distances through the 3-D scene.

---

[2]WIMP = Windows, Icons, Menus, and Pointers

126

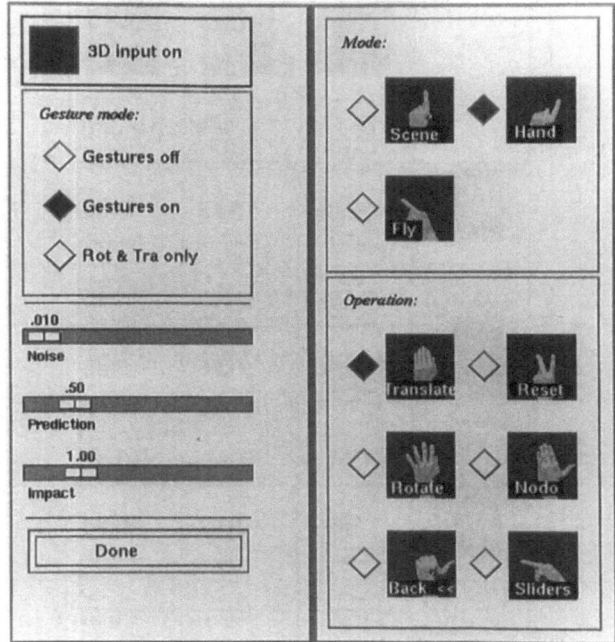

Fig. 6. Using several hand-shapes to steer a 3-D widget.

3.1 The Trinocular Metaphor

Fig. 7. The mirror-box.

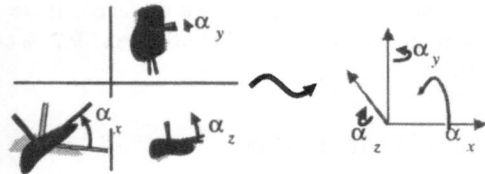

Fig. 8. Mapping 2-D orientations of the three 2-D views onto 3-D Euler angles.

One of our first approaches was quite simple: we took three orthogonal views of the user's hand and mapped the 2-D centers of gravity calculated by first order moments onto the 3-D center of gravity of the hand. To obtain three 2-D views the user interacts in 3-D space by moving his hand into the *"mirror-box"* (figure 7). Two mirrors are arranged in an approximate angle of 45 degrees to the camera plane. Therefore the three views of the scene intersect nearly rectangularly.

The hand's 3-D orientation can be determined by directly mapping the three 2-D orientations of the three views onto 3-D Euler angles (figure 8). Details can be found again in [6].

127

3.2 The Screw Metaphor

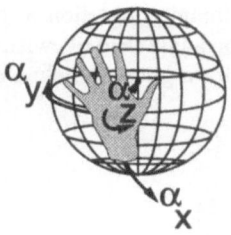 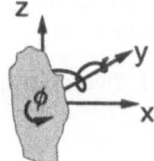

Fig. 9. Screw metaphor.

In order to avoid the necessity to put a rather large mirror box onto the desktop monocular metaphors were investigated more closely. As it will be shown in the evaluation section these monocular metaphors were also found to be more efficient. Monocular metaphors generally steer the operation to perform by a dedicated hand symbol as in the examples on figure 9: the straddled hand is used to rotate things; the closed hand translates them. The screw metaphor got its name from the concept for translations (right side of figure 9): the user translates in x- and z-direction by moving his hand into the appropriate direction. For y-translations one thinks of turning a screw: turning right means increasing y-coordinates, turning left decreasing y-coordinates. The rotational case, shown on the left of the figure, is a straight forward adaptation of the rolling-ball metaphor [14] for three-dimensional input devices:

The 2-D x- and y-translation of the center of gravity of the hand (c_x, c_y) steer the rotational angles α_y and α_x. The hand's 2-D orientation ϕ is mapped directly onto the rotation α_z about the z-axis. The metaphorical concepts, especially for translations, require some training time (≈ 1 min) before they can be used efficiently. But once learned, the metaphor has a decisive advantage, especially for desktop applications: since the hand rests for all manipulations in the x-y-plane it is quite unfatiguing.

3.3 The Thumb Metaphor

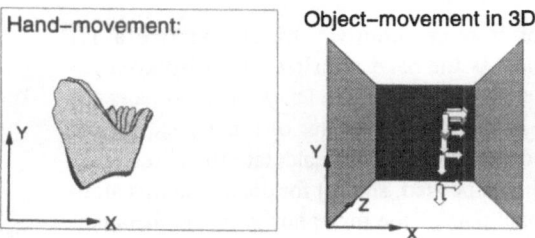

Fig. 10. Thumb Metaphor.

The metaphor is equal to the screw metaphor in its rotational part. For translations the y-translation is specified by the abduction angle of the thumb. This angle can again be calculated by means of signature-correlation. Translations are then characterized by two sample hand-shapes: one for the totally closed hand (σ_1), and another one for the thumb abducted (σ_2). Let denote $\kappa_{\sigma_i,\sigma_k}$ the maximum correlation of two given hand-shapes. Then we are able to calculate the abduction angle (and likewise any other hand-shape alteration, in particular finger movement) for a given signature σ_k by the following definition:

Definition 1 *Two-class specific signature distance:*

$$\tau(\sigma_k) := \left| \frac{\kappa_{(1),k} - \kappa_{(2),k}}{2 - 2\kappa_{(1),(2)}} + \frac{1}{2} \right|.$$

As in the screw metaphor the hand rests in the x-y-plane for all manipulations. Furthermore the user has no problems with unvoluntary changes of the 2D-orientation of his hand induced by x- and z-translations. Figure 11 shows an example plot of a two-class specific signature distance as defined in definition 1.

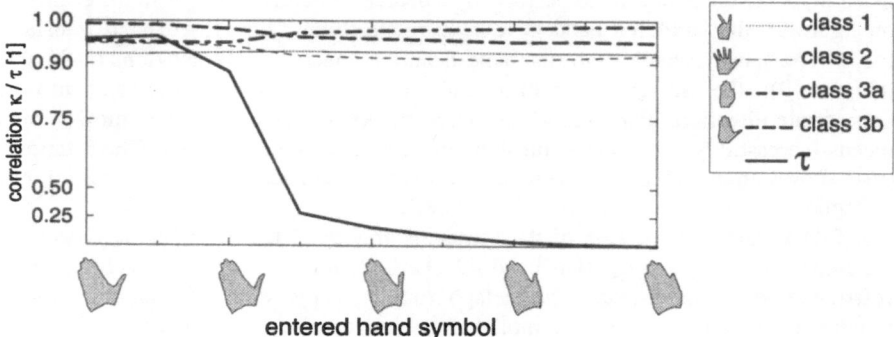

Fig. 11. Example of a two-class specific signature distance.

3.4 The Gear Metaphor

The gear metaphor is more intuitive: translations are a 1:1 metaphor, that means as the hand translates, the displayed geometries are translated. The changes in (x, y, z) coordinates are obtained from the changes of the center of gravity c_x, c_y and the area A of the depicted hand. To calculate this, a camera-calibration algorithm is needed, see [6] for details on this algorithm. The rotational part of the metaphor gave the metaphor its name: it is a 1:4 metaphor, i.e. turning the hand about an angle of 45° implies a rotation of the displayed geometries about

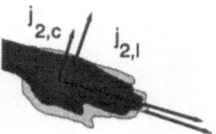

Fig. 12. Changing moments of inertia under rotation.

$4 \times 45° = 180°$. The reason for doing so is the fact that there is no means of determining the 3-D orientation from a 2-D image unambiguously [23]. But if we restrict the allowed rotations to an interval of $[-45°, 45°]$ we can make the following observation (see figure

12): as the hand is rotated about its major inertia axis the last ($\dot{j}_{2,l}$) and current ($\dot{j}_{2,c}$) inertia moments change with the rotation angle approximately linear to the sine of the angle. The same applies for rotations about the second inertia axis and all combinations of these rotations. One problem remains: we do not know the sign of the rotation's sine. To avoid this problem we put the camera at an Euler angle of $(-45°, -45°, 0)$ and restrict the allowed rotations to $[-45°, 45°]$.

Now we know that all rotations within that interval have a bijective effect on the inertia moments. Setting a to the sine of the rotation about the major axis of inertia, b likewise for the minor axis of inertia and f to the unknown depth of the hand along the focal axis of the camera, we obtain the following nonlinear system of equations:

$$\left\{ s_c = \frac{a\,b\,s_l}{f}, \dot{j}_{1,c} = \frac{a\,\dot{j}_{1,l}}{f}, \dot{j}_{2,c} = \frac{b\,\dot{j}_{2,l}}{f} \right\}, \tag{4}$$

where s_c and s_l stand for the current and last length of the hand contour. The solution of this system is:

$$\left\{ b = \frac{s_c\,\dot{j}_{1,l}}{\dot{j}_{1,c}\,s_l}, f = \frac{s_c\,\dot{j}_{2,l}\,\dot{j}_{1,l}}{\dot{j}_{1,c}\,\dot{j}_{2,c}\,s_l}, a = \frac{s_c\,\dot{j}_{2,l}}{\dot{j}_{2,c}\,s_l} \right\} \tag{5}$$

Thus we are able to compute the angles of rotation about the axis of inertia from the moments of inertia and the contour length. Together with the 2-D hand orientation ϕ and the rotational part of the camera-calibration matrix we can transform these parameters into Euler angles in world coordinates.

4   Carving Metaphor

head and hand movements: objects movements in 3–D:

Fig. 13. An example of the carving metaphor.

The metaphors above can be used in parallel for several extremities. Figure 13 shows a composition of these metaphors: the left and right hand operate the screw metaphor, the head only operates in the rotational part of the screw metaphor, since it is not possible with the approaches stated above to do a face-gesture classification. Nonetheless the change of area A of the head's contour can be mapped onto a scaling factor of the displayed geometries. Thus the total number of degrees of freedom is $4 + 2 \times 6 = 16$. In the middle of the figure, the extracted contour curves and the flow of these is depicted. The right part of the figure shows the effects of the left hand on the manipulated object (represented by the dark 3-D axes) and the effects of the right hand onto the tool (represented by the light 3-D axes). The black dots on the floor and side-wall represent the translation of these objects. The effects of the head-movements are not superimposed for illustrating purposes.

5 Evaluation

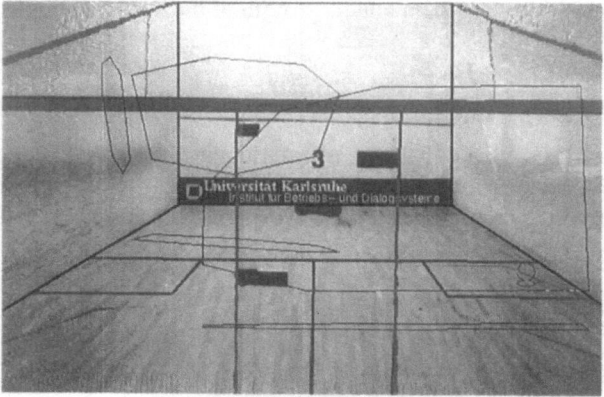

Fig. 14. Virtual squash-court.

To evaluate the video-based 3-D input method it was compared directly to the space-ball, *the* alternative device for desktop 3-D interaction. Therefore a network-distributed *Virtual Squash* game was implemented. The graphics output was quite simple: the squash-rackets were modeled by polygons and superimposed onto a digitized picture of a real squash-court. In order to enhance the 3-D impression shadows of the rackets were plotted on the walls of the squash-court. To get many contacts of the symbolic racket and target the size of the rackets was chosen big. This avoids rare and randomly distributed evaluation data.

5.1 Results

The following figure summarizes the results of the squash experiment. The results were obtained from 12 individuals during a 15-minute game composed of a training phase and three phases where the speed and the translation's and rotation's precision were used to calculate the final-score for each player. The figure shows the results obtained for each phase, respectively. The abbreviations are: s-b = space-ball, s-m = screw metaphor,

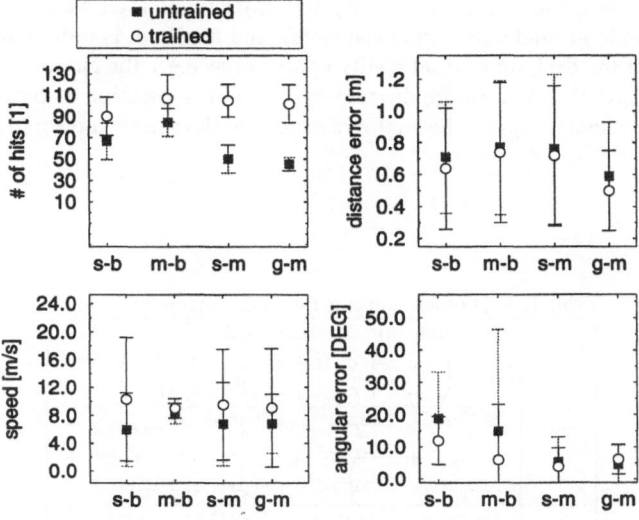

Fig. 15. Results.

g-m = gear metaphor and m-b stands for the mirror-box. One interesting result was found with this device: it was possible either to use translation and rotation isolated or in combination (i.e. 6 DOF), again triggered by different hand-shapes. The decision which variant should be taken was left to the user. Averaged for all users and operations in 3-D only in 20.3 % of all cases the 6 DOF variant was taken, all other operations were split into rotations (34.5 %) and translations(45.2 %). One explanation are the average Euler angles that were induced during translations by the rotational joints of the human arm and hand: for each translation an average of (3.44, 3.83, 5.76) degrees of rotation was measured, for unique rotational tasks we found an average of (4.51, 5.02, 7.56) degrees. Thus nonvoluntary rotations during translations make up more than the half of those for voluntary rotations. Both facts together are a strong hint for the hypothesis 1 in the introduction. Concerning the claim of real-time capability, here only one number is presented to give an estimate of the computational resources needed for the carving metaphor: on an *Intel 486* processor at a clock speed of 50 MHz we obtained a frame rate of 10.6 Hz.

6 Conclusion

Taking all results into consideration it reveals that the precision of translations is slightly worse (factor 0.90), the number of hits (factor 1.19) and the velocity of the Virtual squash-racket (factor 1.25) is slightly better, and the precision of rotations (factor 2.00) is supreme for video-based hand-gesture 3-D input. Thus the results show that video-based 3-D input techniques — even if we use metaphors as simple as the screw metaphor — are competitive to the space-ball. Especially for defining rotations, one even can claim superiority of these techniques. The thumb metaphor seems to be the ideal candidate for the 3-D input device extension to our 3-D widget system, since it is easy to implement, robust towards varying lighting situations (if we use a mouse-pad-sized black underground where the hand rests), and finally, it is unfatiguing. For 3-D interaction off the desktop (virtual reality applications e.g.) the carving metaphor is a promising approach. As a future development a color separation as proposed in [21] should be used here to extract the contours instead of the simple threshold method used above.

Appendix

Table 1. First order moments for cubic polynomial splines.

Parametric equation, $t \in [0, 1]$:
$\gamma(t) = \begin{pmatrix} c_{x,0} + c_{x,1}t + c_{x,2}t^2 + c_{x,3}t^3 \\ c_{y,0} + c_{y,1}t + c_{y,2}t^2 + c_{y,3}t^3 \end{pmatrix}$

$m_{0,0}$	$\frac{c_{x,2}c_{y,1}}{3} + \frac{c_{x,3}c_{y,1}}{4} + \frac{3c_{x,1}c_{y,3}}{4} + c_{x,0}c_{y,2} +$ $c_{x,0}c_{y,3} + \frac{2c_{x,1}c_{y,2}}{3} + c_{x,0}c_{y,1} + \frac{c_{x,2}c_{y,2}}{2} +$ $\frac{3c_{x,2}c_{y,3}}{5} + \frac{2c_{x,3}c_{y,2}}{5} + \frac{c_{x,1}c_{y,1}}{2} + \frac{c_{x,3}c_{y,3}}{2}$
$m_{0,1}$	$\frac{3c_{x,2}c_{y,3}^2}{8} + \frac{3c_{x,1}c_{y,3}^2}{7} + \frac{2c_{x,3}c_{y,2}^2}{7} + \frac{c_{x,0}c_{y,3}^2}{2} +$ $\frac{c_{x,2}c_{y,2}^2}{3} + \frac{2c_{x,1}c_{y,2}^2}{5} + \frac{c_{x,3}c_{y,1}^2}{5} + \frac{c_{x,0}c_{y,2}^2}{2} +$ $\frac{c_{x,2}c_{y,1}^2}{4} + \frac{c_{x,1}c_{y,1}^2}{3} + \frac{c_{x,0}c_{y,1}^2}{2} + \frac{c_{x,3}c_{y,3}^2}{3} +$ $c_{x,0}c_{y,0}c_{y,1} + c_{x,0}c_{y,0}c_{y,2} + c_{x,0}c_{y,0}c_{y,3} +$ $\frac{4c_{x,3}c_{y,3}c_{y,1}}{7} + \frac{5c_{x,3}c_{y,3}c_{y,2}}{8} + \frac{5c_{y,3}c_{x,2}c_{y,2}}{7} +$ $\frac{5c_{y,3}c_{x,1}c_{y,2}}{6} + \frac{2c_{y,3}c_{x,2}c_{y,1}}{3} + \frac{c_{y,3}c_{x,3}c_{y,0}}{2} +$ $\frac{c_{y,2}c_{x,3}c_{y,1}}{2} + c_{y,3}c_{x,0}c_{y,2} + \frac{4c_{y,3}c_{x,1}c_{y,1}}{5} +$ $\frac{3c_{y,3}c_{x,2}c_{y,0}}{5} + \frac{3c_{y,3}c_{x,2}c_{y,1}}{5} + \frac{2c_{y,2}c_{x,3}c_{y,0}}{5} +$ $c_{y,3}c_{x,0}c_{y,1} + \frac{3c_{y,3}c_{x,1}c_{y,0}}{4} + \frac{3c_{y,2}c_{x,2}c_{y,1}}{4} +$ $\frac{c_{y,2}c_{x,2}c_{y,0}}{2} + \frac{c_{y,1}c_{x,3}c_{y,0}}{4} + c_{y,2}c_{x,0}c_{y,1} +$ $\frac{2c_{y,2}c_{x,2}c_{y,0}}{3} + \frac{c_{y,1}c_{x,2}c_{y,0}}{3} + \frac{c_{y,1}c_{x,1}c_{y,0}}{2}$
$m_{1,0}$	$\frac{3c_{x,2}c_{x,3}c_{y,3}}{8} \qquad + \qquad \frac{2c_{x,2}c_{x,3}c_{y,2}}{7} \qquad +$ $\frac{c_{y,1}c_{x,1}^2}{6} + \frac{c_{y,1}c_{x,0}c_{x,2}}{3} + \frac{c_{y,1}c_{x,2}^2}{10} + \frac{c_{y,2}c_{x,1}^2}{4} +$ $\frac{2c_{y,2}c_{x,0}c_{x,3}}{5} + \frac{c_{y,2}c_{x,2}^2}{6} + \frac{3c_{y,3}c_{x,1}^2}{10} + \frac{3c_{y,3}c_{x,2}^2}{14} +$ $\frac{3c_{x,0}c_{x,1}c_{y,3}}{4} + \frac{c_{y,3}c_{x,1}c_{x,2}}{2} + \frac{c_{y,3}c_{x,0}c_{x,3}}{2} +$ $\frac{3c_{y,3}c_{x,1}c_{x,3}}{7} + \frac{c_{y,2}c_{x,1}c_{x,3}}{3} + \frac{c_{y,1}c_{x,1}c_{x,3}}{5} +$ $\frac{2c_{y,2}c_{x,1}c_{x,2}}{5} + \frac{2c_{x,0}c_{x,1}c_{y,2}}{3} + \frac{3c_{y,3}c_{x,0}c_{x,2}}{5} +$ $\frac{c_{y,1}c_{x,1}c_{x,2}}{4} + \frac{c_{y,1}c_{x,0}c_{x,3}}{4} + \frac{c_{y,2}c_{x,0}c_{x,2}}{2} +$ $\frac{c_{x,0}c_{x,1}c_{y,1}}{2} + \frac{c_{x,2}c_{x,3}c_{y,1}}{6} + \frac{c_{x,0}^2c_{y,3}}{2} + \frac{c_{x,0}^2c_{y,2}}{2} +$ $\frac{c_{x,0}^2c_{y,1}}{2} + \frac{c_{x,3}^2c_{y,2}}{8} + \frac{c_{x,3}^2c_{y,3}}{6} + \frac{c_{x,3}^2c_{y,1}}{14}$

References

[1] A. Azarbayejani, T. Starner, B. Horowitz, A. Pentland. Visually Controlled Graph-

133

ics. *Transactions on Pattern Analysis and Machine Intelligence*, 15(6):602–605, June 1993.

[2] R. Azuma, M. Ward, R. Bennett, S. Gottschalk, H. Fuchs. A Demonstrated Optical Tracker With Scalable Work Area for Head-Mounted Display Systems. In *Proceedings of the 1992 Symposium on Interactive 3D Graphics*, S. 43–51, 1992.

[3] R. Bolt, E. Herranz. Two-Handed Gesture in Multi-Modal Natural Dialog. In *Symposium on User Interface Software and Technology*, S. 7–14. ACM, November 1992.

[4] U. Bröckl, A. J. Klingert, A. Schmitt. Towards Standardized User Interfaces for Three-Dimensional Interaction: the Development of 3D Widgets Based on PEX and Motif. In *Proceedings of the Fourth Annual Conference of the European X User Group (EXUG)*, 1992.

[5] U. Bröckl-Fox. *Untersuchung neuer, gestenbasierter Methoden für die 3D-Interaktion*. Verlag Shaker, Aachen, FRG, 1995.

[6] U. Bröckl-Fox, L. Kettner, A. Klingert, L. Kobbelt. *Artificial Life and Virtual Reality*, Kapitel XII, Using Three Dimensional Hand-Gesture Recognition as a New 3D Input Technique, S. 173–187. Wiley and Sons, 1994.

[7] Michael Chen, S. Joy Mountford, Abigail Sellen. A Study in Interactive 3-D Rotation Using 2-D Control Devices. *Computer Graphics*, 22(4):121–129, August 1988.

[8] M. Dai, P. Baylou, M. Najim. An Efficient Algorithm for Computation of Shape Moments from Run-Length Codes or Chain Codes. *Pattern Recognition*, 25(10):1119–1128, 1992.

[9] T. Darrell, A. Pentland. Space-Time Gestures. In *IEEE Conference Computer Vision and Pattern Recognition*, S. 294–299, New York City, June 15–17 1993.

[10] Wolfgang Felger. How Interactive Visualization Can Benefit from Multidimensional Input Devices. In *Proceedings of the SPIE - The International Society for Optical Engineering*, Band 1668, Visual Data Interpretation, S. 15–24, 1992.

[11] Martin Friedmann, Thad Starner, Alex Pentland. Device Synchronisation Using an Optimal Linear Filter. In *Proceedings of the 1992 Symposium on Interactive 3D Graphics, Special Issue of Computer Graphics, Band 26*, S. 57–62, 1992.

[12] R. C. Gonzalez, P. Wintz. *Digital Image Processing*. Addison-Wesley, Reading, MA, 2 edition, 1987.

[13] A. Goshtasby, F. Cheng, B. A. Barsky. B-Spline Curves and Surfaces Viewed as Digital Filters. *Computer Vision, Graphics, and Image Processing*, 52:264–275, 1990.

[14] Andrew J. Hanson. The Rolling Ball. In David Kirk (Hrsg.), *Graphics Gems III*, S. 51–60. Academic Press, 1992.

[15] H. Heuser. *Lehrbuch der Analysis, Teil 2*. B.G. Teubner Stuttgart, 1983.

[16] X. Y. Jiang, H. Bunke. Ein konturbasierter Ansatz zur Berechnung von Momenten. In *Informatik Fachberichte 290*, S. 143–150. Bernd Radig, October 1991.

[17] B. Klaus, P. Horn. *Robot Vision*. The MIT Press, McGraw-Hill Book Company, 1986.

[18] M. W. Krueger. *Artificial Reality*. Addison-Wesley, 1981.

[19] Jia-Guu Leu. Computing A Shape's Moments from Its Boundary. *Pattern Recognition*, 24(10):949–957, 1991.

[20] P. Maes, T. Darrell, B. Blumberg, S. Pentland. Interacting with Animated Autonomous Agents. In *Announced paper for SIGGRAPH 94, Orlando, FL*, 1994.

[21] C. Maggioni. A Novel Gestural Input Device for Virtual Reality. In *Proceedings of IEEE 1993 Virtual Reality Annual International Symposium, VRAIS*, S. 118–124, 1993.

[22] C. Maggioni. Non Immersive Control of Virtual Environments. In *Virtual Reality, Anwendungen & Trends, IPA/IAO-Forum*, S. 129–142, Stuttgart–Vaihingen, 9–10 Februar 1994. Springer Verlag.

[23] J. S. C. Yuan. Mukundan. Estimation of Quaternion Parameters from Two Dimensional Image Moments. *Graphical Models and Image Processing*, 54:345–350, 1992.

[24] B. A. Myers, M. Rosson. *Survey on User Interface Programming*. Number (#77629) in RC 17624. IBM Research Division, January 1992.

[25] M. Nadler. A Note on Coefficients of Compass Mask Coefficients. *Computer Vision, Graphic, and Image Processing*, 51:96–101, 1990.

[26] P. Nahim. The Theory of Measurement of a Silhouette Description for Image Processing and Recognition. *Pattern Recognition*, 6(2):85–95, 1974.

[27] F. Quek. Toward a Vision-Based Hand Gesture Interface. In *Conference on Virtual Reality Software and Technology*, Singapore, August 23-26 1994.

[28] J. Rehg, T. Kanade. DigitEyes: Vision-Based Human Hand Tracking. *File: CMU-CS-93-220.ps.Z ftp:reports.adm.cs.cmu.edu:/usr0/anon/1993*, S. 1–17, 1993.

[29] I. Rothe, K. Voss. *Orientierungsbestimmung von Objekten durch Momentinvarianten*, S. 42–49. Informatik Aktuell. Springer Verlag: S. Fuchs, R. Hoffmann, 1992.

[30] D. Rubine. Specifying Gestures by Example. *Computer Graphics*, 25(4):329–337, 1991.

[31] C. Ware, S. Osborne. Exploration and Virtual Camera Control in Virtual Three Dimensional Environments. In *ACM Transactions On Computer Graphics*, S. 175–183, Oct. 1990.

The Virtual Treadmill:
A Naturalistic Metaphor for Navigation in Immersive Virtual Environments

Mel Slater, Anthony Steed and Martin Usoh[1],
Department of Computer Science, and
London Parallel Applications Centre,
QMW University of London,
Mile End Road,
London E1 4NS UK.

Abstract. This paper describes a metaphor that allows people to move around an immersive virtual environment by "walking in place". Positional data of participants' head movements are obtained from a tracking sensor on a head-mounted display during a training session, where they alternate between walking in place and a range of other activities. The data is fed to a neural net pattern recogniser that learns to recognise the person's walking in place behaviour. This is used in a virtual reality system to allow people to move through the virtual environment by simulating the kinds of kinesthetic actions and sensory perceptions involved in walking. An experiment was carried out to compare this method of navigation with the familiar alternative that involves using a hand-held pointing device, such as a 3D mouse. The experiment suggests that the walking in place method may enhance the participant's sense of presence, but that it is not advantageous with respect to the efficiency of navigation.

Keywords. Immersive virtual environments, virtual reality, navigation, 3D mouse, neural networks.

1. Introduction

In Immersive Virtual Environments (IVEs), commonly called "virtual reality", participants operate in an extended virtual space, created by the interaction between the human perceptual system, and computer generated displays. The displays provide sensory information in the visual, auditory and tactual modalities. In *immersive* VEs (IVEs) sensory input to the human from the external world is, ideally, wholly provided by the computer generated displays. This affords the possibility of participants maintaining a *sense of presence* in the VE, that is the (suspension of dis-) belief that they are in a world other than where their real bodies are located [2, 6, 8, 11, 5, 16]. Presence is the unique possibility that IVEs offer: just as computers are general purpose machines, IVEs may be considered as general purpose presence-transforming machines. We take the same standpoint as Steur, in regarding presence as the central issue in "virtual reality": "A virtual reality is defined as a real or simulated environment in which a perceiver experiences telepresence" [18].

---

[1] emails: mel, steed, bigfoot @dcs.qmw.ac.uk. URL: http://www.dcs.qmw.ac.uk/

A major feature of IVEs is that this form of human-computer interaction can be "naturalistic", with the participant carrying out activities in a manner much as in everyday life. Indeed, where the IVE is used in a training context, such a naturalistic form of interaction is an absolute requirement: for, in this case, operations within the IVE must be similar enough to the real world so that the learning in the virtual environment can transfer to the real world. On this point, Loomis has suggested that the degree of presence and distal attribution[2] might be assessed according to the degree of accuracy that observers can perform visually directed tasks, requiring the perception of distance, in virtual environments as compared to real environments [9].

In practice naturalistic interaction is made difficult by the typically limited tracking information possible with today's equipment - usually only from the head and the dominant hand. Electro-magnetic sensors operate within a small field, so that it is not possible for participants to wander around a large VE by physically walking, unless there are systems specifically designed for that purpose alone, such as roller skates [7] or a treadmill [1]. In general, the gap between actions that are required (such as navigation over large distances) and the sensor information available, means that just as in 2D interfaces, metaphors are required.

Mackinlay et. al. [10] pointed out that there are four requirements that need to be considered for navigation in virtual spaces:

(a) General - for example exploring a building interior;
(b) Targeted - that is, aiming at a particular visible point;
(c) Specified coordinate - that is, moving to a point specified relative to a coordinate system;
(d) Specified trajectory - that is, moving along a position and orientation trajectory, as with a movie camera.

In this paper we consider mainly case (a) - that is, a metaphor for navigating through an environment, without any specific target or location in mind, but according to the temporary and changing whims of the navigator.

Previous investigations have concentrated on metaphors in the context of navigation in 3D VEs viewed through a 2D display using 2D input devices or six degrees of freedom input devices such as the Flying Mouse [19]. Three metaphors for navigation were introduced by Ware et. al.:

(1) eyeball in hand - where the viewpoint is directly controlled by the movements and orientation of the input device;

(2) scene in hand - where the viewpoint is stationary and movements of the scene are controlled by the movements and orientation of the input device;

(3) flying vehicle control - where the user flies in a virtual vehicle and the input device is the vehicle control mechanism, for example, controlling acceleration and velocity, but not directly absolute positioning.

---

[2] Attribution of the objects of our sense perceptions to the external world, or non-self.

Here we are interested in "naturalistic" interaction, so we rule out (2): our requirement is that participants are able to wander around the VE, seeing through their "virtual eyes" which are located in more or less the normal place in their heads. By "naturalistic" in this context, we mean that participants can move through the virtual space in a manner that is similar to how they would do so in everyday reality.

In Section 2 we briefly discuss various methods previously adopted, in Section 3 we outline the new approach, in Section 4 a discussion of some experimental results, and conclusions in Section 5.

2. Navigating in IVEs

A standard solution for navigation in IVEs is to make use of the hand-held pointing device. VPL used the DataGlove [3]: a hand gesture would initiate movement, and the direction of movement would be controlled by the pointing direction. Velocity was controlled as part of the gesture: for example the smaller the angle between thumb and first finger the greater the velocity.

DIVISION's ProVision system typically employs a 3D mouse (though it supports gloves as well). Here the direction of movement is determined by gaze, and movement is caused when the user presses a button on the mouse. There are two speeds of travel controlled by a combination of button presses.

In a previous experiment [14, 15] we adjusted the ProVision's standard interface, and based direction of movement on the pointing direction of the 3D Mouse. This disassociation of gaze and direction of movement gives the participant an extra degree of freedom in exploring the VE. However, we still had no direct control over velocity; this makes accurate navigation quite difficult, people frequently overshooting or under-reaching targets.

In our earlier studies we found that although people did quickly get used to using the 3D Mouse as a navigation device, it was far from ideal. We found that this use of the mouse introduced a "mixed metaphor" - subjects in the experiments moved partially by using their bodies in the normal way, and partially by use of the pointing device. Two of the subjects wrote:

> "Sometimes [I had] a desperate need to actually walk when virtually walking, there does seem to be a conflict between what the eyes see and the body feels - e.g., my feet appear to be floating but I can feel my feet on the ground."

> "Trying to separate virtual and physical movement: constantly being aware - my initial response was to make the physical move then forcing myself to use the mouse instead... The amount of concentration I had to use was something I remember particularly. Moving around with the mouse, forwards and backwards - and with the helmet turning around - it was difficult to reconcile the two ways of moving."

There are important problems here:

• sensory dissonance - a contradiction between different modes of sensory data (visual and kinesthetic);

• the participants moving in two quite different ways: by actually moving their bodies as they would in real life - for example, to move over short distances - or alternatively by pressing a button, with direction controlled by pointing.

In each of the methods discussed above, there is no explicit metaphor that is given to the participant. Many years of research in human-computer interaction in the context of point-and-click interfaces on workstations have made it clear that such metaphors are invaluable [12].

There is some anecdotal evidence that navigation by pointing and button pressing might reduce participant's sense of presence in the IVE. For example, in one of our experiments, subjects stood at the edge of a precipice. Some of them noted that they were unable to physically move themselves forwards by actually taking a step, owing to their fear of heights. However, they were able to move forward by pressing the mouse button. Another subject noted that he was not disturbed by moving into and through walls if this was caused by use of the 3D mouse. However, he was disturbed when he pressed the button to move forward while simultaneously using his legs as if he were actually walking. In this case, he found walking into walls "scary". Generally, analysis of our earlier experimental results suggests that the sense of presence is reduced when actions are not carried out realistically - at least in the context of architectural walkthrough [14]. In the next section we introduce a metaphor that attempts to resolve these problems.

3. A Metaphor for Navigation

Brooks [1] noted that "Physical motion powerfully aids the illusion of presence, and actual walking enables one to feel kinesthetically how large spaces are..." As part of the Building Walkthrough project at the University of North Carolina, a steerable treadmill was constructed, that allowed users to actually experience walking through virtual buildings and building sites. Here we explore a similar idea, implemented in software rather than a real physical treadmill.

3.1 Doing the Impossible

In a sense what we are trying to do is really impossible. We have the following information: at any moment in time the position (x,y,z) of the head-mounted sensor relative to a coordinate system with origin at the receiver, and the direction vector (dx,dy,dz) of gaze. With these two pieces of information we are trying to construct a navigation system that:

• allows the navigator to go anywhere (at ground level) in the VE (we rule out flying);

• is consistent across senses - so that what the navigator sees does not contradict other sensory input (of course, this is not completely possible with today's IVE systems);

• is integrated - does not require switching between different metaphors.

3.2 Let Them Walk

If we want people to be able to navigate the environment - let them walk. Here the metaphor is walking - appropriate to, for example, an architectural walkthrough application. However, they cannot literally walk, because this would lead them outside of sensor range. Instead, let them "walk in place". So the metaphor is: for the participants to go somewhere, they would stay in the same place but carry out actions that for them mean walking - e.g., lift one leg, and then the other, reminiscent of walking, but not actually covering distance in the real world. The direction of walking may be a function of direction of gaze. To stop walking - just stop walking in place. Velocity could be controlled by the frequency of oscillations in the tracking data.

The advantages of this metaphor are:-

(a) Our system presents participants with a virtual body. While they are walking we also show their legs moving up and down. Hence the problem of sensory dissonance could be reduced, although by no means eliminated.

(b) Virtual ground is covered in this metaphor by almost really walking, or by taking one or two actual physical steps: each case involving whole body movements similar to those of walking in everyday reality. Contrast this with the usual method, which is sometimes moving by actually walking, and other times using a mouse or glove.

(c) There is no use at all for a hand-held pointing device such as mouse or glove in this method of navigation. It therefore is less a "computer interface" metaphor. It does not rule out other metaphors that do rely on the pointing device (such as flying vehicle control).

The disadvantage - as usual - is that the relative sophistication of the metaphor is at the cost of extra computation, and it could increase the lag time slightly. However, in our current implementation on the equipment that we are using this has not been noticeable at all. In fact, in walking in everyday reality, there is a lag time between the intention to walk, the act of first moving ones legs, and the viewpoint actually changing.

3.3 Implementation

The method requires the detection of specific behavioural activity of participants - that is, whether they are walking in place or doing something else. An obvious solution to this problem is to use more trackers, at least one on each leg. However, this is not usually feasible for several reasons:

• cost in terms of the additional trackers required;

• cost in terms of two extra streams of data to process, which also slows down the overall system network speed;

• the extra burden to participants of "suiting up" before entering the IVE.

If it is possible to efficiently determine this behavioural activity without extra trackers, then this must surely be preferable.

We have used a neural net pattern recogniser that detects whether participants are "walking in place" or doing something else based on data supplied by the HMD tracker. This solution and a corresponding analysis of the performance of the pattern recogniser is fully described in [17].

4. Experiments with Participants

4.1 Experimental Procedures

In this section we describe the first of our experimental case-control studies to assess the walking in place technique. The experiment had two main purposes related to participant performance:

(a) To assess whether, in the context of the experimental scenario, the walking metaphor is preferred by subjects to the method based on navigation using hand gestures and pointing;

(b) To assess the impact of the walking metaphor on the reported sense of presence of the subjects.

Subjects for the experiment were recruited mainly through informal contacts, by asking people on the QMW campus whether they wish to take part in a "virtual reality" experience. Most of those who participated were post-graduate students or researchers though not in computer science, and all but one had never experienced virtual reality.

The experiments described in this paper were implemented on a DIVISION ProVision200 system. The ProVision system consists of a DIVISION 3D mouse (a hand held input device), and a Virtual Research Flight Helmet™ as the head mounted display (HMD). Polhemus sensors were used for position tracking of the head and the mouse. Scene rendering is performed using an Intel i860 microprocessor (one per eye) to create an RGB RS-170 video signal which is fed to an internal NTSC video encoder and then to the displays of the Flight Helmet™. These displays (for the left and right eye) are colour LCDs with a 360×240 resolution and the HMD provides a field of view of about 75 degrees along the horizontal with a consequent loss of peripheral vision.

Each person was invited to alternate "walking in place" and other activities (while wearing the HMD) for a ten minute data gathering process. This data was used to train a pattern recogniser to recognise "walking in place" behaviour, which does differ from person to person. During walking in place, some people move their heads much more than others. Clearly the recogniser requires rather more data for those who move their head slightly compared to those who move their head a lot. The average stride length of subjects in reality was also measured during this period. This was used to adjust the distance they moved forward for each step of "walking in place". The subjects were invited back for the main part of the experiment a few days later.

Each subject was first given a short description of the procedures, which included a warning that virtual reality can result in symptoms akin to travel sickness for some people. They were given the opportunity to withdraw prior to the start of the experiment. One potential subject withdrew because of this warning.[3]

The experimental scenario consists of a corridor with a room at either end. The first room contains many blocks laying on the floor, and one distinct small red cube at the end of the room furthest from the doorway. The second room, at the other end of the corridor is on two levels. The main level is at normal floor height, but this ends at an edge to a deep drop to a lower level which contains some tables and chairs. There is, in addition, one single blue chair suspended on a wall at the main floor level, across the chasm of the room. There is a plank leading out from the main floor towards this chair, but the end of the plank is too far away from the suspended blue chair for anyone to reach it.

After entering the IVE, the subjects were placed first in the corridor, and given a brief training session. They were shown how to move through the environment, and how to pick up an object. All subjects had the 3D mouse in their right hand; this is held somewhat like a gun - it has four buttons, of which at most two are used in the experiment. The forefinger button, equivalent to the trigger of a gun, is used to select and lift an object. The thumb button, following the analogy of a gun, is in the position of the hammer. Depressing this thumb button would move participants through the scene at ground level, along a path determined by the direction in which their hand was pointing. All other buttons are disabled.

All subjects saw a representation of their hand, and their thumb and first finger activation of the buttons would be reflected in movements of their corresponding virtual fingers. The hand was attached to an arm, that could be bent and twisted in response to similar movements of the real arm and wrist. The arm was connected to an entire simple body representation, complete with legs and left arm. The virtual body seems to be an important factor in enhancing the sense of presence [14, 93b] and so was included for all subjects.

During the training session, the subjects were asked to estimate the distances between each of two pairs of lines, two red lines, and two blue lines. They then moved to the doorway leading to the first room, and the task for the remainder of the experiment was explained. This was to go to a certain small red cube at the far end of the room, pick this up, and take it to the room at the other end of the corridor, and place it on the blue chair. (At this point, the subjects had not seen inside either of the rooms).

Subjects were randomly assigned to one of a control or experimental group. Those in the control group moved through the environment by using the mouse: that is, they moved by pressing the thumb button, and they moved in the direction of pointing. Those in the experimental group, moved by "walking in place". Direction of

---

[3]In past experiments we have not given such a warning, on the grounds that merely alerting people to the possibility may induce the result. However, we have come to believe that it is unethical to subject people to this possibility without prior warning.

movement was determined by gaze. (The subjects were not explicitly told that direction is determined by gaze, but all realised this immediately). There were finally eight subjects in each group, though full data was not obtained for all subjects.

Subjects repeated the task twice. Those in the control group first carried out the task using the mouse method of moving. They then exited from the IVE and were given Part I of a questionnaire to answer. They then returned after a few minutes and repeated the experiment using the walking in place method of moving. They then completed Part II of the questionnaire, which asked them to compare the two experiences on a number of criteria. Those in the experimental group did the same, except that their first experience was by walking in place, and the second was with the mouse. They answered exactly the same questionnaires. Note that after their first entry, each subject had only properly experienced one method - the control group using the mouse, and the experimental group walking in place.

The main problem with these procedures was that the pattern recogniser performed ineffectively for a proportion of the subjects assigned to the experimental group. There was one fallback for this - we have a "standard" recogniser that many casual visitors to the laboratory are able to use without the necessity of one trained for their personal style of walking. If their personal recogniser did not work for a subject, then we tried them with the standard recogniser. If this did not work, then they only completed the control half of the experiment.

4.2 Results with the Pattern Recogniser

There were 16 subjects who completed the experiment. There were three in the control group who were unable to successfully use the walking in place technique so that there is incomplete data for these three.

One earlier subject was unable to successfully move at all either by walking in place or by using the mouse. We have had probably more than 50 people experience our system using the mouse for navigation in the course of the past year, and every one has been able to use the this method of navigation. We therefore decided to eliminate this person from the experiment, she being so unusual in this regard compared to the norm. A full analysis of the pattern recogniser results is given in [17].

4.3 Results on Navigation

Part I of the questionnaire contained three questions relating to navigation, distributed throughout the questionnaire. The results are shown in Table 1.

We were interested in three aspects of navigation: the general process of moving around, the task of getting specifically from one place to another, and whether or not the process seemed "natural". From Table 1 we can observe that on all three criteria, the average scores for walking in place were slightly higher for general moving, getting from place to place, and the extent to which the method seemed "natural", although the samples are too small to do formal statistical testing. These are the results immediately after the first part of the experiment. There were 13 subjects who completed both parts of the experiment. Their part II answers, where they make a direct comparison between the two methods, gives the advantage with respect to general movement and also for getting from place to place to the method using the mouse (Table 1). This was to be expected, in comparison with the recogniser used, navigation could be more easily controlled when using the mouse. Also, use of the mouse is certainly easier in the sense that it requires less energy - pressing a button instead of the whole body activity involved in walking in place. With respect to the sense of the method being "natural" the subjects were equally split between the two methods.

Table 1
Moving Through the World: response to questionnaire

General Moving	Getting from place to place	Natural/unnatural					
Did you find it relatively "simple" or relatively "complicated" to move through the computer generated world?	How difficult or straightforward was it for you to get from place to place?	The act of moving from place to place in the computer generated world can seem to be relatively "natural" or relatively "unnatural". Please rate your experience of this.					
To move through the world was...	*To get from place to place was ...*	*The act of moving from place to place seemed to me to be performed ...*					
1. very complicated	1. very difficult	1. very unnaturally					
...	...	...					
7. very simple	7. very straightforward	7. very naturally					
Group	Mean	Med.		Mean	Med.		Mean	Med.
Exp.	5.1	5.5		5.5	6.0		3.9	4.0
Cont.	4.6	4.5		4.5	4.5		3.1	2.0
n	8	8		8	8		8	8
Part II comparison:/13 prefer: walking: 4 same: 1 mouse: 8	Part II comparison:/13 prefer: walking: 1 same: 2 mouse: 10	Part II comparison:/13 prefer: walking: 5 same: 3 mouse: 5					

4.4 Results on Presence

All subjects but one carefully avoided colliding with objects distributed over the floor in the first room, on their way to pick up the red cube. There seemed to be no difference between the methods of moving in this regard. However, this may have little to do with the sense of presence. Just as a matter of interest we asked one subject, who had been especially careful not to collide into objects in the first room, to repeat the process of moving through the room (after the final completion of the formal experiment) but this time without immersion - by using the mouse and holding the HMD, while watching the results on the TV monitor. Again, he carefully navigated around the objects. His explanation was that it is "normal" not to go through objects.

Table 2

Subjective Reporting on Presence

Being there	Real or present	Seeing/visiting
Please rate your sense of being there in the computer generated world...	To what extent were there times during the experience when the computer generated world became the "reality" for you, and you almost forgot about the "real world" outside?	When you think back about your experience, do you think of the computer generated world more as something that you saw, or more as somewhere that you visited?
In the computer generated world I had a sense of "being there"...	*There were times during the experience when the computer generated world became more real or present for me compared to the "real world"...*	*The computer generated world seems to me to be more like...*
1. not at all	1. at no time	1. something that I saw
...	...	...
7. very much	7. almost all of the time	7. somewhere that I visited

Group	Mean	Med.		Mean	Med.		Mean	Med.
Exp.	5.6	5.5		4.9	5.0		5.0	4.5
Cont.	5.1	5		3.5	3		4.4	4.5
n	8	8		8	8		8	8
Part II comparison:/13 **prefer:** walking: 6 same: 5 mouse: 2			**Part II comparison:/13** **prefer:** walking: 7 same: 5 mouse: 1			**Part II comparison:/13** **prefer:** walking: 7 same: 6 mouse: 0		

The purpose of the scenario in the second room was to repeat some aspects of the "visual cliff" experiment, in which young children and animals were encouraged to move across a visual chasm to (for example) reach their mother. The chasm in fact was covered by a sheet of glass, so that there was no real danger to the subject. This famous experiment, concerned with the visual guidance of human actions reported in [4], suggested that humans and animals are hard-wired to avoid deep drops - the youngsters could not be goaded into crossing the gap. Our previous informal observations and results of a pilot experiment [13] suggested that this phenomenon also operates in IVEs. It may be related to the sense of presence, since subjects who do not experience presence would be unlikely to experience the danger indicated by the virtual visual chasm.

We found no difference in observed behaviour between those in the experimental or control group as a whole. Most of the subjects hesitated, some for a long time, before venturing out over the chasm (they did not virtually fall!) to place the cube on the chair. Most attempted to reach the chair by stretching out their arms. One subject in the control group never went out to the chair.

We also asked three questions relating directly to presence, distributed through the questionnaire. The questions and a summary of the responses are shown in Table 2. These particular questions were derived from our earlier work on presence: Presence concerns the extent of "being there", the extent that the VE becomes more real than everyday reality, and the sense of visiting somewhere rather than seeing something.

All three indicators, in Table 2, suggest that the walking in place metaphor may be associated with a higher sense of presence than using the mouse. This is further supported by the comparisons made in Part II of the questionnaire. With respect to the three presence indicators, a very small proportion of subjects reported that use of the mouse enhanced presence compared to the walking in place technique.

4.5 Other Issues

Motion sickness and nausea is observed in about 40% of all people who have used our system. The experimental evidence suggests that there little difference in the level of reported nausea between the two groups. The median level of reported nausea on a 1 to 7 scale (1 = "not at all", 7 = "very much so") was 2 for the control and 3 for the experimental group.

We asked subjects to estimate the distances between each of the two sets of lines in the corridor, following the possibility that subjects who virtually *walked* over the lines would be in a better position to estimate the distance compared to those who *glided* over the lines by using the mouse. However, we found no difference in the estimates. In fact we have to judge this part of the experiment as a failure, since subjects did not generally notice the lines until we pointed these out to them. This is because of the lack of peripheral vision afforded by the HMD.

When we examine the Type I errors (the probability that the recogniser infers incorrectly that the subject is walking in place) of the recogniser successfully used by the subjects, and compare these with their responses on navigation and presence, the data indicates that the lower the Type I error, the greater the tendency to report a higher sense of presence, and greater ease of navigation. Of course, this is based on a very small amount of data. If it is the case, however, it is important especially with regard to navigation. It implies that if we can reduce the Type I error sufficiently, by improving our data gathering and training methods, then it is possible that the walking in place metaphor may be preferable to the use of the mouse, even in the case of navigation

5. Conclusions

In this paper we have introduced a walking metaphor for navigating through a virtual environment. We have discussed how this requires recognising a participant's walking in place behaviour pattern, based on data gathered from the tracking system for the HMD. Our provisional results indicated that such a recogniser can be successfully trained, and that this metaphor may enhance the sense of presence, in comparison to the more usual method of navigation using a hand-held pointing device. Of course, this is based on a small amount of data. Subsequent experimental results based on a more sophisticated theory of presence and a larger experiment suggest that the positive link between the walking in place technique and presence is strong [17].

It is less clear whether people prefer this walking method to using the mouse, purely from the point of view of actually getting around the environment. As Brooks (op. cit.) noted in the case of the real treadmill: "The steerable treadmill provided quite a realistic walking experience, and it neatly solved the problem of the limited range of the head sensor on the head-mounted display. Nevertheless, it proved to be too slow a tool for exploring extensive models. The user wore out with the exercise and grew frustrated at the slow pace. The flying metaphors proved more useful for this kind of rapid survey."

The utility of any metaphor depends on the application context. Clearly, just as in real life, walking is not a good method for exploring large spaces. We observed that some of our subjects did become physically tired as a result of walking, and we would not recommend it to be used for a long time. However, it is a cheap additional tool in the range of interface metaphors available in virtual reality, and there are circumstances where the sense of presence would outweigh the costs of relative inefficiency and tiredness. For example, consider an application for training simulation of emergency service personnel in hazardous conditions such as a fire: the fact that users would become tired and frustrated as a result of the additional exercise involved in a whole body movement is realistic. In real life, they would not move around a hazardous environment by using a mouse.

Acknowledgements

We would like to thank Ben Kavanagh for helping with the experiments reported in this paper. This work is funded by the U.K. EPSRC, and Department of Trade and Industry, through grant CTA/2 of the London Parallel Applications Centre. The work formed part of a collaborative project with Thorn Central Research Laboratories (CRL Ltd), and DIVISION Ltd. Anthony Steed is supported by an EPSRC research studentship.

References

1. Brooks, F.P. et. al. (1992) Final Technical Report: Walkthrough Project, Six Generations of Building Walkthroughs, Department of Computer Science, University of North Carolina, Chapel Hill, N.C. 27599-3175.

2. Ellis, S.R. (1991) Nature and Origin of Virtual Environments: A Bibliographic Essay, Computing Systems in Engineering, 2(4), 321-347.

3. Foley, J.D. (1987) Interfaces for Advanced Computing, Scientific American, October, 126-135.

4. Gibson, E.J. and R.D. Walk (1960) The "visual cliff", Scientific American, 202, 64-71.

5. Heeter, C. (1992) Being There: The Subjective Experience of Presence, Telepresence, Presence: Teleoperators and Virtual Environments, 1(2), MIT Press, 262-271.

6. Held, R.M. and N.I. Durlach (1992) Telepresence, Presence: Teleoperators and Virtual Environments, 1, winter, MIT Press, 109-112.

7. Iwata, H. and K. Matsuda (1992) Haptic Walkthrough Simulator: Its Design and Application to Studies on Cognitive Map, The Second International Conference on Artificial Reality and Tele-existence, ICAT 92, 185-192.

8. Loomis, J.M. (1992) Distal Attribution and Presence, Telepresence, Presence: Teleoperators and Virtual Environments, 1, MIT Press, 113-119.

9. Loomis, J.M. (1992) Presence and distal attribution: Phenomenology, determinants and assessment, SPIE 1666 Human Vision, Visual Processing, and Digital Display III, 590-595.

10. Mackinlay, J.D., S.K. Card, G.G. Robertson (1990) Rapid Controlled Movement Through a Virtual 3D Workspace, Computer Graphics (SIGGRAPH) 24(4), 171-176.

11. Sheridan, T.B. (1992) Musings on Telepresence and Virtual Presence, Telepresence, Presence: Teleoperators and Virtual Environments, 1, winter, MIT Press,120-126.

12. Shneiderman, B. (1987) Designing the User Interface: Strategies for Effective Human-Computer Interaction, Addison-Wesley Publishing Company.

13. Slater, M. and M. Usoh (1992) An Experimental Exploration of Presence in Virtual Environments, Department of Computer Science, QMW University of London, Technical Report no. 689.

148

14. Slater, M. and M. Usoh (1993) The Influence of a Virtual Body on Presence in Immersive Virtual Environments, VR 93, Virtual Reality International, Proceedings of the third annual conference on Virtual Reality, Meckler, London, 34-42.

15. Slater, M. and M. Usoh (1993) Presence in Immersive Virtual Environments, Proceedings of the IEEE Conference - Virtual Reality Annual International Symposium, Seattle, WA, 90-96.

16. Slater, M., M. Usoh, A. Steed (1994) Depth of Presence in Immersive Virtual Environments, Presence: Teleoperators and Virtual Environments, MIT Press 3(2), 130-144.

17. M. Slater, M. Usoh, A. Steed (1995) Taking Steps: The Influence of a Walking Metaphor on Presence in Virtual Reality, ACM Transactions on Computer Human Interaction (TOCHI) Special Issue on Virtual Reality (in press).

18. Steuer, J. (1992) Defining Virtual Reality: Dimensions Determining Telepresence, Journal of Communication 42(4), 73-93.

19. Ware, C. and S. Osborne (1990) Exploration and Virtual Camera Control in Virtual Three Dimensional Environments, Proceedings of the 1990 Symposium on Interactive 3D Graphics, ACM SIGGRAPH, March 1990, 175-183.

Interaction Models, Reference, and Interactivity in Speech Interfaces to Virtual Environments

Jussi Karlgren, Ivan Bretan, Niklas Frost, Lars Jonsson

Swedish Institute of Computer Science, KISTA, Stockholm, Sweden

diverse@sics.se

Abstract. The enhancement of a virtual reality environment with a speech interface is described. Some areas where the virtual reality environment benefits from the spoken modality are identified as well as some where the interpretation of natural language utterances benefits from being situated in a highly structured environment. The issue of interaction metaphors for this configuration of interface modalities is investigated.

1 Introduction

Virtual reality interfaces sometimes seem to be thought of as embodying a return to a natural way of interaction – the way we interact with the real world[1]. The interaction metaphors already introduced for VR (with some trimming and tuning and the addition of proper tactile feedback...), would then be sufficient for interaction. No learning would be required, as opposed to traditional interfaces – the natural interaction mechanisms are all there. This is a familiar mistake: it has been made repeatedly in the natural language-processing community. Not until recent years has it been widely acknowledged that conventions from other human activities do not always carry over directly to interactions with computer systems. We will give some examples to show similar oversimplifications regarding virtual reality technology.

1.1 The Naming Of Things Is A Serious Matter

"This" and "that" used deictically are physical world concepts easily defined and formalized for virtual reality interfaces in the form of direct manipulation mechanisms. However, they constrain their users to the here and now, even if "here" and "now" may be defined differently than in the physical reality. Human languages are by design a step beyond "this", "that", "here", and "now". They allow the user to refer to entities other than concrete objects, using set conventions: abstract concepts ("reality"), actions ("eating"), objects that are not here ("the dog Pim"), objects that are not present now

---

[1]"[We are] on our own again, after the long mediation of top-down authored experience (...)": Brenda Laurel, WIRED 1.6

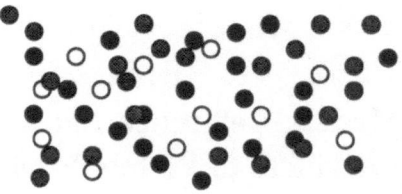

"Select the grey marbles."

Figure 1: Just point and click.

("last month's salary"), objects that cannot exist ("perpetuum mobile"), and objects selected for a property ("slow things"). In general, rendering the domain of interaction in terms of physical objects is not always appropriate – many things are difficult to portray[2].

"Where is the paper about virtual reality I sent to CHI last fall?"

Figure 2: Try this with gestures.

1.2 Virtual metaphors are conventions

The virtual world does not need to obey the laws of the physical: in the real world, language is a means to change the world, and in a virtual world the world will be easier to change. Take something as simple as a virtual table. Unlike its physical relative, it can change to accommodate the preferences of the user. Similarly, the virtual world can be instructed to transport us to somewhere in the virtual space. Naturally, metaphors – a virtual saw, a virtual pot of paint, a flying carpet, superpowers – to do this with could be introduced, but they will not be more natural or less conventionally bound than use of language would be, on the contrary.

"Paint the table red and make it round."
"Take me to the moon."

Figure 3: Manipulating the world with language.

2 System sketch

Our system – DIVERSE (DIVE Real time Speech Enhancement) – is a speech interface to a generic virtual environment based on DIVE (Distributed Interactive Virtual Environment) that can be used with complex worlds modelled in a variety of formats [8]. DIVERSE allows a user to select and manipulate objects in the world and move about

---

[2]This is the point of playing charades.

in it. DIVERSE is implemented as a cascaded sequence of components. Speech recognition is done by means of a Hidden Markov Model system – HTK – which has been trained for the domain [21]. Text processing is performed by a general-purpose surface syntactic processor – ENGCG – which identifies syntactic roles and dependencies in the text [16, 17]. A resulting dependency graph is translated to a logical representation, which in turn is inspected for references to entities and objects and matched to the set of conceivable and possible actions. The resulting queries or commands are then sent to DIVE which manipulates or queries the world accordingly.

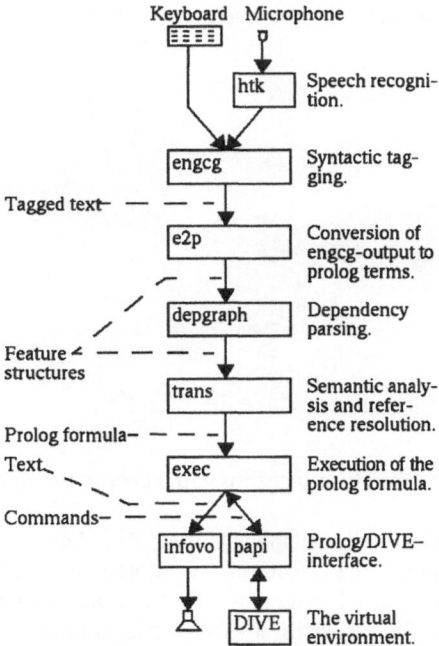

Figure 4: System architecture.

3 Interaction Metaphor

There is no obvious counterpart to the user for dialog with a system in a speech controlled virtual environment. There are several conceivable interaction models:

The basic metaphor of virtual environments is that of **Personal Presence**: the user is embodied in the real world through an actor or entity in it. This model poses problems for speech interaction – who will the user address? ("I now want to paint the house red...") This metaphor can be extended to that of **Proxy**, where users in effect ride on the back of a virtual entity. Users share the perspective, and can address and control their proxies at will "Sindbad: paint the house red!". An alternative similar to that of the proxy are the closely related metaphors of **Divinity**, where users give commands *as* a god to no obviously present counterpart but instead to the world itself: "Paint the house red!" or even "Let the house be red!"; or that of **Prayer** where users address commands in a similar fashion *to* a god.

Another extension of the basic metaphor of personal presence is that of **Telekinesis** where the objects and entities of the world themselves can be counterparts and interlocutors to users: "House, open your door!". Drawbacks include (1) the ability of an object or set of objects to participate in a dialog is far from obvious; (2) talking to objects not yet in the world will not be natural: "Three small red cubes, create yourselves!"; and (3) the need for object independent communication "Take me home". Of course, the last types of message could be addressed to some type of meta-object: a creation object or transportation object – in any case, the counterpart would be highly convention-bound.

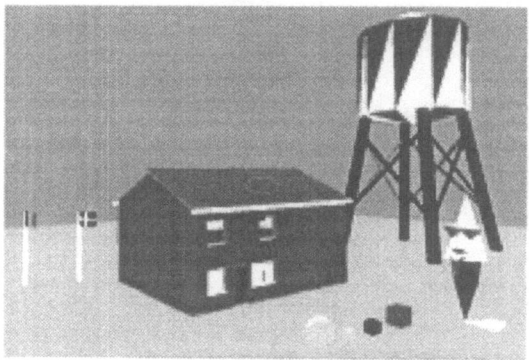

Figure 5: Interface snapshot with agent to the right.

A different type of interaction metaphor is that of an **Agent**. The agent model is different from other models in that it requires a separately rendered autonomous entity with communicative capabilities. The users will find a virtual, visually present, assistant or agent to interact with. This is necessary to be able to integrate visual and spoken feedback naturally; with no feedback or interlocutor, the interaction situation would most likely be very unfamiliar and difficult to make use of. This is the interaction model we have chosen for our implementation of DIVERSE. A consequence of machine use of a single interlocutor is that the system's linguistic competence can be modelled in this agent through its visual characteristics, its gestures, its language, and so on – this will encourage convergence in one direction. Accordingly, the DIVERSE agent has been provided with a simple vocabulary and a small set of gestures.

4   Reference resolution – pragmatics

One of the most challenging problems of language understanding is that of reference resolution: of tracking what referents referential expressions refer to.

We are not even sure of what the characteristics of referents are: we have reasonable evidence from text studies that referring expressions in the text do not refer directly to other expressions in the text itself, but to referents outside it (see e.g. Brown & Yule, [7]); similarly we have reasonable evidence that referring expressions do not refer directly to the "world", "knowledge base" or whatever we posit be the "reality" that the discourse is "about", but to some intermediate level, usually referred to as *discourse referents* [18]. We will make no claims about the characteristics of such referents: in our implementation, with the exceedingly simple task and object structure, we have yet had no need to implement an intermediate level. Our operations apply directly to the world. We may well have to add to the discourse representation in this respect if we try to add competence to the system beyond what we have now: the problems we are addressing at present will remain the same.

Resolving which discourse referent a speaker or writer refers to is non-trivial: usually there are several possible candidates. In the general case, knowledge of the domain in addition to syntactic information and access to the discourse and other aspects of the situation that the language use occurrs in are usually necessary. Brown and Yule, e.g., mention several approaches involving multiple knowledge sources [7]; an implementation by LuperFoy lists nine different sources her algorithms utilize, including Recency, Global Focus, various grammatical and lexical features, and some knowledge oriented features [20].

The knowledge sources used in the various approaches can roughly be categorized into two types: 1) situation specific features: recency, focus, and formal features of the referring expression; and 2) encyclopædic features, involving different kinds of world knowledge.

In DIVERSE we only have partial encyclopædic information. We have full knowledge of what objects exist in the world, and we have a certain hierarchical organization of objects with subparts, but there is no representation of object relations, roles, and world characteristics. We put most of our work into discourse tracking, to analyze multimodal focus.

Figure 6: "Paint the house black." – What does "the house" refer to?

To concretize, the problem we need to solve is that of resolving what the referring expression "the house" in the user utterance "Paint the house black." refers to as in figure 6, and what the referring expressions "a cube" and "it" refer to in figure 7. This is not simple in a purely text based system. Imagining that the picture were not available in figure 7: this would leave the discourse state much less explicit, and assuming a referent for "a cube" and "it" would be a risky prospect. In a visually oriented situation such as with DIVE, the attentional state of the system can be modeled by using the visual focus and highlighting mechanism of DIVE; this means that where a pure text based system might have to deliberate about different candidate cubes a multimodal system may have a less vague situation using the mutually salient information in the pictorial accompaniment.

In DIVERSE we give each object in the world a focus grade, based on recent mention, highlightedness, gestural manipulation by the user, and above all, visual awareness. So, primarily, if an object is in the perceptual focus in the virtual environment, i.e. the agent has a high degree of *awareness* of it [1, 2, 3, 12], it is a prime candidate for reference while it is visible. This effect declines rapidly when the object is not visible any more.

One of the actions available to users is to *manipulate* or *point at* an object. An object which the user points at gets a high focus grade, with a rapid rate of focus decline after the pointing gesture has been completed. Similarly, the command "Select *object!*" or even just "*Object!*" highlights the object. This is intended to be a method for users to pick out referents before issuing commands that process them.

Thirdly, we keep track of which objects have been referred to recently. If an object is in the textual discourse focus, i. e. in the recent *dialog history* it is a strong candidate for reference. An important design issue is how the dialog history is represented. To encourage users to refer to previously mentioned or manipulated objects, the discourse history can be made explicit: presumably the representations of likely candidates for reference will influence the actual references made. This will be studied empirically, with various varieties of DIVERSE implementations being compared to one another. The current version of the implementation shows a list of references above the agent's head, as can be seen in figure 8.

The evidence from gestures, awareness status, previous commands, and discourse history is weighted together to determine which object is the one most likely to have been referred to. We expect that it will be near impossible to find a weighting of these different factors that will satisfy all users performing all kinds of tasks: instead of aiming at an "optimal" weighting we will work to find a way communicating the system evaluation to the user. We expect this to be much more efficient than trying to tune the system to accommodate users with potentially very disparate preferences and needs.

Typical problems for text based reference studies are that the prototypical case, where a definite noun phrase refers to previously introduced referents and indefinites introduce new referents, is not that frequent [13]. Thus, any algorithm for finding a referent for a definite noun phrase will need a fair amount of world knowledge to pick a contextual sponsor or anchor for the referential expression. We have found that the visual awareness factor overrides the importance of most other channels, so that in an interaction, objects can be introduced as salient just by looking at them. If the user moves to look at a tree, and then says "Move the tree to the left." it is clear which tree is meant. And, if the visual awareness is given priority over other sources, the feedback

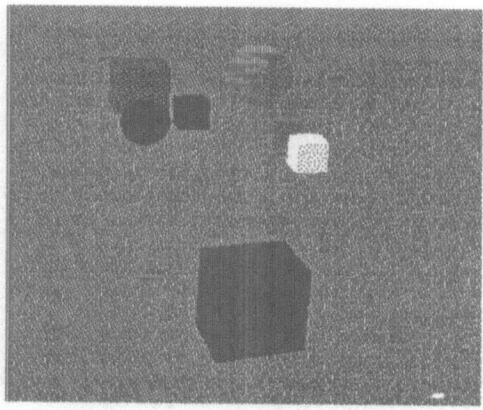

Figure 7: "Move me to a cube. Paint it black."– Now, what does "a cube" refer to?

given the users will always give users information of what is going on.

A typical view of the drawbacks of natural language as an interface tool, be it keyboard entered or spoken, compared with direct manipulation is given by Cohen: "... another disadvantage [of natural language input] is that reference resolution algorithms do not always supply the correct answer in part because systems have underdeveloped knowledge bases, and in part because the system has little access to the discourse situation the user finds himself in, *even if the system's prior utterances and graphical presentations have created that discourse situation.* ... These ... world knowledge limitations undermine the search for referents of anaphoric expressions and provide another reason that natural language systems are usually designed to confirm their interpretations." [10].

Bos *et al* have implemented EDWARD, a text and direct manipulation operating system for workstations [4]. They note that users sometimes lose track of selected objects: "we found ... users not always being aware of the state of the model world: the markedness of objects selected a while ago was sometimes forgotten or overlooked." In DIVERSE we may be able to expect slightly better user attention – visual awareness is much better determined; the view is fixed in EDWARD, whereas the user can change the view in DIVERSE, and as the visual focus overrides selection and highlighting of objects, a DIVERSE user can be expected to be more aware of the state of the model world and markedness of objects. Whatever the case may be on that count, Bos *et al* note that the mistakes the system makes do not seem to faze users; the errors are interactive enough for the user to accept them. Thus they partly answer Cohen's objections: in a highly interactive environment, errors do not matter; at least if the interface is honest about its abilities and cooperative as to displaying them. In our design, feedback is not a matter of asking the user for confirmation, but a view of system actions.

Figure 8: Snapshot of a DIVERSE scenario.

5   Errors do not matter

The interactive design of the DIVERSE interface is related to recent trends in natural language interface research, where the underlying problem of interactive interfaces, especially natural language interfaces, today is identified as that of a low degree of interactivity or "one-shot"-interaction, where users believe – regardless of system competence – that systems expect them to pose queries in one go [5].

The conversational competence users expect from computers is extremely simple, which has been shown in a number of studies of natural language interfaces. This is specifically true for discourse structure, which has been shown to be modellable by an exceedingly simple dialog grammar, by examining the discourse structure of material obtained in Wizard of Oz simulation studies [11]. This can be explained by a fundamental *asymmetry of beliefs* between user and system [14]. Users do not expect computer systems to take responsibility for the coherence of a discourse, but expect to take full responsibility for the discourse management themselves. This is in contrast with naturally occurring dialog which is not only interactive but also *incremental*, i.e. in a form where both parties cooperatively build up referents and references during the course of a discourse.

To change this, the system must somehow display and make explicit what information it has for the user to refer to, and what assumptions about user intentions it makes; at the current point of sophistication, a high degree of interactivity and added communication channels to the system is arguably a better tool for raising system usefulness than adding functionality or intelligence to the existing channel, be it text, speech, or a rule based system [9, 15, 19].

As indicated in the previous section, in DIVERSE we make use of the errors-do-not-matter principle to the extent that we will not worry about the system misinterpreting the occasional user utterance: as long as the interface is interactive we do not expect misinterpretations to be too crucial a problem. More important than error handling is a broad acceptance of user utterances: every utterance should produce some effect.

The representation of the utterance is matched to representations of possible actions in the domain. If no good match is found, any referents that have been identified in the utterance are highlighted anyway, to facilitate users to continue the discourse, rather than starting from square one again. This is similar to recent ideas about how to generally design a natural language interface, using "non-threatening error messages that reiterate vocabulary and phrases the processor understands." as formulated by Zoltan-Ford [22].

6   Conclusions

Language is not only about conveying information[3]: it is a tool for acting in the world. Without immediacy with respect to the world it is used in, it is not natural language. Conversely, VR interaction without language does not take place in a natural or intuitive world. We are working on overcoming some of the most fundamental weaknesses of these two areas of interactive system design – through merging them.

---

[3]In fact, as an experiment, the reader is invited to approximate how large a percentage of language use the reader personally uses for conveying information.

7 References

1. Benford, Steve, John Bowers, Lennart Fahlén, and Chris Greenhalgh. 1994. "Managing Mutual Awareness in Collaborative Virtual Environments" *Proceedings of VRST'94*, Singapore. New York: ACM.

2. Benford, Steve, John Bowers, Lennart Fahlén, and Chris Greenhalgh. 1995. "User Embodiment in Collaborative Virtual Environments" *Proceedings of the ACM Conference on Human Factors in Computing Systems (CHI'95)*, Boston. New York:ACM.

3. Benford, Steve and Lennart Fahlén. 1993. "A Spatial Model of Interaction in Large Virtual Environments" *Proceedings of 3d ECSCW* Milan: Kluwer.

4. Bos, Edwin, Carla Huls, and Wim Claassen. 1994. "EDWARD: full integration of language and action in a multimodal user interface" *International Journal of Human-Computer Studies*, **40**:473-495.

5. Bretan, Ivan and Jussi Karlgren. 1993. "Synergy Effects In Natural Language-Based Multimodal Interfaces" *Proceedings of 1993 ERCIM Workshop on Multimodal Human-Computer Interaction*, Nancy:INRIA. (also available as *SICS Research Report R94:04*.

6. Bretan, Ivan and Jussi Karlgren. 1994. "Worlds without Words", *Proceedings of ERCIM Workshop on VR*, Stockholm:SICS.

7. Brown, Gillian and George Yule. 1983. *Discourse Analysis*. Cambridge: Cambridge University Press.

8. Carlsson, Christer and Olof Hagsand. 1993. "DIVE, a Platform for Multi-User Virtual Environments", *Computers & Graphics*, **17**:6.

9. Chandrasekar, R. and S. Ramani. 1989. "Interactive communication of sentential structure and content: an alternative approach to man-machine communication", *International Journal of Man-Machine Studies* **30**:121-148.

10. Cohen, Philip. 1992. "The Role of Natural Language in a Multimodal Interface", *In Proceedings of the ACM Symposium on User Interface Software and Technology (UIST)*, Monterey: ACM.

11. Dahlbäck, Nils, Arne Jönsson, and Lars Ahrenberg. 1993. "Wizard-of-Oz Studies — Why and How", *Proceedings of the 1993 International Workshop on Intelligent User Interfaces*, Orlando:ACM.

12. Fahlén, Lennart, Charles G. Brown, Olov Ståhl, Christer Carlsson. 1993. "A Space Based Model for User Interaction in Shared Synthetic Environments" *Proceedings of the ACM Conference on Human Factors in Computing Systems (InterCHI'93)* Amsterdam:ACM.

13. Fraurud, Kari. 1990. "Definiteness and the Processing of NP's in Natural Discourse." *Journal of Semantics* **7**:395-433.

14. Joshi, Aravind. 1982. "Mutual Beliefs in Question-Answering Systems", in N. V. Smith (ed), *Mutual Knowledge*, London:Academic Press.

15. Karlgren, Jussi, Kristina Höök, Ann Lantz, Jacob Palme, and Daniel Pargman. 1994. "The Glass Box User Model for Information Filtering", *Proceedings of the 4th International Conference on User Modeling* Cape Cod:ACM. (A longer version available as SICS Technical Report T94:09).

16. Karlsson, Fred. 1990. "Constraint Grammar for Parsing Running Text". *Papers presented to the Thirteenth International Conference On Computational Linguistics (COLING -90)*, H. Karlgren (ed.), Helsinki:University of Helsinki.

17. Karlsson, Fred, Atro Voutilainen, Juha Heikkilä, and Arto Anttila (eds.) 1995. *Constraint Grammar* Berlin: Mouton de Gruyter.

18. Lauri Karttunen. 1969 (1976). "Discourse Referents". Paper presented to the International Conference On Computational Linguistics (COLING -69), Sånga-Säby. Stockholm:KVAL. Also in James D. McCawley (ed.) Notes from the Linguistic Underground. Syntax and Semantics, Vol 7. Pp. 363-385. New York:Academic Press.

19. Lemaire, Benoît and Johanna Moore. 1994. "An Improved Interface for Tutorial Dialogues: Browsing a Visual Dialogue History". *Proceedings of the ACM Conference on Human Factors in Computing Systems (CHI'94)*, Boston:ACM.

20. LuperFoy, Susann. 1991. *Discourse PEGS: A Computational Analysis of Context-Dependent Referring Expressions*. Ph D Dissertation. Austin:University of Texas at Austin.

21. Woodland, P.C., J.J. Odell, V. Valtchev and S.J. Young. 1994. "Large Vocabulary Continuous Speech Recognition Using HTK". *Proceedings of ICASSP'94*, Adelaide.

22. Zoltan-Ford, Elizabeth. 1991. "How to get people to say and type what computers can understand". *International Journal of Man-Machine Studies* **34**:527-547.

Experiment Authoring for Virtual Driving Environments

James Cremer, Joseph Kearney
Computer Science Department, University of Iowa
Iowa City, Iowa 52242, U.S.A.

Michael Bartelme, Michael Booth, Douglas Evans, Richard Romano
Center for Computer Aided Design, University of Iowa
Iowa City, Iowa 52242, U.S.A.

Abstract. Virtual environment applications demand rich, dynamic scenarios populated with objects that exhibit realistic behaviors and interact convincingly with each other and human participants. In addition, applications require scenes that accurately model the geometry and properties real environments to fine levels of detail. In the domain of virtual driving environments, the cost of *experiment authoring*, the process of creating experiment-specific scenes and scenarios, is quite high. In this paper, we examine the challenge of developing scene and scenario authoring tools accessible to non-specialists and outline our approach to meet this challenge.

1   Introduction

Virtual environments provide fundamentally new opportunities for the study of human behavior. In synthetic worlds, experiments can be conducted that are impossible to undertake in real environments because of potential risks to subjects. Virtual places and situations can be crafted to the needs of the experiments in ways that cannot be practically done in the physical world.

Driving simulation exemplifies both the potential and the challenges of using virtual environments for the study of human behavior. Real-time, operator-in-the-loop simulators provide realistic driving experiences under controlled conditions. The computational and algorithmic foundations for dynamic analysis are sufficiently mature to generate high-fidelity simulators of multi-body vehicle models in real time[4]. Recent advances in image generation technology permit the display of high-resolution, textured graphics at video rates[3]. The quality of the images, the fidelity of the motion, and the detail of the scenes combine to create a highly realistic driving experience that can be used to collect vital information on the effects of drugs, disabilities, and aging on driving safety.

To be an effective tool for controlled experimentation, driving simulation must allow experimenters to specify the characteristics of the virtual environment to which subjects will be exposed. We loosely define the *scene* to be

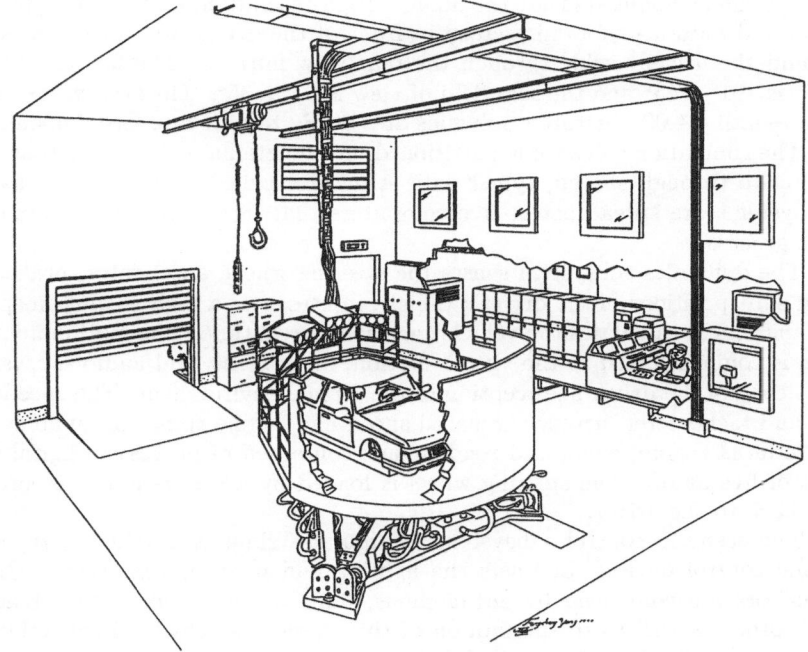

Figure 1: Sketch of the Iowa Driving Simulator facility for real-time operator-in-the-loop driving simulation

a model of the static entities in the virtual environment including the spatial layout of roads; the location, shape, and appearance of buildings, vegetation, and cultural features; and the geometry and material properties of the terrain. We call the model capturing the dynamic characteristics of entities in the virtual environment the *scenario*. The scenario specifies the behaviors of synthetic vehicles, pedestrians, traffic control devices, and variations in weather and lighting. Scene and scenario modeling are difficult and time consuming activities that require substantial expertise in simulation, geometric modeling, and programming. In this paper we examine the problem of creating an *experiment authoring* system for driving simulation that will give the experimenter the ability to specify the scene and scenario to fit the needs of an experiment.

2   Overview of the Iowa Driving Simulator

The Iowa Driving Simulator (IDS) [4] is a high fidelity, ground vehicle simulator that implements multi-body vehicle dynamics in real time using high-speed parallel computers. Figure 1 presents a sketch of the simulator facility. A Ford

Taurus cab is mounted inside the dome[1]. High-resolution, textured graphics are projected onto a panoramic screen in front of the driver and a smaller screen behind the driver visible through the rear view mirrors. The forward field of view is 191° × 45° and the rear field of view is 64° × 35°. The system is capable of presenting 4,000 textured polygons at a 60 Hz refresh rate (see Appendix).

The simulation software is partitioned into functional subsystems that communicate through shared, typed data structures called cells. Twelve distinct subsystems are spread across five computers that incorporate thirty-six separate processors.

The dynamics subsystem senses the steering wheel, accelerator, brake, and gear shift positions of the driver's vehicle, interrogates a high-resolution spatial database, and calculates the vehicle's motion in real time. The motion information is communicated to the visual, motion, instrument, and audio subsystems that control the driver's perception of the virtual environment. The speedometer and tachometer display simulated speed and engine rpm. An audio system reproduces engine, wind, and road sounds composed of processed digital samples of live audio. The steering wheel is loaded by a torque motor to provide feedback to the driver.

The scenario control subsystem manipulates simulated vehicles, regulates traffic control devices, and sets the lighting and weather conditions. Object behaviors are controlled by autonomous, finite state machines that react to each other as well as to the motion of the operator's vehicle. Each vehicle is programmed to obey the rules of the road.

3 Scene Modeling

We have devoted substantial effort to developing methods to represent and tools to construct models of realistic driving scenes. An important aspect of scene modeling for driving environments is the design of the road network. In IDS, each segment of road is represented in three separate, but correlated, databases that support the differing requirements of various simulation subsystems[2]. In the visual database, road surfaces are represented in multiple levels of detail by smooth-shaded textured polygons for effectiveness and ease of rendering. A scenario database represents roads using oriented space curves with attached properties for speed limits, passing zones, and other traffic regulations. The vehicle dynamics terrain database represents the geometry of drivable surfaces in a fine scale, piecewise uniform grid. The geometry of the driving surface must be known with high accuracy to minimize errors in the computations of vehicle dynamics. The three-dimensional location of a point on the roadway is calculated using bilinear interpolation of grid values. In addition to surface shape, the terrain database characterizes the surface type, roughness, friction, and soil properties.

---

[1]Other cabs can be installed in the dome — IDS uses a HMMWV cab for some of its projects.

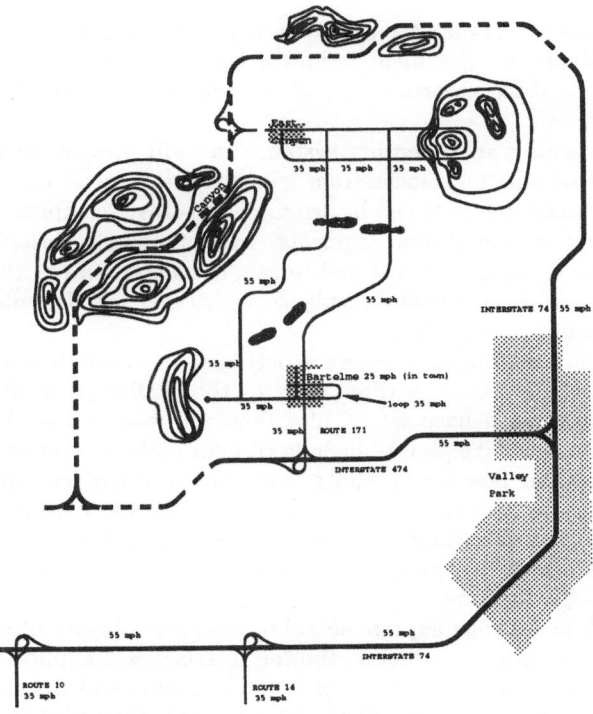

Figure 2: Map of the Orchids2 database of the Iowa Driving Simulator

3.1 Limitations of the Current Scene Modeling Tools

The design of road networks consistent with civil engineering standards, including banked curves with transition zones, is a difficult and time-consuming process that requires substantial expertise. It takes approximately six person-months of effort by scene database experts to go from an initial plan for a scene to an implemented, debugged database for a moderately complex scene with 50 miles of roadway, a freeway interchange, a town, rural areas, and appropriate cultural features. A map of an IDS database currently in use is shown in Figure 2. It is impractical to train experimenters in the construction of complex, spatial databases and it is unreasonable to expect that they pay for costly development fees for customized scenes that may take months to prepare. The compromise that experimenters are currently forced to accept is that they must design their experiments around the available scene models that may be inappropriate to test their hypotheses.

3.2 The Design of a Scene Authoring System

To support the variety of experiments for which IDS was designed, we need the capability to construct, modify, refine, and debug scene databases much more quickly. At the minimum, it should be possible for scene database experts to quickly create new scene databases. More ambitiously, we want to provide scene database creation tools that are usable by experimenters or other non-experts. The tools available to experimenters may not have the full expressive power of those used by database experts but should be sufficient to generate a wide range of complex scenes.

We are designing an authoring system that will present an experimenter with a library of building blocks from which scenes can be created. Experts will construct scene tiles that can be assembled to create complex roadways. To simplify interconnection of road segments, a set of standard interfaces for road modules will be developed. Road and terrain characteristics at tile boundaries will be constrained to simple and regular forms so that seamless blends between tiles can be easily accomplished.

We envision a system that allows experimenters to interactively select, instance, and arrange database tiles. One of the challenges in developing the system is identifying a base set of tiles that will meet a broad spectrum of experimenters' needs. We plan to include tiles for highway and urban road segments, two and four lane roads, and a variety of road surface types. The tiles will be designed to provide a variety of connectable road segments including straight sections, curves, hills, intersections, and interchanges. The tiles will include standard markings on roads, surrounding cultural features, and scenery appropriate to the location.

In addition to allowing experimenters to design the layout of roads and the surrounding landscape, the scene authoring interface will support specification of the attributes of roads, locations of critical objects, and the sites of critical actions. The authoring system will graphically display the tiled scene and allow the experimenter to interactively specify traffic density on roads, the locations of traffic signs and regulatory devices, and identify sites to be communicated to the scenario modeling system discussed below. We intend to provide the author with the capability to graphically select locations to place hazards such as fallen trees, potholes, or rocks.

3.3 Implementation Challenges for Scene Authoring

A major challenge to be faced in implementing the scene authoring system is the process of joining tiles that share boundaries to form a single, coherent scene. Scene continuity must be preserved across the tile borders. This includes geometric continuity of road surfaces and surrounding terrain, continuity of surface type and texture, and continuity of traffic regulations as defined by roadway markings, signs, and control devices. The composite database must consistently merge three separate representations for the visual, scenario, and dynamics subsystems. Furthermore, the visual database constructed by combining scene tiles must support efficient, real-time image generation.

Early in the design of the authoring system, we must choose what tile shapes and sizes will be supported. Forcing all tiles to have the same size and shape would facilitate the process of merging tiles. However, we believe there is significant benefit in having a variety of tile sizes to accommodate differ scales of road segments. Thus, a single large tile could be used to model a two mile segment of country road while a small tile might model a block of an urban street. Furthermore, we believe that it will be important to support reuse of authored scenes. We intend to provide the author with the capability to edit, duplicate, and combine previously constructed scenes to create a growing, customized library of scenes.

It is highly desirable to have natural changes in the decorative or cultural features that populate roadsides. We plan to offer the author a selection of transition tiles that contain smooth variations from cityscapes, for example, to rural scenery.

To simplify the elimination of gaps in a patchwork of tiles, we plan to provide some scalable tiles such as variable length segments of straight roads. We also foresee the usefulness of area filling options, analogous to region filling operations in paint programs, that will automatically generate simple landscapes to fill vacant off-road regions. In addition, we plan to provide interactive design assistance to help the author find the set of tiles that can validly be attached to open boundaries of a partially constructed scene.

4 Scenario Modeling

The scenario control subsystem is responsible for controlling the actions of agents and mechanisms in the virtual driving environment. Two, sometimes conflicting, demands must be met in a scenario. On one hand, controlled vehicles must perform normal driving functions and respond to the motions of other vehicles, including the operator's. On the other hand, the experiment may call for a specific set of circumstances to occur, possibly in some prescribed order. The conditions of the experiment must be satisfied without causing aberrant or physically impossible behaviors.

The emphasis of our work to this point has been on defining and implementing basic driving behaviors. Simulated drivers are controlled by autonomous state machines that reactively respond to the evolving state of the virtual world. In response to the demands of experiments, we have developed tools to direct and coordinate object behaviors. However, much work on this important aspect scenario control remains to be done.

4.1 Modeling of Basic Vehicle Behavior

At present, scenario vehicles are controlled by separate instances of a single state machine that encodes basic driving behavior. A simplied version of the driving state machine is shown in figure 3. The state machine shown controls driving on an open road, following behind another vehicle, and intersection behavior for a restricted set of intersection types. The states controlling passing and merging behaviors have been omitted to simplify the diagram.

Variations in the attributes associated with individual vehicles lead to differences in vehicle behaviors. Without these differences, the traffic appears stiff and regimented and many normal traffic patterns cannot occur. Vehicle attributes include preferred driving speed, desired following distance, acceptable

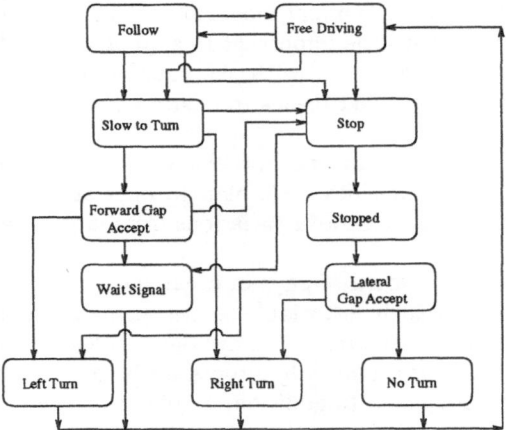

Figure 3: Simplified version of the driving state machine

gap for entry into intersections, reaction time, and aggressiveness. A *scenario* file specifies the statistical distribution of vehicle attributes for different types of vehicles[2]. For example, trucks are assigned, on average, longer gap acceptance intervals than passenger cars. The density of each vehicle type on the roadways is also specified in the scenario file. Figure 4 is a snapshot from the graphical tool used to display the road network and traffic behavior during testing and debugging of the scenario system.

The current scenario control program can manage up to 40 vehicles in real time (single CPU at 60 Hz) on city streets, rural highways, and multi-lane urban freeways. Plausible traffic patterns emerge from the interactions of the autonomously controlled vehicles including traffic clusters at intersections. The behaviors of groups of vehicles demonstrate properties characteristic of actual traffic, such as motion ripples through a chain of vehicles stopped at a controlled intersection. In a related paper[1], Cremer and Kearney describe new framework, HCSM, that extends the basic state machine paradigm by using hierarchical concurrent state machines to facilitate the creation of new behaviors, simplify the modification of old behaviors, and to better accommodate to the concurrent constraints influencing driving behavior.

4.2 Limitations of the Current Scenario Subsystem

Although reasonably convincing traffic can be modeled, it is difficult to generate predictable, repeatable event sequences for experimentation. The behavior of each of the programmatically controlled vehicles depends on reactions to the movements of other nearby vehicles. Since the details of operator behavior will vary from simulation to simulation, there will be some degree of non-determinism in the behaviors of the scenario cars. The experimenter must

---

[2]Specific values for particular vehicles may also be specified.

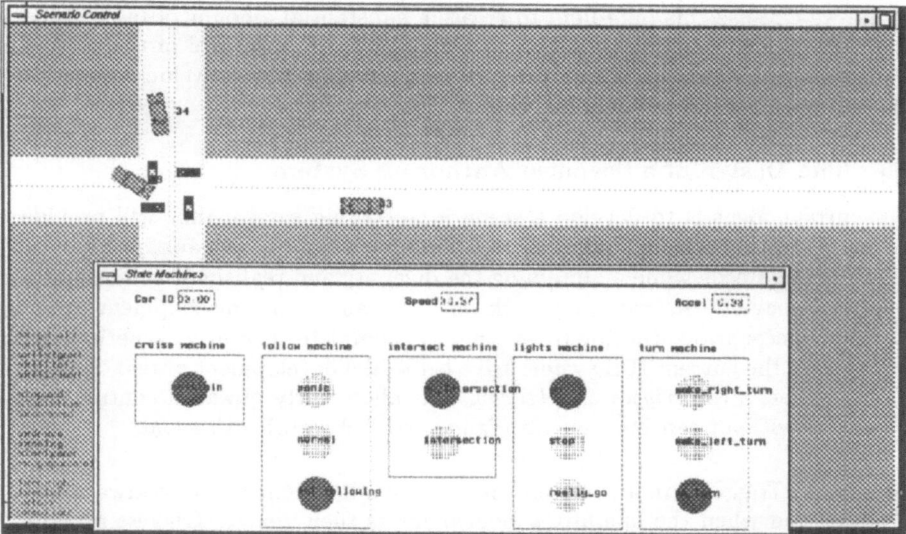

Figure 4: Snapshot from a Silicon Graphics based graphical tool for visualizing, debugging, and interacting with scenarios. The tool can display the road network at various levels of detail, and it provides access to the hierarchical concurrent state machines used to model the behavior of scenario vehicles.

have some ability to specify the nature of situations and occurrence of critical events.

For example, an experimenter may be interested in testing an operator's reaction to an unexpected threat at an intersection. The experiment may call for a stopped car to prematurely leave a controlled intersection in front of the oncoming operator's vehicle. Even this simple scenario is difficult to create using the current method of control. A separate state machine must be created to control the motions of the threatening vehicle. This vehicle must drive to the intersection and arrive shortly before the operator. Given variations in operator performance, it may be difficult or impossible to direct this particular car to make its way through traffic so that it arrives at the intersection at an appropriate moment, and to make sure other vehicles are not in positions that will interfere with the planned situation.

Even when the operator and hazard vehicle are the only cars on the road, there may be difficulties in creating a realistic scenario for this experiment. Motions that are too tightly coupled to the state of the operator's vehicle can appear too artificial to be believable. If the threatening car's approach to the crossing intersection mimics the motions of the operator's vehicle, braking and accelerating to mirror the operator's approach, the operator will perceive the world as too mechanistic.

Thus, the autonomous, reactive nature of the scenario vehicles in the current IDS system is both a blessing and a curse when designing simulation scenarios.

While we can use this paradigm to create a substantial amount of interesting, plausible traffic, it is quite difficult to maintain the natural feel of the driving environment and, at the same time, programmatically control vehicles to meet the requirements of the experimenter.

4.3 The Design of a Scenario Authoring System

Our current focus is to develop a scenario authoring system that will provide a natural framework for designing and building complex scenarios that meet experimental needs while maintaining the diversity and realism of autonomous, reactive behavior. As with the work on scene authoring, development of sophisticated scenario authoring tools is not yet complete. However, experimental demands of the current IDS system have led to the development of two "behavior controllers", the *trigger* and *beacon*, that allow fairly powerful control over a scenario without causing the stiff regimented feel we wish to avoid.

Triggers Triggers are associated with physical locations along roadways and are activated when the operator's vehicle enters their space. Triggers may be either *oneshot* or *permanent*. A oneshot trigger is destroyed when the driver leaves its active region, while a permanent trigger is activated each time the driver enters its space. Triggers control the behavior of a predetermined set of objects by influencing state transitions or changing state variables. For instance, two kinds of state changing triggers have been defined for traffic lights. A *change* trigger causes the associated traffic light to change to the target state, moving through any intermediate states if necessary. Once the target state is reached, the trigger is deactivated allowing the light to resume its normal behavior. A *stay* trigger also causes the traffic light to change to a target state, but then forces the light to remain in that state until the driver leaves the trigger's region. Using a change trigger, an experimenter can cause a traffic light to change to yellow when the operator's vehicle is a critical distance from an intersection. Similarly, a stay trigger can be used to ensure that a traffic light is green when the driver reaches it. Another example of current trigger use in IDS is to generate a simple hazardous lane encroachment. By placing a scenario vehicle on the road shoulder and defining a trigger in the lane at some distance before the vehicle, the experimenter can cause the parked vehicle to pull out onto the road in front of the driver.

Beacons For more complex interactions between the driver and the scenario vehicles, special choreography may be required to cause a given event to occur. For instance, an experimenter may desire all of scenario vehicles to turn left at a particular intersection in order to keep a certain road clear. Another situation may require vehicles to move out of the right lane on a three lane highway. Yet another may require some vehicle (not a predetermined one, but any one that is in a position to do so at the time of the event) to slam on its brakes when it is in front of the driver on a certain road and a certain traffic pattern is present. In such situations a *beacon* controller may be used. Beacons may be placed in the lanes of a road network, and are invisible to the operator's vehicle. Beacons radiate directives to scenario vehicles in order to orchestrate the action according to the experimenter's goals. These directives may be simple, such as "move to the right lane", or "turn left at the next intersection", or they may be complex, requiring the beacon to assess the pattern of traffic surrounding it, select an appropriate vehicle, and supply it with a directive. Any number of beacons may be placed throughout the road network, and they have durations much as the trigger controllers do.

More general scenario authoring tools Using combinations of triggers and beacons, we can create interesting scenarios with controlled experimental situations and events that blend smoothly with the background of autonomous, reactive traffic. To provide a powerful, flexible scenario authoring system, however, further tools and techniques must be developed.

One problem with the current implementation is that new triggers and beacons must be programmed in C and require direct manipulation of internal data structures. Experimenters cannot be expected to define scenarios at this level, so we must develop an authoring interface that facilitates scenario creation at a level of abstraction appropriate for experiment designers. This interface should allow experimenters to control object behaviors using computational mechanisms such as triggers and beacons. The interface should also allow experimenters to coordinate activities by specifying sequences of critical events that are to take place in an experiment.

Furthermore, we are generalizing the trigger and beacon ideas to provide more powerful behavior controllers. One alternative to strict scripting of particular vehicle motions is to wait until circumstances provide natural candidates to perform the required actions. For example, consider the problem of directing a scenario vehicle to threaten the operator's vehicle by prematurely entering an intersection. Instead of scripting the actions of a specific vehicle to pose the threat, the most appropriate vehicle to perform the action can be selected as the operator approaches the intersection. The selection could be done using beacons, but might be done more naturally using a general computational mechanism called a *daemon*. Daemons are processes that need not be associated with particular regions or objects of the scene database. They are activated by the occurrence of specified events, and may have a variety of effects beyond causing simple object state changes, including the creation or destruction of other daemons.

Another form of scenario control, called *experimenter-in-loop* control, allows the experimenter to interact with the simulator as it is running. The experimenter would have a separate experimenter's console, including a graphical display showing bird's-eye and other views of the evolving scenario, and an interface providing access to detailed information about vehicles and other scenario objects. Through this interface, the experimenter can act as a very powerful daemon, monitoring the evolution of the experiment and changing states or scenario variables as required. The experimenter could also temporarily take complete control of any vehicle, overriding its controlling state machine

170

and driving it interactively in order to produce some desired situation.

5   Conclusion

Our experience with high-fidelity driving simulation has demonstrated that scene and scenario authoring are vitally important for the effective use of virtual worlds in the study of human behavior. Experiments in complex virtual worlds offer advantages of both field and laboratory experiment paradigms; virtual environments can approximate the richness of natural experience in a carefully controlled domain. The challenge facing simulator developers is to find techniques that allow experimenters to create the scenes and scenarios appropriate to the needs of their studies. The ability to adapt the experiment to variations in subject performance will lead to more realistic scenarios and replicate the essential aspects of critical events across trials.

References

[1] O. Ahmad, J. Cremer, S. Hansen, J. Kearney, and P. Willemsen. Hierarchical, concurrent state machines for behavior modeling and scenario control. In *Proceedings of the 1994 Conference on AI, Simulation, and Planning in High Autonomy Systems*, Gainesville, December 1994.

[2] Douglas Evans. Correlated database generation for driving simulators. In *Proceedings of the IMAGE VI Conference*, pages 353–361, July 1992.

[3] Volkhard Schill and Hannsjoerg Schmieder. Car simulation – the challenge for a visual system. In *Proceedings of the IMAGE IV Conference*, pages 343–350, July 1992.

[4] James W. Stoner, Edward J. Haug, Kevin S. Berbaum, Douglas F. Evans, Jon G. Kuhl, Julia C. Lenel, John F. McAreavy, and Fuh-Feng Tsai. Introduction to the Iowa Driving Simulator and simulation research program. Center for Simulation and Design Optimization of Mechanical Systems Technical Report R-86, University of Iowa, August 1990.

Editor's Note: see Appendix, p. 301 for coloured figure of this paper

Simulating Automated Cars in a Virtual Urban Environment

Bruno Arnaldi, Rémi Cozot and Stéphane Donikian

IRISA
Campus de Beaulieu
35042 Rennes Cedex, FRANCE
arnaldi@irisa.fr, cozot@irisa.fr, donikian@irisa.fr

Abstract. Real world simulation by creating virtual environments is indispensable when you need to design complex entities which have to evolve in the real urban world. For example, testing control algorithms of autonomous vehicles needs an environment composed of a variety of active, moving entities and different kinds of vehicles. Virtual simulation environments have to provide this capability during the design step.

To perform a realistic simulation of a real environment composed of a large set of vehicles (where some of them are autonomous, the others are controled by the user or by some specific control law), we need to implement different models : geometric modeling of the environment, mechanical simulation of the vehicles, motion control models, driver models for autonomous vehicle, captor models to manage the interactions between objects, and visualisation algorithms. We present a simulation platform which complies with our needs.

Keywords: Virtual Environment, Simulation, Behavioural Animation

1 Introduction

Context. The Praxitele Project has in charge the design of a new kind of transportation in an urban environment, which consists in a fleet of electric public cars. These public cars are capable of autonomous motion on certain displacements between stations. The realization of such a project requires experiments of the behaviour of autonomous vehicles in the urban environment. Because of the danger of this kind of experiments in a real site, it is necessary to design a virtual urban environment in which simulations can be done.

Organization of the paper. The Praxitele project is presented in more details in the next section. The section 3 presents a simulation platform which complies with our needs for the testing of automatic motion control algorithms of vehicles evolving in a complex environment. The section 4 is devoted to the general presentation of the virtual urban environment, while the section 5 will focus on the description of an automatically driven dynamic car. A first proto-type of Real-Time Driving Simulation is shown in the section 6, and then in the last section we will discuss about the evolution of this work.

2 Aims and goals of the Praxitele Project

The Praxitele project combines the efforts of two large government research institutes, one in transportation technologies (INRETS), the other in computer science and automation (INRIA), in cooperation with large industrial companies (RENAULT, EDF, CGEA). This project designs a novel transportation system based on fleet of small electric public cars under supervision from a central computer [1]. These public cars are driven by their users but their operation can be automated in specific instances. The system proposed here should bring a solution to the congestion and pollution in most cities through the entire world.

The concept of a public transport system based on a fleet of small elec-tric vehicles has already been the subject of experiments several times but with poor results. The failure of these experiments can be traced to one main fac-tor : poor avaibility of the vehicles when a customer needs one. To solve this main problem, Praxitele project develops and implements automated cooper-ative driving of a platoon of vehicles, only the first car is driven by a human operator [2]. This function is essential to move easily the empty vehicles from one location to another. The realization of such a project requires experiments of the behaviour of autonomous vehicles in an urban environment. Because of the danger of this kind of experiments in a real site, it is necessary to design a virtual urban environment in which simulations can be done. Unfortunately, existing driving simulators [3, 4, 5, 6, 7] differ in two points with the Praxitele Project requirements:

- They are all realized to integrate a real driver in the simulation loop, and all the simulation is based on this aspect (movement restitution, realistic driving interface, ...).

- The simulated environment is not urban.

Our simulation platform permits to simulate a platoon of vehicles evolving in a virtual urban environment and so to test control algorithms of the automated cars.

3 A Simulation Platform

Introduction. Motion control models are the heart of any simulation system that determines the friendliness of the user interface, the class of motions and deformations produced, and the application fields. Motion control models can be classified into three general families : descriptive, generative and behavioural models [8]. Descriptive models are used to reproduce an effect without any knowledge about its cause, thus a subset of instantaneous states are expressed either absolutely or relatively over time, and by interpolation a spatio-temporal trajectory is obtained in the system description space. Unlike preceding models, generative models are interested by a causal description of objects movement (describe the cause which produces the effects) for instance their mechanics. The goal of behavioural models is to simulate organisms (plants) [9, 10] and living beings (animals and persons) [11, 12], their action and their response to stimulation. One goal of behavioural models is to provide the user with a higher level control of movement. With the intention of making these three kinds of models work together, we are interested by their integration into a same simulation platform. This integration of the three kinds of models in the same platform permits to offer to each dynamic entity a more realistic and richer environment, and thereby will increase possible interactions between an agent/actor and its environment.

Logical architecture. The simulation platform is composed of a set of agents/actors whose synchronization and communication are managed by a real-time kernel (cf figure 1). The main part of this kernel is the general controller. Communication between the agents is both synchronous and asynchronous. The synchronous part is data-flow based where each agent has its own frequency and is managed by the general controller. So, the data-flow communication channels include all the mechanisms to adapt to the local frequency of the sender and receiver agents (over-sampling, sub-sampling, interpolation, extrapolation, etc...). The asynchronous part is based on event based communication between agents and the general controller.

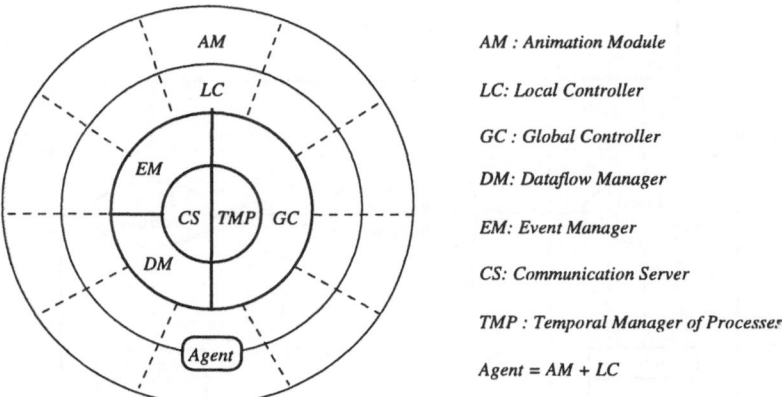

AM : Animation Module

LC: Local Controller

GC : Global Controller

DM: Dataflow Manager

EM: Event Manager

CS: Communication Server

TMP : Temporal Manager of Processes

Agent = AM + LC

Fig. 1. layers of the logical architecture of the platform.

Time is the most important element of our simulation platform either during the specification or during the execution phase. The figure 2 show a structural view of two communicating agents in the platform. At each component is associated a specific task:

Global controller: it is the centralised controller of an animation/simulation. It performs the scheduling of the agents execution in order to respect the real time constraint. It is responsible of the initialization and dynamic configuration of the set of agents through communications with the agent using events. The dynamic configuration depends of events generated by the agents or of the analysis of an external script describing the animation/simulation.

Local controller: this controller has to manage the communications by events to the global controller and by data-flow to the other agents. The temporal control of the animation module is also performed by this controller according to the global controller directives.

Animation module: this module is the effective computation module performing the animation task as user interaction, physically based models calculation, trajectories application, image synthesis and so on. Each animation module has a local frequency according to its functionality.

Communication channel: the communication channel connects two agents with potentially different local frequencies. It has to adapt the data-flow communication according to these known frequencies by temporally stamping messages between agents.

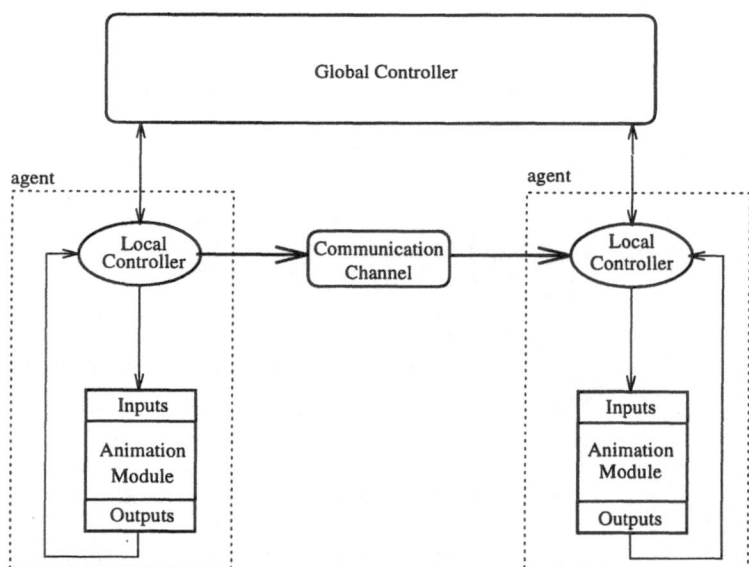

Fig. 2. Structural view of the platform.

4 Simulation of an Urban Environment

An urban environment is composed of many dynamic entities evolving in a static scene. These dynamic entities have to be both autonomous and controllable and also realistic in term of behaviour. It is necessary to combine the three motion control models to describe dynamic entities of the environment. For example to describe traffic lights it is not necessary to use a generative model when a descriptive model (finite state automata) is sufficient. On the other hand, for a realistic car driving, we need both generative and behavioural models (the first one to simulate the dynamic of the vehicle and the second one to simulate the driver).

4.1 The static scene

As we want to control entities evolving, we need to link dynamic entities with the static scene in which they are moving. This link requires a semantic knowledge on the scene. If we want to simulate as completely as possible the life of a city, we need a lot of semantic informations. For the car driving simulation example, we are particularly interested by the life in the streets and less by what is happening inside buildings (cf figure 3). Informations required for the simulation are:

1. Geometric:

    − the geometry of the town,
    − roadsigns,

2. Topologic:

    − the road network (network of trajectories),
    − a visibility grid,

3. Semantic:

    − road informations: roadsigns, color of traffic lights, qualitative aspect of the road, ...
    − city informations: name of streets, quarters, particular buildings, squares, ...

To describe such a scene, an urban modeling system is currently in development. This system is an extension of the Scriptography (Declarative Design System) [13], in which geometric, topologic and semantic informations are mixed.

4.2 Dynamic entities

To take into account natural phenomena, the first work is to choose a physical model to represent the object. From a high level description of articulated rigid body systems [14], a simulation blackbox is generated whose inputs are torques and outputs are position and orientation parameters. We have now to determine

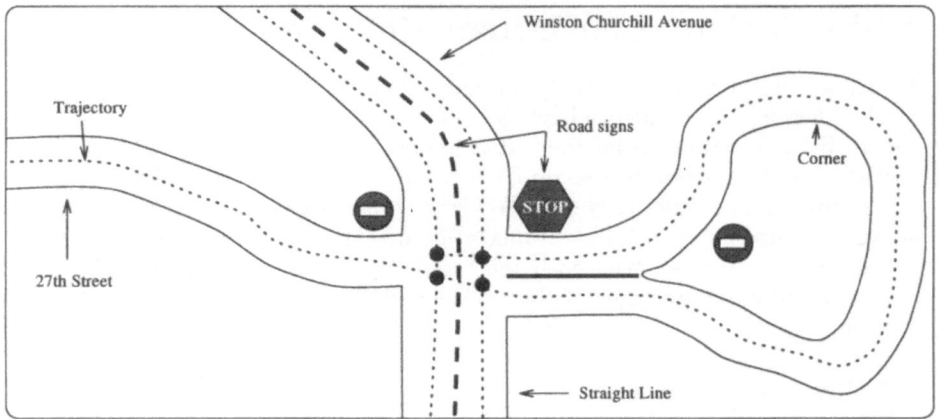

Fig. 3. Geometric, Topologic and Semantic Informations.

how to control this physical model that is to say, depending on the actual state of the entity what kind of torque must we apply to it to obtain the desired motion ? In the case of an automatic motion control, this question can be decomposed in two parts:

1. how control the physical model ?

2. what is the desired motion ?

The answer to the first question consists in using motion control algorithms [15] well known in the automatic and robotic communities, which can permit to build a library of elementary actions. The behavioural model tries to answer to the second question by defining actions and reactions of an entity [16, 17, 18]. The behavioural model is based on two kinds of relationships between the object and its environment: perception and action (cf figure 4).

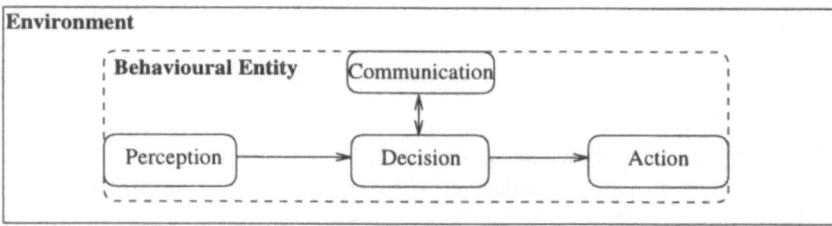

Fig. 4. A behavioural agent immersed in its environment.

Different approaches have been studied for the decision part: Sensor-Effector [19, 20, 21], Behaviour Rule [22, 23, 24, 25, 26, 27, 16], Predefined Environment [28, 29] and State Machine [30]. The general statement about actual systems using these different approachs is that they are *ad hoc* models designed to be applied in some particular cases, in which the simulated environment is very simple. Possible interactions between an object and its environment are very simple, and sensors and actuators are reduced to minimal capabilities which, most of the time, permit only to avoid obstacles in a 2D or 3D world. Another conclusion is that none of these models are able to take into account the explicit management of time, either during the specification phase (memorization, prediction, action duration, etc.) or during the execution phase (synchronization of objects with different internal times).

We have chosen to define a multi-agent system [31, 32] in order to implement a cooperation between the different behavioural approaches in one decisional model. So, this decisional model is decomposed in a set of specialized agents who use themselves some experts before proposing their diagnostic to the decisional agent (supervisor). The work of this supervisor is to integrate all the local decisions according to the desired behaviour of the system. The supervisor is principally constituted of hierarchical parallel automata, whose transitions depend on sensor data and on event generated by lower level agents. Therefore, the supervisor decides to activate some of the specialized agents and this decision depends on its own state and on sensor data (cf figure 5). The use of hierarchical parallel automata allows us to take into account concurrency and abstraction in the description of the behaviour, like Kearney et al. with their hierarchical concurrent control state machines [18]. Because of the integration of our behavioural model in a simulation platform, we have also the ability to deal with a real time during the specification and the execution phase.

5 An Automatically Driven Dynamic Car

A vehicle is an articulated rigid object structure if we do not consider the deformations of the tires and the component flexibility [33]. The vehicle is defined by a generative model which is parametrized by a state vector and two torques (motor and guidance). In the case of an automatic control of the vehicle, we have to describe the behaviour of a virtual driver depending on how is its perception of its environment. A feedback state control algorithm [34] determines what torques are applied to the vehicle from actions decided by the virtual driver.

The decisional module has to make the choice of what kind of action to perform, depending on its actual state and on its own perception of its environment (cf figure 6). This operation is decomposed in six stages:

1. The supervisor (the driver module) reads received messages and makes an analysis of data received from sensor(s).

2. The supervisor activates specialized agents.

3. Execution of specialized agents (itinerary, road signs, obstacle detection and state feedback control) which can also activate, if necessary, more specialized agents (here the obstacle detection module can activate both the moving obstacles module and the stationary obstacles module).

4. The supervisor analyses diagnosis of specialized agents.

Fig. 5. One point of view: one car is stopping at the crossroad because the traffic light is red, another one is now out of the corner.

5. The supervisor decides to act.

6. *Actions.*

Stages two, three and four are corresponding to the calculation of the new state of the world from the point of view of the agent. To deal with complex and concurrent behaviours, stage five is performed by hierarchical parallel automata (cf figure 7). Transitions on automata are functional expressions depending on the actual state of the world. Each state of each automaton is either an automaton itself or an elementary state. Each elementary state has in charge to propose an action to execute.

The *road signs* module is, at the moment, in charge of determining the value of three parameters:

- speed limitation (real value),

- overtaking (YES | NO),

- crossroads priority (right of way | priority to the right way | stop | traffic lights),

The *itinerary* module is in charge of determining the new direction at each crossroads, so this module is only activated when the vehicle is near one of them. The *obstacle detection* module has to determine if there is some possible intersections between the vehicle desired trajectory and predicted trajectories of other

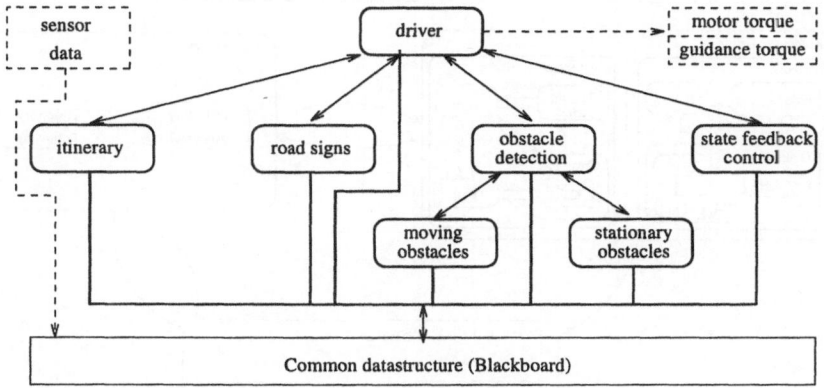

Fig. 6. Hierarchical structure of the driver decisional model.

vehicles, and if so to propose a new trajectory. Actions managed by the *state feedback control* module are:

for the guidance torque:

 − *follow_trajectory(actual position, desired trajectory, circle radius),*

and for the motor torque:

 − *accelerate(desired speed),*

 − *brake(),*

 − *stop(distance),*

 − *cover(distance,delay),*

 − *follow(preceding vehicle actual speed, distance).*

In order to simplify calculation, the human vision is not completely simulated but is replaced by a global knowledge on the scene geometry and on the location of objects, then by using visual sensors we obtain qualitative informations about objects in the vision cone.

6 A first Prototype of Real-Time Driving Simulation

A first implementation of this system has been realized as part of the car driving example. It is a modular system whose synchronization and control are specified in the synchronous real-time language SIGNAL [35]. Data communication between agents is realized by using the notion of Blackboard (common data structure).

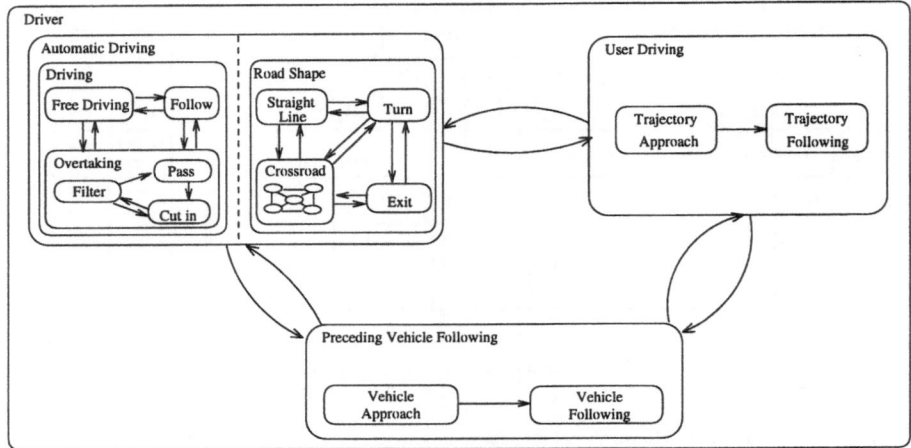

Fig. 7. Hierarchical Parallel Automata of the Driver.

We describe now an example of a little town composed of some different kinds of buildings (appartment buildings, separated houses, church), a eight shaped road, a crossroads with traffic lights and seven ground vehicles (cf figure 8). There is three kinds of vehicles: one of them is driven by a user (by using a mouse) and corresponds to the first vehicle of the platoon; three of them represent other vehicles of the platoon and the three last one describe the dynamic environment.

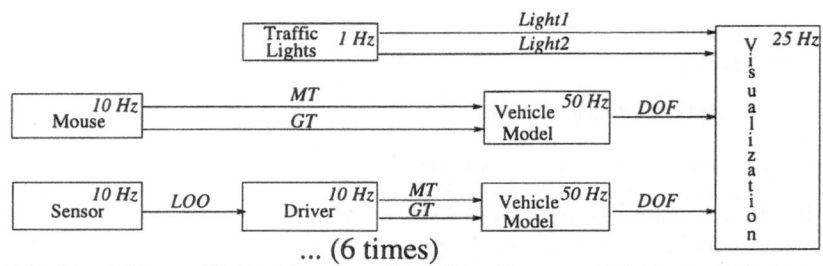

LOO: List of Objects   MT: Motor Torque   GT: Guidance Torque   DOF: Degrees of Freedom

Fig. 8. Driving example composition.

Internal frequencies of these modules are relatively different: the vehicle module has an internal frequency that can not be less than 50 Hz because of numerical convergence while sensors have an internal frequency of 10 Hz and the visualization frequency must be ideally of 25 Hz. The traffic lights module does not require a higher frequency than 1 Hz. It is necessary to synchronize the execution of all these modules to offer to real and virtual drivers a *realistic world*.

The figure 8 show synchronous dataflow communications between modules of the example. There is also some asynchronous event based communications between the mouse module and the others:

Mouse ⇒ Traffic Lights: A *reinitialization()* message can be sent at anytime, according to the user decision.

Mouse ⇒ Visualization: Different kinds of message are sent to the visualization module to control the point of view. For example, a message *set_view(front | behind | right | left | upon | driver)* changes the viewpoint whereas a message *set_vehicle(1 | 2 | ... | 7)* changes the view reference point.

Mouse ⇒ Global Controller: A message *termination()* is sent to the global controller when the user decides to terminate the simulation.

Fig. 9. One example of obtained simulation: the traffic light being red on his way, the user decides to stop the first car of the platoon, then the three others decelerate also, while an automatically driven car is passing through the crossroad.

7 Future Works

In the actual version of our system, the interaction of more than one user with the simulated environment is not possible. We are actually working on the generalization of this model to deal with communicating processes. Our goal is to permit the platform execution whatever the hardware configuration may be, and to offer a high quality multiuser interface. In addition, a general reflection is done to characterize a language which offer the ability to specify both agents and their different kinds of relations.

8 Conclusion

We have presented in this paper a platform which permits to simulate a line of autonomous vehicles in an urban environment. The integration of descriptive, generative and behaviourals models in the same simulation platform offer to each dynamic entity a more realistic and richer environment, and thereby increase possible interactions between an agent and its environment. This work is directly applied as part of the PRAXITELE project. Our work will permit to first simulate the line of vehicles evolving in a virtual environment with the intention of giving experimenters the ability to test their control algorithms whose inputs are informations from virtual sensors.

References

[1] M. Parent and P.Y. Texier. – A public transport system based on light electric cars. – In *Fourth International Conference on Automated People Movers*, Irving, Texas, U.S.A., March 1993.

[2] M. Parent and P. Daviet. – Automatic driving for small public urban vehicles. – In *Intelligent Vehicle Symposium*, Tokyo, Japon, July 1993.

[3] G. Malaterre and D. Lechner. – Expérimentation de manœuvres d'urgence sur simulateur de conduite, comportement des conducteurs. – Technical Report 104, INRETS, November 1989.

[4] T. Suetomi, A. Horyguchi, Y. Okamoto, and S. Hata. – The driving simulator with large amplitude motion system. – Technical Report 910113, SAE, 1991.

[5] E.J. Haug. – Feasability study and conceptual design of a national advanced driving simulator. – Technical report, University of Iowa, 1990.

[6] P. Gauriat and D. Lechner. – Les simulateurs pour la recherche dans le domaine de l'automobile. – *Recherche Transports Sécurité*, (30):43–51, 1991.

[7] A. Kemeny and J.M. Piroird. – A simulator for cooperative driving. – In *Drive Conference*, Bruxelles, 1991.

[8] G. Hégron and B. Arnaldi. – *Computer Animation : Motion and Deformation Control*. – Eurographics'92 Tutorial Notes, Eurographics Technical Report Series, Cambridge (Grande-Bretagne), September 1992.

[9] Phillippe de Reffye, Claude Edelin, Jean Francon, Marc Jaeger, and Claude Puech. – Plant models faithful to botanical structure and development. – In John Dill, editor, *Computer Graphics (SIGGRAPH '88 Proceedings)*, volume 22, pages 151–158, August 1988.

[10] Przemyslaw Prusinkiewicz, Mark S. Hammel, and Eric Mjolsness. – Animation of plant development. – In James T. Kajiya, editor, *Computer Graphics (SIGGRAPH '93 Proceedings)*, volume 27, pages 351–360, August 1993.

[11] N. I. Badler, C. B. Phillips, and B. L. Webber. – *Simulating Humans : Computer Graphics Animation and Control*. – Oxford University Press, 1993.

[12] Norman I. Badler, Bonnie L. Webber, Jugal Kalita, and Jeffrey Esakov, editors. – *Making them move: mechanics, control, and animation of articulated figures*. – Morgan Kaufmann, 1991.

[13] S. Donikian and G. Hégron. – A declarative design method for 3d scene sketch modeling. – In *EUROGRAPHICS'93 Conference Proceedings*, Barcelona, Spain, September 1993.

[14] R. Cozot, B. Arnaldi, and G. Dumont. – A unified model for physically based animation and simulation. – In *Applied Modelling, Simulation and Optimization*, Cancun, Mexico, June 1995. IASTED.

[15] Ch. Lecerf. – *Contrôle du mouvement de systèmes mécaniques en animation.* – PhD thesis, Université de Rennes 1, September 1994.

[16] Xiaoyuan Tu and Demetri Terzopoulos. – Artificial fishes: Physics, locomotion, perception, behavior. – In *Computer Graphics (SIGGRAPH'94 Proceedings)*, pages 43–50, Orlando, Florida, July 1994.

[17] S. Donikian and B. Arnaldi. – Complexity and concurrency for behavioral animation and simulation. – In G. Hégron and O. Fahlander, editors, *Fifth Eurographics Workshop on Animation and Simulation*, Oslo, Norvège, September 1994.

[18] J. Kearney, J. Cremer, and S. Hansen. – Motion control through communicating, hierarchical state machines. – In G. Hegron and O. Fahlander, editors, *Fifth Eurographics Workshop on Animation and Simulation*, Oslo, Norway, September 1994.

[19] Michiel van de Panne and Eugene Fiume. – Sensor-actuator networks. – In James T. Kajiya, editor, *Computer Graphics (SIGGRAPH '93 Proceedings)*, volume 27, pages 335–342, August 1993.

[20] Jane Wilhelms and Robert Skinner. – A "notion" for interactive behavioral animation control. – *IEEE Computer Graphics and Applications*, 10(3):14–22, May 1990.

[21] M. Travers. – Animal construction kits. – In *artificial life*, pages 421–442. Addison-Wesley, 1988.

[22] B. Coderre. – Modeling behavior in petworld. – In *artificial life*, pages 407–420. Addison-Wesley, 1988.

[23] D. Kalra and A.H. Barr. – Modeling with time and events in computer animation. – In A. Kilgour and L. Kjelldahl, editors, *Eurographics*, pages 45–58, Cambridge, United Kingdom, September 1992. Blackwell.

[24] R. Mouli, S. Duthen, and R. Caubet. – Un modèle de simulation comportementale orienté objet pour l'animation intelligente. – In *Interface des mondes réels & virtuels*, pages 111–121, Montpellier, France, March 1992.

[25] Craig W. Reynolds. – Flocks, herds, and schools: A distributed behavioral model. – In Maureen C. Stone, editor, *Computer Graphics (SIGGRAPH '87 Proceedings)*, volume 21, pages 25–34, July 1987.

[26] Hanqiu Sun and Mark Green. – The use of relations for motion control in an environment with multiple moving objects. – In *Graphics Interface*, pages 209–218, Toronto, Ontario, May 1993.

[27] T. Widyanto, A. Marriott, and M. West. – Applying a visual perception model to a behavioural animation system. – In *Eurographics Workshop on Animation and Simulation*, pages 89–98, Vienna, Austria, September 1991.

[28] Michael F. Cohen. – Interactive spacetime control for animation. – In Edwin E. Catmull, editor, *Computer Graphics (SIGGRAPH '92 Proceedings)*, volume 26, pages 293–302, July 1992.

[29] Gary Ridsdale and Tom Calvert. – Animating microworlds from scripts and relational constraints. – In N. Magnenat-Thalmann and D. Thalmann, editors, *Computer Animation '90 (Second workshop on Computer Animation)*, pages 107–118. Springer-Verlag, April 1990.

[30] M. Booth, J. Cremer, and J. Kearney. – Scenario control for real-time driving simulation. – In *Fourth Eurographics Workshop on Animation and Simulation*, pages 103–119, Politechnical University of Catalonia, September 1993.

[31] J. P. Haton, N. Bouzid, F. Charpillet, M. C. Haton, B. Lâasri, H. Lâasri, P. Marquis, T. Mondot, and A. Napoli. – *Le raisonnement en intelligence artificielle. Modèles techniques et architectures pour les systèmes à bases de connaissances.* – InterEditions, 1991.

[32] I. Lapierre, C. Laurgeau, J.M. Drappier, and M. Vezzoli. – Un automate de compréhension de l'environnement routier pour l'assistance à la conduite automobile. – In *L'interface des mondes réels & virtuels*, pages 533–548, Montpellier, March 1992.

[33] B. Arnaldi and G. Dumont. – Vehicle simulation versus vehicle animation. – In *Third Eurographics Workshop on Animation and Simulation*, Cambridge, September 1992.

[34] Ch. Lecerf, B. Arnaldi, and G. Hégron. – Mechanical systems motion control for computer animation. – In Bulent Ozguc and Varol Akman, editors, *First Bilkent Computer Graphics Conference on Advanced Techniques in Animation, Rendering and Visualization, ATARV-93, July 12-14, 1993*, pages 207–222. Bilkent University, Ankara, Turkey, jul 1993.

[35] Patricia Bournai, Bruno Chéron, Thierry Gautier, Bernard Houssais, and Paul Le Guernic. – Signal manual. – Technical Report 745, IRISA, July 1993.

A Shared Virtual Workspace for Constraint-based Solid Modelling

Terrence Fernando, Peter Dew, Mingxian Fa, John Maxfield and Neil Hunter

School of Computer Studies, University of Leeds,
Leeds LS2 9JT, U.K.

Abstract. This paper presents a shared virtual workspace in which geographically separated groups can collaborate on the design of constraint-based solid models. Iris Inventor graphical toolkit has been extended to support the shared virtual workspace. An interactive constraint-based solid modeller is used as a server within this shared virtual workspace to support collaborative constraint-based solid modelling and assembly modelling. The interactive constraint-based solid modeller integrates the direct interaction techniques and geometric constraints to support the intuitive construction of constraint-based solid models.

1. Introduction

The success of modern manufacturing companies increasingly depends on reducing the time taken to design and manufacture new products. A strategy used by many of these companies is to split a product into parts that can be designed and even manufactured in parallel. Each part can then be produced by a small group of experts with specialised knowledge and machinery, reducing the time to market a product. However, such groups conducting this *parallel product development* need to be very carefully managed since it is vitally important that a group does not become isolated from developments within any other groups. The design of each individual component is constraint-oriented and much of the design process involves the recognition, formulation and satisfaction of constraints arising from diverse engineering and management areas [33]. This becomes a greater concern in concurrent group design activities. If a group (or a member) has decided to change original design specifications, such changes should be immediately communicated to other groups and agreed upon since they may have an impact on other parts.

Traditional CAD tools do not support such dynamic constraint information exchange amongst designers, and do not support collaborative working among groups. Therefore there is a need for CAD environments which can support effective communication, coordination and negotiation among designers who are involved in concurrent design activities. In addition, powerful design tools should be made available in such environments to achieve a significant improvement, not only in the individual designer's performance, but also in the performance of the design team as a whole.

The purpose of this research work is to develop a shared virtual workspace for geographically separated groups to collaborate on the design of constraint-based solid models. The main goals of this research are as follows :

- To develop 3D design tools together with advanced 3D interaction techniques to provide an intuitive virtual design environment, instead of the 2D tools commonly used in existing CAD systems.

- To investigate techniques for managing geometric constraints in a multi-user virtual workspace. This work involves mechanisms for maintaining consistency and negotiation amongst participants during collaborative design activities.

- To exploit various technologies such as VR, multi-media, high speed networks (ATM) and advanced workstations to develop a highly interactive virtual workspace to support collaborative working.

- To evaluate this virtual workspace against realistic case studies from industry.

2. Background

Related work for this research comes from several areas such as *constraint-based solid modelling*, *direct manipulation techniques* and virtual environments. A brief description of the related work is presented in this section.

2.1. Constraint-based Solid Modelling

In recent years, there has been a considerable amount of interest in the development of constraint based solid modelling systems to support parametric design of mechanical parts in terms of dimensions [25, 15]. These systems provide a natural and efficient way for specifying and modifying geometry. Importantly, they provide an explicit means of representing dimensions, tolerances and form features which are essential elements of a product model [15, 17]. Good reviews of the current state-of-the-art in constraint-based solid modelling systems can be found in the literature [17, 31, 28]. These current systems can be classified into four categories: *direct parameterisation approach* [25], *algebraic approach* [19], *geometric reasoning approach* [1], and *procedural constraint propagation approach* [15, 29, 42]. The majority of these systems employ 2D interactive techniques and use complex menus. The result is that the user is faced with non-intuitive, repetitive procedures for specifying constraints and with limited 2D graphical interaction for performing 3D construction of the solid model [30, 26]. Recent advances in 3D graphical interaction devices (e.g. spaceball, 3D mouse and dataglove) are encouraging researchers to take seriously the issue of using 3D interaction techniques for constructing constraint-based solid models. However, as Rossignac [30] has recently pointed out, the subject is still in its infancy.

2.2 Direct Manipulation Techniques

In the past, a variety of direct manipulation techniques [4, 22], to support the graphical construction and modification of 3D objects through the use of 2D input devices, have been investigated. These techniques employ snapping operations to aid in specifying relative positions and orientations between objects. However, the relationships derived from snapping operations are neither explicitly represented nor automatically preserved. It is the user's responsibility to maintain them during subsequent editing. Several attempts have also been made to develop a set of modelling tools to improve 3D interaction [13, 21]. Tools such as a subtractive tool that cuts away material, and an additive tool that adds material, have been implemented to create 3D objects simply by direct manipulation of these tools. However, the models created are not precise, so the techniques are not appropriate for modelling mechanical parts [13].

The advent of 3D input devices has made it feasible for the user to directly interact with 3D models in a virtual environment, thus offering the potential to significantly speed up the model creation time. Examples of such VR systems for 3D modelling are 3D Modeller [5] and 3-Draw [32]. However, these systems are not concerned with constraint-based 3D design.

Several research efforts [43, 23] have been focused on the positioning of 3D objects by 3D input devices. They have revealed that the six degrees of freedom provided by the 3D input device should be constrained in some way to help the user to correctly move a 3D object to a desired 3D position [23].

Various attempts have been made to integrate the constraints and direct manipulation techniques to develop more powerful and intuitive constraint-based modelling systems [14, 35, 36]. However, these systems are limited to 2D interactive techniques, and support a limited number of constraint types.

2.3 Distributed Virtual Environments

Several distributed virtual environments have been developed. The VR systems described in [34, 6, 9] are based on some form of client/server model. Systems such as DIVE [8] and VEOS [6] are heterogeneous VR systems and use a peer to peer distribution between processes as opposed to a client/server architecture.

2.4 Environments for Collaborative Product Development

The current research work in environments for collaborative product development has been targeted at providing effective collaboration among team members, through services such as communication, coordination and information sharing. This section summarises several research projects which are exploiting multi-media and VR technologies to support collaborative product development.

Several engineering notebooks [20, 41] have been developed to enable project teams to record the status and history of a project to establish a *shared understanding* and to enhance the productivity among collaborative work groups. The Electronic Design Notebook (EDN) [41] enables the project members to capture their daily notes and thoughts and provides mechanisms to maintain links with a Shared Information Model. The Virtual Notebook System (VNS) [20] manages notebooks and pages which hold information objects. Objects may be images, text, audio, pointers to programs and other files, and links to other pages and notebooks. SHARE [10] is a much more sophisticated design book which is being developed at the Stanford University. In addition to the tools for creating and sharing multimedia engineering documents, SHARE provides tools such as MovieMail and Xshare. MovieMail allows the project members to capture a work session as a series of screen dumps and video clips, narrated with mouse gestures and spoken comments, which can then be e-mailed to another member. Xshare provides real-time conferencing and application sharing facilities.

A case study of building a prototype of a collaborative working environment using a virtual environment is discussed in [39]. The current implementation enables two operators to directly grasp, move or release stereoscopic computer graphics images by hand.

Several research attempts to support collaborative working in product design are reported in [33, 44, 37, 24]. Important issues such as architectures, constraint management, representational issues, organisational issues etc are being studied.

3. A Virtual Workspace for Constraint-based Solid Modelling

Our initial research work was targeted at developing a constraint-based solid modeller which could perform interactive constraint-based solid modelling and assembly modelling by exploiting 3D manipulation techniques and VR technology. As a result of this research, an Interactive Constraint-based Solid Modeller (ICBS Modeller) has been developed, based on novel 3D interactive techniques. A virtual environment has been implemented to enable the user to interact with the ICBS Modeller using a 3D input device such as a dataglove or a spaceball. This section briefly explains this constraint-based solid modelling environment.

3.1 ICBS Modeller

The ICBS Modeller has been developed by integrating direct 3D manipulation and procedural constraint propagation approaches. This has enabled the ICBS Modeller to deliver the power of these two techniques. For example, the 3D design of constraint-based solid models is carried out in a more intuitive and effective way by directly manipulating the solid models.

Direct 3D manipulation of solid models is supported by the ICBS modeller through 3D interaction techniques developed by the authors [11, 12]. An *automatic constraint recognition* process is used to recognise assembly relationships and geometric constraints between entities (such as against, coincidence, tangency, and concentricity, cylindrical fit, gear fit, screw fit) from 3D manipulations. This process continuously checks for the possible constraints between the solid model which is being manipulated, and the other solid models in the virtual environment. It provides a more intuitive way for specifying constraints than conventional techniques such as textual specification, menu interaction and 2D snapping [18, 27, 36, 7, 2]. Constraints recognised from 3D manipulation are maintained in a Relationship Graph (RG) and evaluated using an extended form of the *procedural constraint propagation* approach [29]. An *allowable motion* process is used to compute the allowable motion of the under-constrained solid model from its constraint information in the RG. These allowable motions are then used to automatically constrain the subsequent 3D manipulation of the solid model without invalidating its associated constraints. (see [11, 12] for a detailed description of these 3D interaction techniques.)

Such techniques are necessary if we are to apply VR technology to support the model construction within virtual environments. As it has been pointed out in [3, 23], the precise positioning of models within a virtual environment, using 3D input devices, is difficult and therefore such techniques are needed for automatically constraining the six degrees of freedom provided by the 3D input devices. In our approach we have achieved precise positioning in terms of geometrical constraints.

3.2 A Virtual Environment for the ICBS Modeller

The ICBS Modeller has been integrated with a virtual environment to build an intuitive virtual workspace for interactive constraint-based solid modelling. (We use the term *virtual workspace* to refer to the integrated environment, i.e. ICBS Modeller and the virtual environment). The paradigm presented to the user, within this virtual workspace, is that of designing constraint-based solid models directly in 3D space with a set of *virtual design tools*. Two types of virtual design tools are available to the user: *virtual modelling tools* and *virtual drafting tools*. Virtual modelling tools include *block, cylinder, sphere* and *cone* tools. Drafting tools include *3D T-square* and *3D Protractor*. These tools are maintained in two separate boxes. These virtual design tools have been implemented as functional 3D objects associated with several pre-defined modelling functions. For example, modelling tools are associated with functions to perform operations such as *drilling, gluing, intersection,* and *fitting.* Drafting tools are associated with functions to create construction planes, or to define dimensional constraints (e.g. distance and angle) between the geometric elements of the solid models. The manipulation of these tools is supported by the 3D interaction techniques to achieve precise 3D positioning in terms of geometric constraints. By interpreting its constraint information and the user's manipulation, the modelling functions of the tool can be automatically triggered [11].

The ICBS Modeller is also able to support interactive constraint-based assembly modelling. Several assembly relationships, such as against, coincidence, concentric, cylindrical fit, spherical fit, screw fit and gear fit, are supported by the ICBS Modeller. A number of industrial case studies have been used to demonstrate the capability of this virtual workspace to perform intuitive assembly modelling, purely by 3D manipulations [45].

3.3 System Implementation

As shown in Figure 1, the system comprises of two sub-systems : ICBS Modeller and Virtual Environment (VE). This section briefly explains the implementation of the VE and the interface between the VE and the ICBS Modeller. The virtual environment has been implemented using a 3D toolkit library called IRIS Inventor [16, 38] and therefore a brief description of this toolkit is given first.

3.3.1 IRIS Inventor Toolkit

IRIS Inventor is an object-oriented toolkit for developing interactive 3D graphics applications. This toolkit provides a general and extensible framework for representing 3D scenes so that applications can integrate their data with graphical objects. An event model that enables direct interaction with 3D objects is also provided.

IRIS Inventor provides a scene database to store dynamic representations of 3D scenes as graphs of objects called *nodes*. These nodes are *shape nodes* that represent geometric objects, *property nodes* that describes various attributes of those objects, and *group nodes*, which connect other nodes into graphs and sub graphs. The database provides a set of actions that can be applied to scenes or parts of scenes. Examples of actions are rendering, picking, computing a bounding box, handling an event, and writing to a file. The *interaction* section of the 3D toolkit introduces event classes and *smart* nodes that process events. Event classes define an extensible set of abstract events such as *ButtonEvent* and *Motion3Event*. (The latter refers to 3D motion events generated by a 3D input device such as a spaceball). An example of a smart node is the *manipulator* node, which responds to interaction events and edits other nodes (for example, transform nodes) in a scene database. In addition, callback mechanisms are provided that allow callback functions to be registered with various interaction events or nodes of the scene graph. These callback functions can be used to invoke application specific operations.

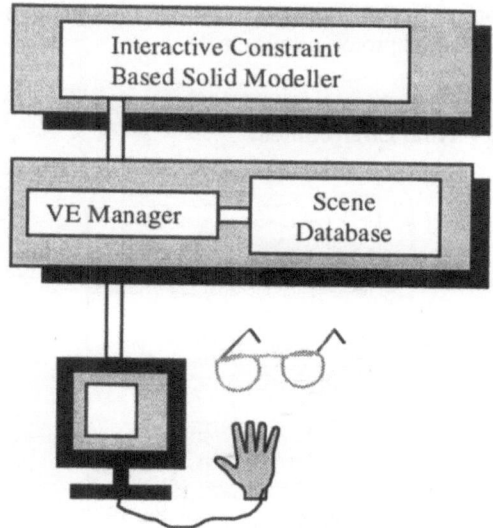

Fig.1. Software Architecture of the Virtual Workspace

3.3.2 Interface between the VE and the ICBS Modeller

As shown in Figure 1, the main components within the virtual environment are the VE Manager and the Scene Database. The VE Manager, based on IRIS Inventor, handles the user events and provides an interface to the ICBS Modeller. The Scene Database maintains various 3D objects as graphs. The VE Manager invokes the necessary functions to create shape nodes in the Scene Database, on request from the ICBS Modeller. For example, functions are available to create a sub graph for a CSG primitive, or to create a shape node for a face set. Links are maintained between these shape nodes in the Scene Database and their corresponding CSG solid models in the ICBS Modeller. Thus, whenever a 3D object in the Scene Database is selected, its corresponding CSG solid model can be found in the ICBS modeller which can then receive and process any 3D motion events. When an object is being manipulated, motion events of the 3D input device are continuously transmitted from the VE Manager to the ICBS Modeller through callback mechanisms. These motion events are processed by the allowable motion and automatic constraint recognition processes to support modelling operations. If an allowable transformation or a

192

modelling operation is carried out within the ICBS Modeller on the solid models as a result of the motion event, the Scene Database is updated accordingly.

4. A Shared Workspace for Constraint-based Solid Modelling

The single-user virtual workspace for constraint-based solid modelling has been extended to support a shared workspace for parallel product development. This section describes our initial prototype system.

4.1 A Distributed Virtual Environment

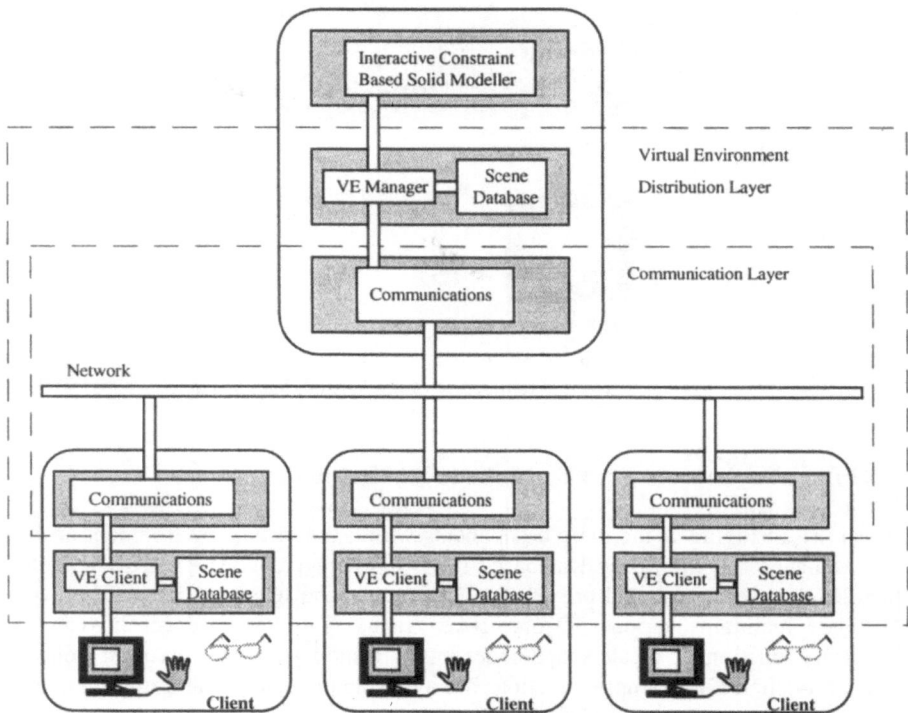

Fig.2. Software Architecture of the Shared Workspace

The first phase towards developing a shared workspace for constraint-based solid modelling was the design and implementation of an architecture to handle the distribution of virtual environments. The architecture that was developed is based on the well established, client-server model and consists of two basic layers (Figure 2):

- *The Communications Layer* : which provides the functions required for message passing between processes over a physical network, raising the next layer above any particular network hardware dependencies.

- *The Virtual Environment Distribution Layer* : which provides the facilities for distributing and managing changes within a virtual environment.

The communications layer controls the creation and maintenance of the communications channels between separate components of the system. The present communication layer is based upon the Unix operating system socket mechanisms. The layer is implemented using C++ classes, starting from a base class containing a simple two way socket connection, building up to a message passing system.

The virtual environment is automatically distributed by the *virtual environment distribution layer*. This layer may contain one of two processes, namely the Virtual Environment Server (VE Server) or Virtual Environment Client (VE Client). The VE Server performs the role of the VE Manager with extra server specific tasks. For example, the VE Server is responsible for managing Clients, resolving mutual exclusion, passing the Clients' motion events to the ICBS Modeller and broadcasting the updates to Clients in order to maintain an up-to-date copy of the virtual environment. The function of a VE Client is very similar to the VE Manager. However, in this case, interaction with the application module (ICBS Modeller) is done through remote procedure calls via the communication layer and the VE Server.

Given these two layers, an application that makes use of a virtual environment may be fitted on top of the virtual environment distribution layer in the Server. Since the distribution of the virtual environment is transparent to the application, it can interact with the environment as if it is serving a single user. The virtual environment distribution layer in the Clients enables multiple users to view and interact with the environment.

4.2 Interaction Scenario

The interaction scenario within this shared virtual workspace is as follows :

- The VE Server receives the initial scene models from the application, creates a copy in its Scene Database, and broadcasts a copy to all the Clients. The VE Server also maintains a database of Clients that are connected to the virtual environment.

- A VE Client requests a *lock* on an object from the VE Server in order to interact with the object.

- The VE Server sends a reply to the VE Client giving permission to select the requested object, if it has not already been locked for another Client.

- When the object is being manipulated by a user, the VE Client continuously transmits the motion events of the 3D input device to the VE Server. The VE Server passes on these motions to the ICBS Modeller to be processed.

- The ICBS Modeller receives this motion information which is then processed as explained in section 3. The Scene database of the Server is then updated accordingly.

- The VE Server then broadcasts the changes to the VE Clients to update their own copy.

- If a new Client requests to join in, the VE Server sends an up-to-date copy of its Scene Database and enters the new Client into its database.

4.3 Current Prototype System

The current shared workspace runs on a network of SGI workstations and enables several users to perform concurrent constraint-based modelling activities, interactively. This environment runs in parallel with Inria Video-conferencing System (IVS) [40] to demonstrate the concept of collaborative working. IVS is a groupware tool that supports audio and video conferences over the Internet. The system makes use of compression algorithms for both audio and video signals to reduce the bandwidth required on the network, and provides colour video and high quality audio communications between clients in the virtual environment. The current prototype system enables the designers to discuss their design ideas and carry out simple constraint-based solid modelling and assembly modelling activities within a shared virtual workspace.

5. Conclusion and Future Work

As a result of this research programme, novel 3D interaction techniques have been developed to support the construction of constraint-based solid models within a virtual environment. An Interactive Constraint-based Solid Modeller has been implemented based on these novel interaction techniques. This ICBS Modeller has been integrated with a distributed virtual environment to demonstrate the *proof of concept* of distributed collaborative working within a shared virtual workspace.

This work is now being extended to develop a *multi-perspective distributed virtual environment* that supports collaboration among members of a geographically dispersed multidisciplinary team, who are engaged in concurrent product development [44].

6. Acknowledgement

The authors wish to thank Dr.Neal Juster and Jim Baxter in the Mechanical Engineering Department for their many helpful suggestions. Thanks also go to Mudarmeen Munlin, Feng Gao, Richard Drew and Jim Hughes for their software development support. Many thanks to Dave Morris for his technical support.

7. References

1. Aldefeld, B.: Variation of Geometries Based on a Geometric-Reasoning Method, CAD, 20(3), pp.117-126, April 1988.

2. Alpert, S.R..: Graceful Interaction with Graphical Constraints, IEEE CG and A, pp. 82-91, March 1993.

3. Badler, N.I., K. H. Manoochehri, and Baraff, D.: Multi-Dimensional InputTechniques and Articulated Figure Positioning by Multiple Constraints. 1986 Workshop on Interactive 3D Graphics, pp. 151-169, 1986.

4. Bier, E.A.: Snap-Dragging in Three Dimensions. 1990 Symposium on Interactive 3D Graphics, pp. 193-204,1990.

5. Butterworth,J., Davidson, A., Hench, S. and Marc Olano, T.: 3DM: A Three Dimensional Modeller Using a Head-Mounted Display, 1992 Symposium on Interactive 3D Graphics,1992.

6. Coco, G.P.: VEOS 2.0 Tool Builders Manual. Technical report, University of Washington, 1992.

7. Structural Dynamics Research Corp. I-DEAS PartDesign, 1991.

8. Fahlen, L.E. (et.al), The MultiG Distributed Interactive Virtual Environment. Proccedings of the 5th MultiG Workshop, December 1992.

9. Appino, P.A. (et.al). : An Architecture for Virtual Worlds. Presence, vol.1,1991.

10. George, T. (et.al) : SHARE: AMethodology and Environment for Collaborative Product Development. To Appear in the Proceedings of the Second Workshop on Enabling Technologies:Infrastructure for Collaborative Enterprises, 1993.

11. Fa, M., Fernando, T., and Dew, P.M. : Direct 3D Manipulation Techniques for Interactive Constraint-based Solid Modelling. Computer Graphics Forum, Proc. of EuroGraphics'93, 12(3), pp.237-248, September 1993.

12. Fa, M., Fernando,T., and Dew, P.M.: Interactive Constraint-based Solid Modelling using Allowable Motion, Proc. of ACM/SIGGRAPH Symposium on Solid Modelling and Applications, pp. 243-252, May 1993.

13. Galyean, T.A, and Hughes, J.F.: Sculpting:An Interactive Volumetric Modelling Technique, SIGGRAPH 91, 25(4), pp.267-274, July 1991.

14. Gleicher, M.: Integrating Constraints and Direct Manipulation.1992 Symposium on Interactive 3D Graphics, pp. 171-174, 1992.

15. Gossard, D.C., Zuffante, R.P., and Shakurai, H.: Representing Dimensions, Tolerance and Features in MCAE Systems. IEEE CG and A, pp. 51-59, March 1988.

16. Juster, N.P.: Modelling and Representation of Dimensions and Tolerances: a Survey. CAD, 24(1), pp.3-17,January 1992.

17. Light, R.A.: Symbolic Dimensioning in Computer Aided Design. Master's thesis, Massachusetts Institute of Technology, 1980.

18. Lin, V.C., Gossard, D.C., and Light, R.A.: Variational Geometry in Computer Aided Design. SIGGRAPH 81, 15(3), pp.171-175, August 1981.

19. Long, K.B., and Gorry, A.: The Virtual Notebook System:An Architecture for Collaborative Work.Hypertext 91 Conference Proceedings, pp. 417-418, December 1991.

20. Naylor, B.: SCULPT: An Interactive Solid Modelling Tool. Graphics Interface'90, pp. 138-146, 1990.

21. Nielson, G.M.: Direct Manipulation Techniques for 3D Objects Using 2D Locator Devices, 1986 Workshop on Interactive 3D Graphics, pp. 175-182, 1986.

22. Prime, M.J.: Human Factors Assessment of Input Devices for EWS. Technical report, Rutherford Appleton Laboratory, April 1991.

23. Reddy, Y.V.R., Srinivas, K., Jaganathan, V., and Karinthi, R.: Computer Support for Concurrent Engineering, IEEE Computer, pp. 12-15, January 1993.

24. Requicha, A.A.G.: Representations of Tolerances in Solid Modelling: Issues and Alternative Approaches, In Solid Modelling by Computers From Theory to Applications, 1984.

25. Requicha A.A.G., and Rossignac, J.R.: Solid Modelling and Beyond. IEEE CG and A, 12(5), pp. 31 45, September 1992.

26. Roller, D.: An Approach to Computer Aided Parametric Design. CAD, 23(5), pp.385-391, June 1991.

27. Roller, D., Schonek, F., and Verroust, A.: Dimension-Driven Geometry in CAD: A Survey. In Theory and Practice of Geometric Modelling, pp. 509-523, 1989.

28. Rossignac, J.R.: Constraints in Constructive Solid Geometry, 1986 Workshop on Interactive 3D Graphics, pp. 93-110, 1986.

29. Rossignac, J.R.: Through the Cracks of the Solid Modelling Milestone. Eurographics'91 State of the Art Report on Solid Modelling, pp. 23-109, 1991.

30. Roy, U., Liu, C.R., and Woo, T.C.: Review of Dimensioning and Tolerancing: Representation and Processing, CAD, 23(7), pp. 466-483, September 1991.

31. Sachs, E., Roberts, A., and Stoops, D.: 3-Draw:A Tool for Designing 3D Shapes, IEEE CG and A, pp.18-25, November 1991.

32. Serrano, D.: Managing Constraints in Concurrent Design: First Steps, In Proc.of the 1990 ASME International Computers in Engineering Conference, pp. 159-164, 1990.

33. Shaw, C., Green, M., Liang, J., and Sun, Y.: The De-coupled Simulation Model for Virtual Reality Systems, In Proc. of CHI'92, 1992.

34. Sistare, S.: Graphical Interaction Techniques in Constraint-based Geometric Modelling. Graphics Interface'91, pp. 85-93, 1991.

35. Sohrt, W., and Bruderlin, B.: Interaction with Constraints in 3D Modelling. International Journal of Computational Geometry and Applications, 1(4), pp. 405-425, 1991.

36. Sriram, D.: Computer Supported Collaborative Engineering, Technical report, Intelligent Engineering Systems Laboratory, M.I.T., May 1993.

37. Strauss P.S., and Carey, R., An Object-Oriented 3DGraphics Toolkit, 92, 26(2), pp.341-349, July 1992.

38. Takemura, H., and Kishino, F.: Cooperative Work Environment using Virtual Workspace. In Proc. of the ACM Conference on CSCW'92, Toronto, October 1992.

39. Turletti, T.: H.261 software codec for videoconferencing over the Internet : Report No.N1834, Technical report, Institut National de Recherche en Informatique et en Automatique, 1993.

40. Uejio, W.H., Carmody, S., and Ross, B.: An Electronic Project NoteBook from the Electronic Design NoteBook, 3rd Annual National Symposium on Concurrent Engineering, CALS and CE, pp. 527-535, 1991.

41. Van Emmerik, J.: A System for Graphical Interaction on Parametrized Models, Eurographics'89, pp. 233-242, 1989.

42. Ware C., and Jessome, D.R.: Using the Bat:A Six-Dimensional Mouse for Object Placement, IEEE CG and A, pp. 65-70, November 1988.

43. Wong, A., Sriram, D., and Logcher, R.: SHARED: An Information Model for Cooperative Product Development, Research in Engineering Design, September 1993.

44. Maxfield, J., Fernando, T., Dew, P.M.: A Distributed Virtual Environment for Concurrent Engineering, Proceedings of IEEE VRAIS'95, pp. 162-170, March 1995.

45. Fernando, T., Fa, M., Dew P.M. and Munlin, M.: Constraint-based 3D Manipulation Techniques for Virtual Environments, Proceedings of International State of the Art Conference (BCS) on Virtual Reality Applications, June 1994.

An interactive virtual world experience - the cyberspace roadshow

Peter Astheimer and Wolfgang Felger

Fraunhofer-Institut für Graphische Datenverarbeitung (IGD)
Demonstration Center for Virtual Reality
Wilhelminenstr. 7, D-64283 Darmstadt, Germany
phone: ++49 6151 155 121 & 122, fax: ++49 6151 155 399
email: {astheime, felger}@igd.fhg.de

Abstract. The goal of this paper is to describe a virtual reality application which requires a mobile installation, and the experience gathered during the preparation, realization, and execution of this project. Recently, high-end virtual reality (VR) receives much attention in the marketing field. Professional advertisment agencies are trying to exploit the fascination in this technology raised within the public. IGD was approached by such an agency and requested to prepare a high-quality VR application, serving as marketing event for the Schweizerische Bankgesellschaft / Union de Banques Suisses (SBG/UBS), the largest swiss bank. SBG wanted to attract the swiss youth, in order to promote its junior bank card.

This event was held in twelve major swiss cities during four weeks in May/June 1994 with daily presentations. The time schedule and the marketing concept required a mobile installation. As Cyberspace Roadshow the event was advertised in newspapers and radio spots. This was worldwide the first mobile, immersive, high-quality VR installation. The complete VR infrastructure was installed in a huge truck as well as the presentations were performed inside the truck. The hardware infrastructure comprised: image generator (SGI Crimson/RealityEngine), VR peripherals (head-mounted display, data glove, body tracking systems), sound generator (SGI Indigo), and a large screen, stereoscopic rear projection, using polarizing light. Using such an immersive environment, approx. 40 persons can be covered. Wearing 3D glasses the audience can experience stereoscopic viewing and follow passively, what one active person is controlling by utilizing the VR devices.

For this event IGD created several entertaining virtual worlds, using its proprietary VR system. The main idea was that one active player is flying through a tunnel, approaching a switch room with three alternatives: riding through a jungle, playing music instruments, or exploring a space labyrinth. Each player had a time limit of approx. 5 minutes.

Keywords. Virtual reality, roadshow, case study.

1 Introduction

Almost continuously during the last couple of years since the foundation of IGD's virtual reality demonstration center a variety of VR presentations have been realized. The presentations cover demonstrations at scientific conferences, in-house consulting, museum exhibitions as well as fairs and commercial exhibitions. The main goal of all performed contract-based VR presentations was to attract the audience by featuring VR technology. This shows the potential of VR as a marketing instrument in business management [8].

In late 1993 the advertising agency Bosch & Butz approached IGD with the concept idea of a special marketing event for the Schweizerische Bankgesellschaft (SBG), the largest swiss banking institute. In order to address its young clients, the swiss youth, the SBG has currently a marketing concept, which concentrates on the realization of a few pretty big and unique events per year rather than numerous small events. The motto for the year 1994 was entitled "the year of adventures" and should provide exciting and thrilling experiences. The previous event was the European premiere of the Disney movie Aladdin in an outdoor cinema-setup on top of a mountain in the swiss alps with a screen carved into a glacier. The basic idea for the next event was to exploit the fascination of VR technology for marketing and promoting the SBG. In several Swiss cities people should be able to self-experience VR. The realization of a roadshow was the ultimate goal. Although the initial enthusiasm for VR has diminished, media and the general public are still excited, open, and eager for a new experience [5].

The paper represents a case study and is organized according the following structure: First, preparation activities und basic thoughts are presented. Afterwards, realization aspects are discussed, showing the problems of the project. Later, experiences in the execution phase of the project gained during the public presentations are summarized. The paper closes with an outlook on future work and the conclusions.

2 Preparation phase

The project started in late February 1994 and should have been on the road around mid May 1994. This gave us only less than three months for the project preparation and realization.

After initial negotiations about costs and considerations about the feasibility of the planned event we decided to take the chance to explore new terrain. Our partners at the bank and the advertising agency neither posed any restrictions on us nor enforced or suggested specific solutions (only the glove was a must, because it was the central component of the advertisement campaign, symbolizing VR). We "only" had to realize something exciting and thrilling. This left us with complete freedom for our work, but also caused some troubles and a lot of headache.

We started to tackle the project with a team of computer graphics and design people (supported by students of course). Although we only had few weeks left for designing and modeling the virtual world and specifying and integrating new features in our VR system we were confident about the realization of the event. Soon we decided on the kind of the overall system interaction: exploring an adventure world. Shoot and quick reaction scenarios were abandoned because of ethic and technological (body tracking latency) reasons. Think and learn contents are not explicitly thrilling for everyone.

We had to meet two basic challenges:

1) Logistic and technology challenge: For the purpose of this marketing event a mobile installation had to be planned, which could tour some ten major swiss cities during a month's time. Adequate locations had to be found and prepared (e.g., administration clearance, power supply, local support people, catering for guests). The installation had to be so robust to run a continuous six hour show per day and endure the intermediate transport. To even complicate the organization, three showmasters had to be trained because there are three different languages regions in Switzerland (French, German, and Italian). Furthermore, customs and insurance issues had to be solved.

2) System challenge: The experience had to be tailored for use by any people with any education and any experience around the age of 17 (i.e., SBG's junior bank card holders). The major demands for the virtual world and the system were:
   - Continuous motion in order to create interesting worlds. No pure walkthrough or flythrough.
   - Provide an athmosphere beside the pure geometric architecture of a world.
   - Dynamic worlds rather than static worlds.
   - Easy, intuitive interaction, which doesn't requires training or longer introduction (self-explaining content).
   - Exciting and thrilling content (for users of this age/generation).
   - Participation of a larger audience (more than 20 persons).
   - Quick turnaround times for players.

All these aspects had been taken into consideration in order to realize an attractive mobile, immersive, and high-quality VR installation. For further reading [4, 6, 9, 10] are recommended.

3 Realization phase

This chapter covers the realization aspects for the roadshow, dealing with hardware components, interaction issues, and the overall story of the presentation. The used VR system is IGD's Virtual Design [3].

3.1 Hardware Components

To fulfil the requirement of touring accross the country and minimizing the time without presentations lead to the idea for an VR installation inside a huge truck (figure 1, see Appendix). This enables times of approx. one hour to start-up or shutdown the complete infrastructure at each show location. It was intented to run the shows on public open-air places and in large halls. As a larger audience should be able to watch the active players and their behaviour within the virtual worlds the truck was open at one side during show times. To avoid the brightness of sun light, the open side could be covered by a tent-like curtain.

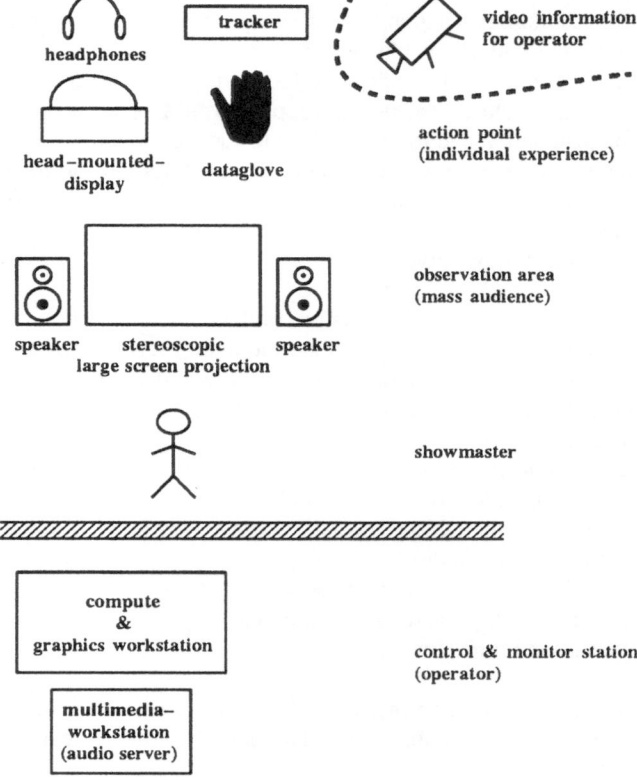

Figure 3: VR infrastructure

The basic VR equipment per player with a powerful graphics workstation and peripherals (head-mounted display, navigation device, tracking system) is very expensive. For this reason we decided to install one high-quality VR station for the active player and a stereoscopic large-screen rear projection, utilizing polarizing light, for passive observation by the audience (figure 2, see Appendix). Figure 3 shows the VR infrastructure of the installation. It comprises: image generator (SGI

Crimson/RealityEngine1 with Multi-Channel Option), VR peripherals (Virtual Research FlightHelmet, VPL DataGlove, Polhemus Fastrak), sound generator (SGI Indigo), and stereoscopic rear projection (NEC/TAN). Using such an immersive environment, approx. 40 persons can be covered. Wearing 3D glasses the audience can experience stereoscopic viewing and follow passively, what one active person is controlling by utilizing the VR devices.

The Multi-Channel Option delivers a high-resolution video signal (1280 x 1024 pixel) to drive the stereoscopic projection in highest quality. With a scan converter one signal is transformed into a standard low resolution NTSC signal to feed the HMD. To reduce the image generation complexity we decided to run the HMD in monoscopic mode, because former presentations proofed that due to the poor resolution of the used HMD, the appealing thing is its wide field of view and not the stereoscopic viewing. This will certainly change when HMD's with higher resolution are available/affordable.

Being aware of the fragile VR peripherals in use, a replacment for the HMD and the tracking system was always on board. Having our experience in mind with VPL's fibre optic glove for public presentations, it was purly used as a platform to mount the hand tracker [7]. No gesture interfacing was applied and it was expected that the glove will not survive the entire event. Clearly spoken, it was only integrated because it was the central component in the nation wide advertisment campaign.

3.2 Interaction with the virtual world

Various actions should be available for the players when they experience a virtual world. This considers interactions with objects representing the virtual world as well as navigation within the world.

Static worlds, observed in typical walkthrough applications, can get boring very soon. To create a vivid environment, dynamic object behaviour has to be integrated in a virtual world. We introduced animations for lights, camera and any world object. Although these animations have to be precalculated (mostly) and thus the objects do not react in an intelligent manner to the players' action this makes the worlds much more interesting. Animations can be triggered or combined with user interactions or run continuously as long as the players visit the virtual world. With these features the resulting presentation becomes a mixture of preprocessed animation show and high-interactive virtual reality, both running in harmony under realtime requirements.

Navigating in virtual worlds requires in this special setup some new thoughts. As the DataGlove has to be integrated in any manner because it symbolizes VR technology for the lay audience, we have to work around its inherent deficiencies. The DataGlove may cause problems, because it has to be calibrated to each player's hand and the applied fiber optic technology is not robust enough for permanent public use. Hygiene still is another issue. Another lesson learned from previous events and also strongly recommended by Prof. Henry Fuchs from UNC during his talk at IGD in April 1993 is: Don't fly !!!

People have problems with standard navigation mechanisms based on the DataGlove (point & fly). Thus we realized a carpet metaphor for navigation, where the players can move freely with respect to the constraints of cable length and tracker range (i.e., physical borders of the action point limit the movements) to perform small-scale navigation. To travel longer distances they are transported or beamed in a predefined manner. This is similar to the Aladdin realization at EPCOT done by Disney Imagineering except that we do not use a real carpet and do not have the capability to control the carpet.

The players trigger the movement over long distances in general by touching an appropriate object in the virtual world. This object represents the movement behaviour (e.g., moving along a specific path for a certain time). Moreover, such a basic interaction mechanism is generic and can be applied and configurated for different virtual worlds (no explicit programming necessary). This is realized as a list of touchable (triggerable) objects with associated actions. Initial actions can be started when entering or switching to a new virtual world. The following actions can be distinguished (combinations are possible too):

1) Animation of objects and lights in terms of transformations. Animations can loop endless or according a given repetition counter.
2) Animation of the camera (view of the observer) in terms of transformations. Various modes are possible:
   - Additional head movement is allowed, yes or no.
   - Interpolation from a current camera view to a given starting view is enabled, yes or no.
   - Accelerate or slow down the camera movement.
   - Camera animations can loop endless or according a given repetition counter.
3) Trigger a sound event.
4) Switch between to virtual worlds.
5) Switch the visibility of objects between visible and invisible.
6) Animate an object in terms of changing its geometric representation. An alternating object sequence can loop endless or according a given repetition counter.

3.3 Presentation story

The idea of the story was to generate an eventful and complex adventure world consisting of several subworlds which were connected by a simple transition structure. Furthermore, with respect to the expected players and audience, the junior bank card should play a major role in the story. With the integration of special effects (see below) a certain athmosphere or mood is created for each world. Due to the soon deadline, only a few ideas could be realized (e.g., virtual rain was skipped). In general, sound helps a lot to create a typical mood and is used throughout the adventure world [1].

At the beginning, the players are flying helicopter-like around the truck (figure 4, see Appendix) until they are transported towards the action point inside the truck. This symbolizes the shift from the real world into the virtual real world and represents the start of the virtual journey.

After arriving at the action point the players face a contomat (SBG's teller machine, figure 5, see Appendix). Until here they are completely guided by the system which changes to the interactive mode at this point. By touching the contomat with the hand the players trigger the transition from the virtual real world (truck with environment) to the virtual imaginative worlds.

The players are sucked into the card feeder and find themselves flying through a tunnel (figure 6, see Appendix). For a certain time they proceeded in the tunnel with good (blue sky texture) and bad (yellow/red texture) objects (cubes) approaching them. They should try to touch the good objects and avoid to get in contact with the bad ones. Appropriate sound signals are generated in both cases. The bank card is always flying ahead, guiding the players through the tunnel and releasing particles, never reachable.

Next, the players approach a switch room (figure 7, see Appendix) where they select one out of three alternative worlds in order to proceed the journey. The bank card dissolves into three parts which disappear in these three worlds. The choice between the corresponding virtual worlds is symbolized by colour and a typical object from this world (palm tree indicating the jungle world, trumpets indicating the stage world, planet indicating the space world). The players make their selection to enter one world simply by touching one of the big arrows just beneath them. We called this switch room the "tower of fate" , because its design is inspired by the star-wars scene, where the yedi master fought Darth Vader on a narrow bridge overlooking a precipice. Here, spaceship-like flashing control lights are performed.

In the jungle world (figure 8, see Appendix) an elephant ride through a jungle is simulated. The players can touch animals which live in this jungle. By doing so they are collecting parts of the bank card, whose fragments were attached to the back of the players' hand. Each successful hit is signalized by a sound event.

The stage world (figure 9, see Appendix) provides a scenario where the players fly accross a fictive audience onto a stage, being surrounded by phantastic instruments (e.g., keyboard, guitar, chorus). Furthermore, a light show is performed on the stage. By touching the instruments a short melody fragment from a song is played and the instruments start moving as long as the music plays. Keeping the instruments randomly playing rewards the players with parts of the bank card. (Our original idea was to force the players to remember and replay a given melody sequence. But this was too restrictive to be solved by everyone.)

The space world is placed in an universum with moving asteroids and planets. It is designed as a labyrinth with five nodes and multiple connections (e.g., tube, staircase) between these nodes (figure 10, see Appendix). Each node consists of four exits. Touching one exit means selecting this connection to the neighbor node and being moved along its path. In some nodes parts of the bank card are placed, which can be collected.

Finally, after a certain time the entire experience ends with a colorful and loud firework (figure 11, see Appendix).

4 Execution phase

4.1 Show procedure

The roadshow toured across Switzerland from May 16 until June 15, 1994 with stops in Zurich (May 16-18), Winterthur (May 19), Aarau (May 20-21), Geneva (May 24-26), Lausanne (May 27-29), Sierre (May 30), Bern (May 31 - June 2), Zug (June 3-5), St. Gallen (June 6-7), Chur (June 8-9), Lugano (June 10-12), and Lucern (June 13-15). In each city a local group of volunteers from the SBG supported the event. At some locations the show was held inside a festival or exhibition hall, at others direct in front of the SBG building or on a public place. The entrance regulation was at the discretion of the local group. Some charged bank card holders 5 SFR and non-holders 15 SFR, others gave card holders free entrance. Mostly one free drink was included.

A typical presentation day featured 50 minutes shows with a 10 minutes break between two shows, running from 4 pm until 10 pm. Mostly, IGD staff gave a very brief introduction to VR technology and its applications at each show start [2]. A show master was guiding the players and the audience with respect to multi-lingualistic Switzerland, either in French, German, or Italian language. Performing one VR experience together with some interviewing of the player took approx. 5 minutes time. Most of the time an audience between 10 and 50 persons attended one show. We had days with a total of roughly 400 persons sharing the presentations. Players were selected by the show master or by means of a lottery. The players started with the sequence of the virtual truck, and the approach to the contomat; followed by the tunnel flight, the switch room, and either the space labyrinth, the stage, or the jungle ride; and concluding with the final firework. Each player was rewarded with a unique "Cyberspace Roadshow T-Shirt".

4.2 Media Coverage

The roadshow was promoted by a nation-wide advertisment campaign. This included poster walls, radio spots in the local radio stations, and a preview in SBG's newsletter "megascene". Furthermore, two press conferences were held, one at the tour start in Zurich, and the other one later in Geneva.

The echo in the media was enormous and very positive. Already, during the first week the roadshow had coverage in most major Swiss newspapers and the public TV station. This continued steadily over the full runtime of the event. In total, approx. 100 press articles can be counted, as well as four TV spots (even one in the Austrian TV station), and five radio interviews.

4.3 Observations

After watching the large-screen stereoscopic projection in highest resolution many players were disappointed about the poor resolution of the HMD (90k primary pixels). Some complained about the integrated system guidance or expressed the feeling, that they were not really mastering the world (sometimes the operator "helped" to interact via keyboard function keys). Another complaint was about the jaggy motion due to low frame rates (approx. 5-10 frames/sec depending on the world complexity) and tracker faults, which resulted worst case in still frames for a short time.

As in numerous earlier presentations it was very hard to explain, that all computations and computer graphics is done online under realtime requirements and no prerecorded tape or video is involved. On the other hand many people were very interested, starting some PC-level discussions to figure out the enormous computational work load.

We got all types of persons (e.g., from kids in kindergarten age to retired adults, male/female, computer-educated/non-computer-educated). Most people did like the experience, a few were enthusiastic, a few did not like it at all. Groups cheered group members playing. Some people were very passive and showed a TV-like stiff behaviour, some were very active (too active in fact for the tracking system). Very tall or small people (kids) did not match our predefined settings and they sometimes had extraordinary perspectives. The most wanted final world was the space labyrinth and there especially surfing the staircase up or down was appealing.

4.4 Lessons learned

A roadshow and its show locations have to be planned very carfully. Luckily, we did not have to face unsolvable problems but it seems to be wise to check the locations well in advance by the truck driver. Although the enormous size of the truck was known to everybody sometimes its delicate manouverability was not considered adequate.

If you want many people coming by to see the show, it is very important to place it somewhere on a central open air place, rather than at a remote location. For example, at Geneva the show was held on the fairgrounds (Palexpo) at the city periphery and appeared like an insider event. At Lugano the truck stopped at the main square near the lake front (Piazza Riforma) and it was almost impossible to handle the crowds waiting in the surrounding street cafes.

Expect a great variety of people joining the show. Even when the target audience seems to be of a certain age (junior bank card holders age is less 20), be prepared for everybody. Make a comprehensive dry test of your software and the created worlds with such a variety and not only with people being avaiable in your lab. If possible, be flexible enough to adjust your software or world during the show.

Set aside enough time for the design and creation of your virtual worlds. Spend at least half of the development effort and you will get creative worlds. Less than three month for the preparation and realization of such a project is extremly short and can only be tackeld by a fine-cooperating team.

Our biggest surprise was not having any major problem with the VR infrastructure. The complete equipment ran without failure during the roadshow. There was not one show which has to be delayed or cancelled. But it will be soothing to have redundant equipment with you, then running the hardware over months and years in our lab tells us that you can not expect such a nice behaviour.

Although HMD and DataGlove are the classical VR symbols think twice if the intended presentation will really need it. For this roadshow it was a requirement and we dealt with it by implementing dedicated interaction techniques which worked fine. If you have the freedom to choose the equipment wait for really robust and comfortable HMD's and gloves, or avoid its use.

5 Future Work

During the roadshow and the weeks after the roadshow IGD received many inquiries about this Cyberspace Roadshow. Many had the same goal, to use a mobile VR system for marketing purposes. With a few companies, which can afford such an installation, further negotiations are ongoing. You can expect one future event in mid 1995 in Germany. Confidentidility reasons prohibit a disclosure at this time.

As IGD is a research institute, we are always looking for new challenges and don't want to duplicate a finished project. We are improving our VR system with respect to requirements from entertainment and leisure applications. The integration of a personal motion platform lies within a medium-term time scale.

6 Conclusions

This paper described the Cyberspace Roadshow which was performed for the Schweizerische Bankgesellschaft (SBG) in Switzerland. The associated work in preparing, realizing, and executing this roadshow were described in detail as case study.

For this project the interaction concept of IGD's VR system was redesigned and extented. Interactions can be specified in a data file referencing world objects and predefined actions. Thus interesting living or reacting worlds can be easily defined and evaluated. It has been proofed that a mobile and high-quality, immersive VR installation is feasable. Moreover, recently a mobile driving simulator has been prototyped [11].

For the SBG this marketing event was a big success, although the resonance was not as big as prognostized. As usual for marketing events, SBG did a questionaire along with the roadshow, but the results are not available to the authors. According to the SBG, especially the extensive media coverage accross Switzerland has strenghten significantly SBG's image of dealing with innovations and being known for new ideas off the beaten track. SBG spent about 250.000 SFR to enable this event [12].

7 Acknowledgements

We acknowledge our very ambitious and hard-working team (in alphabetical order): Peter Frisch, Torsten Fröhlich, Wolfram Kresse, Rolf Kruse, Stefan Müller, Uli Spierling, and Johannes Strassner. We are grateful to Werner Vieth for his permanent care of the projection system and to the truck driver Hans Scheidt for doing such a good job and sometimes even making impossible manouvers possible. We would like to thank the show masters Nicole Calame and "Rookie" D. Ruckstuhl for their great help. Our gratitude belongs to Stefan Merz from the agency Bosch & Butz, as well as to Simon Stauber and D. Zoppi from the SBG for having the roadshow idea, supporting it, and their believe in its success. Special thanks to Mike Sokolewicz for proof-reading. He is responsible for much of the readability and none of the faults.

References

1. Astheimer, P.: "What you see is what you hear - Acoustics applied to Virtual Worlds", Proc. of IEEE Symposium on Research Frontiers in Virtual Reality, San Jose, USA, October 1993, pp. 100 - 107

2. Astheimer, P., Dai, F., Felger, W., Göbel, M., Haase, H., Müller, S., Ziegler, R.: "Virtual Design II - an Advanced VR System for Industrial Applications", Proc. Virtual Reality World 95, Stuttgart, February 1995

3. Astheimer, P., Felger, W., Müller, S.: "Virtual Design - A Generic VR System for Industrial Applications", Computers & Graphics, Pergamon Press, vol. 17, no. 6, November 1993, pp. 671 - 677

4. Blinn, F.F.: Animation Tricks, Siggraph course notes no. 1, 1994

5. Cohen, M.: "Cybertokyo: A survey of public VRtractions", Presence 2(4), 1994

6. Dodsworth, C. et al.: Digital Illusion: Distributed Interactive Entertainment, Siggraph course notes no. 7, 1994

7. Felger, W.: "How interactive visualization can benefit from multidimensional input devices", In Proc. of SPIE/IS&T Symposium on Electronic Imaging Science and Technology, Conference 1668: Visual Data Interpretation (San Jose, USA, February 9-14) 1992

8. Felger, W.; Waehlert, A.: "Employment Potential and Application of Virtual Reality in the Domain of Business Management", Proc. of Virtual Reality World '95, Stuttgart, February 1995

9. Giles, W., Schroeder, R., Cleal, B.: "Virtual Reality and the Future of Interactive Games", Proc. VR '94, Stuttgart 1994

10. Helman, J. et al.: Designing Real-Time Graphics for Entertainment, Siggraph '94 course notes no. 14, 1994

11. Latham, R.: "Illusion Technologies REAL DRIVE Simulator", Real Time Graphics, Vol. 3, No. 4, 1994, pp. 1,3,14

12. N.N.: "Der Kunde im Wunderland", acquisa, August 1994, pp. 32-34 (in German)

Editor's Note: see Appendix, p. 301 f. for coloured figures of this paper

Improving the Legibility of Virtual Environments

Rob Ingram and Steve Benford

Department of Computer Science
The University of Nottingham
Nottingham, NG7 2RD, UK

Tel.: +44 602 514203
Email: s.benford, r.ingram @cs.nott.ac.uk
Fax: +44 602 514254
http://www.crg.cs.nott.ac.uk/

1. Introduction

Years of research into hyper-media systems have shown that finding one's way through large electronic information systems can be a difficult task. Our experiences with virtual reality suggest that users will also suffer from the commonly experienced "lost in hyper-space" problem when trying to navigate virtual environments.

The goal of this paper is to propose and demonstrate a technique which is currently under development with the aim of overcoming this problem. Our approach is based upon the concept of *legibility*, adapted from the discipline of city planning. The legibility of an urban environment refers to the ease with which its inhabitants can develop a cognitive map over a period of time and so orientate themselves within it and navigate through it [Lynch60]. Research into this topic since the 1960s has argued that, by carefully designing key features of urban environments planners can significantly influence their legibility.

We propose that these legibility features might be adapted and applied to the design of a wide variety of virtual environments and that, when combined with other navigational aids such as the trails, tours and signposts of the hyper-media world, might greatly enhance people's ability to navigate them. In particular, the primary role of legibility would be to help users to navigate more easily as a result of experiencing a world for some time (hence the idea of building a cognitive map). Thus, we would see our technique being of most benefit when applied to long term, persistent and slowly evolving virtual environments. Furthermore, we are particularly interested in the automatic application of legibility techniques to information visualisations as opposed to their relatively straight forward application to simulations of the real-word. Thus, a typical future application of our work might be in enhancing visualisations of large information systems such the World Wide Web.

Section 2 of this paper summarises the concept of legibility as used in the domain of city planning and introduces some of the key features that have been adapted and applied in our work. Section 3 then describes in detail the set of algorithms and techniques which are being developed for the automatic creation or enhancement of these features within virtual data spaces. Next, section 4 presents two example applications based on two different kinds of virtual data space. Finally, section 5 presents some initial reflections on this work and discusses the next steps in its evolution.

2. What is legibility?

Legibility, in the context of navigation and wayfinding, is a term which has been used for many years in the discipline of City Planning. Work on legibility in this area has been concerned with the way in which people are able to 'read' an environment and hence perform wayfinding tasks. In his book "The Image of the City" [Lynch60] Kevin Lynch defines the legibility of a city as: "...the ease with which its parts may be recognised and can be organised into a coherent pattern..." Here, Lynch is referring to the formation of a *cognitive map* within the persons mind [Passini92], a structure which is an internal representation of an environment which its inhabitants use as a reference when navigating to a destination. The Image of the City describes experiments carried out in a number of major US cities which show how the cognitive map is built up over time through experience of the city. The experiments involved obtaining information from long term inhabitants of the cities in the form of, for example, interviews, written descriptions of journeys through the city and drawn maps. By examining this data Lynch identified five major elements of urban landscapes which are identified by the inhabitants and used as the building blocks of the cognitive maps. These features are:

- **Landmarks.** Static and recognisable objects which can be used to give a sense of location and bearing
- **Districts.** Sections of the environment which have a distinct character which provides coherence, allowing the whole to be viewed as a single entity
- **Paths.** Major avenues of travel through the environment such as major roads or footpaths
- **Nodes.** Important points of interest along paths, e.g. road junctions or town squares
- **Edges.** Structures or features providing borders to districts or linear obstacles

3. Legibility techniques for virtual environments

The aim of ongoing research at Nottingham University is to apply the work described above not to real environments but to the artificial spaces of virtual reality systems. More specifically we are developing techniques to automatically construct the five legibility features in the abstract spaces produced by data visualisation systems such as database or document store visualisers. One of our main aims is to accomplish this with without requiring the users of the system to perform the placement of the features manually. Essentially the system should, wherever possible, identify and place the features using information available from the database and visualisation systems alone.

To do this we have constructed a prototype system called LEADS (LEgibility for Abstract Data Spaces) which is designed to provide a layer on top of existing visualisation systems and which performs the addition of legibility information to the space. LEADS acts on the position of data items provided by this underlying system, as well as accessing the raw data where necessary, to add and emphasise the objects which are used to improve the legibility of the environment.

LEADS is designed to be applied to spaces which satisfy three main criteria. They should: be persistent over relatively long periods of time; be relatively stable so that they evolve over their lifetime and are rarely disturbed by major upheavals in the database; be accessed repeatedly by a number of independent users. An example of a large space to which application of LEADS techniques might be appropriate is the WWW space, which is constantly evolving but which rarely undergoes global scale restructuring.

To place the legibility features LEADS uses districts as a starting point as this allows for a number of relatively simple techniques to be used to form the other features. Districts are areas of cities which are identified as a single unit because of some common theme which runs through the buildings contained within them. In a data space this idea maps onto clusters of items which have some sort of similarity to each other which they do not share with nearby items in the rest of the space. In order to identify districts within an arbitrary data space the LEADS system uses the technique of cluster analysis. In this area a number of algorithms have been developed to carry out just this task. For the initial prototype of the system we needed to identify one of these algorithms which would have a relative simple basis, making it easy and quick to implement, but which carried out the task effectively, and generally, enough to be able to identify natural clusters in a wide range of data without being too computationally expensive. The particular algorithm which was eventually chosen is Zhan's Minimum Spanning Tree Algorithm [Zhan71].

This clustering technique is basically a two stage process. In the first stage a minimum spanning tree of all the items in the space is formed using any well-known algorithm. This assumes that the space contains some sort of graph structure from which the spanning tree may be produced. Whether this occurs naturally depends on the type of space being visualised, for example a visualisation of a large computer network will necessarily contain a graph structure already but this is may not be the case with a representation of a document store. In such cases we would assume the space to be fully connected, with each item having a link to all others. This has an impact for the amount of computation required to form the tree but has not proved a major problem with the size of spaces examined so far. To form the minimum spanning tree all of the links must have a weight associated with them which is their value. In a space which already contains a network these values may already exist but where they do not it is necessary to compute some measure of the 'distance' between the data items. How this is carried out must depend on the contents of the database itself and the structure of the data items, and so cannot be determined in a general sense for all spaces. Comparison methods for different types of data have been developed in the area of cluster analysis and seem appropriate to be applied to this problem [Jain88].

The second stage of the clustering process involves walking through the spanning tree and comparing the length of the links with those nearby. If the link is found to be significantly larger than those nearby it is marked for elimination. This removal of links leaves a number of disconnected subtrees whose items will form the clusters. It is necessary to provide the algorithm with criteria with which to decide if a link should be eliminated. The system at the moment uses as its default measure criteria similar to those used by Zhan in the referenced paper, that a link should be eliminated if it is greater than 2.5 times the standard deviation of the average length of the neighbouring links *longer* than that average and also the overall length of the link is twice that of the average. Links used to form the average are those within two steps of the candidate edge. Every effort has been made to allow these values to be changed easily to adapt to different data spaces.

The requirements of landmarks are that they form stable reference points in areas of the space where they will be most useful. A number of methods of placing landmarks based on the district data were considered. The most simple solution would be to position the feature at the centre point of each district. Two possible values exist for this point, the geometric centre of the area and the centroid of the cluster based on the values of the data. The latter is a useful value to discover, being the mean point of all the data in the cluster and therefore in some respects being the value that most accurately represents the *character* of the cluster. It was felt however that this positioning may not be the most useful as it takes no real account of any local conditions or variations of the data. A second suggestion places landmarks at points where more than two districts intersect. This method was thought more useful as the landmarks will provide useful external references for observers within the clusters but again it does not really take account of the actual data nearby. The solution that was finally chosen was to find groups of three clusters which were mutually adjacent and compute their centroids. The landmark would be placed in the centre of the triangle formed by these centroids as is illustrated in Fig. 1. This has the advantage of providing useful external references but only where clusters are measurably adjacent, and therefore relatively dense.

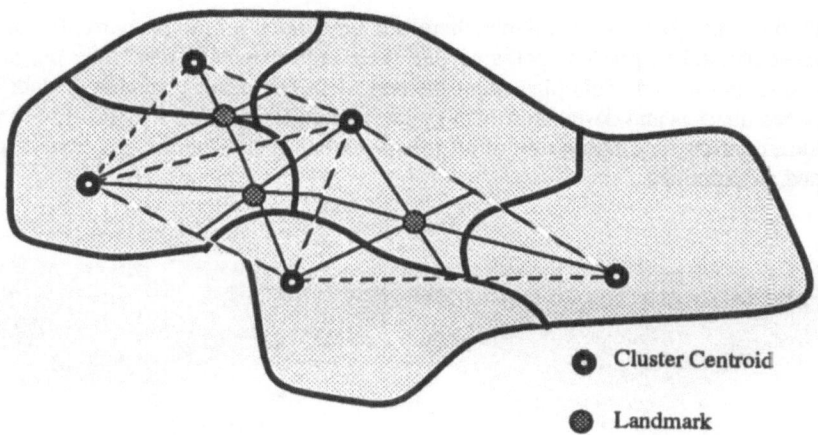

Fig.1. The Centroid Triangulation Method of positioning Landmarks

Edges in LEADS are structures which help to define the borders of districts. They are placed in the space between those districts which are 'significantly' large. The value of significance is currently defined in a simple manner as 'having more than a single entry' although this measure could easily be changed to some more complex criterion. Ideally, edges would be relatively complex surfaces which follow the shape of the edges of the clusters they divide. For the purposes of the initial prototype concept demonstrator of the system a simpler method was chosen where edges are placed between the nearest neighbours in adjacent clusters and aligned along the line that joins them. In most cases, especially where the clusters are essentially spherical, this results in an edge placement which effectively separates the space but does not cut into the individual districts.

Finally the system must place the path and node elements. These features are very strongly linked in the real world and so in the LEADS system they are co-dependant. The eventual aim is to develop method whereby the paths will evolve from the data space on the basis of the way in which the users interact with the database and move through the environment. This means that all access and modification of the database will be logged and this usage information used to form the paths, therefore placing these thoroughfares along the most accessed routes though the data. Nodes will be formed at the intersection of paths and at very well used items along them. From this it can be noted therefore that while paths form additional objects in the space the formation of nodes will be accomplished by enhancing or highlighting data items which already exist in the virtual environment.

This method of developing paths is not viable at the current stage of work and with the data sets now available therefore the initial prototype currently uses an interim method to produce paths so that their impact in the space may be, at least visually, considered. This placement method identifies nearest neighbour data items between districts and designates them as gateway nodes, placing a path between them. Within districts a spanning tree of all the nodes is produced and these edges are also added as path links.

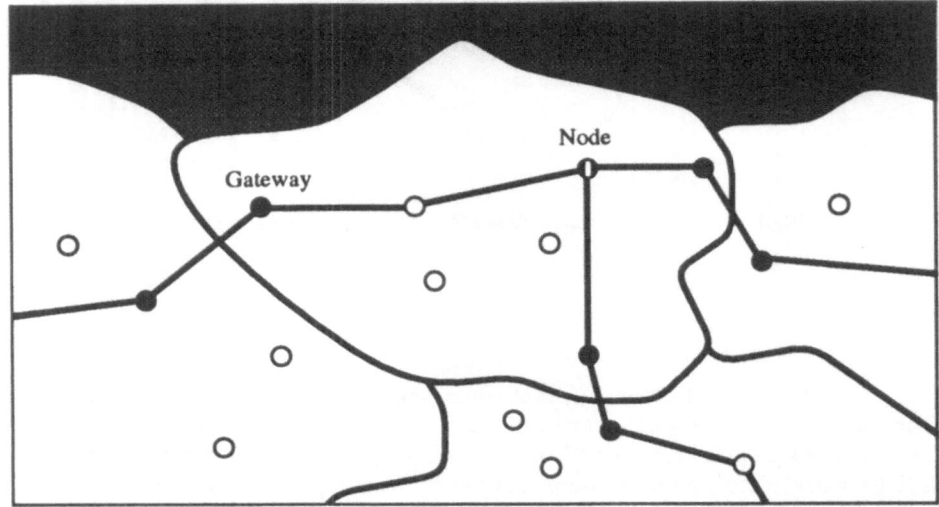

Fig.2.Paths joining four Districts

3.1 Other Navigation Devices

In addition to the legibility features LEADS also contains other devices to aid navigation which we will describe here briefly. In the field of city planning signposts are often considered to be something of an admission of failure [Canter84], that the planner was unable to produce a sufficiently legible environment, but we concur with the view of Passini that they are in fact a useful, even invaluable tool during wayfinding tasks. For this reason we are endeavouring to include signposts in our environments where possible. Currently these appear attached to the paths near to the node objects and identify the item to which the path leads but the use of signs will continue to be expanded as the system develops.

Another tool in the space is an optional axis object which floats near the occupant of the space and remains constantly aligned to the three major axes. The purpose of this object is to allow users to maintain bearing in spaces where there may be none of the references we are familiar with such as a horizon line. It is also planned to extend this object to become something like a 'portable sign' by annotating it with text to indicate interesting nearby objects in the direction in which the axes are pointing.

Finally, we wish to allow users to backtrack and move to interesting places by providing history mechanisms and the ability to store 'bookmarks' such as those widely used in hypertext systems.

4. Two example applications

We have so far applied LEADS to the visualisation produced by two existing information visualisation tools. The first of these, Q-PIT, is a system which works on databases where the items have a number of well defined fields [Benford94]. Three of these fields may be chosen so that the values they contain are mapped onto the three major axes of the space to give the position of the data items in a scatter-graph style layout. The remaining fields may be used to define aspects of the representation of the items such as their shape, colour or speed of rotation. This system could be used to visualise a variety of databases having the ability to map both numerical and string values to the axes and could provide a number of different visualisations of the same data by changing which fields are chosen to give the object positions. This gives the users of the system the ability to choose the visualisation which best represents their interest in the data. Q-PIT also allows multiple users to simultaneously access the data space and interact with the data. Any changes thus made to the underlying database are animated in real time in the visualisation.

The second system, FDP (Force Directed Positioning), is a 3D graph drawing tool. This takes a representation of an arbitrary network and produces a 3D visualisation by representing the nodes as masses and the links as springs. Initially the items will be placed randomly and the system will then go through a cycle of repositioning the nodes based on the tension in the springs until a relatively stable formation is found. Each link in the graph can be given a weight which will alter the way in which the tension value is calculated. This system also allows multiple users to enter the data space and query the values given to the nodes. Each user can therefore see which other people are interested in the data and on which items they are focusing their attention, which could potentially lead to interaction around a common subject.

LEADS attempts to enhance the legibility of both systems through the above techniques. Figure 3[1] shows before and after shots from Q-PIT. The data shown is around 120 items which represent people, having fields such as name, location, age and occupation. LEADS identifies a number of significant districts in the data as indicated by the different shapes (and colours) of objects and the presence of the edges and paths. One landmark is placed between a cluster of three districts. Figure 4 shows before and after shots from FDP where the space is a randomly generated test file of more than 200 simple nodes and unit weight links. The second image shows a close up of the intersection between two of the clusters found in this space and the edge that is

---

1. Because of the extensive use of colour in LEADS these plates can not fully demonstrate the effectiveness of the enhancement. We hope however that the do give some idea of the effect of the addition of legibility features.

placed between them.

5. Reflections

Our initial experiences of developing and testing LEADS have been largely positive and we suspect that this approach does have the potential to significantly improve the legibility of virtual environments. However, we have encountered a number of difficulties which suggest some immediate improvements to the system:

First, legibility features such as paths seem to sit uncomfortably with 6 degrees of freedom navigation. Paths in a city are actually travelled along and the environment is therefore experienced from the perspective of the path. We suspect that users of our legible virtual environments should also directly experience paths as part of navigation. Thus, we need to develop simple interface techniques to support navigation via paths (e.g. "take me along the nearest path in this direction").

Second, automatically determining an appropriate scale and appearance for legibility features has not always been easy. In particular, features such as landmarks and edges must be visible without being intrusive. Creating useful edges has proved to be a particularly difficult task as an edge should ideally follow the contours of a district. In a 3-D space, determining a sensible size for edges has been difficult. At one extreme an edge might be a hull completely surrounding a district. At the other it might be a thin flat surface dividing two districts. The former is likely to be visually intrusive; the latter is likely to provide an insufficient sense of separation between districts.

Third, other features and tools are clearly needed to help people navigate. For example, the use of textual information in the form of signposts is an important part of navigating conventional urban environments. We can imagine adding signposts to virtual environments and placing them at nodes pointing along paths. Furthermore, we can imagine that signposts might refer to districts and landmarks that lie along a path. However, this gives rise to the problem of how to name districts and landmarks. More specifically, given that districts and landmarks are automatically created by LEADS, we are left with the problem of automatic name generation or alternatively the use of non-textual symbolic identifiers on signposts.

Finally, we need to be careful that by adding additional objects to an information visualisation, we do not increase the rendering overhead thereby degrading system performance. However, we suspect some extensions to LEADs might enable it to actually improve system performance. Specifically, LEADS might enable a general distancing effect for data spaces by allowing the individual objects in a district to be replaced by an overall representation of the district when viewed from a distance.

6. Summary

We have described a number of general techniques for improving the legibility of virtual environments so that their users might more easily construct cognitive maps to help them navigate. Our work has adapted techniques from the discipline of city planning where decades of experience have identified key features of urban landscapes which are critical to their legibility. The primary goal of our work has been to develop a set of algorithms for *automatically* creating or enhancing these features within information visualisations. These include:

- the use of clustering algorithms to create districts;
- the creation of edge objects separating districts;
- the placement of landmark objects at a central point between districts;
- emphasising nearest neighbour node objects within districts and creating paths between them.

We have implemented these techniques in a system called LEADS which is intended to provide an additional legibility layer sitting on top of current information visualisations. So far, we have applied LEADS to two existing and contrasting information visualisation tools. Our paper included some before and after screen-shots to show the overall effect of LEADS on these systems.

Our early experiences have been positive and suggest that this approach is promising. However, we have encountered several difficulties including the need to experience paths when navigating; the difficulty of getting an appropriate scale for features such as edges and landmarks; and problems with automatically naming features so that they may be referred to by signposts.

Longer term work will include combining LEADS with larger scale, more widely used information sources (e.g. visualising the World Wide Web) and carrying out a more formal evaluation of our work. For the latter, we intend to revisit and adapt the initial experiments carried out by Lynch within real cities, but this time within virtual environments.

7. References

[Benford94] Steve Benford, John Bowers, Lennart Fahlén, Chris Greenhalgh, John Mariani and Tom Rodden, *Networked Virtual Reality and Co-operative Work*, Presence, MIT Press, (in press).

[Canter84] David Canter, Way-finding and Signposting: Pennance or Prosthesis, Nato Conference on Visual Presentation of Information, published as Information Design (Easterby and Zwaga eds.), Wiley, 1984

[Jain88] Anil K. Jain and Richard C. Dubes, *Algorithms For Clustering Data*, Prentice-Hall, 1988

[Lynch60] Kevin Lynch, *The Image of the City*, M.I.T. Press, 1960

[Passini92] Remedi Passini, *Wayfinding in Architecture*, Van Nostrand Reinhold, 1992

[Zahn71] Zahn, C.T., *Graph-theoretical Methods for Detecting and Describing Gestalt Clusters*, IEEE Transactions on Computers, C 20, 68-86

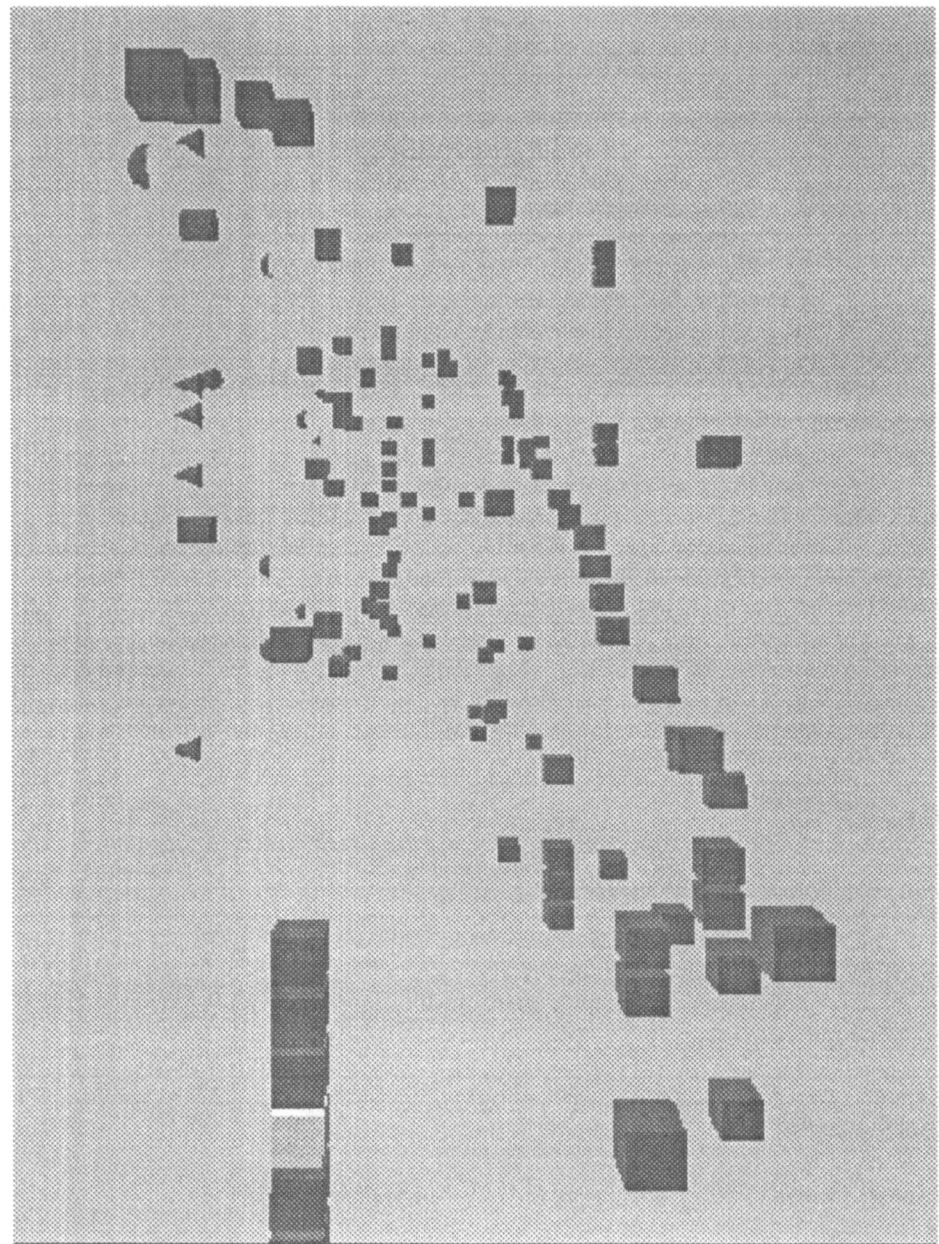

Fig.3(a). A space generated by Q-PIT, before application of LEADS

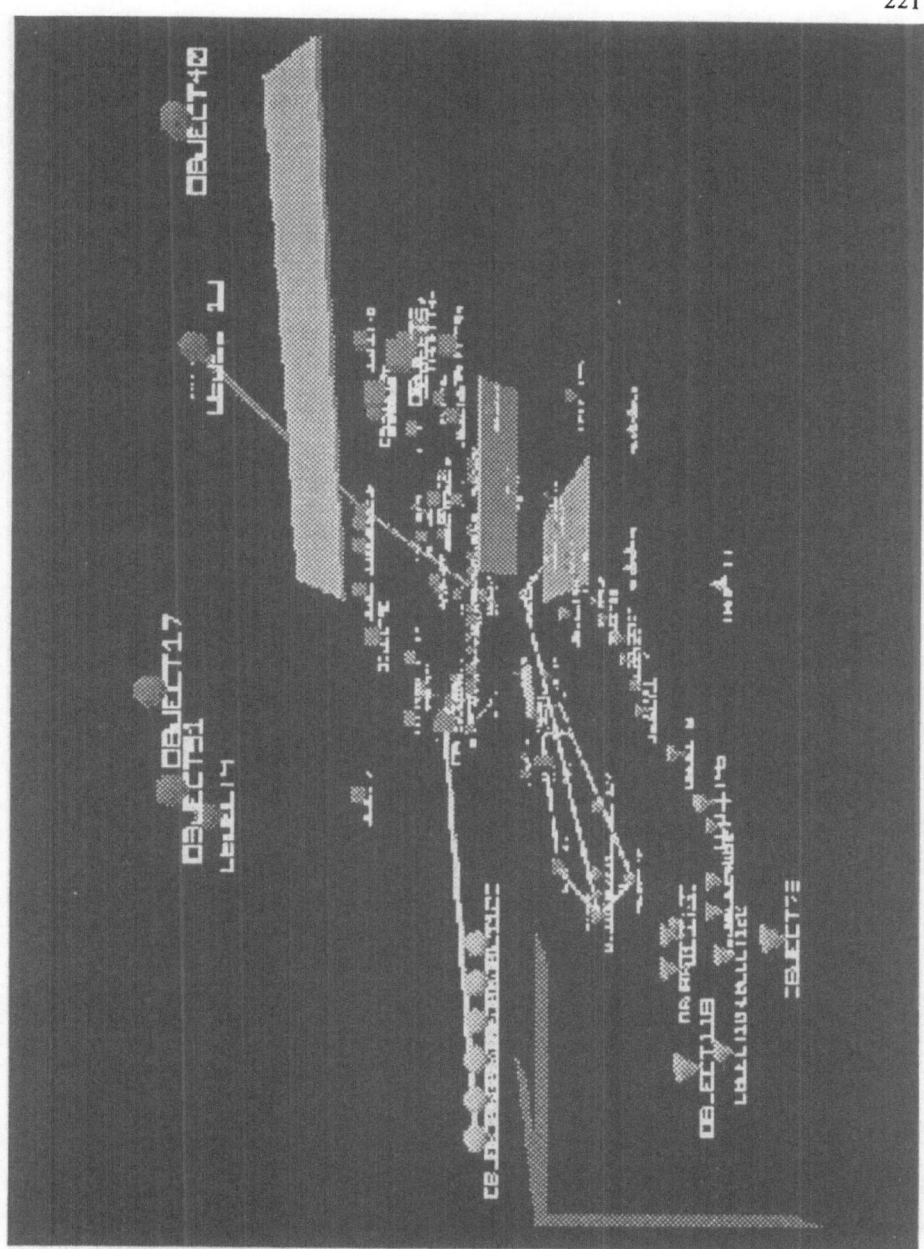

Fig.3(b). The same Q-PIT space after application of LEADS

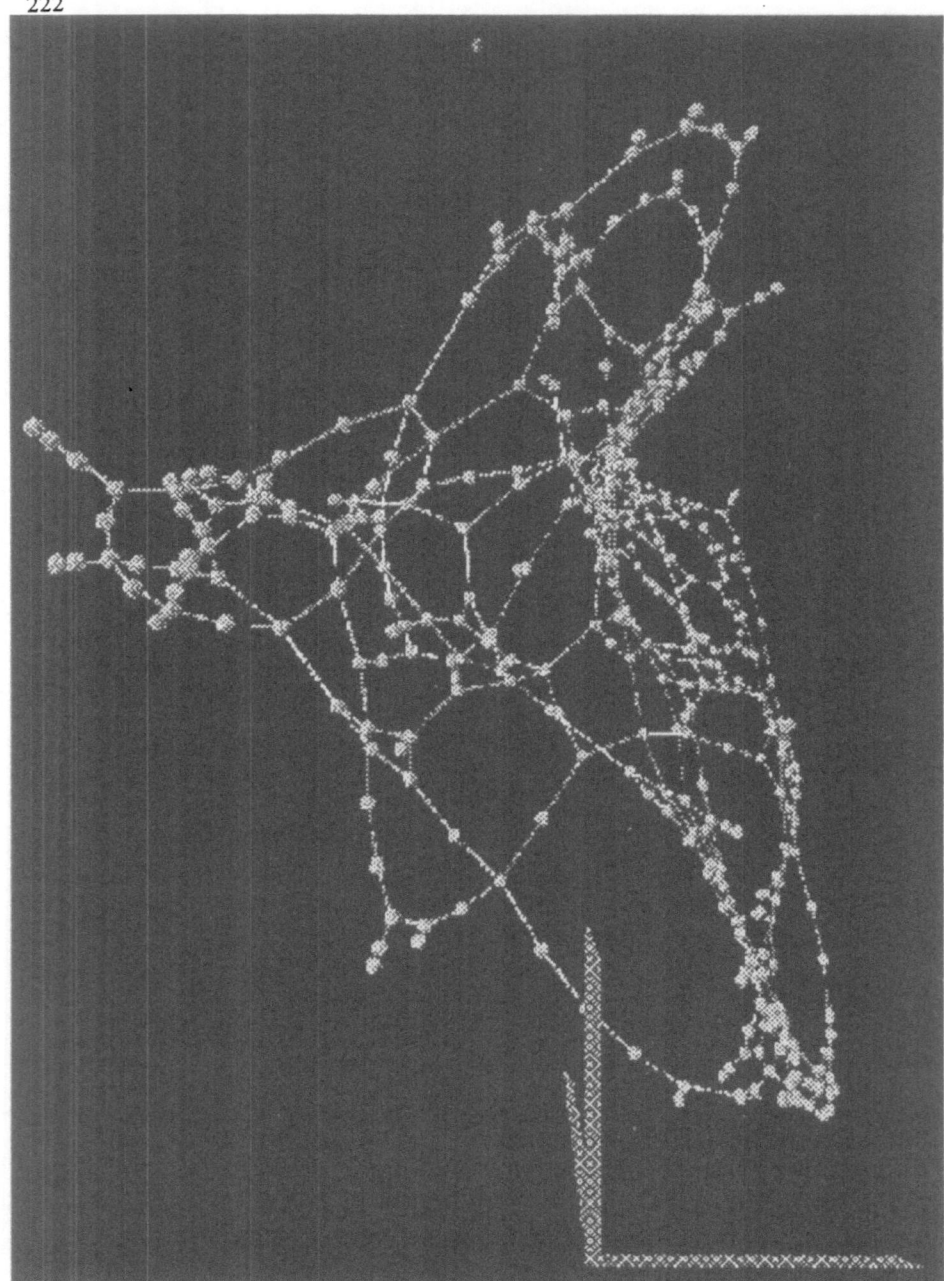

Fig.4(a). A space generated by FDP, before application of LEADS

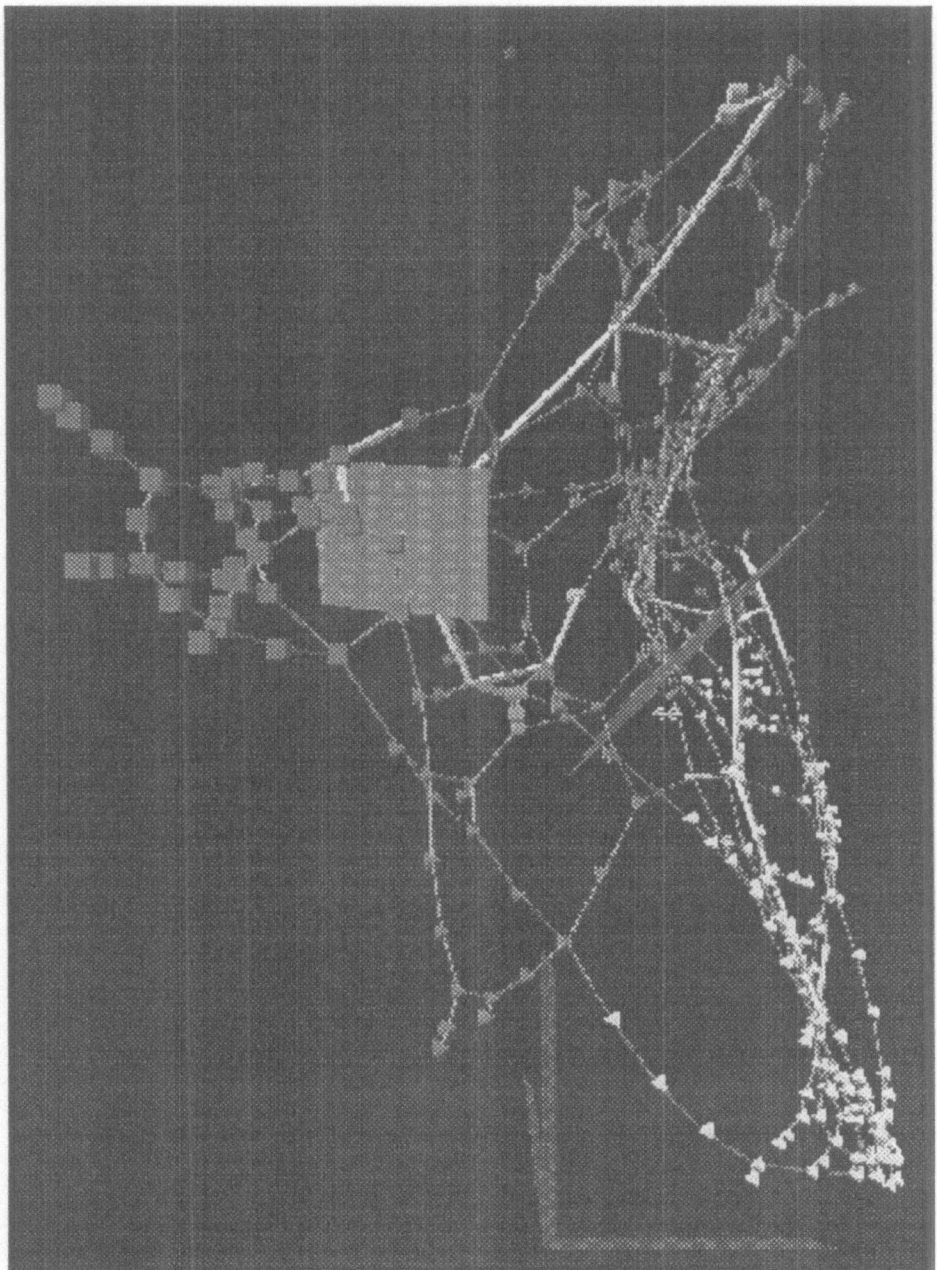

Fig.4(b). The same FDP space after application of LEADS

Design Issues for Virtual Reality Systems

Roger Hubbold, Alan Murta, Adrian West, Toby Howard

Advanced Interfaces Group
Department of Computer Science, University of Manchester
Oxford Road, Manchester M13 9PL, UK

Abstract

In this paper we describe a number of issues which are central to the design of a software architecture for a distributed, generic, virtual reality system. These include support for diverse and demanding applications, the management of time to provide high-quality interaction with tightly controlled closed-loop feedback, and the need for continuity of the experience presented to the user. These issues are being addressed in the design of a generic VR system called AVIARY.

1 Introduction

An interesting feature of VR is that it is not based on any fundamentally new technology. Input devices based on direct interaction, such as the light pen, joystick and mouse have been around for a long time. Similarly, displays capable of rendering 3D scenes have also existed for many years, and indeed these things have been routinely coupled in CAD packages, flight and military simulators, and computer graphics research laboratories.

What makes VR a radical approach to HCI is not the technology (although evolutionary progress has eased the task) but its application. It is a subtly new way of using established technology and techniques, but with dramatic implications for HCI.

The new feature that VR brings to the HCI scene is the removal of the computer as an object of perception, allowing the user to *interact directly* with the generated environment. Whilst technically similar to flight simulation, this is psychologically radically different as we are no longer looking into a window, but are actually in the environment. Although in its infancy, the potential for solving some of the thornier HCI problems, such as natural interaction with 3D objects, is clear.

Exciting though this all is, we are not there yet. Although the potential has been demonstrated, we are far from having a mature technology capable of dealing with the large scale use of VR for significant applications, with any degree of richness. Some issues are implementation-specific, others – to a far greater degree than in previous interfaces – belong to the realm of psychology and perception.

If we stand back and consider what is necessary to bridge the gap between the existing state of the art and a future mature technology, we begin to see the range of issues that is raised, and the nature of some of the interesting problems that must be addressed.

In the Advanced Interfaces Group at the University of Manchester we have been addressing this area. The prototype AVIARY system deals with some of the software architecture issues and is described elsewhere[1, 2, 3, 4]. In 1993 we established a VR laboratory in which to conduct experiments and to explore the application of VR techniques to real-world applications. Details can be found on the world-wide web at http://www.cs.man.ac.uk/aig/aig.html.

In this paper we raise some problems that we consider important, and which will need to be addressed if VR is to progress. Two particular threads can be distinguished: the importance of addressing human perceptual mechanisms, and the new perspective that VR brings to existing implementation issues.

1.1 Engaging perceptual mechanisms

In our everyday existence we cope with, and filter out, tremendous amounts of information almost effortlessly and with very little conscious thought. Indeed, if the same information, in all its detail, were to be presented in a form that we had to think about consciously, then we would be overwhelmed quite easily. Spatial awareness, pattern recognition, information filtering, coordination of multiple information streams, are things we take for granted. Rather than look for a solution in AI, part of the VR thesis is that information presented in a suitable way can be processed far more effectively and directly by people.

Traditional interfaces are suited to, and have largely relied on, human cognitive abilities with relatively low bandwidths between operator and machine. Interfaces that engage perceptual skills have potentially far higher bandwidth. Used in this way the machine marshalls and presents information, a task to which it is generally well-suited, and the operator's perceptual mechanisms filter and abstract behaviour of interest – a task to which they are well-suited. This information is then processed cognitively and acted upon. VR offers a means of engaging these perceptual skills far more directly and effectively than is generally offered by traditional screen-based interfaces.

One of the primary goals of VR research must be to discover how to engage human perception most effectively. The technological priorities may not be the obvious ones. For example, players soon adapt to quite unsophisticated graphics in some video games, and become deeply engaged in the scenario, provided certain levels of cues and interactions exist. Conversely, even good photo-realistic images fail to retain attention if there is little that can be done with them, or if the interaction lags are substantial.

The quality of an interface in these terms is notoriously difficult to quantify, or even to describe to others. Research can therefore all too easily become focussed on measurable issues such as frames per second, or number of primitives in the scene, which may ultimately be of only secondary importance.

For example, one issue that we regard as central to the success of large scale VR systems is that of coherency. We believe it is important that some degree of consistency is maintained between different virtual worlds and applications if users are to develop skills for inhabiting environments and navigating between them. Total consistency is neither practical or necessary, but what degree of coherency is required for users to perceptually orient themselves in the complex environment?

Engaging human perceptual skills and perceptual coherency are, we believe, keys to the success of VR.

1.2   A new solution space for old problems

A second feature that seems generally characteristic of VR issues is presented here in the form of an observation. Many of the problems involved in the implementation of a VR system are those of well-studied areas of computer science. This is most clearly true with computer graphics, parallel processing, discrete event simulation, multimedia and HCI. Whilst problems in these areas have been extensively studied, and certain tasks are known to be difficult, VR brings a sufficient perspective shift to allow us to seek new solutions to these problems. In this way the subtly different requirements of VR may help us to see beyond some of our current computational preoccupations, such as (for example) the emphasis on photo-realism in many areas of computer graphics.

VR also provides an opportunity to bring together techniques which have been developed for specialised applications, but have not as yet been integrated in a more general environment. Examples include different strategies for model culling and rendering, and synchronisation of simulation and interaction. These are discussed later in this paper.

With this background, we will now present some of the central issues with which we are concerned. These arise from our desire to construct a VR 'operating system' as a base for real applications. They range over the abstract and the concrete but are all real issues that we must address.

2 Generic or specific support – can they be reconciled for VR?

The goal of our research is the design of a generic VR system capable of supporting a diverse range of large-scale applications within a single, coherent environment.

The need for a general approach is highlighted by considering the wide range of disparate applications which may benefit from the integration of VR-style interfaces. Three-dimensional CAD packages, for example, may exploit novel VR input techniques for model building. Scientific visualization systems may be greatly enhanced by allowing the user to explore and manipulate complex data representations 'from within'. Other applications, such as air traffic control systems, or surgical training simulators, require a mix of 3D viewing capabilities coupled with unobtrusive means of interacting with real-time environments.

It is clearly not possible to build a single VR system that addresses all the requirements of these different applications. Instead what is required is a framework which takes advantage of common elements, such as techniques for 3D interaction, but allows the system to be customised for individual behaviour.

For a future, mature, general purpose VR system it will not be sufficient merely to provide a single world and an object-oriented environment, requiring users to tailor the class hierarchies for their own applications. Whilst this approach is useful in smaller systems, for more ambitious environments it is rather limited and difficult to manage. The diversity of applications for which VR seems appropriate suggests that a variety of world models are required[1]. It is not possible to provide all features within a single world, not only due to the contradictions that would ensue, but also because of the performance implications of such an approach. This is an interesting challenge to reconcile with the need for coherency of experience in the system as a whole.

2.1 The distinction between application and system

In considering a generic large scale environment of the future, one detailed issue that is raised is the distinction between the system and its applications. Exactly where does the boundary between application and system lie? This is much more clearly an issue if we consider multiple active applications within a single virtual world. Here, there is a direct analogy with operating system/application interfaces which have evolved over the last few decades.

Separating what is application from what is virtual world is not simply an academic exercise, as clear distinctions will be needed if the users' conceptual model of a complex system is also to be clear. In practice elegant distinctions of this kind tend to be compromised for all sorts of reasons, but there is no reason why a clean conceptual model should not be devised to which the system as a whole should aspire.

3 Perceptual consistency and display performance

Maintaining an illusion of a perceptually consistent world places quite stringent demands upon its implementation. Unless a system can respond rapidly and without distracting artifacts, the advantages of immersive environments may be unattainable. This area is complex, because consistency does not necessarily imply, for example, real-time behaviour for all tasks. More important is the creation of an environment in which the user remains comfortable and well oriented. In some cases this may demand real-time response, but in others it may be more important to maintain a sense of continuity[5]. We are used to dealing with a real world in which some actions may take a finite time to complete. Thus, when calling a lift, we do not necessarily expect that the lift will arrive instantaneously. On the other hand, the movement of objects attached directly to our hands, or the performance of head tracking, must occur in real-time if we are to maintain the illusion of reality.

Thus, a key issue for any immersive VR system is that of the 'closed loop' feedback time for tracking the user's movements – for both head and limbs[6]. Most low-cost VR systems are woefully inadequate in this respect, which is the primary reason that many VR demonstrations portray very simple models. Rapid feedback during navigation is central to the tight coupling of users' actions to the system's response. There are actually two separate factors which affect the closed loop response time: the rate at which pictures can be animated, and the rate at which inputs from the human participants can be decoded and acted upon.

Smooth animation. The simplest way to characterise the speed of animation is to count the number of frames per second required to create an illusion of continuous smooth motion, as users move through a world, or objects in the world move and change. This varies between individuals, but is generally at least 20. In practice, frame rates of less than 60 Hz may produce ghosting effects, whereby an observer sees multiple images of objects due to discrete changes in their positions. A classic example of this is to watch the telegraph poles in some of Silicon Graphics' simulations of driving a vehicle around a landscape. At less than 20 Hz the scenes appear as a series of separate frames, and the illusion of smooth motion is lost. At faster rates, such as 30 Hz, the frames merge to provide a smooth sequence, but the telegraph poles appear to be duplicated! Only at rates approaching 60 Hz does the motion appear completely smooth.

Sensor tracking. It is essential that inputs can be processed sufficiently rapidly to avoid delays between actions by users and the system responding accordingly. In slow systems it is possible to get completely out of synchronisation, so that the displayed image of a user's waving hand, for example, is completely out of phase with its true position. We will return to this point again in section 4.

Some researchers take the view that solving these problems is only a question of building faster hardware. However, if we are to build portable VR systems which work well with a range of applications, and on equipment which is cost effective – which means cheap, if VR is to be widely used – then we must examine the problem from a more fundamental viewpoint. We also need to take account of the characteristics of 'real' applications, which are often quite complex – support of these must be a central goal of our research.

3.1 Animation rates for high-performance workstations

To understand better the issue of scene complexity and its effect on animation, we have considered the rendering speeds of current high-performance 3D workstations, such as the Silicon Graphics VGXT and Reality Engine[7], and the Evans and Sutherland Freedom Graphics Series for Sun workstations[8]. The usual way manufacturers quote rendering performance is in terms of some number of notional triangles, quadrilaterals (or triangle or quadrilateral strips), with various shading options (flat, Gouraud, Phong etc.). Impressive rates, in the order of 1 million or more triangles per second can be achieved in theory. But for real applications, with all of the constraints which apply when designing and writing code – and here we exempt very special cases such as military simulators – rates in the order of 10% to 20% of the peak performance are more realistic. If we assume a speed of 200,000 triangles per second (i.e. 20%), and a minimum required frame rate of 20 Hz, then we must limit our model to at most 10,000 triangles.

Generous though this may sound, in many applications it is inadequate. In one application we are studying, 3D CAD models contain as many as 800,000 primitives[9, 10]. These primitives include shapes such as planes, boxes, cylinders, spheres, and cones. Some of these generate many polygons, taking us three orders of magnitude beyond the 10,000 triangle limit for a 20 Hz display rate. A relatively simple example is shown in Figure 1, which contains less than 2,000 primitives. The right-hand picture shows a closer view, in which the complexity of the primitives can be more readily appreciated. Even an optimised display algorithm can only achieve about 4 or 5 frames per second with this model on an SGI Crimson VGXT workstation. Although alternative algorithms exist for direct rendering of primitives such as quadrics (e.g. ray-casting), these are not supported in current display hardware, so that everything must be reduced to polygons. Curved surfaces, and even mathematically simple shapes such as spheres, eat up polygons at an alarming rate, dramatically reducing the complexity of models which can be displayed at adequate frame rates.

3.2 Culling and level of detail processing

One approach to this problem is to use tailored rendering techniques, so that only those parts of the model within the field of view are rendered, and only those close to the observer are shown in detail[1]. However, solutions to this are frequently specific to particular applications and to particular hardware platforms[14]. This issue is closely related

---

[1] Since the original version of this paper was presented, there have been several developments in the area of culling and level-of-detail algorithms. See[11, 12, 13] for example.

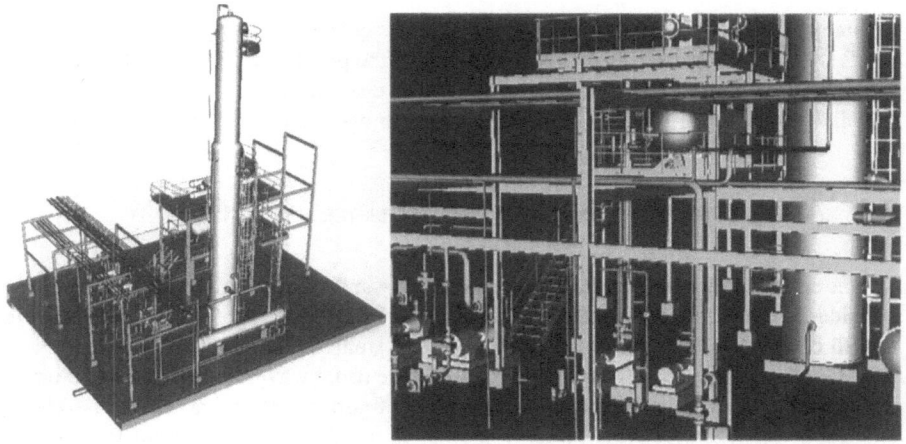

Figure 1: An overview and a zoomed view of a simple process plant

to the problem of hidden surface removal, and experience with this suggests that the use of application knowledge is a major factor in solving it effectively. For example:

- In an architectural walk-through, we can use knowledge of a building's layout to cull parts of the model which are known not to be visible from the current viewing position. Thus, if we know that the walls are solid, we need only display objects visible within the room, and perhaps a further subset visible through open doors or windows[15].

- In flight simulators it is common to employ a pre-processing step, based on binary space partition (BSP) trees and backface culling, in order to determine in a view-independent way those objects which are potentially visible from different view-points. Then, at runtime, only the subset of potentially visible objects requires processing, selected according to the real viewpoint[16, 17]. Additionally, levels of detail – usually applied as texture maps – can be made dependent on the distance of the observer from each surface. Mipmaps offer one way to introduce greater detail as the observer moves closer to a surface[18, 14].

- With finite element models, we can use connectivity information in the element data structures to quickly determine a subset of potentially visible element faces.

In each of these cases, we can use application-specific knowledge to provide an efficient solution, but these solutions cannot necessarily be applied in other situations. For example, in the case of an airport or terrain model, only a small part of the model will change between frames. This may not be the case for other applications, and the BSP pre-processing step is very time-consuming for models of any complexity. A general VR system must attempt to provide a framework for solving this problem in a flexible manner.

3.3   The influence of perceptual issues on rendering

Any solution which involves the selective display of information must strive to maintain a perceptually smooth transition between levels of detail. Objects which pop on and off a display can be highly distracting. Picture complexity is often viewpoint-dependent, so that turning one's head can produce very sudden changes in the quantity of data to be processed graphically. The characteristics of different hardware platforms may vary widely in this respect. If displays cannot deliver the required performance then methods are required which degrade gracefully. Even if display performance continues to improve dramatically, a solution for this problem will still be needed for the low-cost end of the market.

Factors other than mere speed are also important here. Many displays can draw 3D vectors faster than filled polygons, suggesting that during manipulation, or navigation, a wireframe mode may be used. Unfortunately, switching modes in this way can be unsettling for the user, and a wireframe view often results in considerable clutter for models of any complexity. Extensive testing will be required to establish the most effective ways of culling a model to achieve acceptable frame rates allied to consistent data presentation. Research into such techniques has been pursued for many years in the flight simulator market, but its application to a much wider range of tasks is still needed.

It is worth observing that it is not obvious what cues require optimising in order to create a convincing world. Anyone who has played a video game in an arcade will know that fast system response is a key element in engaging the player, and this can overcome limitations in the way information is presented. However, in other areas more faithful rendering of the scene may be required, an example being a surgical training system. It is clear that the *quantity* of information which can be displayed depends on the speed of the display system, but the choice of *what* to display will be application-dependent, and not necessarily based solely on distance from the observer.

4   Temporal consistency

The issues of frame rates and device input lag are examples of a more fundamental problem which a general-purpose VR system must solve, namely, the provision of a consistent framework for managing time in an environment where the goal is, at least, to effectively simulate real-time processing.

The determination of input sensor locations, the simulation of virtual world events and the generation of visual and other sensory representations all require finite amounts of time. As a result, input handling, simulation and rendering all occur within effectively different time-frames. This creates two problems: the skew in action and observation can be perceptually disturbing to the user[19], and the lack of a global frame of reference may impair the integrity of the world simulation.

One method which is currently used to tackle the cognitive skew problem is to use predictive algorithms to calculate the location and motion of input sensors at some small temporal offset in the future in order to bring sensor time in-step with simulation or rendering completion time[20]. This has been shown to be more acceptable to the human perceptual system, although the shortfalls of this method can become apparent when the user is drawn to the temporal discrepancies (by hand-clapping in the real and virtual world, for example). The only completely effective solution to this problem is to keep accumulated latencies below the minimum which can be perceived (around 25 msec for interactive tasks[21]), and this should become less of an issue as VR technologies improve.

The rational handling of time within a simulated environment is a more difficult issue. It is a problem which has been addressed many times in the computing field, in the context of electronic circuit simulations, event profiling in distributed systems, physical modelling, and so on. In many respects, the problem of temporal management in a VR system is more demanding, as solutions must be found in real-time. As a result, many of the computationally expensive solutions which are applied in other areas are inappropriate. However, some aspects of VR modelling may allow certain degrees of freedom with respect to event synchronisation, unlike related disciplines such as electronic simulation, which must adhere to strict rules of causality. Identifying where in the system such tolerances are allowed is an interesting research area.

A closely related issue is the maintenance of deterministic behaviour. Virtual interactions should behave consistently, whether they are carried out in real time, in slow motion, or on a platform incapable of the fine grained simulation of a more powerful system. The problems of synchronism may also have a fundamental effect on the meaning of user interactions. An example of this is a command such as 'delete this', where the command is uttered into a speech recognition system and the 'this' is indicated by pointing or touching an object in the virtual world.

The principles of synchronisation, latencies, and local time frames within a VR system must therefore be understood in order to devise coherent methodologies for time management which can deliver a conceptually consistent behaviour to the system users. Some groundwork in this area has already been undertaken in the multimedia field, in which time-augmented Petri nets are used to assess synchronisation problems in the delivery of multimedia presentations[22].

Many existing VR systems are somewhat restrictive in their support for temporal management, and simply coordinate events with respect to some specific aspect of the VR platform, such as frame delivery rates. We believe a better approach is to consider time as a completely independent resource, effectively using a time server to manage coordination, synchronisation and the rate of flow of time itself within the virtual world. This is a more general solution, since it allows greater flexibility in the handling of virtual time (allowing multiple rates of flow within the system, for example), and separates world behaviour from specific performance-related metrics imposed by the underlying hardware.

5 The AVIARY system

AVIARY is the generic VR support environment being developed by our group[1, 2]. This system provides a basis for us to explore many of the design issues addressed within this paper. The AVIARY system supports:

A hierarchical world model constructed using object-oriented methods. This permits the tailoring of new worlds by software re-use, and also provides a framework for the design of consistent techniques for interaction and presentation across a range of applications.

Multiple, concurrently active applications with well-defined interfaces to the virtual world manager, and between applications.

Platform independence. A prototype version of the system has been developed and executes on a 64-processor, transputer-based parallel machine, or alternatively on one or more networked Sun workstations. Ports to other platforms are currently in progress (see below).

Distributed processing. AVIARY was designed from the outset to operate in parallel and distributed environments. We believe the exploitation of concurrency to be an important research issue for a number of reasons. Firstly, virtual environments are inherently concurrent in nature, requiring the simultaneous processing of many different input, output, simulation and sensory rendering tasks. Secondly, such an approach allows us to tackle large-scale applications which would be considered unmanageable on uniprocessor systems. Another important factor is that the implementation issues of distributed synchronisation are closely tied to the problems of temporal management within virtual worlds; a research area which we are already addressing.

Distributed graphics processing. The need for high-performance means that dedicated graphics hardware is required. In order to minimise communication in a distributed environment we use retained mode graphics, with picture information held in a local display list (or structure) store. For example, the prototype AVIARY system uses PHIGS[23] for the graphics. This allows small changes, such as altering a viewpoint, to be communicated very efficiently, but runs counter to the direct mode graphics used by many workstations. To maintain platform independence, an internal graphics protocol is employed so that the system is not dependent on a specific graphics system.

In 1993 we established a VR laboratory, equipped with high-performance Silicon Graphics workstations and a complement of VR input and output devices including Eyegen-3 head-mounted display, Sharp large screen stereoscopic projection system, Division-Polhemus 3D input sensors, audio I/O, and speech recognition hardware. We are fortunate in having access to a 64-processor Kendall Square Research KSR1 – a parallel, virtual shared-memory computer[24]. This machine has 2 gigabytes of memory, an inter-processor communication speed of 1 gigabyte per second, and a theoretical peak computation rate of 2.4 gigaflops. This raw power is allowing us to explore computationally demanding applications such as scientific simulation and visualization, and medical imaging. The AVIARY environment will enable us to use the KSR1 for simulation and virtual world modelling, with input processing and rendering tasks being off-loaded to specialised equipment in the VR laboratory. The system as a whole will permit us to further develop the AVIARY prototype in its support for a range of 'real world' applications.

6 Conclusions

In this paper we have tried to show that building a generic VR system, which can support a broad range of applications, requires much more than software and hardware technology. Even today's most expensive displays are quite limited in the amount of information they can portray, at frame rates fast enough to create the illusion of a 'realistic', continuous world.

One of the major strengths of immersive environments is their capacity to engage their users' perceptual skills in solving problems. This involves a complex set of issues: it is the way that users perceive their environment which should determine the crucial performance measures for an implementation, and we should not blindly assume that just building faster hardware will provide the solutions to the problems. In any case, for many users ultra-fast hardware is simply too expensive.

Human beings are remarkably adaptable. An attraction of virtual environments is that we can suspend the 'real' world. Not only can we change our size – from the galactic to the microscopic – we can alter time, so that events move faster or slower. In effect, we can create slow-motion worlds, and replay events, so that we can study them in detail, and we can speed up time, as when carrying out simulations of phenomena such as the weather. The concept of time within a VR system is central to managing these problems, providing a framework for resolving the different time-bases involved in tracking user inputs, synchronising displayed images, and interfacing to simulations of various phenomena.

From a computer science perspective, the inherently concurrent nature of virtual worlds, and the issues of synchronisation and management of time, make parallel and distributed solutions to these problems an interesting topic for research.

Acknowledgements

Our CAD applications research is part of a collaborative project with CADCentre Ltd in Cambridge, England, whose enthusiasm and support for our work is gratefully acknowledged. Our large-screen stereoscopic projection system was supplied to us as part of a collaboration with Sharp Laboratories of Europe and we thank Dr David Ezra for his support. The AVIARY system was the result of a collaborative effort by our group; the prototype implementation of the system and many details of its design were the work of David Snowden, forming part of his Ph.D research.

References

[1] A.J. West, T.L.J. Howard, R.J. Hubbold, A.D. Murta, D.N. Snowdon, and D.A. Butler. AVIARY – A Generic Virtual Reality Interface for Real Applications. In R.A. Earnshaw, M.A. Gigante, and H. Jones, editors, *Virtual Reality Systems*, chapter 15, pages 213–236. Academic Press, March 1993.

[2] David N. Snowdon, Adrian J. West, and Toby L. J. Howard. Towards the Next Generation of Human-Computer Interface. In *Informatique'93: Interface to Real & Virtual Worlds*, pages 399–408, March 1993.

[3] D.N. Snowdon and A.J. West. AVIARY: Design Issues for Future Large-Scale Virtual Environments. *Presence*, 3(4):288–308, 1994.

[4] David N. Snowdon and Adrian J. West. The AVIARY VR System: A Prototype Implementation. In *6th ERCIM Workshop*, June 1994.

[5] George G. Robertson, Jock D. Mackinlay, and Stuart K. Card. Cone trees: Animated 3D visualizations of hierarchical information. *Communications of the ACM*, 34(2):189–194, February 1991.

[6] Roy S. Kalawsky. *The Science of Virtual Reality and Virtual Environments*. Addison-Wesley, 1993.

[7] Silicon Graphics Inc., 2011 N. Shoreline Boulevard, Mountain View, CA 94043, U.S.A. *Workstation Product Documentation*.

[8] Evans and Sutherland Design Systems Division, 580 Arapeen Drive, Salt Lake City, Utah 84108, U.S.A. *Freedom Graphics System*.

[9] CADCentre Ltd, High Cross, Madingley Road, Cambridge CB3 0HB. *PDMS, Piping Design Management System*.

[10] R.J. Hubbold and N.P. McPhater. The use of virtual reality for training process plant operatives. In *Proceedings of EPSRC Conference on Virtual Reality and Rapid Prototyping for Engineering (James A. Powell (Ed)), EPSRC Information Technology Awareness in Engineering, DRAL*, pages 31–41, January 1995.

[11] Seth J. Teller and Pat Hanrahan. Global visibility algorithms for illumination computations. In *Proc. ACM SIGGRAPH '93*, pages 239–246, August 1993.

[12] Seth J. Teller and Carlo H. Sequin. Visibility preprocessing for interactive walkthroughs. In *Proc. ACM SIGGRAPH '91*, pages 61–69, August 1991.

[13] John Rohlf and James Helman. IRIS performer: A high performance multiprocessing toolkit for real-time 3D graphics. In Andrew Glassner, editor, *Proceedings of SIGGRAPH '94 (Orlando, Florida, July 24–29, 1994)*, Computer Graphics Proceedings, Annual Conference Series, pages 381–395. ACM SIGGRAPH, ACM Press, July 1994. ISBN 0-89791-667-0.

[14] Silicon Graphics Inc., 2011 N. Shoreline Boulevard, Mountain View, CA 94043, U.S.A. *Iris Performer reference manual*.

[15] John M. Airey, John H. Rohlf, and Frederick P. Brooks Jr. Towards image realism with interactive update rates in complex virtual building environments. *ACM Computer Graphics*, 24(2):41–50, March 1990.

[16] I.E. Sutherland, R.F. Sproull, and R.A. Schumacker. A characterisation of ten hidden-surface algorithms. *ACM Computing Surveys*, 6(1):1–55, March 1974.

[17] Henry Fuchs. On visible surface generation by a priori tree structures. *ACM Computer Graphics*, 14(3):124–133, July 1980.

[18] Lance Williams. Pyramidal parametrics. *ACM Computer Graphics*, 17(3):1–11, July 1983.

[19] R. Held. Correlation and decorrelation between visual displays and motor output. In *Motion sickness, visual displays, and armoured vehicle design*. Aberdeen Proving Ground, Maryland, Ballistic Research Laboratory, 1990.

[20] Martin Friedmann, Thad Starner, and Alex Pentland. Device synchronization using an optimal linear filter. In R.A. Earnshaw, M.A. Gigante, and H. Jones, editors, *Virtual Reality Systems*, chapter 9, pages 119–132. Academic Press, March 1993.

[21] S.K. Card, T.P. Moran, and A. Newell. *The Psychology of Human-Computer Interaction*. Lawrence Erlbaum Associates, Publishers, Hillsdale, New Jersey, 1983.

[22] T. Little. Managing time in multimedia. In J. Rosenberg, editor, *SIGGRAPH '91 Panel Proceedings*. ACM, 1991.

[23] T.L.J. Howard, W.T. Hewitt, R.J. Hubbold, and K.M. Wyrwas. *A Practical Introduction to PHIGS and PHIGS PLUS*. Addison-Wesley, Wokingham, England, 1991.

[24] Steven Frank, Henry Burkhardt, and James Rothnie. The KSR1: bridging the gap between shared memory and MPPs. In *Proceedings of Compcon93*, pages 285–294, February 1993.

Further Development of the Responsive Workbench

Bernd Fröhlich, Berthold Kirsch, Wolfgang Krüger, Gerold Wesche

Dept. of Visualization and Media Systems Design
German National Research Center for Information Technology
D-53754 Sankt Augustin, Germany
http://www.gmd.de/
E-mail: bernd.froehlich@gmd.de

Abstract. The Responsive Workbench [8] is designed to support end users as scientists, engineers, physicians, and architects working on desks, workbenches, and tables with an adequate human-machine interface. Virtual objects are located on a real "workbench". The objects, displayed as computer generated stereoscopic images are projected onto the surface of a table. The participants operate within a non-immersive virtual environment. A "guide" uses the virtual environment while several observers can watch events by using shutter glasses. Depending on the application, various input and output modules have been integrated, such as motion, gesture and voice recognition systems which characterize the general trend away from the classical multimedia desktop interface.

The system is explained and evaluated in several applications: A virtual patient serves as an example for non-sequential medical training. The car industry benefits from areas like rapid prototyping for exterior design and interactive visualization and examination of flow field simulations (virtual windtunnel, mixing processes). Visualization and verification of experiments with mobile instrument deployment devices in outer space missions are another fascinating application. Architecture and landscape design are another discipline well suited for the workbench environment.

1 Motivation

The standard metaphor for human-computer interaction arose from the daily experience of a white-collar office worker. For the last 20 years desktop systems have been enhanced more and more, providing tools such as line and raster graphics, WIMP(Window Icon Mouse Pointer) graphical user interfaces and advanced multimedia extensions. With the advent of immersive virtual environments the user finally arrived in a 3D space. Walkthrough experiences, manipulation of virtual objects, and meetings with synthesized collaborators have been proposed as special human-computer interfaces for the scientific visualization process. Specific interfaces, originally developed for pilots and telepresence tasks, became available to the ordinary user (see [7], for example).

The dream of the ultimate medium, which uses all channels of human perception, has guided the efforts of user interface design towards these virtual reality systems. Unfortunately, head-mounted displays, body-tracking suits, and force-feedback exoskeletons are obstrusive. These systems separate the users from each other. Especially in scientific visualization applications, comprehensive attempts have been made to overcome these drawbacks. The BOOM systems allow for easy-to-use walkthrough and object manipulation experiences [3]. The surround-screen projection-based virtual environment CAVE [2] was designed for several users to become immersed with their whole body in a virtual space.

All these approaches to future user interface systems have one point in common: design of an (almost) universal interface based on the most advanced computer and display technology available.

Another approach to the design problem for future human-computer interfaces is rigorously centered on the users's point of view. Myron Krueger pioneered this attempt with his work on non-immersive responsive environments [7]. Application-oriented visualization environments have been proposed and built to support a specific problem-solving process. The computer acts as an intelligent server in the background providing necessary information across multi-sensory interaction channels (see [4], [10], for example).

We developed the Responsive Workbench concept, first described in [8], as an alternative model to the multimedia and virtual reality systems of the past decade. Analyzing the daily working situation of such different computer users as scientists, architects, pilots, physicians, and professional people in travel agencies and at ticket counters, we recognized that there is only small acceptance of a simulation of working worlds in a desktop environment. Generally, users want to focus on their tasks rather than on operating the computer. Future computer systems should use and adapt to the rich human living and working environments, becoming part of a responsive environment.

2 System description

During the analysis of the working environment and of the behaviour of the specialists, we recognized that the (cooperative) tasks of this class of users relies on a "workbench" scenario. The future impact of desk-like user interfaces in general has been discussed in [9]. Using a beamer, a large mirror and a special glass plate as table top, we built an appropriate virtual environment.

Virtual objects and control tools are located on a real "workbench" (see Figure 1). The objects, displayed as computer generated stereoscopic images, are projected onto the surface of the workbench. The projection parameters are tuned such that the virtual objects appear above the table. Depending on the application, various input and output modules can be integrated, such as motion, gesture and speech recognition systems. A responsive environment, consisting of powerful graphics workstations, tracking systems, cameras, projectors and microphones, replaces the traditional multimedia desktop workstation.

The most important and natural manipulation tool for virtual environments is the user's hand. Our environment depends on the real hand, not a computer-generated representation. The user wears a data glove with a Polhemus sensor

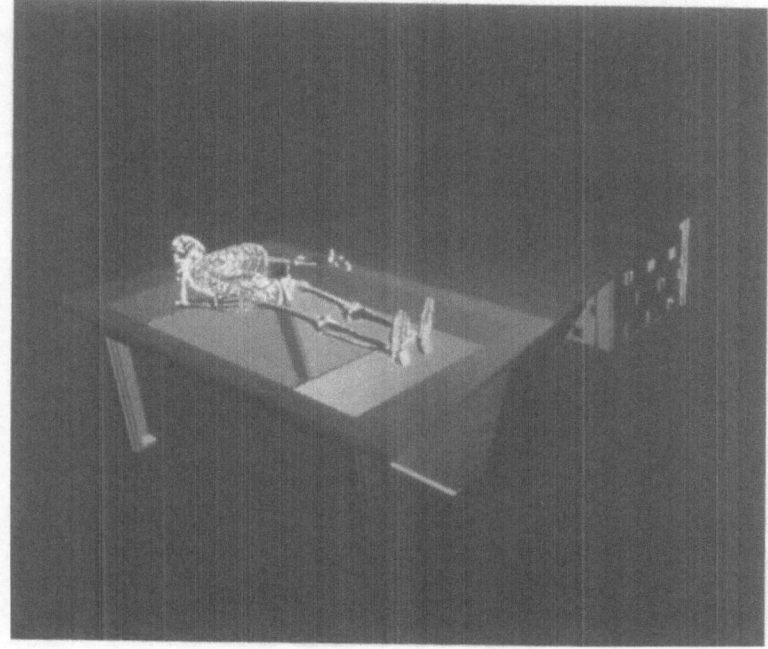

Figure 1: Set-up for a stereoscopic display of virtual objects

mounted on the back. Gesture recognition and collision detection algorithms, based on glove and Polhemus data, compute the user's interaction with the virtual world objects.

To get correct stereoscopic rendering from any location around the workbench the system must keep track of the guide's eye positions. We realized this by mounting a Polhemus sensor on the side of the shutter glasses. It delivers position and orientation data for the head, allowing the system to calculate the position of each eye. Additional collaborateurs see the stereoscopic images with only slight distortions as long as they stay close to the guide.

The Responsive Workbench setup generates a very effective 3D impression which is due to the negative parallax, the wide angle of view and the head tracking. None of the users suffered from motion sickness using the workbench which happens often with head mounted displays. This seems due to the non-immersive nature of our approach. People still have fix points in their environment so their senses don't get irritated.

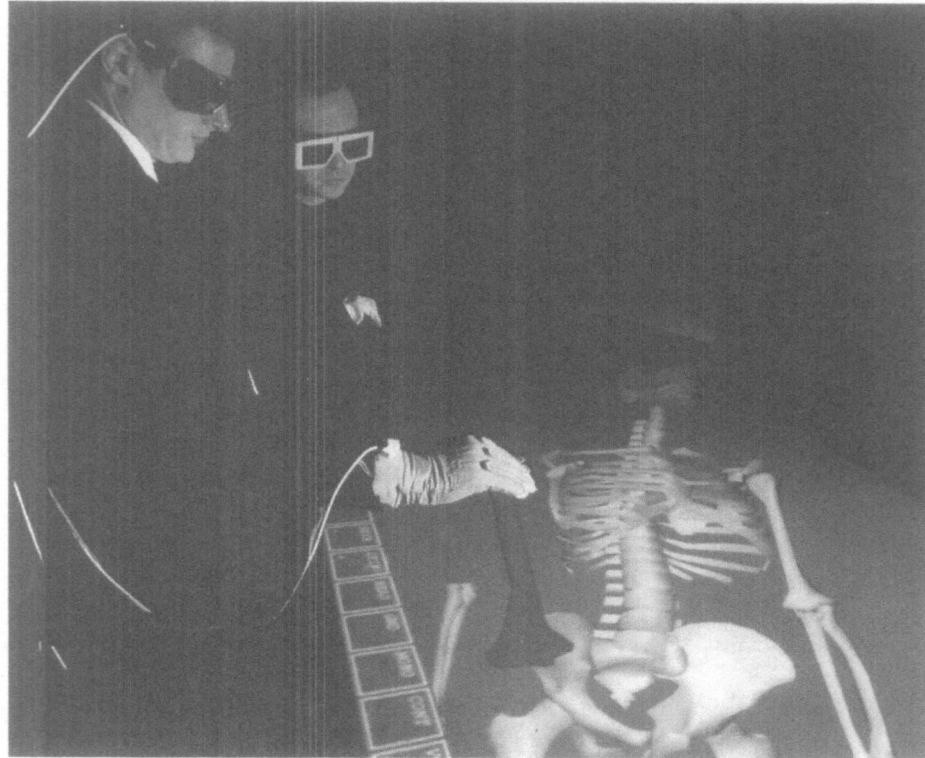

Figure 2: Cooperative work of a physician and a student

3 Applications

Based on current research projects in the field of computer graphics, human computer interfaces and visualization, the following applications have been embedded in this new type of environment following the suggestions of the involved end users.

3.1 Medicine

Nonsequential training This scenario is based on a real sized model of a patient. Figure 2 shows the model in a teacher/student scenario. The patient's skin can become transparent, making the arrangement of the bones visible. Now the surgeon or student can pick up a bone with the data glove and examine its joints, or take a closer look at the bone itself. The virtual patient could be examined in any detail through the zoom operation. Covered parts could be set free by removing the obscuring bones or organs with the hand or by making them transparent. Especially important for the understanding of many processes inside the human body are their dynamic aspects. We implemented two primary cases: the spatially exact reconstruction of the beating heart and the blood flow inside the transparent heart.

Simulation system for ultrasound heart examinations This research project has been developed in close cooperation with the Center for Pediatry of the University of Bonn, Department for Cardiology, Germany. A typical user team is made from a radiologist, a surgeon and a visualization specialist.

Originally, the project was designed on a multimedia workstation. Recently we started to implement the system on the Responsive Workbench to meet the requirements of the surgeons for a virtual environment. They want to see the organ of interest and the measurement process in real or magnified size from all points of view in 3D space. They also would like to compare the simulation with the images on TV screens originating from the scanning process.

Detailed visualizations of the beating heart can be explored as interactive animations. The user can rotate the model in order to examine the structural and dynamic features of the heart. Different visualization modes (i.e., transparent, with/without blood circulation) are available. The complex interior structures and dynamics of the heart, valves, and blood can thus be examined (see Figure 3).

3.2 Architecture and design

For the design and discussion process in architecture, landscape and environmental planning we implemented a basic testbed for demonstrations.

An architectural model is shown on the workbench, in our case the area around the buildings of our research institute. In front of the table two architects discuss the model, moving around buildings or other objects, such as trees in the virtual world. Additionally, lightsources can be set by the data glove to simulate different times of the day.

3.3 Automotive industry

In cooperation with scientists and engineers of the research department of Daimler-Benz AG, Stuttgart, we implemented two applications concerned with fluid dynamic simulations on supercomputers.

Virtual windtunnel This application realizes the virtual windtunnel scenario [1] (see Figure 4) in the Responsive Workbench setting. The simulation data is taken from a finite element program running on a supercomputer or a highend workstation. In a preprocess the data points from the finite element mesh are resampled to a regular grid to speed up particle tracing. Particle tracing directly on finite element meshes is more accurate, but the additional computational cost restrict the number of particles, which could be handled simultaneously. The geometry data is also extracted from the finite element mesh and somewhat

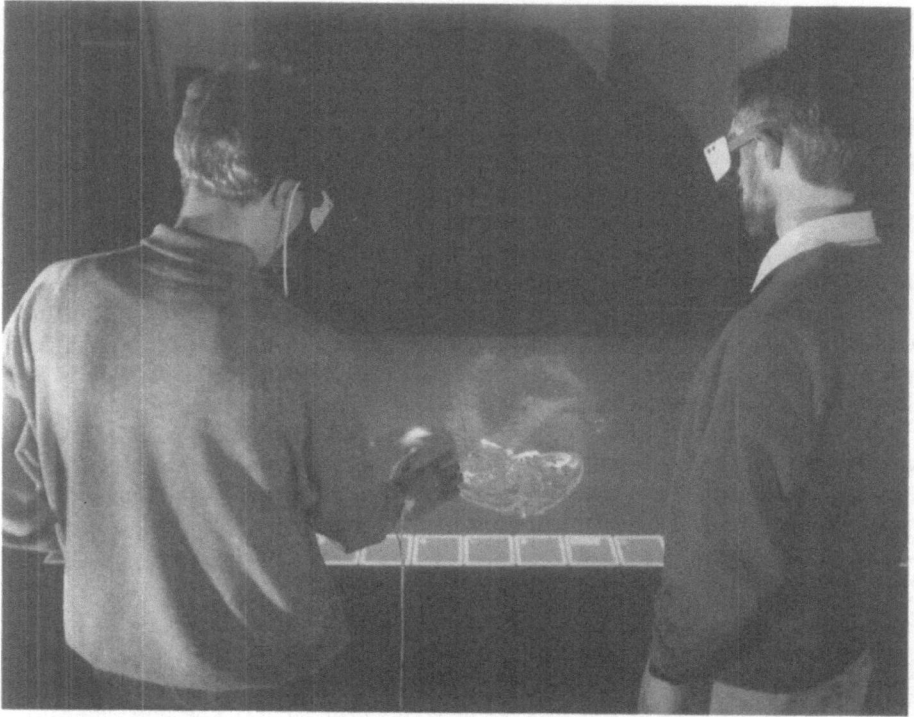

Figure 3: Examination of the blood flow in a human heart

polished by a modeling system, e.g. by adding textures. A few precomputed streamlines are added as an overview of the flow field.

The stylus serves as a particle injector to examine any area around the car in detail. The particle generation rate and their lifetimes are adjustable. The velocity values of the flowfield are globally scalable even if this is physically not realistic.

Mixing process The dynamics of the mixing process, generated by a super-computer simulation, are visualized with the aid of fluid particles as rendering primitives. The essential physical properties to be visualized are the velocity field, pressure, temperature and fuel distribution. The mixing process is strongly time-dependent, so the data rate is much higher. The visualization shows the particle flow with color coded temperature during the injection process. These particle paths are precomputed during the finite volume simulation. The current implementation focusses on the interactive real-time exploration of the temperature and pressure distribution inside the cylinder with arbitrary cutting planes. The cutting plane is attached to the stylus which allows easy positioning. The finite element data is again converted to a regular grid, which serves as a 3D texture

**Figure 4: Virtual windtunnel scenario for car manufacturing applications
(aerodynamical study model ASMO-II)**

on the SGI Reality Engine 2 rendering system.

3.4 Simulation and control of outer space experiments

In cooperation with Deutsche Forschungsanstalt für Luft- und Raumfahrt e.V.
(DLR) and other partners a mobile instrument deployment device prototype
(IDD) will be developed.

A mobile IDD is a small microroboter for positioning of instruments on Mars
or other space bodies to explore the near vicinity of the landing location. It is
not possible to test the IDD under martian conditions or to control it on Mars
directly. The first project stage studies the possible walking styles of an IDD
and identifies the necessary data for a precise simulation of its behaviour. In
a later stage the Responsive Workbench is meant to display remotely sensed
terrain data including the position of the IDD and the lander for simulation and
planning of experiments.

An IDD prototype vehicle has been developed by Transmash, St. Petersburg.
It consists of three container segments which are coupled by two traverses. In
its smallest position the size of the IDD is about 35x20x7 cm. The IDD moves

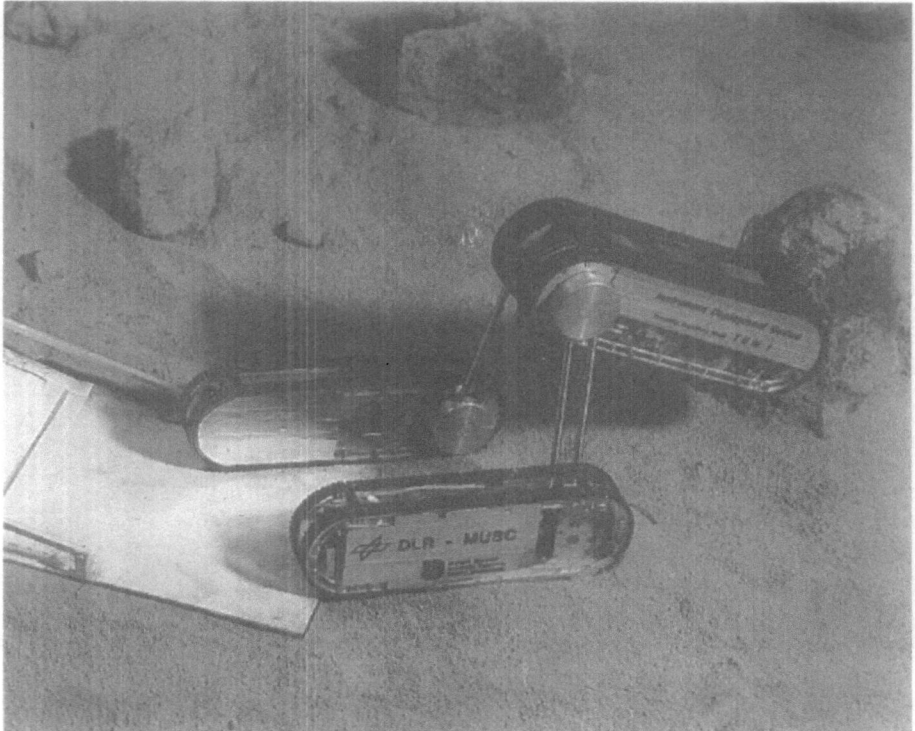

Figure 5: IDD TEM1 implemented by DLR and Uni Duisburg

by rotation of the container segments which hold the instruments. The IDD has been further developed by DLR and the University of Duisburg (see Figure 5). Dynamics and kinematics are simulated using "MOBILE" [5], a multibody modeling system.

A computer controlled crawling or walking style can be developed in the Responsive Workbench environment. The main problems are: which moving styles are possible, which information (input sensors) is needed to control speed, direction and walking style or to program autonomous movement (reaction on obstacles, keep a given direction etc.) of the IDD robot [6].

Following the successful simulation of a save walking (crawling) path in the virtual environment at the ground station, the driving code is sent to the IDD operating on an other planet. Data measured by the IDD and the lander will e sent back to calculate the next steps and to update the visualization. This control loop is necessary to syncronize the remote and the virtual environment.

Typical operating sequences for an IDD are the approach to a preselected site, appropriate positioning of the instruments at the object, preparation of the object for measurements, measurement procedure, aquisation of a surface sample and analysis, digging to acquire a sub-surface sample and analyse it,

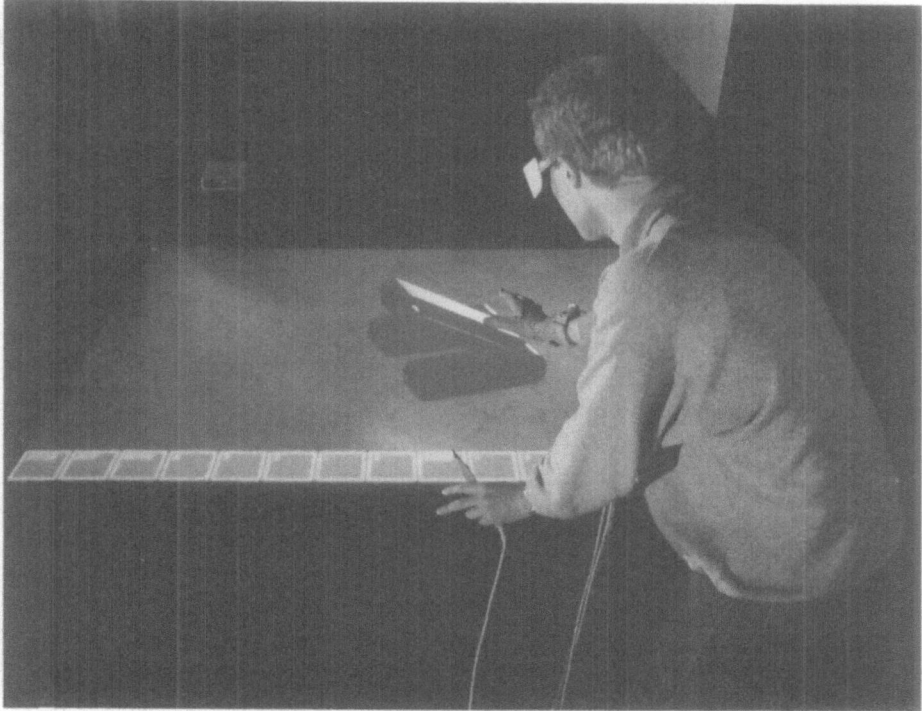

Figure 6: The computer model of the IDD

return material to the lander for further analysis, provide additional information for the selection of the next site.

The operating sequences are prepared and tested in the virtual environment. The lander station sends its data to the ground station. These data is used to construct the actual virtual world where the scientist acts. The scientist decides on the next action, teaches the new goal by i.e. pointing to the target site and runs the experiment within the virtual world. If the experiment has been successful the appropriate commands are sent to IDD on the planet. When the new situation on the planet has been incorporated into the virtual world the next sequence can start.

4 Conclusions

The Responsive Workbench system is designed to demonstrate the ideas and power of future cooperative responsive environments. Further applications under consideration running on this virtual workbench will be the simulation of air and ground traffic on airports, a training environment for complicated mechanical tasks, e.g., taking apart a machine for repair, landscape design and environmental studies via terrain modeling, and physically based modeling of virtual objects ("virtual clay"). These applications also rely on the workbench metaphor, but require specific interaction and I/O tools.

5 Acknowledgments

This work relies on the discussion with scientists and engineers of the research department of Daimler-Benz AG, Stuttgart, and physicians of the Centre for Pediatry of the University of Bonn. Especially, we are grateful to Prof. Redel for his involvement in this new field.

We thank our colleagues and students Stefan Banse, Manfred Berndtgen, Thorsten Fox, Klaus-Jürgen Quast, Peter Rohleder, Thomas Sikora, Josef Speier, Wolfgang Strauss, Jürgen Wind and Jürgen Ziehm for their extraordinary involvement in SW/HW management and modeling.

This work is partly supported by the Department of Research and Technology (BMFT) and the European Space Research and Technology Centre (ESTEC).

References

1. S. Bryson, C. Levit: The Virtual Windtunnel. *IEEE CG&A '93*, July 1992, 128–137
2. T.A. De Fanti, D.J. Saudi, C. Cruz-Neira: A Room with a View. *IEEE Spectrum*, Oct. 1993, 30–33
3. I.E. Dowall, M. Bolas, S. Pieper, Fisher, J. Humphries: Implementation and Integration of a Counterbalanced CRT-based Stereoscopic Display for Interactive Viewpoint Control in Virtual Environment Applications. *Proc. SPIE* 1256
4. M. Green, R. Jacob: SIGGRAPH '90 Workshop Report: Software Architectures and Metaphors for Non-WIMP User Interfaces. *Computer Graphics*, July 1991, 229–235
5. A. Kecskemethy: MOBILE User's Guide and Reference Manual. Fachgebiet Mechatronik, Universität Duisburg, 1993
6. B. Kirsch, U. Schnepf, I. Wachsmuth: RoboVis - a Scenario for Using Virtual Reality Techniques in Learning Robot Development. *VISWIZ Report 4*, GMD, 1993
7. M. Krueger: Artificial Reality II. *Addison-Wesley*, Reading, Massachusetts, 1991
8. W. Krüger, B. Fröhlich: The Responsive Workbench. *IEEE Computer Graphics and Applications*, May 1994, 12–15
9. W. Newman, P. Wellner: A Desk Supported Computer-based Interacting with Paper Documents. *Proc. of ACM SIGCHI*, May 1992, 587–592
10. J. Nielson: Noncommand User Interfaces. *Communications of the ACM* 36, No. 4, (April 1993), 82–99

This article was processed using the LaTeX macro package with LLNCS style

Editor's Note: see Appendix, p. 303 ff. for coloured figures of this paper

Virtual Design II -
an advanced VR development environment

Peter Astheimer, Martin Göbel

Fraunhofer-Institute for Computer Graphics (IGD)
Wilhelminenstr. 7, 64283 Darmstadt, Germany
phone: ++49 6151 155 121, fax: ++49 6151 155 199
email: (astheime,goebel)@igd.fhg.de

Abstract. This paper presents an overview of virtual reality system technology and its application within the Fraunhofer Demonstration Centre for VR. The Virtual Design II development environment including various pre-processing and editing tools is introduced and its benefit for the realization of efficient and high-quality virtual worlds is highlighted. A broad range of applications realized with Virtual Design II demonstrate the usability of virtual reality technology, which enables new dimensions in computer-supported applications.

Keywords. Virtual reality, acoustic simulation, photorealism, radiosity, virtual prototyping, scientific visualization.

1 Introduction

Virtual environments (VEs) (also called virtual reality (VR) or cyberspace) are regarded as one significant step forward in man machine communication. Following non-interactive, command-driven and graphical-interactive sytems, virtual environments now allow an easy-to-understand presentation and more intuitive interaction with data. The computer internal worlds, consisting of data and processes, represent various aspects of a natural environment or even a totally artificial world outside any human experience. The main building blocks of virtual environments - presentation, interaction, and simulation [1] - require realtime performance. The integration of visual, auditory and other stimuli are evidently needed in future man machine interaction.

The first generation of peripherals and systems for building Virtual Environments like gloves, helmets, and commercial software packages are already widely available. Many applications [2] - not only architectural design - are going to use and evaluate available VE tools. As the accuracy, usability, and effectiveness of this new technology are still insufficient, many application requirements are adjusted according to the capabilities of VE components. Research activities [3,4] aim to overcome the limitations and to improve the acceptance of VE techniques. New paradigms in computer-supported human communication are under development.

To foster the badly needed applied research a strategic initiative of the Fraunhofer Society was launched, which established demonstration centres for virtual reality in three different institutes [10], including the IGD. These demonstration sites are fairly well equipped with VE devices and high end graphics workstations, and provide consultancy in VEs and integration of VEs in industrial applications in cooperation with small and medium size companies.

Virtual environments are defined as realtime interactive graphics with three-dimensional models, when combined with display technology that gives the user immersion in the model world and direct manipulation [11]. When he can not decide, whether the world he is in is real or fake, the virtual environment successfully imitates reality (modified turing test). This definition comprises not only purely computer-generated worlds but also all kinds of simulators, e.g. the arthroscopic training simulator of IGD which will be discussed later. The availability of VE techniques has initiated discussions about the benefits and impacts of VEs for different application areas and led worldwide to many experiments on VEs in these areas.

Many available tools developed in the CAD and animation area are not directly applicable for VR purposes, because they neglect the realtime requirement. Out of this reason a virtual environment development system has to comprise its own tools with dedicated functionality or which pre-/postprocess data produced of other systems.

In this paper the rationales and goals of the Fraunhofer Demonstration Centre for Virtual Reality/Virtual Environments is presented and the hard- and software system installation of the Demonstration Centre in Darmstadt (Germany) is explained. Finally we introduce to various projects carried out within the Demonstration Centre in different application areas.

2 Demonstration Centre

In the beginning of the nineties, virtual reality was regarded to be more a toy than a tool. The use of new, but today well known virtual reality peripherals, the head mounted diplays and gloves, in the entertainment business has established this image. Press article and TV contributions on 'cyberspace' reported on virtual worlds as compute, generated alternatives to the real world. This created more a fascination about the new possibilities with virtual reality technology and supported science fiction impression more than providing information. The social impacts of virtual reality were discussed and critisized very intensively even before first results were available from scientific-technical research and development work.

2.1 Organization and Services

This situation has launched the VR Demonstration Centre initiative of the Fraunhofer Gesellschaft in Germany, one of the biggest research organizations carrying out applied research with industry. The project has started 1993 for a period of 5 years.

The Demonstration Centre for Virtual Reality has been established in Germany at four research institutes from different application areas. Each institute participates in this overall project with a local technology and competence centre presenting VR devices, systems and applications. The institutes involved are IAO (Institute for Industrial Engineering), IBP (Institute for Building Physics), IGD (Institue for Computer Graphics) and IPA (Institute for Manufacturing Engineering and Automation). They operate in Stuttgart and Darmstadt focussing on specific VR relevant issues like acoustical simulations (IBP), realtime computer graphics and intuitive interaction (IGD), robotics and production environments (IPA) and ergonomic studies (IAO).

The demonstration centres aim to create local contact points for all questions concerning virtual reality and to demonstrate the industrial feasibility of virtual environments. Thus, especially for small and medium-sized compagnies, solutions for future production and process developments are provided. The local competence centres offer:
- Consultancy on application problems related with VR.
- Training for industry staff.
- Seminars, workshops, inhouse-demonstrations.
- Presentation and evaluation of commercial and R&D systems.
- Testing and evaluation of available virtual reality products.
- Application prototyping.
- Technology development.

The main goal is to demonstrate that virtual environments are an innovation in man machine communication and to communicate the advantages and perspectives of virtual environmnets. The research infrastructure available at the institutes is used more efficiently and consistently to improve prevailing conditions and to strengthen the competitiveness of medium-size enterprises.

2.2 Hardware

The demonstration centre provides current virtual reality products, such as datagloves, stereo displays, and sound processors. The use of this technology in existing systems is demonstrated by competent staff members in training and demonstration rooms. The research and development teams at the demonstration centre implement specific virtual reality solutions efficiently. The following hardware components are currently in use at the institutes involved:

- machines for numerical computations like Convex C3220;
- massive parallel machines for realtime simulations MANNA;
- advanced graphics workstations, e.g. SGI single, dual and triple headed VGX, VGXT and RE, RE2;
- multi media workstations: NEXT, SUN, SGI, Apple;
- gloves like the DataGlove (VPL) and the CyberGlove (Virtex);
- stereo displays: EyePhone (VPL), CrystalEyes (Stereographics), Flight Helmet, VR4 (Virtual Research), nVision;
- stereo rear screen projections;
- tracker: 3Space, FASTRAK (Polhemus);
- audio-equipment: Convolvotron, Alphatron (Crystal River Eng.), 3D-Audio (Focal Point), Midi equipment (AKAI, Alesis);
- industrial robots: Stäubli;
- further input devices like 6D-track balls, flying joysticks, etc.

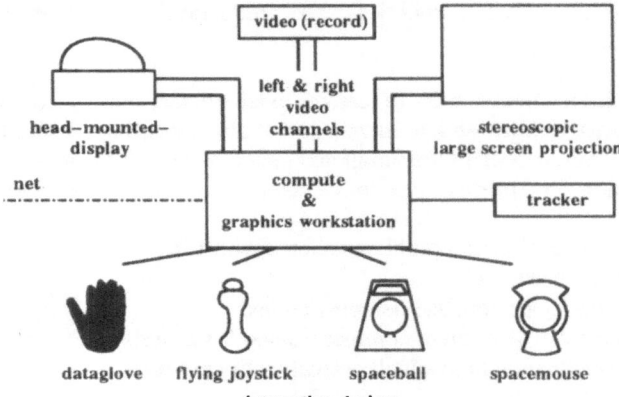

Figure 1: IGD DC - graphics part

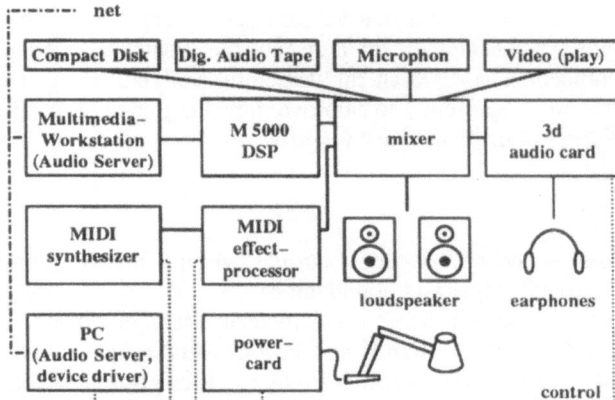

Figure 2: IGD DC - acoustic part

In the demonstration centre at IGD a number of hardware devices (figure 1 and 2) is installed: SGI machines for model visualization, VPL DataGlove and Virtex CyberGlove, spaceball, DLR spacemouse for interaction, the Polhemus Fastrak for position and orientation detection, Midi-equipment (Akai S1000 digital synthesizer, Alesis QuadraVerb effect processor), SGI Indigo/Indy and Crystal River 3d audio cards for audio rendering.

2.3 Software

At the software side, the centre accesses
- commercial Virtual Reality systems (VPL, Division's dVS, Sense8's WorldToolkit [14]);
- commercial systems for modelling, simulation and visualization, like TDI Explore, Prisms, AutoCAD, Catia, Bravo4, GeoMod;
- inhouse developments, such as Virtual Design [15], GIVEN [16] or VR4Robots [17] and planning tools, control systems, sound simulations, high speed rendering systems, which form a virtual reality development platform.

3 Virtual Design II

IGD has developed its own VR development environment with a number of pre- and postprocessors, realtime visual and acoustic rendering system and an interaction toolkit, which wraps and hides device details. Very early already the decision was made to develop and maintain a proprietary system in order to be independent of any manufacturer and to be able to integrate any new modules or tools anytime. Virtual Design II bases on our own experience with its predecessor Virtual Design, which has successfully been applied over a couple of years and with which many demonstration events have been realized, and commercial systems like SGI Performer.

3.1 Rendering system

Y is the realtime rendering system applied in Virtual Design II. It uses a hierarchical scene graph consisting of different types of nodes. The basic node classes are polyhedra (geometry), assemblies (grouping of other nodes), level-of-detail, viewer, lights, environment and callback nodes.

Some important constraints apply to all node types. They are motivated by the needs of predictive lod handling. For predictive lod handling during culling the part of the scene has to determined, which matches the given time constraint. Thus, each lod has to be able to render itself independently from its parents or any other node. This is achieved by accumulating the transformation matrices from the lod node to the root.

As it would be too expensive to calculate this matrix for every frame, it is calculated once and stored at the node. As an extensive bounding volume scheme had to be integrated for collision detection, each node would have a specific overhead to keep its bounding volumes up to date. This forced a design that reduced the number of nodes as much as possible.

Reducing the number of nodes without loosing expressive power required the nodes to become more powerful. Thus every node has a list of primitive transformations like translation, rotation or scale, so that no additional nodes are necessary just to build up a complicated transformation sequence. Each node contains a local, a model and a world coordinate system. As each of these coordinate systems has an associated matrix to convert the local points into it (except for the local coordinate system itself), there are two different matrices and their inverses important to every node. These matrices are evaluated only if they are needed, and they have to be updated when changes to the defining structure occur. The bounding volumes are represented in each of these coordinate systems, too.

Generally only a few transformations will change during the execution of the program. To avoid unnecessary computation, transformations can be tagged as static and preprocessed, i.e. the object's transformation is evaluated and applied to the point coordinates of the object. All transformations up to and including a node that has a dynamic brother can be flushed. Their parents can not be flushed, because flushes cannot cross dynamic transformations. These flushed transformations are not eliminated but merely flagged, so that the flushing could be reversed if needed.

Other general information common to each object includes a unique id that is used to identify the object to and from the outside (e.g. in files or over networks) and a name. Furthermore each object carries a pointer to a collection of object class specific methods. Typical methods include self destruction, transformation, output and reaction to invalidation of own or children data structures. Rendering is a method too, so that once the setup is completed, a single call to the root node to render itself will render the whole tree.

Polyhedra

These are the internal representations of the FhS's geometry nodes. They are designed to be both flexible in that they can be used on different and non-optimal representations like concave polygons using pooled points, each with a different material, but also be fast when they encounter well behaved data, like stripes sorted by materials and points that are consecutive in the points array. It should also be possible to have wireframe and filled versions of different types of polygons in one object. In general it should never be needed to use two polyhedra to generate one object.

This was achieved by giving each face a pointer to a rendering function that is able to render a group of those faces. During the update after changing the polyhedron, faces are grouped together according to this function and their material attributes. The resulting face blocks are the smallest handled rendering unit, and they can become as big a the whole object, thus minimizing overhead.

These rendering functions are made for every possible combination of face and vertex attributes like colors, normals or texture coordinates, and for interesting special cases like faces with consecutive points, wireframe stripes (which need a special handling to look good), triangles, quadrangles or stripes with important lengths. This results in a huge number of functions that are very similar.

Assemblies

Assemblies are the general grouping node, all other grouping nodes are derived from them. They handle a list of children and normally just forward the actions done on them to all of their children.

Rendering is a special case, though. Assemblies check each of their children for visibility, before they let them render themselves, if the assembly itself is not totally visible. This can be enhanced, for assemblies with many children, by hierarchies of bounding volumes built on top of the list of children to reduce the needed bounding volume tests. Different types of hierarchies have been realized and tested (independent nodes, Kay-Kajiya's bisecting box algorithm, Goldsmith-Salmon's iterative growth algorithm, approximated octree).

Level-of-detail

Level-of-detail nodes are derived from assemblies, but they differ from them so far, that they only render one of their children. To guarantee a constant frame rate a predictive algorithm has been realized. It estimates the time needed to render the static parts of the scene and of each level of detail of a lod node. To do that, the number of polygons, vertices and associated information is calculated after changing the polyhedra. This number is multiplied by the times needed per element, depending on the current machine. The times have been measured by a separate program with special test scenes to isolate the individual aspects.

The importance of each object is associated with it's formfactor. The time each object is allowed to consume is the amount of time that is available for the levels-of-detail after the static parts are drawn, multiplied by it's formfactor and divided by the sum of all formfactors.

Viewer

The viewer itself is also a node in the tree. This allows easy movement and attachment to other objects in the scene and it allows a clean interface to an important special effect. The viewer does not render its children when its rendering method is called, this is delayed until all other objects have been rendered. At this time, the z-buffer is optionally cleared, the viewing transformation is taken from the stack and the viewers children are rendered. Thus, it is possible to create objects that maintain a fixed position within the field of view and do not interfere with the scene.

This is interesting for things like menus or constant informations like a clock or a map, or for virtual representations of things that are attached to the viewer in the real world, like his hand.

Lights

Lights have been made nodes, too. This makes a light an object as any other object, and allows movement of lights like the movement of any other object. This allows lights also to render themselves, in the current implementation as a unit circle facing the viewer.

As lights should have influence on the whole scene, their position must be known at the very beginning of the frame, so that the lighting hardware can correctly account their influences. So before anything is rendered the light positions are transformed into world coordinates and are send to the graphics hardware (if the position have changed).

Environments

Environment information, like ambient light level or background color, has also been moved to an own node. Thus, all information needed to define the scene visually is set inside the tree. This allows a convenient and simple way to switch between parts of scenes. The renderer just has to be informed that a specific subtree is no longer rendered, but another one instead. Then he can search for the lights, viewer and environment nodes and set up the graphics state correctly.

Callback Nodes

Callback nodes are nodes that simply call a user defined function when they are rendered. This gives the user access to the graphics hardware for making mode changes not supported by the system itself. It is his responsibility to restore the mode afterwards.

As the system may want to change rendering order, and this might interfere with the callback's intention, all pending state changes (like flushing material slots or lazily popped matrices are made before the callback is invoked. After the pre-draw callback the children of the callback node are rendered and before the post-draw callback is called all pending actions are executed.

Rendering

Rendering is mostly handled by the nodes themselves, i.e. the renderer just calls the rendering method of the root node and the rest works for itself. This greatly enhances flexibility and makes the addition of a new node very easy.

The rendering module provides a layer on top of the underlying graphics library (SGI's GL), that matches the functionality of the rendering lib very closely. This indirect use of the lib allows easier portability (after the window is set up there is only one function that accesses the graphics hardware) and it is a must for decoupled drawing, for which all issued commands are entered into a display list to be executed by the drawing process. This is also a convenient way of hiding optimizations and other special cases.

The typical optimization is the buffering of faces with the same material. Before rendering, the faces are collected in slots for each material. Some operations, like activating a different matrix, force these slots to be flushed. This is done by activating the material and sending all the faces with this material at once. This prevents unnecessary material changes and in combination with lazy popping transformation matrices may achieve to activate each material exactly once for a given scene. This may result in speedups of 2 or more, depending on the scene.

Transparent faces as a special case have to be retained and rendered at last, possibly in a depth-sorted order. The application just sends them like any other faces, the renderer takes care of them. Optionally the drawing can be handled by one (or more, for multipipe machines) drawing processes. The protection against changes in the polyhedron's data is left to the application so far, this be handled in the near future.

3.2 FHS model data exchange format

FHS is the Fraunhofer standard to exchange model data. It is an ASCII format for simplicity, debuggability and most importantly for transfer to any kind of machine over any kind of connection (and may it be mail). Scanning and parsing is handled via lex/yacc. The general structure consists of a header (name of the model) followed by the object tree.

Surfaces

The surface description used is based on the Phong lighting model used by nearly every hardware supported graphics library today, with extensions for radiosity simulations. Surfaces have color for ambient, diffuse and specular lighting (specified as RGB triples) and scalar factors for transparency and specular coefficients. Optionally surfaces may be textured or have an emitting radiosity or even a BRDF description reference.

Their scope is meant to be global and thus double definitions are illegal. To prevent the need for two pass parsing they are accessible beginning from the point they are defined, which for practical reasons should be near the beginning of the file.

General Objects

Every object has a unique name for identification purposes. This allows the direct identification of objects between the different systems. Furthermore to place an object relative to its father it has a transformation, which can either be dynamic or static. Static tranformations are just for modelling purposes and removed from the scene graph by being applied directly to the coordinates of the children. Dynamic transformations are meant to be changed during the execution of the program and thus have to be kept in the scene graph.

The transformations can be specified in different ways, either as matrices or by a number of primitive transformations like rotation, translation and scaling, which are applied to the objects on the order of their appearance.

Geometry objects

Geometry objects represent the typical leaves of the tree. They are the only objects that actually have a renderable representation and thus form the whole visible part of the scene. The simplest form of a geometry node is the polyhedron. It is just a list of polygons (or alternatively triangle and quadrilateral stripes for better rendering performance). These polygons can either be specified using references into a point pool which is local to the geometry node or explicitly by giving the vertex coodinates, normal, color and/or texture coordinates.

Each of these polygons can have its own material and its own rendering specifications like with or without vertex normals or colors etc. This gives maximum flexibility and thus the need to have more than one geometry node for any logical object should never arise.

Instead of the simple polyhedron more complex primitives can be used, e.g. spheres, cones, bodies of extrusion or revolution etc.. These are used for faster modelling and easier conversion from other CAD-related formats. At load time they can be decomposed into simple polyhedra.

For purposes of radiosity simulations each geometry node can specify an alternative representation in the form of regular or quadtree-strutcured patches with geometry and radiosity information. These radiosity structures prevent a direct multiple use of geometric data, as they can never be replicated. To prevent repetive specification of geometric data a geometry node may specify its non-radiosity parts to be taken from another geometry node. This does only make sense as long as the referencing node uses a transformation (otherwise the two objects would be in the same place). The data is dereferenced and copied at load time, thus every node uses its own copy of the geometry.

Assembly Objects

Assembly objects (and their descendents) are the interior nodes of the tree. They have a list of children who are transformed relative to the assembly in order to build hierarchically linked structures (e.g. robot arms). The differences between the descendants of assembly objects manifest themselves in the way they treat their children during rendering (normal, level-of-detail, billboards).

Lights & Environments

Light sources are also put into the tree as nodes. This allows the same mechanisms that manipulate other objects to manipulate light sources. The types of light sources supported are the types usually supported by the graphics hardware (direct, point, spot) and additionally one type used for lighting simulation of real light sources.

Environment nodes collect all the global information for the whole environment like background color and ambient light. Light sources and environments influence the whole scene, not only the parts that follow them in the tree. This is much more intuitive than alternative as they can be placed at any position in the tree that is logical in contrast to special places on the far left of the tree.

3.3 Collision detection

Collision detection has many different applications, e.g. in physically based simulation, where moving objects are simulated. In order to determine their behavior over time, the most basic information needed is the time and position of collision together with the exact point of collision. Only if this information is known exactly, the collision response can determine how objects will react, according to their mass, mass distribution,
velocities, etc.

In virtual reality collision detection can be used to facilitate intuitive interaction, natural manipulation of the environment, any kind of physically based simulation, and modeling. In general, collision detection with appropriate collision response can make a virtual reality application look more believable (which is supposedly why it is called virtual *reality*), because collision detection is usually the first step towards objects behaving more *real*.

In virtual reality, the requirements are most severe. Under all circumstances, the collision detection must be real-time in order to attain the effect of immersion. For physically based simulation within a VR environment, it is also highly desirable to have exact and accurate collision detection, because there won't be a second chance to tweak if the output of the simulation module is not satisfactory. Although interaction in virtual environments (e.g., pressing 3D buttons) might not really need the exact point of collision, a detection too inaccurate (e.g., only bounding box tests) disturbs the impression of realism.

There are several difficulties that commonly arise when the ultimate goal is real-time exact collision detection:

- pairwise tests, on the object level as well as on the edge-/face-level; a naive algorithm has to test all possible pairs of edges and faces, and also all possible pairs of objects.

- discrete time; this makes it hard to compute the exact time of collision. Dynamic graphical systems display all objects at certain time intervals, usually as soon as the application is done with all the computation, like gathering input data, simulating the environment, moving objects, etc. If the collision detection module "sees" the environment only at these time steps without any further information about the future, then it can only check whether there is a collision or not. If speeds (translational and rotational) and maybe acceleration are provided, too, then the module can also compute the exact time of collision (or an approximation thereof), either by computing the next collision in the future, or by back-tracking and recursive interval bisection (of the time interval). Recursive interval bisection is in fact a sort of a root-finding algorithm, which could fail if objects moved too fast. However, this is usually not a problem, since dynamic systems always try to make time steps as small as possible.

- concave polyhedra, or, even worse, polyhedra which do not consist of convex polygons and which are not closed. There are many possible ways to tackle the collision detection problem with convex polyhedra; for non-convex polyhedra, very few algorithms seem to be known. For closed polyhedra, we can still resort to algorithms for convex polyhedra only, by partitioning them into convex pieces; if they are not closed, there is little we can do.

Several algorithms have been implemented for fast, exact collision detection on the level of object pairs. By utilizing many different prechecks, conventional algorithms have gained considerable speed. Further speed-up has been obtained by pre-phases which collect relevant polygons, and by lazy evaluation which avoids calculating normals or bounding boxes which are not needed.

Probabilistic algorithms have been developed to be tied together with conventional algorithms, thus yielding speed-up in cases where conventional algorithms are rather slow. A new algorithm has been developed to solve the $O(n^2)$-problem on the edge-polygon level. It uses a hierarchical, adaptive data structure (the box-tree) to discard quickly un-interesting polygons.

Few approaches so far have attempted to provide an integrated solution which addresses fast exact pairwise collision detection as well as fast retrieval of potentially colliding objects. In order to overcome the n^2-problem on the global level, algorithms for octree and grid have been developed; these have been designed with special regard to highly dynamic scenes. Several variants of both of them have been evaluated.

3.4 Into interaction toolkit

InTo is a sensor independent interaction toolkit applied by Virtual Design. It features logical input classes, which enable applications to communicate with physical input devices in an abstract manner. To echo users' interactions various feedback actions are available, which addresses not only the visual sense but also others, like the auditory and haptic sense.

InTo is represented as a library with a procedural interface. An application using InTo can be executed on one single workstation or over a network with sensor handling represented by autonomous processes. Different operation modes may be used to communicate with the devices; either the application polls the sensors or input events are generated and user-defined callback functions are executed. With this a flexible platform is available to investigate 3D interaction techniques in virtual environments.

3.5 Sound server

Up to now VR systems have emphasized on visual graphics and display technology. With audio hardware and system software readily available it is now possible to take the next evolutionary step and use acoustic processing to enhance virtual worlds. An audiovisual system addresses two important human senses at the same time and increases the level of realism towards an ideal immersive system significantly.

The sound server addresses several acoustic devices (multimedia workstations, MIDI equipment) and hides device specifics in a common library. The server offers a network protocol (different kinds of sockets) and a client library, which enables Virtual Design II to render and manipulate arbitrary sound samples. Several applications can access the server at the same time.

4. Pre- and Postprocessors

A VR system requires a number of pre- and postprocessors to manage, filter, convert and group input data, e.g. the output from modelers. In IGD's development environment Genesis serves as a tool for data preparation and lighting, RKS provides object behaviour, ISVAS preprocesses finite element and volume data, ICV provides flow propagation, the level-of-detail editor allows interactively to create arbitrary object simplifications.

4.1 Genesis

The interactive program Genesis [18] was developed to overcome a number of problems:

- Modelers often produce flat object lists (geometry, topology and material properties). VR requires a hierarchical data structure in order to speed up the rendering process.
- There is no standardized vr scene description exchange format. Furthermore, it can be difficult to convert the information needed (CSG-representation, IGES).
- For illumination the geometry has to be reprocessed, e.g. to subdivide large surfaces into a number of patches.
- Change of material can be expensive, so the order and object hierarchy is important.

Genesis can be used to convert scenes from several CAD or modeling systems and to prepare them for a presentation in virtual reality. With the help of Genesis one can ensure a high frame rate, by interactively deleting redundant or unimportant polygons and defining object hierarchies. The rendering quality can be improved by defining material properties, binding textures and using a radiosity approach for diffuse lighting. The output of Genesis is the FHS data format needed by the VR system. Interfaces for the following data formats have been implemented in Genesis:

- CGRG (used by several animation systems).
- icf (info component file of Applicon's Bravo 4+).
- dxf (used by AutoCad and supported by most architectural CAD programs).
- neu (neutral file of Pro-Engineer).
- nff (used by several ray tracing and rendering systems).
- FHS (Fraunhofer VR standard).

The user can redefine the hierarchy of objects by re-grouping polygons. This is very important to make interaction feasible in the virtual environment. If the data set is too complex and only a low frame rate can be achieved by the renderer, Genesis can be used to split the data set in several scenes or to decrease scene complexity by interactively deleting polygons or object groups. For an illumination simulation, the patch resolution can be defined for polygonal surfaces. The scene can also be varied by moving or rearranging objects.

For improving image quality, material-, light- and texture editors are integrated. Thus, the user can define surface properties for polygons or polygonal groups. Raster images can be imported into Genesis, e.g. digitized photographs from building details, and texture coordinates assigned to the polygonal model by interactively placing and changing the polygonal shape on top of this image.

Finally a radiosity simulation can be started to precompute color values for patch vertices. For some applications, it proved to be very convincing to simulate only the direct illumination by using a kind of "faked radiosity" algorithm. From each virtual point light source, a shadow feeler is sent towards each surface patch; if the patch is visible, its illumination is computed by evaluating the cosine between this ray and the patch normal.

4.2 Robot Kernel System (RKS)

The behavior of the objects is very important for the realism of the virtual environment. Our real world is dynamic. Things change over time according to physical laws. Human recognizes not only the form, color and sound, but also these changes. Additionally, manipulation of virtual objects is only realistic, if these objects respond correctly to the users actions.

Recently, first approaches are known showing the possibilities of integrating dynamic objects into virtual worlds (e.g. [19]). Generally, there are two ways to do that: off-line and integrated simulation of dynamics. The off-line approach allows to process even very complex dynamic scenes.

RKS is an example of external simulation systems [20]. It is a software system consisting of a framework and core functions which build a graphical interactive environment for planning of flexible robotics applications. Using RKS, from individual 3D parts to complex scenario can be modeled with functional properties and motion data. One can specify both functional relationships and spatial motions with basic actions which define dependencies and interactions between the components of a scene, and interactively simulate 3D motions and actions with its mouse-menu driven interface. The generated data can be imported into the VR system. Additionally, RKS is used to build kinematics models for integrated simulations in VR.

4.3 ISVAS

ISVAS[1] [21] is a monolithic visualization system for finite element and volume data. It supports methods that allow interactive analysis of very large data sets. Among the features offered by this system are support for time dependent data sets, user defined mapping transfer functions, flexible means for mathematical manipulation of the data, data probing, cutting, flow field analysis, real time visualization with steering of the data source, and hybrid display of FE and voxel data.

Visualization objects which have been created with ISVAS (e.g., surface with color mapping, vector arrows, cut plane, etc.) can be written to a file in a format that allows to load these geometries into the Virtual Environment system and to investigate them immersively.

---

[1]ISVAS is a registered trademark of Fraunhofer IGD

4.4 Level-of-Detail Editor

The performance of graphics workstations is limited in the maximum number of polygons which can be processed in realtime. Complex world models (which are of prime interest) exceed this limit easily. A set of rendering techniques allow to handle and conquer complex worlds, where level-of-detail techniques prove to be most promising and successful. Level of detail means the generation of several variations of the objects with different complexity. Depending on a decision criterion a variation is selected and displayed, e.g. depending on distance to the viewer.

A straight-forward approach for a level-of-detail is the substitution of the object with its bounding box. This obvious solution is immediately rejected when observing the jerky transition between the box and the object. Simplified object variations, whose shape match closer the original provide a much better solution. In our tool we provide a set of algorithms which operate on points, edges, angles, face areas or normals or a combination of that [22].

Selection criteria determine the current level-of-detail to be rendered and displayed. Distance, view angle and movement criteria can be applied. When changing the viewpoint it may be necessary to switch from one level-of-detail immediately to another one. This transition between two different object representations can be of constant, switch, fade or morph type.

The generation of multiple levels-of-detail of objects can be controlled either to match a given quality (shape, appearance) or a given quantity (number of points, faces). All available techniques in this editor tool provide quality control to meet application demands especially in interior design and architecture. With inappropriate parameter values the resulting levels-of-detail can either be still very complex (almost no reduction) or they can be heavily distorted (no similarity between original and level-of-detail). Because the visual results of applied techniques and parameter values are not always predictable the generation is an interactive process requiring an interactive tool. Figure 3 (see Appendix) depicts the original and two lower resolutions of a bust of Beethoven.

5 Applications

Within the last years, many applications had been realised with Virtual Design and Virtual Design II [15], IGD's VR development environment. Especially in the field of architecture and interior design, lots of models have been prepared and imported into the system [23]. Some models originally have been created from a number of furniture companies, others have been designed from architects, from ship construction or have been reconstructed from ruins. Advanced VR examples had also been implemented in the field of medicine, scientific visualization, virtual prototyping and marketing. Besides these commercial applications several prototypes have been realized showing advances in the research and development domain.

5.1 Architecture

Several architectural models have been prepared and imported into the VR system. The models originally have been created from a number of CAD companies or the architects itself.

In figure 4 an example from the field of architecture is shown. It is the new building of the Fraunhofer Institute for Computer Graphics in Darmstadt, which should be finished at 1996. The 3D model was created by the Computer Graphics Center Darmstadt (ZGDV) with the help of Mr. Seidel, the architect of the building.

Architectural concepts are very difficult to explain using standard presentation methods. In VR, the user is able to experience the design and concept by himself by walking through the virtual house and exploring it.

5.2 Interior Design

VR applications in interior design are typically more complex, then in the field of architecure. Here, not only walk-through systems are required. The users and costumers need interactive systems, in order to change their design, move furnitures or present alternative concept. Here, VR is not only used for the presentation of the design concept; it is already used as an interactive tool during the planning phase.

One of the most important features of our VR system is the integration of simulated lighting data. In figure 5 (see Appendix), the virtual model of our VR demonstration center in Darmstadt is shown. At the walls, we can see the simulated illumination and shadow situations. Thus, the customer is able to imagine, how the design will look like.

In the middle of the room, we see the visualization of the illumination at a virtual working plane of 80 cm height. This representation is very important for the light engineer. The red colour at the desk prooves enough light for the people working their. The green and blue colours on top of the chairs demonstrate less light - the people are not disturbed by watching the screen.

This kind of visualization bridges the gap between the presentation of illumination for an unexperienced observer (photorealistic images) and and lighting expert (working plane).

5.3 Urban Planning

The model of the city of Darmstadt, Erfurt, Rostock and Frankfurt have been prepared and imported in our VR-system. For the presentation of Frankfurt (figure 6, see Appendix), a 2D polygonal model has been gained by applying image processing programs to land-register data. A fixed height was assigned to each building layout in order to automatically generate a 3D model and important buildings had been re-modelled using a CAD-system.

Photographs of building facades had been scanned and retouched (in order to get rid of disturbing picture elements like cars and people in front of the buildings) and mapped to the virtual model.

Virtual models of cities are mainly used for the evaluation of visual appearance of new buildings to fit in a existing area (especially in historic parts of cities). New applications have been developed to visualize the electro-magnetic field for portable telephones in a city.

5.4 Medicine

Since minimally invasive surgery, especially arthroscopical diagnosis, is increasingly applied in operating theatre, training is becoming an important issue. Arthroscopy is a special endoscopical diagnosis method to recognize pathological changes and diseases of joints (e.g., knee, hip, shoulder, etc.). The arthroscope, supplied with optic and light source, and the exploratory probe are inserted for example into the knee joint through two small incisions located underneath the kneecap. So far, the skills required for an arthroscopy have been taught the learning-by-doing way. In addition, the various orthopedic operations have been practised using a plastic replica of the knee joint. However, with training on synthetic knees only, the first surgical operation on the human knee is very critical.

Against this background, the Fraunhofer Institute for Computer Graphics, in cooperation with the "Berufsgenossenschaftliche Unfallklinik (BGU)" in Frankfurt am Main, developed a prototype based on the idea of using computer simulation applying Virtual Reality (VR) techniques for training and establishing of arthroscopic techniques [41].

The main intention of the project was to develop a training simulator as an enhanced alternative to conventional training systems (i.e. plastic replica of the knee joint). The surgeons are criticizing the insensitiveness of the plastic replica with regard to incorrect handling of the instruments. Furthermore the conventional training system does not provide any mechanism to verify (and protocol) the training progress.

Our representation of the knee joint has been derived from a MRI (magnetic resonance imaging) data set. The VR interface of the arthroscopy training simulator consists of two main components: the 3D interaction, realizing the piloting of the instruments, and the 2D user interface for the visual feedback and the control of the training session. One advantage in comparison to conventional training systems is the possibility to verify the training progress by recording the session.

Applying VR techniques the training simulator can provide the necessary interactive realism. The 3D interaction of the system simulates a real arthroscopy. An original exploratory probe and a replica of an arthroscope are inserted into a synthetic model of the knee through two small incisions located underneath the patella.

Three tracking sensors are used in the arthroscopy simulator. One sensor is fixed on the arthroscope in order to simulate a virtual camera, optics and lightsource located on the tip of the arthoscope. The sensor on the exploratory probe enables the integration of this instrument in the virtual environment. The third sensor is located on the lower leg of the synthetic knee. According to the current position of this sensor the attitude of the knee joint is computed and rendered in the scenery. Now the trainee is able to bend the knee joint similar to a real arthroscopy.

We had very positive assessments of the training simulator (figure 7, see Appendix). The simulator is well suited for the training of the 2-axis-coordination. The main drawback of the simulator is the missing of resistance, which we call force feedback. In cooperation with the Department of Electro-Mechanical Construction at the Darmstadt Technical University we have finished a conceptual study. Based upon the results of this study we are working on the realization.

5.5 Scientific Visualization

3D presentation techniques and interaction methods using a "conventional" (mouse-menu driven) user interface have some disadvantages: spatial relationships are often difficult to recognize and navigation is only indirectly possible. Virtual Reality techniques offer new possibilities of presentation and investigation of multidimensional data. Immersive exploration of scientific data is the natural next step after interactive real time visualization.

Small scale cellular radio networks

In a project for German Telekom, a VE system is being used to investigate measured and simulated propagation data of small scale cellular radio networks. An X windows based mapping program is employed to map propagation data to geometric objects. Data like received power or delay spread determine size and color of spheres, cylinders, etc., representing locations of measured or simulated data.

Combination of full size VE and SciVis System

To be able to utilize as many VE and SciVis techniques as possible in one application, two systems designed at IGD, ISVAS and Virtual Design, have been linked to each other. The two systems run separately as individual processes. Communication between them is achieved by means of a UNIX pipe, allowing for two way communication.

In a simple application, the user is immersed within a finite element data set in Virtual Design. He can position a particle source interactively by means of his data glove. This position is transmitted to ISVAS which uses the precomputed flow field to simulate the movement of a particle within this finite element data set. The particle positions are returned to Virtual Design which visualizes the moving particle in its proper context. Another possible application of this configuration is data probing.

The advantage of this approach is that the full power of an advanced visualization system as well as of a state-of-the-art VE system are available without having to reimplement every feature again for a given application. Figure 8 (see Appendix) shows an example of a virtual wind tunnel.

Molecular Modeling

The aim of this system is to investigate the relationship of complex molecules interactively in an immersive environment. Molecule data can be imported in form of the common pdb file format (Broohaven Protein Data Bank). Since this file does not contain the linkages directly, they must be infered from the data available. This makes it neccessary to include a complete table of all possible linkage atoms for each amino-acid.

The corresponding surface model is read from an additional file. Several molecules can be loaded into the system in order to compare them or to combine them at will. The molecules are displayed in any combination of ball-and-stick- and semitransparent, color-coded surfacemodel. A level of detail technique with several levels is used to achieve fast rendering while still showing as many details as possible due to resolution. Size and position of a molecule can be perceived due to a shadow which is cast onto a "floor" (figure 9, see Appendix. Data courtesy Dpt. of Chemistry, Technical Univ. Darmstadt).

Visual examination of the surface structure of molecules can be used e.g. to find out which substratum and which inhibitor fit a certain enzyme. Therefore, a molecule can be grabbed with the data glove and moved arbitrarily in order to determine if a molecule fits to another one.

5.6 Virtual Prototyping

In virtual prototyping a product data model is used to build a virtual model, which can be handled like its physical representation. This idea is based on the integration of computer supported modeling, simulation and presentation of products. Virtual prototype means not only the product data model itself, but also includes the user's imagination upon viewing and manipulating this model. It is essential that the human senses are provided with information which represent the data model as realistic as possible. For this purpose VR techniques are required.

Visual evaluation is one of the first application areas of virtual reality. Interior design applications can be regarded as some kind of virtual prototyping too, where audio-visual effects are of primary importance. Typically, a walk through is performed in order to get an impression about the spatial relationship of a 3D model.

Furthermore, first examples in the mechanical engineering domain were performed. The data model of the hospital area inside a huge ship has been visually evaluated. Some parts can be grasped and moved using the dataglove. Due to highly complex pipeline systems inside a ship, pipe interrupts because of planning mistakes can be identified very easily.

A prototype system features interaction techniques for real-time object manipulation. The interaction metaphor is the idea of a potter process. Using a glove a user can point onto the surface of a rotating cube. Real-time collision detection is applied in order to change the form of the cube according to the hand movement. This results in an on-line modification of the geometry.

An assembly system has been implemented for research purpose at IGD. With a glove, a user can grab and assemble objects. A precise collision detection with penetration avoidance is applied. When two objects are aligned properly to each other a snapping mechanism will assemble the parts automatically. Due to the lack of force feedback, acoustic signals give important additional feedback for each action to the user.

A complex factory scenario consists of several active objects, these are: a robot, a car and a milling machine. Motions of these objects are simulated off-line with RKS. The motion data is assigned to the VR objects as actions. The user can play the role of the human worker, who controls the machines via a console.

More sophisticated virtual prototyping requires integrated on-line simulation. An example is presented in figure 10 (see Appendix). During an immersive walk-through the cybernaut can interact with objects of the virtual environment, and these objects expose a realistic (i.e. physically correct) behavior. The lamp is represented by an open kinematic chain. It is mounted on the table and can be moved by grabbing parts of it. According to the constraints of the segment joints and the hand movement the on-line simulation results in a correct behavior of the lamp.

A broad application field is the domain of training and prototype evaluation. The introduction of a new product on the market can be expedited, when last changes are easily possible and the training of involved people, like maintenance workers can be started before a real product is on hand.

For example, the change of a car engine can be done in a dry test and the generation of its appropriate maintenance manual description can be performed at a very early production level. Figure 11 (see Appendix) shows a rotating crank shaft in VR which is a part of the virtual prototype (so called digital mock-up) of a car.

The evaluation of a prototype by potential customers can benefit from the VR technology too. No physical prototype mock-up is necessary and so the potential customers of the product (e.g. a new car) can contribute during the whole development process and not only at its final step, when larger changes are not possible anymore.

5.7 Marketing

In early 1994 an advertising agency approached us to help them realize a special marketing event for the Schweizerische Bankgesellschaft (SBG), the largest swiss banking institute [27]. The SBG currently has a marketing concept, which concentrates on the realization of a few but pretty big events per year rather than numerous small events. This year's motto was entitled "the year of adventure" and should provide exciting and thrilling experiences.

We decided to install one high-quality VR-action-station and a stereoscopic large-screen projection for passive observation by the mass audience. The final adventure world consisted of several subworlds which were connected by a simple transition structure. Each player started flying helicopter-like around the truck until he was attracted into the action point of the truck, here he faced a "contomat" (teller machine). Until then he was completely guided by the system which changed to the interactive mode at this point. By touching the contomat he started the transition from the virtual real world (truck with environment) to the virtual imaginative worlds.

He was then transferred into a tunnel. For a certain time he proceeded in the tunnel with good (blue sky texture) and bad (yellow/red texture) objects (cubes) approaching, the banking card always ahead releasing particles, never reachable. With his hand he could avert hits and score points. In the next world the banking card dissolved into three parts which disappeared in the three final worlds. Here he could choose to enter one world simply by touching one of the big arrows just beneath him. The worlds were symbolized by colour and a typical object (palm tree - jungle world, figure 12, see Appendix, trumpets - stage world, planet - space labyrinth).

We tried to integrate effects to create a certain athmosphere or mood for each world. In the stage world a light show was performed, in the tower of fate spaceship-like controls flashed. The space world was placed in an universum with asteroids and planets. Sound helped a lot to create a typical mood.

Static worlds observed in typical walkthroughs very soon get very boring. To create a living environment we introduced animations for lights, camera and any world object. Although these animations had to be precalculated (mostly) and thus the objects did not react intelligently to the player's behaviour it made the worlds much more interesting. Animations could be triggered or combined with interaction or were continuous.

For this project the interaction concept of our virtual reality system was completely redesigned. Possible interactions can be specified in a data file referencing world objects and predefined actions. Thus interesting living or reacting worlds can be easily defined and evaluated.

With a slightly modified system another marketing event for the chemical enterprise Hoechst was realized to promote a microscopic view of their printing plate (Ozasol) (figure 13, see Appendix).

6 Conclusion

Virtual environments as an enabling technology in man machine communication has been presented and various industrial applications - which already make use of virtual worlds - were shown. Thus, the research and development work and the applied development environment within the Demonstration Centre for Virtual Reality in Darmstadt has been presented. Many application areas are going to install virtual environments as a testbed for the particular application. The first commercial training simulators based on VR are already under development.

During the last two years, Virtual Reality has done a significant step forward with respect to its acceptance as the man machine interface of the future.

7 Acknowledgement

We greatfully acknowledge the support of the Fraunhofer Gesellschaft in establishing Virtual Reality as a key research direction in Europe and the support of the German Ministry for Research and Technology in funding the basics of this centre by the VIS-A-VIS project which focussed on real time computer graphics for complex data for Scientific Visualization.

The Virtual Design II development environment is the work of many individuals: Peter Astheimer (sound simulation, level-of-detail, system design), Fan Dai (RKS, virtual prototyping), Helmut Haase (scientific visualization), Kennet Karlsson and Thomas Frühauf (ISVAS, engineering applications), Wolfgang Felger (InTo, Demonstation Centre Manager), Torsten Fröhlich (InTo, navigation), Martin Göbel (department leader), Stefan Müller (Genesis, Radiosity, FHS), Dirk Reiners (Genesis, Y-Renderer, FHS), Frank Schöffel and Matthias Unbescheiden (Genesis), Gabriel Zachmann (InTo, collision detection, system design), Rolf Ziegler and Wolfgang Müller (medical applications). Besides staff inumerable students contributed to the functionality and applicability of the system, the listing of their names would burst the available space.

8 References

1. Encarnacao, J.L., Astheimer, P., Felger, W., Frühauf, T., Göbel, M., Müller, S.: Graphics and Visualization: The Essential Features for the Classification of Systems, Proceedings ICCG, Bombay, February 1993
2. Göbel, M. (ed.): Virtual Reality, Computers and Graphics, Special Issue, Vol.17, 6, Nov. 1993
3. Encarnacao, J.L., Göbel, M., Rosenblum, L.: European Activities in Virtual Reality, IEEE Computer Graphics and Applications, Vol.14, 1, Jan. 1994
4. Göbel, M. (ed.): Eurographics Workshop on Virtual Environments, Proceedings, Eurographics Technical Report, ISSN 1017-4656, September 1993, Barcelona
5. McCormick, B.H., DeFanti, T.A., Brown M.: Visualization in scientific computing, ACM Computer Graphics, Vol. 21, No. 6, 1987
6. Astheimer, P., Encarnacao, J.L., Felger, W., Frühauf, M., Göbel, M., Karlsson, K.: Interactive modeling in high-performance scientific visualization - the VIS-A-VIS project, computers in industry, vol. 19, no, 2, 1992, North-Holland, pp. 213 - 225
7. Frühauf, M.: Volume Rendering on a Multiprocessor Architecture with Shared Memory: A Concurrent Volume Rendering Algorithm, In: Patrizia Palamidese (ed.): Scientific Visualization - Advanced Software Techniques, Ellis Horwood Press, 1993, pp. 101-114
8. del Pino, A.: Volume Visualization on Distributed Memory Computers, SERC Visualization Community Club Seminar on Parallel Processing for Visualization, University of Manchester, U.K., Nov. 1993
9. Felger, W., Schroeder, F.: The Visualization Input Pipeline--Enabling Semantic Interaction in Scientific Visualization, Proc. EUROGRAPHICS 92, Computer Graphics Forum, 1992
10. Göbel, M., Neugebauer, J.: The Virtual Reality Demonstration Centre, Computers and Graphics, Vol.17,6, Nov. 1993, pp.627-631
11. Bishop, G., Fuchs, H., et al.: Research Directions in Virtual Environments, Computer Graphics, Vol. 26, 3, August 1992, pp. 153-177

12. Cruz-Neira, C., Sandin, D.J., DeFanti, T.A.: Surround-Screen Projection-Based Virutal Reality: The Design and Implementation of the CAVE, Computer Graphics, Proc. SIGGRAPH 93, Anaheim, Aug. 1993, pp. 135-142

13. Sutherland, I.E.: The Ultimate Display, Proc. IFIP 65, 2, pp. 506-508, 582-583, 1965

14. Bauer, W., Bullinger, H.-J., Riedel, O.: Virtual Reaility as a Tool for Office Design, Proceedings HCI, Orlando, Florida, 1993

15. Astheimer, P., Felger, W., Müller, S.: Virtual Design - A Generic VR System for Industrial Applications, Computers & Graphics, Pergamon Press, vol. 17, no. 6, November 1993, pp. 671 - 677

16. Böhm, K., Hübner, W.: Virtual Reality: A new User InterfaceParadigm for Industrial Applications, in Proceedings IMAGINA'93, Monte Carlo, Feb. 1993

17. Neugebauer, J.: Virtual Reality applied to Industrial Robots, in Proceedings IMAGINA'93, Monte Carlo, Feb. 1993

18. Müller, S., Unbescheiden, M., Göbel, M.: Genesis - Eine interaktive Forschungsumgebung zur Parallelisierung des Radiosity-Verfahrens für die virtuelle Welt, Proceedings VR '93, Stuttgart, Februar 1993

19. Astheimer, P., Dai, F.: Dynamic Objects in Virtual Worlds - Integrating Simulations in a Virtual Reality Toolkit, Proceedings ESS '93, the European Simulation Symposium, Delft, October 25 - 28, 1993, pp. 299 - 304

20. Dai, F.: RKS - the Robotics Kernel System, in: Wloka, D.W. (ed.): The International Handbook on Robot Simulation Systems, John Wiley & Sons Ltd., London, 1993

21. Frühauf, T., Göbel, M., Haase, H., Karlsson, K.: Design of a Flexible Monolithic Visualization System, in: Rosenblum, L., Earnshaw, R. (Eds.): Scientific Visualization - Advances and Challenges, Academic Press Ltd., London, UK, 1994, pp. 265 - 285

22. Astheimer, P., Pöche, M.L.: Level-of-Detail Generation and its Application in Virtual Reality, in: Singh, G., Feiner, S.K., Thalmann, D. (eds.): VRST '94 Proceedings, World Scientific, Singapore, August 1994, pp. 299 - 309

23. Astheimer, P., Felger, W.: Virtuelle Realität in der Architektur, Bau-Informatik, Werner-Verlag, Düsseldorf, Heft 2, 1993, pp. 54 - 58

24. Astheimer, P.: Sounds of Silence - How to animate Virtual Worlds with Sound, Proceedings of ICAT/VET, Houston, Texas, May 1993, pp. 191 - 202

25. Astheimer, P.: What you see is what you hear - Acoustics applied to Virtual Worlds, IEEE Symposium on Virtual Reality, San Jose, USA, October 1993, pp. 100 - 107

26. Astheimer, P., Dai, F., Göbel, M., Kruse, R., Müller, S., Zachmann, G.: Realism in Virtual Reality, in: Thalmann, D., Thalman-Magnenat, N. (Eds.): Artificial Life and Virtual Reality, J. Wiley 1994, pp. 189 - 208

27. Astheimer, P., Felger, W.: An Interactive Virtual World Experience - The SBG Cyberspace Roadshow, Second Eurographics Workshop on Virtual Environments - Realism & Realtime, Monte Carlo, February 1995 (see also in this book)

28. Brooks, F.P., Ouh-Young, M., Batter, J.J., Kilpatrick, P.J.: Project GROPE - Haptic Displays for Scientific Visualization, in: ACM Computer Graphics, Vol. 24, No. 4, August 1990, pp. 177-185

29. Carrabine, L.: Plugging into the Computer to Sense, Computer-Aided Engineering, June 1990, pp. 16-26

30. Cohen, M.F., Chen, S.E., Wallace, J.R., Greenberg, D.P.: A Progressive Refinement Approach for Fast Radiosity Image Generation, ACM Computer Graphics, Proceedings Siggraph 1988, pp. 75 - 84, August 1988

31. Cohen, M.F., Greenberg, D.P.: The Hemi-Cube, A Radiosity Solution for complex Environments, ACM Computer Graphics, Proceedings Siggraph 1985, pp. 31 - 40, July 1985

32. Felger, W.: Konzept und Realisierung eines Demonstrationszentrums für Anwendungen der Virtuellen Realität, Proceedings 3. GI-Workshop, Sichtsysteme, Wuppertal, 18./19. November 1993

33. Fisher, S.S., Foster, S.H., Stone, P.K., Wenzel, E.M.: A System for three-Dimensional Acoustic "Visualization" in a Virtual Environment Workstation, in: Kaufman, A. (ed): Proceedings of Visualization '90, IEEE Computer Society Press, Los Alamitos, 1990

34. Goebel, M.: Virtuelle Realit - Technologie und Anwendungen, In: Nastansky, L. (Ed.): Multimedia und Imageprozessing, AIT Verlag, 1992

35. House, D.; Breen, D.; Getto, P.: On the Dynamic Simulation of Physically-Based Particle-System Models, RDRC Techn. Report TR-91035, Renssellaer Polytechnic Institute, Troy, NY, USA (1991)

36. Pentland, A. P.: Computational Complexity Versus Simulated Environments, Computer Graphics, Vol. 24, No. 2 (1990), ACM SIGGRAPH, New York

37. Vaananen, K., Böhm, K.: Gesture driven interaction as a human factor in virtual environments - an approach with neural networks, in Earnshaw, R (eds): Virtual Reality Systems, Academic Press, 1992

38. Väänänen, K.; Böhm, K.: Gesture Driven Interaction as a Human Factor in Virtual Environments - An Approach with Neural Networks, Proceedings Virtual Reality Systems, University of London, London (UK), 20-21 May 1992

39. Wenzel, E.M.: Localization in Virtual Acoustic Display, Presence, vol. 1, no. 1, Winter 1992, pp. 80 - 107

40. Zeltzer, D.: The Concept of Telepresence: Autonomy, Interaction, and Presence. Presence, Vol. 1,1., MIT Press 1992

41. Ziegler, R., Müller, W., Fischer, G., Göbel, G.: Virtual Reality Medical Training System, in: N Ayache (ed.): Computer Vision, Virtual Reality and Robotics in Medicine (CVRMed95), pp. 282 - 286, Springer 1995

Editor's Note: see Appendix, p. 306f. for coloured figures of this paper

Using the GIVEN toolkit for system development in *MuSE*

M. Sokolewicz[*], H. Wirth[†], K. Böhm[*], W. John[†]

[*]ZGDV – Zentrum für Graphische Datenverarbeitung e.V.
[†]Technical University of Darmstadt, Dep. of Computer Science, Interactive Graphics Systems Group
Wilhelminenstrasse 7, D–64283 Darmstadt, Germany
email: {mike, wirth, boehm, john}@igd.fhg.de

Abstract. The development and realisation of complex virtual environments, with functionality beyond walk throughs, will place considerable demands on the software engineer. The use of toolkits is necessary in order to allow the development of virtual environments in a time and cost effective manner. The concepts of our 3D-User Interface toolkit GIVEN (Gesture-based Interactions in Virtual ENvironmenst) will be described. The problems we tackled in GIVEN include *input device independence*, *individual object behavior*, *gesture dialogue and reçognition* as well as *multi–user* and *network transparency*.

The first application of GIVEN is as the virtual reality user interface for the *MuSE* simulator. *MuSE* is an integrated environment for development, verification and simulation of technical systems. The functionality of the *MuSE* hypermedia user interface, the simulation capabilities and the *MuSE* VR user interface are described. An outlook on the future of GIVEN and *MuSE* is given.

1 *MuSE*[1]

1.1 Motivation

During the development of complex technical system like cars, airplanes, or power plants, reliability and security, as well as environmental concerns, play an important role. Validating such systems before they are fully realized is becoming more and more important. The reasons are clear: developers and engineers like to specify parts of a system, even if it is incomplete. They are going to verify and extend their

---

1. *MuSE* is the acronym for the German project name *Multimediale Systementwicklung*. The project is sponsored by the *Deutsche Forschungsgesellschaft* (DFG), grant number He 1170/5–1. *MuSE* is intended to be a long term research project (up to 10 years). The project is constituted as a research group located at the computer science department of the Technical University Darmstadt. Partners are the research groups *Artificial Intelligence, Interactive Graphics Systems, Software Engineering, Integrated Circuits and Systems,* and *Integrated Publication and Information Systems.*

specification step by step. So there is always a tight loop consisting of specifying, testing, evaluating, modifying, testing, and so on. Currently it is possible to do a simulation of some small parts, however other parts or whole systems have to be built in hardware. A lot of time and money is used during these steps.

The *MuSE* environment supports the developer with tools which allow the specification of the system using rapid prototyping, simulation of the system in a virtual environment, evaluation of the results of a simulation, and inquiries about any possible system state.

We do not want to allow only engineers and developers to use a system. There are other people who should be able to access this data; the neighbor of a power plant, for instance. Thus we have at least three different types of users with different knowledge about a system and different interest in the system's functionality. All of them need to obtain information in a certain manner. Various types of information in a system should therefore be accessible through a number of different modes.

We are currently building and extending our libraries of virtual input and output devices. Furthermore, we are integrating the other *MuSE* parts from our partners into a single system. The *MuSE* kernel runs on Sun SPARCstation10's, while the rendering is done on Silicon Graphics computers and, alternatively, on a Sun SPARCstation10 with an Evans & Sutherland graphics accelerator.

As an application example, we are working, in cooperation with Mercedes Benz, with special purpose trucks, called *Unimog*, which have hybrid, electro–hydraulic, rear wheel steering.

1.2 The *MuSE* environment

In the following section we describe briefly the main components of *MuSE*.

Functional modelling

Typically, a technical system consists of various parts or modules. To allow rapid prototyping, each module may be only partially specified. *MuSE* uses high level specification languages for model description. The executable functional language SAMPλE (see [1]) is used to specify the simulation functions. Electronic system components can be modelled using the VHDL language, which allows the description of parallelism even inside single electronic circuits (see [2]). Both, SAMPλE and VHDL can be used at the same time to describe and simulate the system. In addition, the user is able to ask questions about the system, so he is able to find out how it can get into an erroneous state. This is not done by simulation but by deduction. The deduction works on a first order logic description of the model (see [3]).

User interfaces to the simulation

Whereas the functional model describes the properties of the system to be simulated, it contains no description of the interface the user uses to control the simulation. *MuSE* offers two types of user interfaces to the simulation: a 2D, mouse–based UI and a virtual reality user interface. The 2D UI is designed to be used as a method to quickly test individual parameters of the simulated system. The virtual reality user interface offers a virtual environment to the user with which they can interact. For both types of UI, the devices with which the user controls the simulated system and the output of the system have to be modelled. Take, e.g., a car. It needs input devices to control the speed and another input device to control the direction. In the 2D window–based interface, the user controls the car with sliders and a symbolic steering wheel. In the virtual environment, the user can interact with virtual input devices displayed in the scene with the help of VR input hardware like a data glove. For the virtual input devices, a geometry is coupled with constraints (like an axis around which the device can be turned) and a range of values which the device delivers. Only the values produced by the virtual input devices are delivered to the functional simulation. Events like the touching of a virtual input device with the virtual representation of the users hand are handled by the VR toolkit.

A further option is to display internal parameters of the simulated system. These parameters are displayed on virtual instruments (like analog and digital meters or a scope, see [4]). The output devices are configurable, e.g. update time, or axis scale can be varied. The instruments allow input from the user. This can be used to simulate defects while simulating a system. The instruments can either be displayed on the same display as the 2D UI or be used by a second user while the first uses the VR user interface.

There are two types of simulation. One we call an online simulation, the other an offline simulation. In an online simulation, the user controls the system directly through the input devices. The user's actions are recorded in a database. With an offline simulation, the user's actions are taken from the database and fed into the simulation component of *MuSE*. In this case, we get an exact copy of a previously stored simulation and can perform experiments with the system. The user may look at any part of the system and perform little modifications to get information on how the system behaves during error conditions. These features are needed to explore the system's behavior and, finally, to validate it.

Hyper structure

The *MuSE* desktop is the hyper system SEPIA (see [5] , [6] and [7]) which runs on an object oriented multimedia database system, called VODAK. With this interface we organize our environment with a hyper network of multimedia system data. Modules are represented as nodes in the hyperstructure, as well as different versions of the system. A designer can compare different versions easily by clicking on a node. Specifications, simulations and versions can be stored as nodes, as well as documentation, text, and drawings . Links are used to describe relationships between various nodes. Some relationships can be created automatically, e.g. results of a simulation, but others have to be set manually, such as "new version" or "is subpart of".

Each user group has its own space with its own rights to access data. The developers of a power plant, for instance, would not like to give delicate information to everyone. However, it must be possible to simulate the system with all its functionality and features, and to present this simulation to all users. SEPIA takes care of data privacy and presentation.

1.3 Functionality of the *MuSE* VR user interface

The reason why a VR interface was chosen to implement the user interface to the *MuSE* simulation was to give the users a realistic look and feel of the simulated system without having to build special hardware for a simulator which is costly and time–consuming. Another aim was to give the different groups of users, which have different knowledge about computers and simulations, an interface which they all could easily use. The *MuSE* VR interface tries to implement usage metaphors which the users know from their daily life. The software goals in designing the *MuSE* VR user interface were independence from the modelled technical system, ease and usability and input device independence.

The VR interface is based on the "direct manipulation" metaphor and uses virtual input devices. The control devices of the simulated system are modelled in the VR interface in a way that is similar to their real–world behavior. The user is able to control those virtual devices (e.g. switches, knobs or a steering wheel) with multidimensional input devices, like the DataGlove, the CyberGlove or a magnetic position sensor. In principle, *MuSE* is independent of specific input device hardware, but the developer has to take the device hardware into account while designing the VR user interface for simulations because of the limitations of certain input devices. For example, it is awkward for a user to be forced to grab a steering wheel with only a 6D position sensor.

Another development goal of the *MuSE* VR interface was the ability to use different physical input devices at once. This is important in order to give the user the ability to control simulated systems which require ambidextrous input from different virtual input devices at once (e.g. cars).

Functionality of the unimog simulation

The first system which is modelled with the *MuSE* system is a small truck designed for municipal or agricultural use (see [8]). The modelled features of the truck are the external hull, the wheels, parts of the chassis and parts of the cabin (mainly the dashboard). For the driving simulation, the viewpoint of the user is located in the cabin. The environment in which the truck can be driven is a road marked by pylons.

The dashboard consists of a steering wheel and buttons for starting and stopping the engine and for controlling the behavior of the electro–hydraulic rear wheel steering. Accelerator and brake are not modelled within the virtual environment, as it would be awkward for the user to control these with a data glove. The dashboard is partitioned into different objects, which are modelled as virtual input devices in GIVEN. The user is able to grab and turn the steering wheel and press the buttons with a graphical representation of a hand which is controlled by a data glove. Currently, the accelerator and brake pedals are custom–made hardware pedals.

Modelling the VR user interface

In order to build a VR User Interface for a simulation, the systems engineer has to differentiate between the objects in the scene:

- A geometric object is a graphical representation for an object which the user should be able to see but has not any functionality in the user interface of the simulation. This includes objects which are simulated physically (e.g. wheels) as well as objects which are just there for the optical effect (e.g. the cabin of the truck).

- A virtual input device is a geometric object which is extended by constraints. These constraints refer to geometric movement, minimum and maximum output values of the device, type of the output value and flags for collision checking.

- A virtual output device is a geometric object which is extended by definition of a type of input value, a value range and geometric constraints.

At the moment, the behavior of virtual input devices is coded into the VR toolkit software. The geometry is read from a description which also describes the rest of the simulated system and its environment. Methods to define the behavior of a virtual input device with an API are being investigated. Virtual output devices are not used in the *MuSE* simulation at the moment. One could use them, e.g., to display the speed of a car on a speedometer.

2 The 3D user interface toolkit GIVEN

2.1 Motivation

"Virtual Reality", also known as "Virtual Environment", refers to a computer–created and –supported system, space or interactive situation, in which people (the users, or rather, the visitors) can act and interact with objects in a "natural" way. There are two key issues which relate directly to the "Reality" part of the term: high–quality 3D graphical and multimedia images (visual output), and advanced methods of interaction. Visitors to such an environment must receive both visual feedback and natural interaction, or behavior, feedback from the objects they encounter. Therefore, instead of "human–computer" interaction, we should talk about "visitor experiences" in an environment, or "human–environment" interaction. Independent of what we call it, though, it must be carefully modelled in order to achieve believable situations and "feel" for the user. (See [9] and [10] for discussions about human factors in 3D interaction).

Graphical 3D scene output technology and the use of various media, such as audio (speech, sound), are already relatively mature fields. What is lacking are paradigms, techniques and toolkits for 3D input methods which are integrated into the behavior of virtually real environments. This is the field in which we are concentrating our research.

In the following the conceptual model of the 3D user interface toolkit GIVEN is described. The development of the system GIVEN (Gesture–based Interaction in Virtual ENvironments) started in 1991 [11]. We have tried to improve our concepts based on experiences we have made and to introduce new functionalities ever since.

2.2 Features

The following is a list of features we deemed necessary for GIVEN:

- *Input device independence:* Ideally, it should be possible to interchange the input devices. This has the result of minimizing their effects on the functionality of the system. The system , e.g., should be able to change from using a dataglove to using hand–position–sensing cameras without a major rewrite of the input and interaction drivers.

- *Application and object type independence:* Basic interaction techniques and concepts should be applicable and usable by many types of applications.

- *Open (extensible) architecture:* No fixed set of predefined 3D interaction techniques would be sufficient for all applications. Therefore the toolkit must be open and extensible to allow ease of modification of old modules and the addition of new ones.

- *Individual object behavior:* Objects should have knowledge of how certain gestures will affect them, allowing for individualized behavior. In practice this means that under certain conditions and forces of interaction different objects will behave differently from each other.

- *Gesture dialogue:* Hand gestures should be recognized to achieve various tasks. For instance, pointing means to navigate or "fly" within the 3D environment, and grasping and releasing gestures are used to grab and let go of objects. An interactive gesture recognition editor, in combination with a neural network, makes the process of teaching the system easier.

- *Distributed:* We wanted to avoid the various bottle-necks which occur when a graphics application runs on one workstation. Our aim was to be able to split the three major CPU–intensive parts of the program (the renderer, the collision manager and the application number–crunching) onto three different workstations in a network. This would allow applications to take advantage of idle workstations and supercomputers in a network, while rendering on machines especially made for pretty pictures.

- *Network transparency:* Although the system should be distributed, that fact should be as hidden as possible from the applications programmers and users. From their point of view, all system calls and manipulations should seem to be local, when in reality they are being distributed across a number of nodes in a network.

- *Multi–user:* The system should be created from the beginning with the idea in mind that two or possibly many people will be working together in the same "virtual space."

- *Multi–application:* All the users connected to the same system need not be working together. Therefore, the system should allow various users to work on different applications concurrently.

- *Object–oriented programming interface:* The use of an object–oriented language makes the process of application–building much easier through its various inheritance and encapsulation paradigms. The architecture itself (described below) is highly modular and divided, allowing the separate pieces to be developed and tested individually and then, as smoothly as possible, integrated or reintegrated into the complete system.

It was decided that the best way to achieve this flexibility was to split the system architecture into two parts: a low–level, "micro" grouping of processes or logical units, and a way to coordinate a collection of those groups, called the "macro" architecture. The word, "System" below, refers to these two parts of the architecture taken collectively. Section 2.3 describes the group of processes and the ideas behind the "micro" architecture. The higher, "macro" layer is discussed in Section 2.4.

2.3 The "micro" GIVEN architecture

The lower layer of the GIVEN architecture consists of a group, or "Cluster", of processes which control, or expedite the control of, specific objects (called "Entities") in the shared virtual space. Figure 1 shows this "micro" GIVEN architecture graphically.

Managers

The GIVEN Kernel consists of the various Managers. Managers in GIVEN take care of very specific input, output and dataflow tasks. Each Manager keeps its own database of Entities in a way which is most convenient and logical for itself. For example, the Space Manager, which detects collisions, can decide to store information about polygon Entities in an octree structure, but the Output Manager which is responsible for rendering to the workstation screen could store them in a linked list for speed during rendering. The Managers are designed so that they can be separate processes running on different workstations in a network, or bound together into one

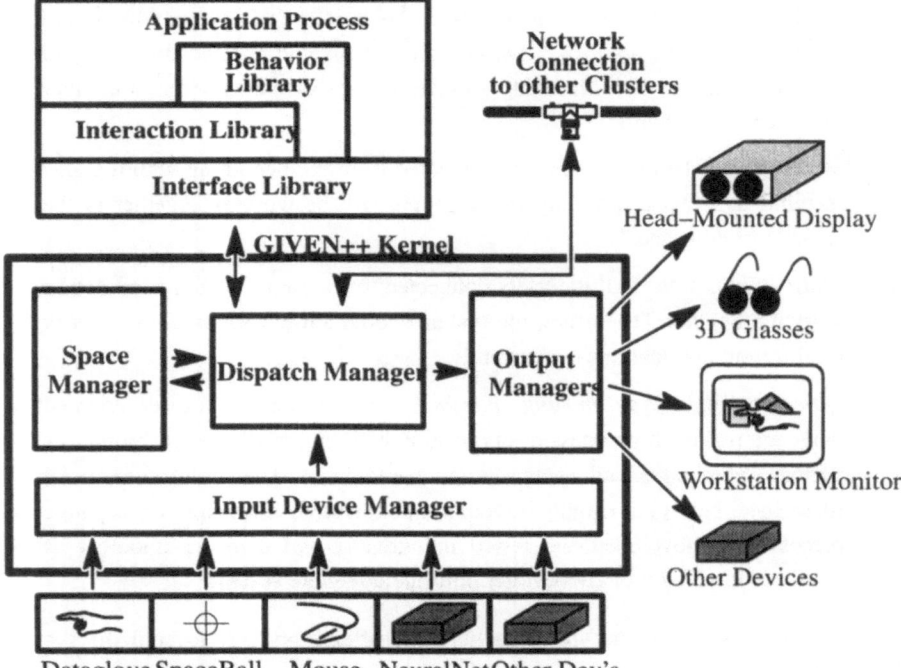

Fig. 1. The "micro" GIVEN architecture: One Cluster

process (so it can run on a PC, for instance). The various Managers and their descriptions follow.

- *Dispatch Manager:* responsible for receiving information from one part of the Cluster and passing it on to other parts (as well as to and from other Clusters);

- *Input Device Manager:* responsible for gathering data from various input devices and giving it to anyone who is interested;

- *Output Manager:* responsible for outputting to a specific output device; e.g., rendering polygons to some graphic device or generating sounds on speakers;

- *Space Manager:* responsible for deciding when collisions have occurred; there is only one Space Manager per complete System; in other words, all Dispatch Managers have to be in contact with the one–and–only Space Manager in the System to send and receive data about collisions;

Libraries

Libraries are collections of classes or routines which make specific use of the general functionality of GIVEN. For instance, GIVEN offers general handling of polygon Entities, such as translation and rotation; a Library, then, could use this functionality to define the behavior of a door: how it would "swing" and stop, etc. After this Library has been written once, all Application programmers could make use of the "Door Library" (but it is more likely that "doors" would be offered as part of a more general Library).

- *Interface Library:* allows the creation and manipulation of data objects; through this library, the data which comes from the Application is moved transparently throughout the entire Cluster and/or System; the Interface Library is described more fully in section 2.5.

- *Interaction Library:* a complete object–oriented framework for the technical specification of components of user interfaces. Each interaction technique can be described as a class in an extendible and configurable hierarchy. All components can be individually designed. Some of these components are as follows: *Prompt* (graphics output to prepare input), *Trigger* (input operation(s) for event firing), *Feedback* (graphics output as an input result), *Semantics* (application–dependent processing instructions for an interaction), and *Dynamics* (control of dynamically changeable dialogue sequences). For the description of complex, Continuous Interactions, a dialogue designer can create a single level of Basic Interactions (using single Triggers or hierarchically structured interactions). The Continuous

Interactions, then, are developed by connecting the input events of separately–specified Basic Interaction objects with predicate–logic or algorithmic–trigger operators (named *and, or, parallel, sequence,* and *repeat*). The result of this is a composite trigger. This approach is based on the work in [12] and [13] and extended for our special requirements.

- *Behavior Library*: contains a predefined set of interactions and objects together with predefined behaviors (e.g., a switch with its behavior when it is touched). The Interaction Library is used for the definition of the interactions. Typical predefined Interactions are those for navigating in 3D–Scenes and simple grabbing/releasing of objects. Application programmers can elect to use or extend these interactions and behaviors or define their own which may be more appropriate for their purposes.

2.4 The "macro" architecture

The "macro" architecture refers to how each Cluster interacts with other Clusters in the System. The Dispatch Managers are responsible for communication within the System. When an Application creates an Entity, it will be broadcast from the original Cluster to the others via the Dispatch Managers. Once it arrives in a foreign Cluster it can be treated like any other Entity, regardless of where it originated. The advantage of this scheme is that Clusters (and, therefore, users) do not need to be physically near

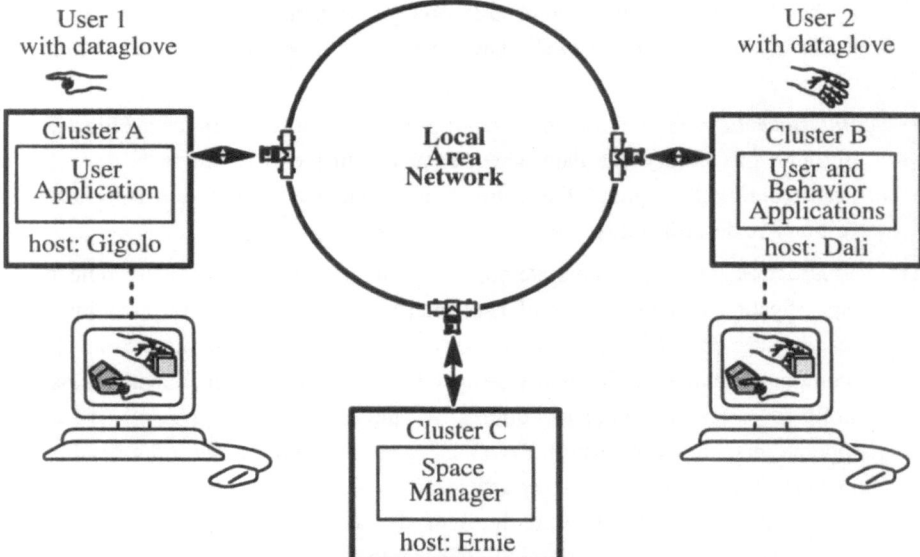

Fig. 2. The "macro" GIVEN architecture

each other in order to work together; they can be as far away as their communications hardware will allow. Figure 2 gives a diagram of this process.

In figure 2, Cluster A contains an Application which is controlled by User 1, who is wearing a dataglove input device. Since this Application is only responsible for the Entities necessary for that user's interaction, this is called a "User Application". Cluster B has the User Application for User 2, but also has an Application which controls Entities directly, without user interference, called a "Behavior Application". Cluster C has no User or Behavior Applications, only the Space Manager (of which there can be only one per System).

If we assume Gigolo and Dali are high–quality graphics workstations and that Ernie is a supercomputer, we can see the advantages of the distributed nature of GIVEN: the computing power of Ernie is used to detect collisions within the System, while Gigolo and Dali can take care of rendering the graphics and manipulating Entities.

2.5 Realizing modularity through the Interface Library

Since we wanted to make the various Managers as modular as possible, we needed an interface technique which was common for all of them. The Interface Library was developed for this purpose. The Interface Library stands between the various parts of the toolkit, allowing them to work almost as if all of them were in the same process.

Just about all Entities begin their lives within the Applications. The Interface Library offers functionality which allows the Application to believe it is working directly with various Managers, when in actuality there could be a number of steps in between. Figures 3 and 4 illustrate this process. Figure 3 shows how the Application "sees" the process of adding a polygon Entity to the System to be rendered by the Output Manager.

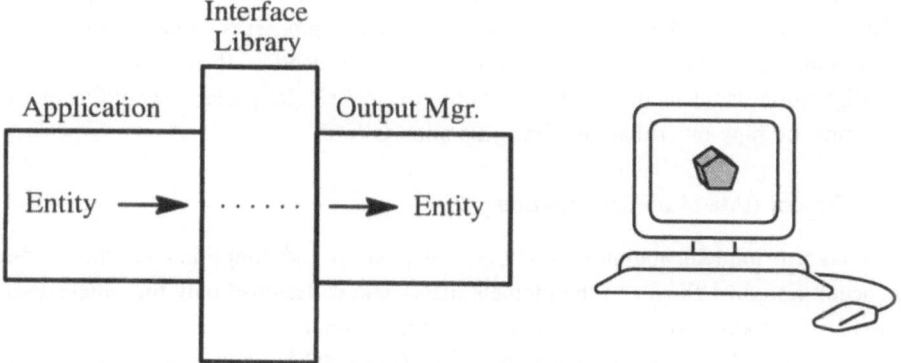

Fig. 3. Path of an Entity from the Application's point of view

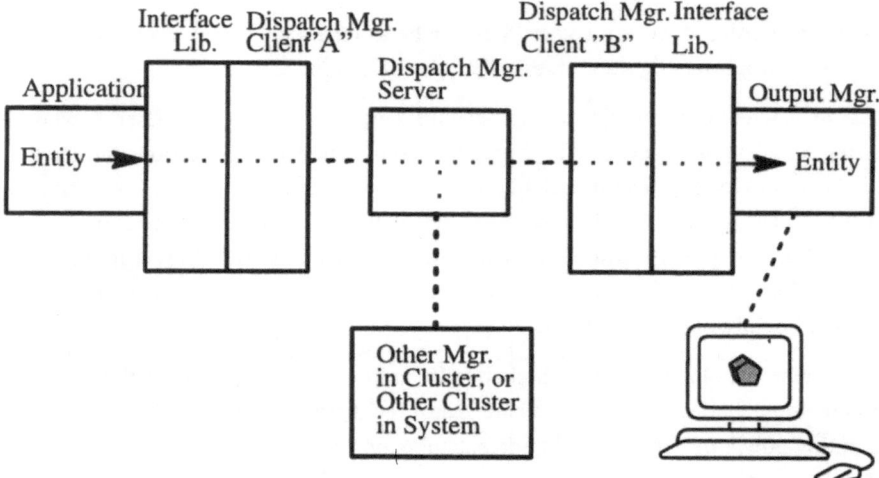

Fig. 4. Actual path of an Entity

However, for a realisation, the Interface Library which is used by the Application can be seen just a front–end for the client–communications part of the Dispatch Manager. The methods which are called by the Application actually send the data, via the Dispatch Manager, to the desired destination. The Dispatch Manager is also responsible for broadcasting the Entity to other Managers and Clusters. Figure 4 shows the actual path of an Entity through the System.

The use of the modular Interface Library above gives us one more advantage, totally for free: the ability to have various runtime configurations just by relinking. Since the Application and the Managers all use the Interface Library to move and manipulate Entities, a decision can be made at any point to link a particular Manager with its Dispatch Manager Client, or to link it directly to the front or back end of the pipeline. This allows any Cluster to be either numerous processes running on many workstations, or just one process running all by itself. If the latter runtime configuration is elected, the functionality of the single process would actually resemble nothing other than the first generation GIVEN.

2.6 Current state of implementation

The current implementation of GIVEN is a reduced and simplified version of the concept described above. At the moment the system is designed only for single–user mode. The toolkit kernel as well as the application are realized in one process. Because of these reasons the development of a Dispatch Manager has been postponed. Nevertheless, multi–user mode will be supported by the end of 1995 and with that all requirements for shared virtual environments are provided.

3 *MuSE* as a GIVEN application

The *MuSE* simulator is an application process of the GIVEN system (see figure 5). All objects of the simulated system are loaded from the *MuSE*–Database and translated into graphical objects in GIVEN. The behavior of the virtual input devices is assigned to the respective objects. While running the simulation, the GIVEN collision checking is only used to detect collisions between an object and the representation of the user (e.g. a hand when the user uses a data glove). Events which are generated by this collision checking (e.g. the grabbing and turning of a steering wheel) are translated to the apropriate values and are delivered to the simulation. Collisions between objects of the physical simulation are not detected by the user interface. Such collisions are, for example, the collision between the truck and a pylon on the street. This is required to keep the physical simulation consistent. The output which is generated by the *MuSE* simulation processes is transmitted to the *MuSE* application process of GIVEN. Objects like the truck itself as well as subobjects like the steering wheel or control lamps have "behaviors" which are not defined in GIVEN itself. Instead, those objects read the values of the simulation output which is used by GIVEN to transform them to their updated state.

3.1 Future work on the VR interface

At the moment, no immersive VR environment with a head mounted display is implemented in *MuSE*. The benefits and drawbacks of immersive VR will be a topic in the future work done in the *MuSE* context because displaying the scene on a flat screen of limited size has several problems (angle of view, perspective etc.). A second topic will be the integration of multimedia information into the VR environment which is stored in the hyper network at the moment. This would enable the user to get information about the simulated system without context switches. Other future work should be done on the extension of the GIVEN implementation of interactions in order to get predefined interaction methods for a wide variety of simulated systems and the development of a toolkit for the interactive construction of virtual environments and their characteristics.

3.2 Future work on *MuSE*

The simulation strategy in *MuSE* is being changed from a synchronous to an event driven simulation. This will eliminate the fixed time steps we have to deal with right now. The basis for the simulation network in *MuSE* is OMG's common request broker architecture (CORBA). We regard this simulation network as an object with an interface to the graphical user interface. The CORBA approach allows us to add one or more user interfaces to the simulation object. Each user interface may present another aspect of the running simulation, each grants its user interactive access to the

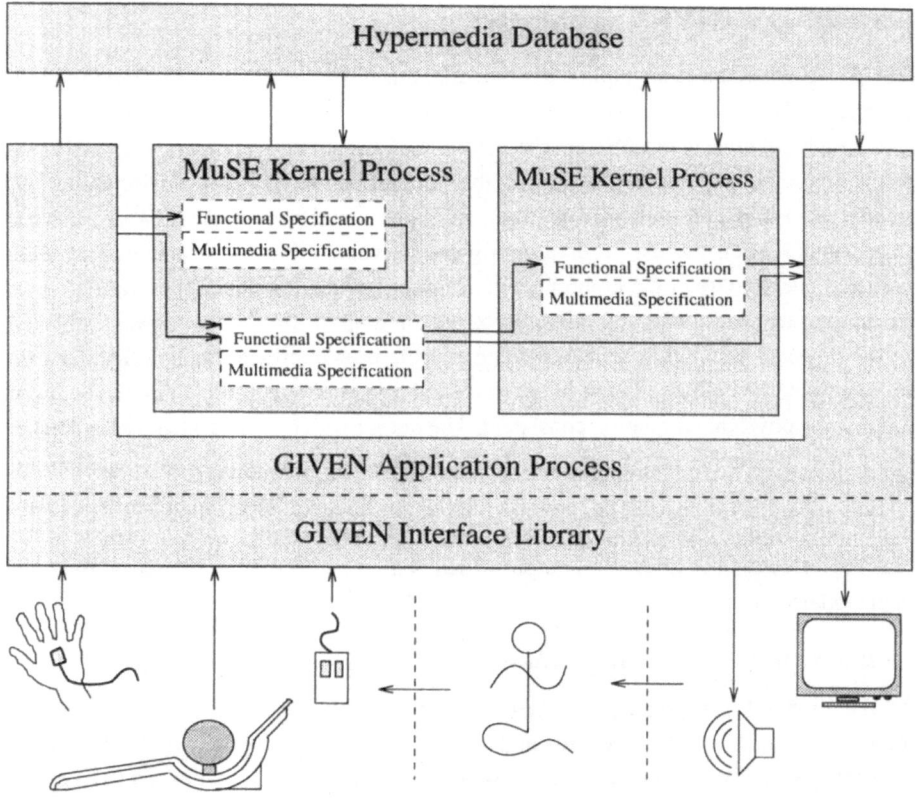

Fig. 5. Combination of the *MuSE* Kernel and GIVEN

simulation. Of course, access to certain simulation parameters has to be moderated in order to avoid conflicts within the simulation itself.

Validation of technical systems plays an important role in the conceptual framework of *MuSE*. Therefore a long term research project is the integration of highly sophisticated methods and tools for validation of technical systems. In this area, we will cooperate with two departments of the mechanical engineering faculty of our university. The aims are to incorporate e.g. product definition standards like STEP into the *MuSE* conceptual framework. Additionally *MuSE* plans to investigate the possible feedback on classical product life cycle models in the area of systems engineering, which will be induced by virtual prototyping tools like *MuSE*.

4 Related work

The "Rubber Rocks" VR environment described in [14] and [15], and the IBM VR DECK described in [16] are similar to the combined *MuSE*/GIVEN system. One of the differences, however, is that the simulation in *MuSE* is much more elaborated because we try to model and simulate complex technical systems. The *MuSE* system is also capable of storing additional information about the simulated system, whereas the IBM system is solely a VR system with the ability to simulate simple physical behavior.

The decoupled simulation model described in [17] is similar to GIVEN concerning the structure of the user interface toolkit, but lacks the simulation capabilities of *MuSE*.

The VR system described in [18] allows the user to create a virtual environment in which he can interact with different objects present. Some of the objects have physical properties, but the simulation of these properties is very restrained and cannot be changed by the user.

The work presented in [19] describes a sophisticated system for constraint based manipulation techniques for objects within virtual environments. This work will be of great importance to *MuSE* in future as it is planned to address further areas of system development. These areas will include interactive construction of systems from predefined parts which can be assembled interactively and interactive changes of the user interface layout of the simulated system in order to enable human factor research.

5 Conclusion

GIVEN was chosen as the toolkit for the simulator *MuSE* because of its 3 dimensional interaction, ease of writing of application code, and flexibility/extensibility. The usefulness and practical applicibility of *MuSE* confirms our belief in Virtual Reality generally as a viable user interface technique, and specifically in our architectural approach to GIVEN.

MuSE and GIVEN together open a whole range of possibilities. Using this combination, simulations of mechanical systems such as special–purpose vehicles and elevators are no longer restricted to 'movies' which can only be watched. The 3D interaction techniques and visualization of GIVEN along with the simulation databases and calculation power of *MuSE* allow the user to actually get into, see and work with the various parts, while they're functioning, as well as answer many difficult "what if " questions: what if this cable is cut? what if the door doesn't close? what if these two buttons are pushed at the same time? etc. And since it is done in a virtual environment, the answers can be found quickly, safely and cheaply. The merging of these two technologies results in a powerful system.

Acknowledgements

The authors would like to thank Prof. Encarnação for his encouragement and for providing an environment that makes this work possible. Also, we thank Dr. Christoph Hornung, Dr. Markus Groß for his insighted comments on this paper, and Dr. Kaisa Väänänen and Constance Belz for proof reading as well as support in the process of writing this paper.

References

1. Jäger, M., Gloger, M., Kaes, S.: SAMPLE – A Functional Language. In: Lectures in Computer Science, volume 328, pp. 202 – 217. Springer, 1988.

2. Deegener, M., Huss, S.A.: Ein Verfahren zur Kopplung standardisierter sequentieller und nebenläufiger Beschreibungssprachen für die Simulation komplexer Systeme. To be published, Technische Hochschule Darmstadt, Fachbereich Informatik, Fachgebiet Entwurfsmethodik und VLSI–Systeme, 1993.

3. Grosse, G., Waldinger, R.: Towards a Theory of Simultaneous Actions. In: European Workshop on Planning, 1991.

4. Quack, J.: Entwicklung eines Systems zur interaktiven Visualisierung und Manipulation von Datenströmen im MuSE–Simulator. Diplomarbeit, Technische Hochschule Darmstadt, Fachbereich Informatik, Fachgebiet Graphisch–Interaktive Systeme, November 1994.

5. Streitz, N.A., Hannemann, J., Thüring, M.: From Ideas and Arguments to Hyperdocuments: Travelling through Activity Spaces. In: Proceedings of the 2nd ACM Conf. on Hypertext (Hypertext'89), pp. 343–364. ACM, November 1989.

6. Streitz, N.A., Haake, J., Hannemann, J., Lemke, A.,Schütt, H., Schuler, W., Thüring, M.: SEPIA: A cooperative Hypermedia Authoring Environment. In: Lucarella D., Nanard J., Nanard M., Paolini P. (eds.): Proceedings of the 4th ACM Conference on Hypertext (ECHT '92), Milano, Italy, pp. 11–22. ACM Press, New York, November 1992.

7. Haake, J.M., Wilson, B.: Supporting Collaborative Writing of Hyperdocuments in SEPIA. In: Mantei M.M. (ed.): Proceedings of the ACM 1992 Conference on Computer Supported Cooperative Work, Toronto, Ontario, pp. 138–146, ACM Press, New York, November 1992.

8. Mercedes Benz AG. Betriebsanleitung UNIMOG 437. Mercedes–Benz AG, Werk Gaggenau, Kundendienst Unimog, 1989.

9. Foley, J.D., Wallace,V.L., Chan,P.: The Human Factors of Computer Graphics Interactive Techniques. IEEE Computer Graphics and Applications, November 1984.

10. Foley, J.D.: Interfaces for Advanced Computing. Scientific American, October 1987, pp. 127–135.

11. Böhm, K., Hübner, W., Väänänen, K.: GIVEN: Gesture Driven Interactions in Virtual Worlds – A Toolkit Approach to 3D Interactions. In: Interfaces to Real and Virtual Worlds, Montpellier, France, 1992.

12. Hübner, W., Lancastre, H.: Towards an Object–Oriented Interaction Model for Graphical User Interfaces. In: Computer Graphics Forum, Vol. 8, No. 3, 1989.

13. Hübner, W.: Entwurf Graphischer Benutzerschnittstellen. PhD, Springer, 1990.

14. Codella, C., Jalili, R., Koved, L., Lewis, J.B., Ling, D.T., Lipscomb, J.S., Rabenhorst, D.A., Wang, C.P., Norton, A., Sweeney, P., Turk, G.: Interactive Simulation in a Multi–Person Virtual World. In: Proceedings of CHI 1992. ACM, May 1992.

15. Lewis, J.B, Koved, L., Ling, D.T.: Dialogue Structures for Virtual Worlds. In: Robertson S.P., Olson G.M., Olson J.S. (eds.): Reaching through technology – CHI 1991 Conference Proceedings, Human Factors in Computing Systems, ACM, May 1991.

16. Codella, C., Jalili, R., Koved, L., Lewis, J.B.: A Toolkit for Developing Multi–User, Distributed Virtual Environments. Research report, to be published, IBM Research Division, T.J. Watson Research Center, February 1993.

17. Shaw, C., Liang, J., Green, M., Sun, Y.: The Decoupled Simulation Model for Virtual Reality Systems. In: Proceedings of CHI 1992. ACM, May 1992.

18. Nomura, J., Ohata, H., Imamura, K., Schultz, R.J.: Virtual Space Decision Support System and Its Application to Consumer Showrooms. In: Kunii T.L. (ed.): Visual Computing – Integrating Computer Graphics with Computer Vision, CGS CG International Series, pp. 183 – 195, Springer–Verlag, 1992.

19. Fernando, T., Fa, M., Dew, P.M., Munlin, M.: Constraint–based 3D Manipulation Techniques within Virtual Environments. In: Earnshaw R., Jones H., Vince J. (eds.): Proceedings of "Virtual Reality Applications", Leeds, June 1994, British Computer Society.

Appendix: Colour Figures

Views of the virtual right arm as a box with shadows is approached (Slater et al., Plates 1, 2)

294

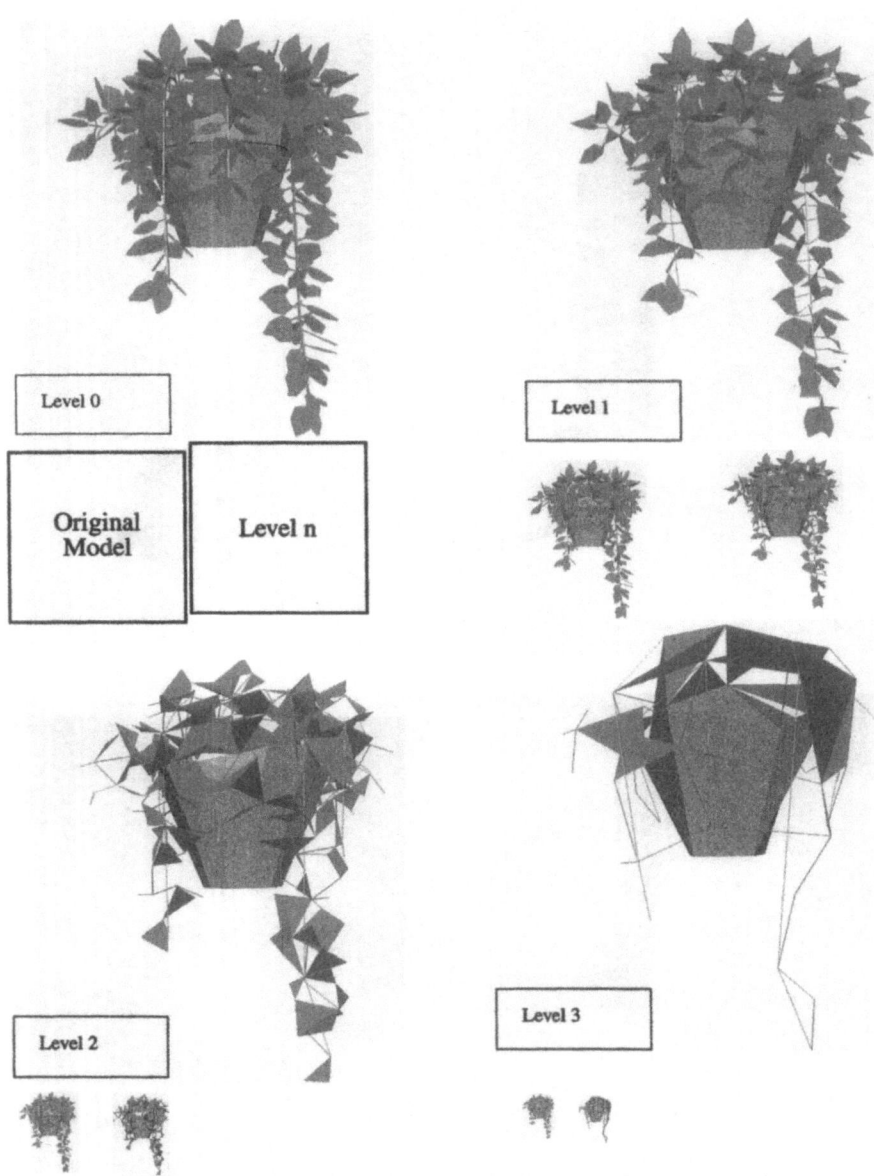

Levels of detail of plant (6064, 3674, 1225, 339 polygons/lines) (Schaufler and Stürzlinger, Fig. 1)

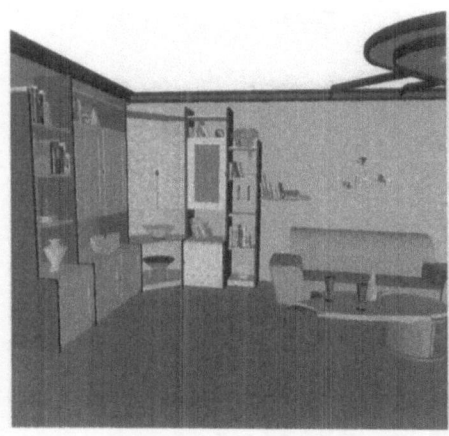
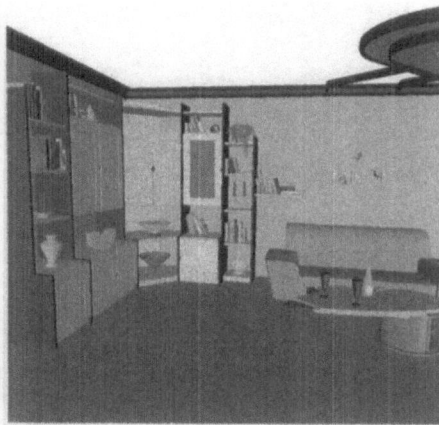

Living room left with, right without LODs (left 6810, right 13847 polygons) (Schaufler and Stürzlinger, Fig. 2)

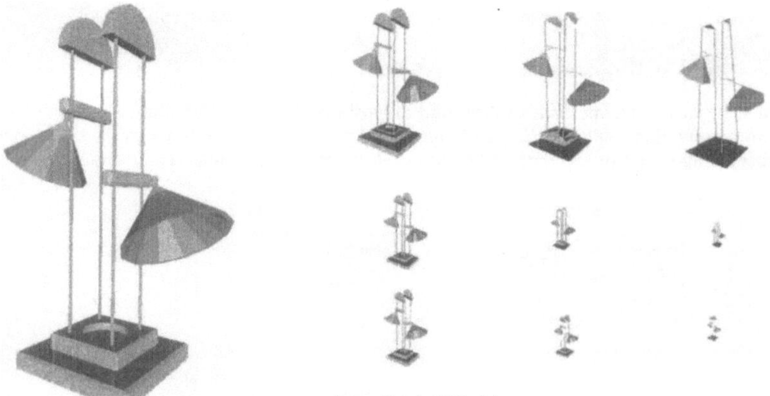

Lamp Original Model

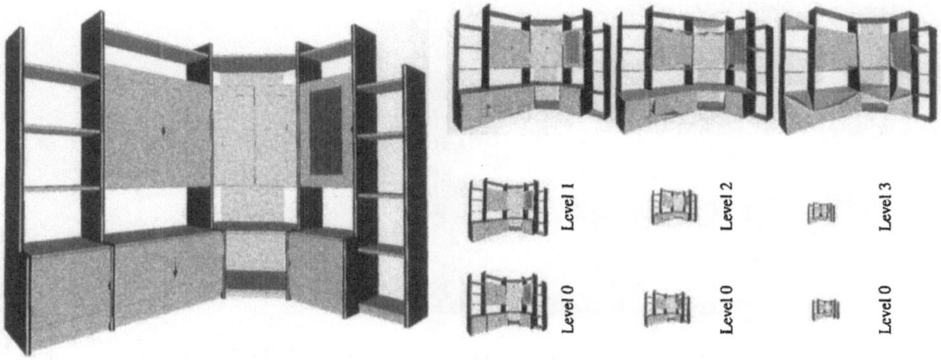

Shelf Original Model

Level of detail close and distant (Schaufler and Stürzlinger, Fig. 3)

Overall view of an enzyme and a substratum (Trypsin & Arginin). Ball-and-stick representation and surface representation combined. $\subset$ and shape of the molecules is also shown by the shadows which are implemented by means of precomputed textures (Haase et al., Color plate 1)

Virtual menu offering several choices for visualization. The menu is invoked by a certain gesture of the data glove. Selection of a menu item is performed by means of the index finger of the glove echo (Haase et al., Color plate 2)

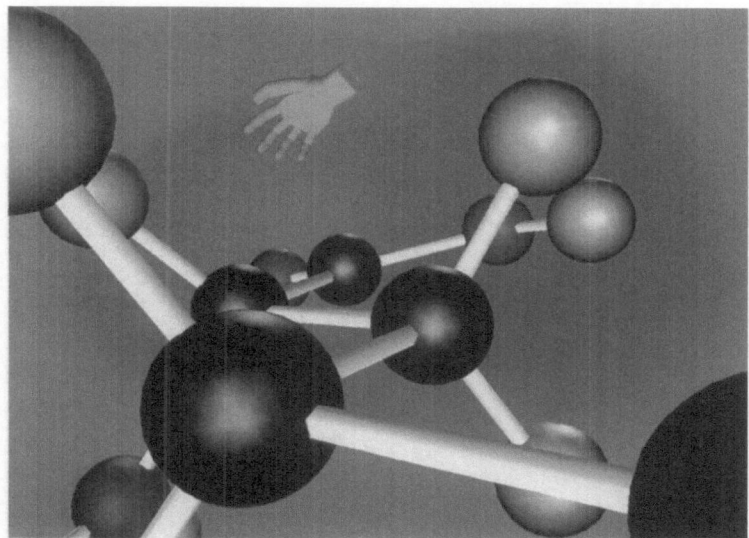

Detail view of an Arginin molecule in ball-and-stick representation. The "sticks" only consist of 5 surfaces; smooth appearance is achieved by Gouraud shading. Spheres have varying resolution depending on their distance from the viewer (level of detail) (Haase et al., Color plate 3)

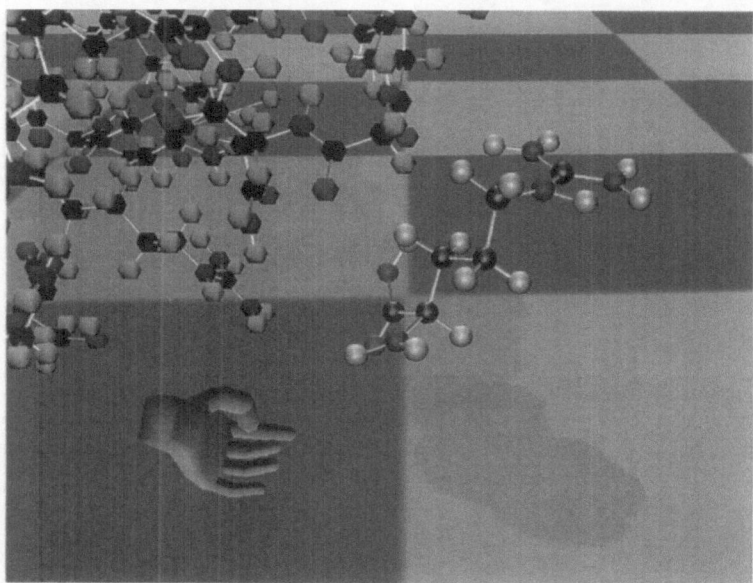

Two molecules in different resolution. Also note the shadows on the floor (Haase et al., Color plate 4)

View from a "pocket" of the Trypsin molecule towards the approaching Arginin. Note that the smaller Arginin surface is rendered without artifacts (due to sorted triangle strips) while in the Trypsin surface there are z buffer problems (e.g., upper left corner of image) (Haase et al., Color plate 5)

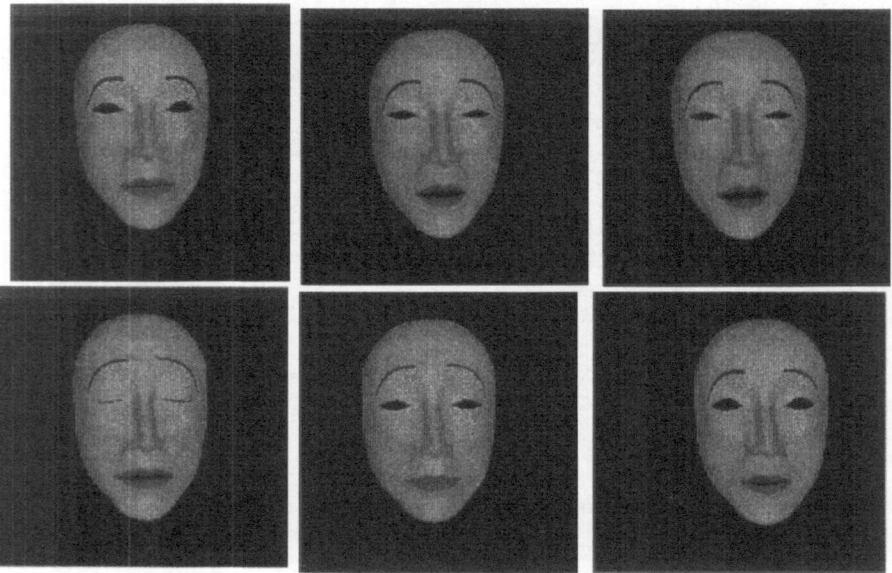

"Amplifier" (Pelachaud and Prevost, Fig. 2)

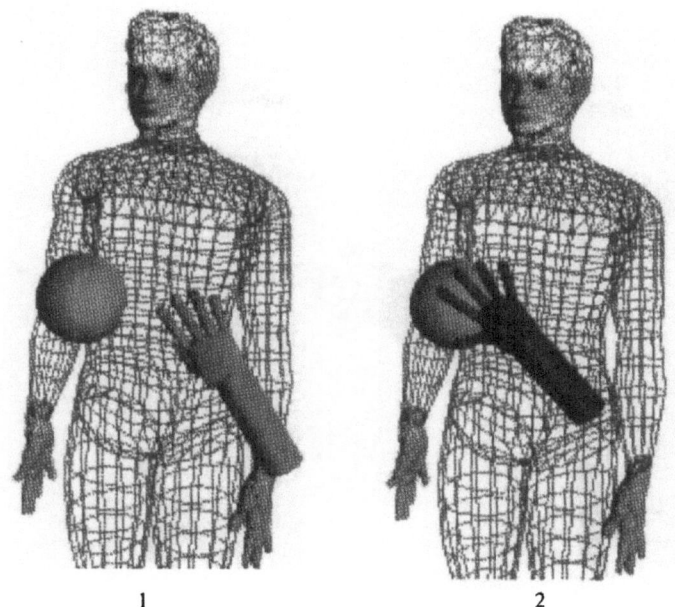

1   2

The operator grasps the ball and...

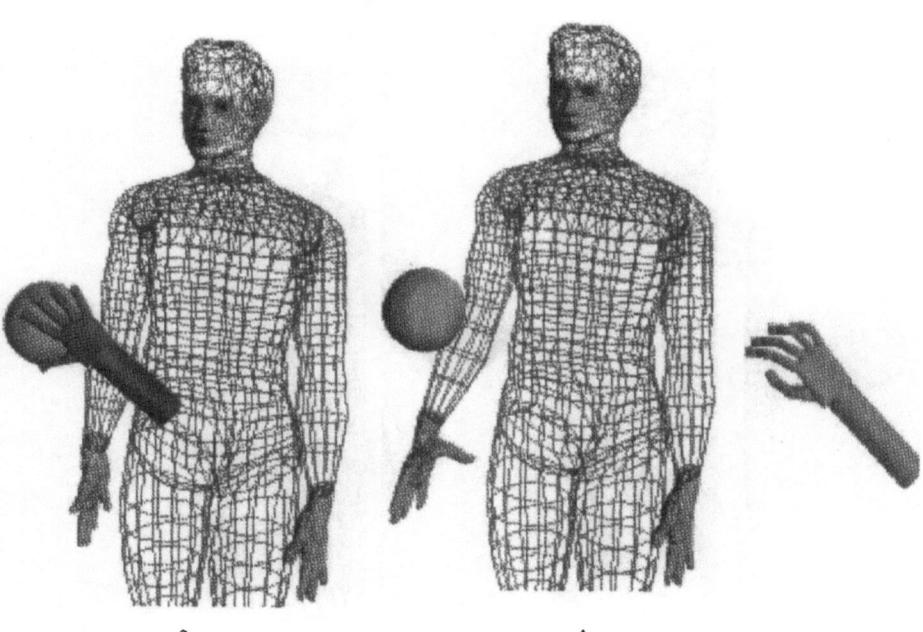

3   4

hands it to the virtual actor who...   (Rezzonico et al.)

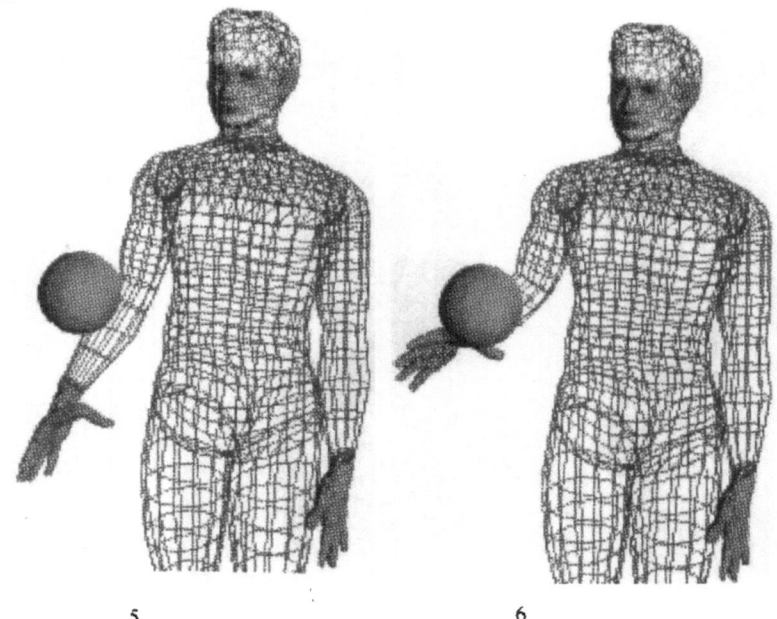

5 6

...automatically grasps it.

7 8

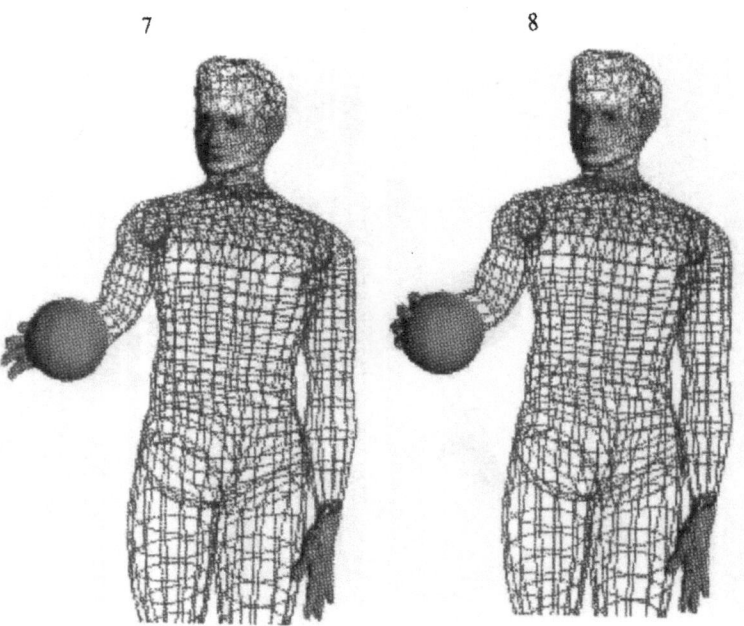

(Rezzonico et al.)

Scene from the inside of the Ford Taurus cab of the Iowa Driving Simulator (Cremer et al., Fig. 5)

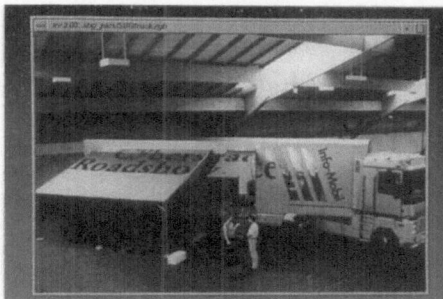

Roadshow truck with VR equipment
(Astheimer and Felger, Fig. 1)

Presentation stage with action point (left) and
stereoscopic rear projection (right)
(Astheimer and Felger, Fig. 2)

Helicopter flight around the virtual truck
(Astheimer and Felger, Fig. 4)

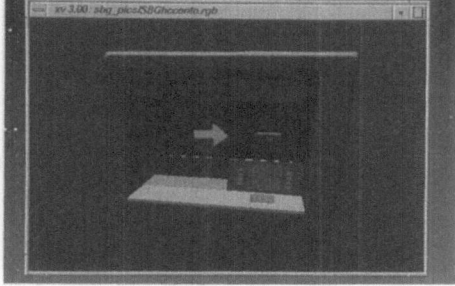

Contomat (teller machine)
(Astheimer and Felger, Fig. 5)

302

Tunnel flight (Astheimer and Felger, Fig. 6)

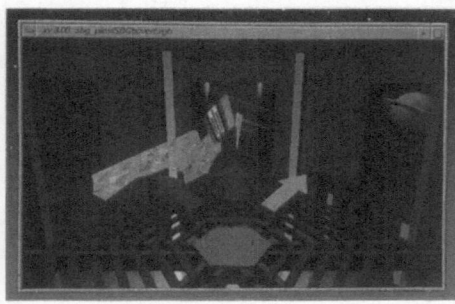

Switch room (tower of fate)
(Astheimer and Felger, Fig. 7)

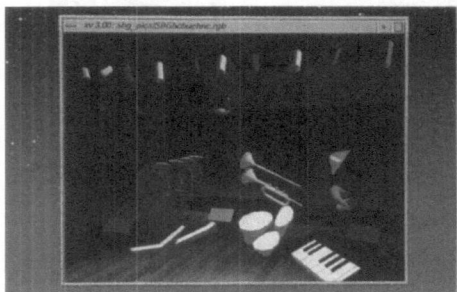

Jungle (Astheimer and Felger, Fig. 8)

Stage (Astheimer and Felger, Fig. 9)

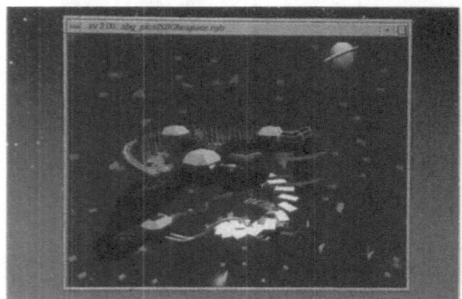

Space labyrinth (Astheimer and Felger, Fig. 10)

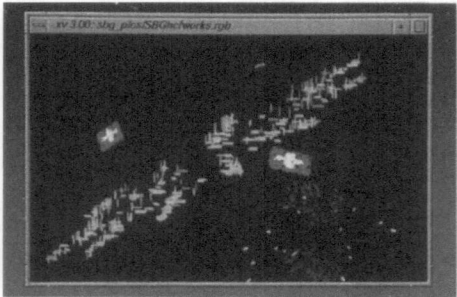

Firework (Astheimer and Felger, Fig. 11)

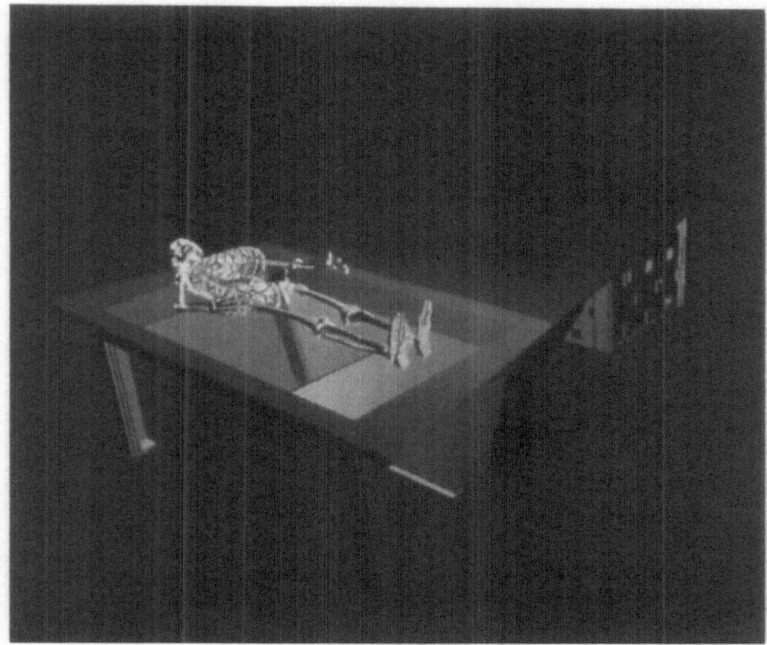

Set-up for a stereoscopic display of virtua' ' ;ects (Fröhlich et al., Fig. 1)

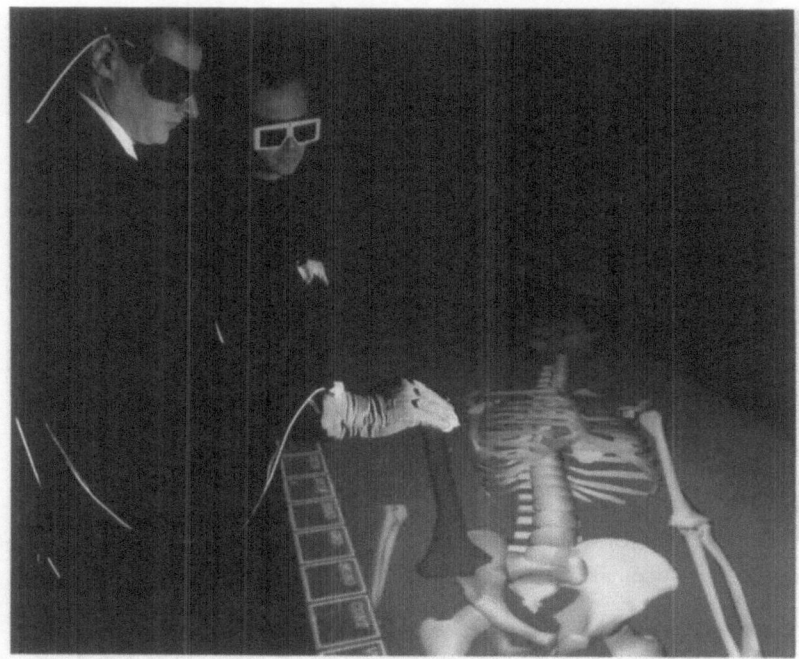

Cooperative work of a physician and a student (Fröhlich et al., Fig. 2)

Examination of the blood flow in a human heart (Fröhlich et al., Fig. 3)

Virtual windtunnel scenario for car manufacturing applications (aerodynamical study model ASMO-II) (Fröhlich et al., Fig. 4)

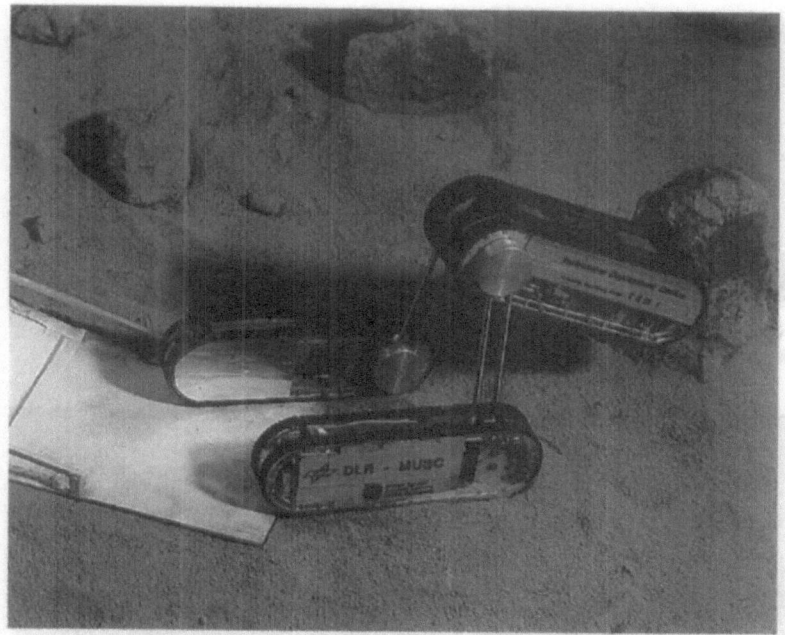

IDD TEM1 implemented by DLR and Uni: ...sburg (Fröhlich et al., Fig. 5)

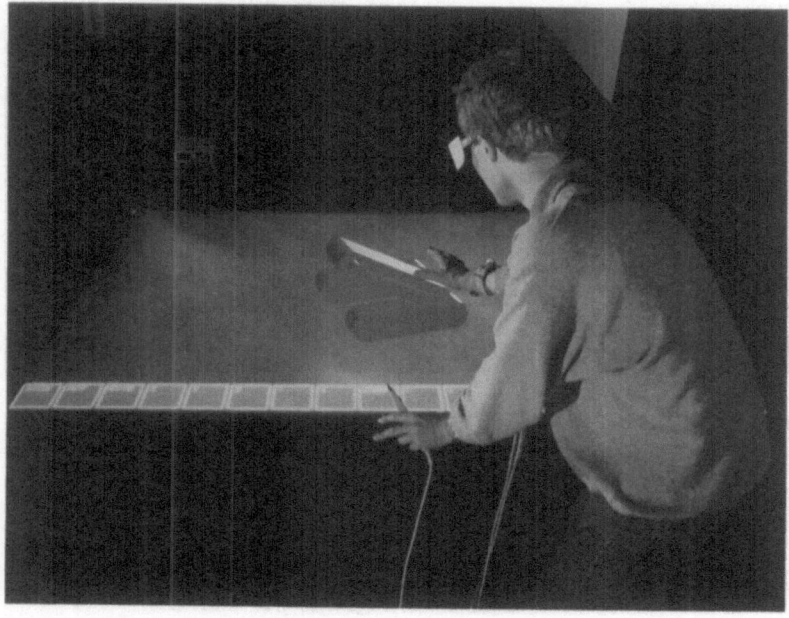

The computer model of the IDD (Fröhlich et al., Fig. 6)

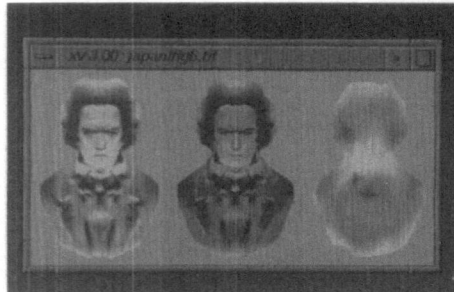

Bust of Beethoven (original, face normal 80%, point 9%) (Astheimer and Göbel, Fig. 3)

The virtual model of IGD's new building (Astheimer and Göbel, Fig. 4)

Illumination at a virtual working plane (Astheimer and Göbel, Fig. 5)

The virtual city of Frankfurt (Astheimer and Göbel, Fig. 6)

Presentation in Frankfurt (Astheimer and Göbel, Fig. 7)

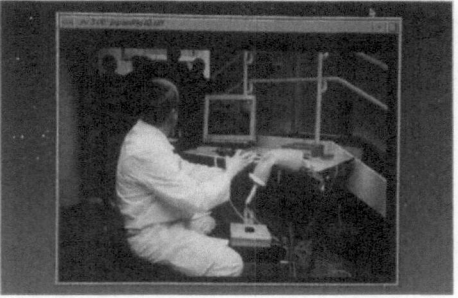

Virtual wind tunnel (Astheimer and Göbel, Fig. 8)

Overall view of an enzyme and a substratum
(Trypsin & Arginin) (Astheimer and Göbel, Fig. 9)

On-line inverse kinematics simulation
(Astheimer and Göbel, Fig. 10)

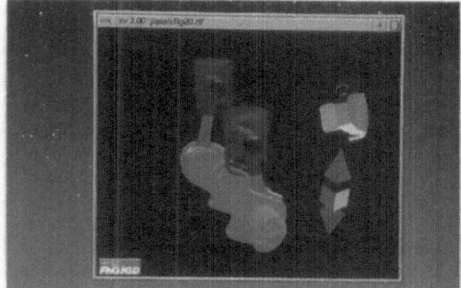

Rotating crank shaft
(Astheimer and Göbel, Fig. 11)

Jungle world (Astheimer and Göbel, Fig. 12)

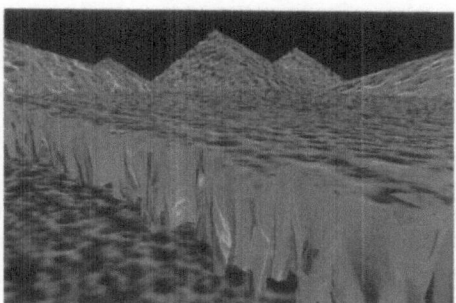

Macroscopic view of a printing plate
(Astheimer and Göbel, Fig. 13)

Philippe Palanque, Rémi Bastide (eds.)

Design, Specification and Verification of Interactive Systems '95

Proceedings of the Eurographics Workshop
in Toulouse, France, June 7–9, 1995

1995. 153 figures. X, 370 pages. ISBN 3-211-82739-0
Soft cover DM 118,–, öS 826,–. (Eurographics)

Twenty-one contributions cover the different aspects of interactive systems, from
formal user modelling to formal techniques for prototyping, and describe the state-of-
the-art on these topics, also giving new directions for future research.
The book is an obligatory piece of literature for all scientists working in the formal
aspects of the interactive systems field, but it is also valuable for the practitioner
involved in the design of reliable interactive systems.

Demetri Terzopoulos, Daniel Thalmann (eds.)

Computer Animation and Simulation '95

Proceedings of the Eurographics Workshop
in Maastricht, The Netherlands, September 2–3, 1995

1995. 156 partly coloured figures. VIII, 235 pages. ISBN 3-211-82738-2
Soft cover DM 89,–, öS 625,–. (Eurographics)

The sixteen papers in this volume present novel animation techniques and animation
systems that simulate the dynamics and interactions of physical objects (solid, fluid,
and gaseous) as well as the behaviors of living systems such as plants, lower animals,
and humans (growth and metamorphosis, motion control, locomotion, etc.). The book
vividly demonstrates the confluence of animation and simulation, a leading edge of
computer graphics research that is providing animators with sophisticated new algorithms for synthesizing dynamic scenes.

Prices are subject to change without notice

Springer-Verlag Wien New York

Sachsenplatz 4–6, P.O.Box 89, A-1201 Wien · 175 Fifth Avenue, New York, NY 10010, USA
Heidelberger Platz 3, D-14197 Berlin · 3-13, Hongo 3-chome, Bunkyo-ku, Tokyo 113, Japan

Riccardo Scateni, Jarke J. van Wijk, Pietro Zanarini (eds.)

Visualization in Scientific Computing '95

Proceedings of the Eurographics Workshop
in Chia, Italy, May 3–5, 1995

1995. 110 partly coloured figures. VII, 161 pages. ISBN 3-211-82729-3
Soft cover DM 85,–, öS 595,–. (Eurographics)

13 contributions cover a wide range of topics, ranging from detailed algorithmic studies to searches for new metaphors. The reader will find state-of-the-art results and techniques in this discipline, which he can use to find solutions for his visualization problems.

Patrick M. Hanrahan, Werner Purgathofer (eds.)

Rendering Techniques '95

Proceedings of the Eurographics Workshop
in Dublin, Ireland, June 12–14, 1995

1995. 198 partly coloured figures. XI, 372 pages. ISBN 3-211-82733-1
Soft cover DM 118,–, öS 826,–. (Eurographics)

31 contributions give an overview on hierarchical radiosity, Monte Carlo radiosity, wavelet radiosity, nondiffuse radiosity, radiosity performance improvements, ray tracing, reconstruction techniques, volume rendering, illumination, use interface aspects, and importance sampling. Also included are two invited papers by James Arvo and Alain Fournier.

Prices are subject to change without notice

Springer-Verlag Wien New York

Sachsenplatz 4–6, P.O.Box 89, A-1201 Wien · 175 Fifth Avenue, New York, NY 10010, USA
Heidelberger Platz 3, D-14197 Berlin · 3-13, Hongo 3-chome, Bunkyo-ku, Tokyo 113, Japan

Martin Göbel, Heinrich Müller, Bodo Urban (eds.)

Visualization in Scientific Computing

1995. 150 figures. VIII, 238 pages. ISBN 3-211-82633-5
Soft cover DM 118,–, öS 826,–. (Eurographics)

Visualization is the most important approach to understand the huge amount of data produced in today's computational and experimental sciences. Selected contributions treat topics of particular interest in current research, for example visualization of multidimensional data and flows, time control, interaction, and volume visualization. Readers may profit in getting insight in state-of-the-art techniques which might help to solve their visualization problems.

Wolfgang Herzner, Frank Kappe (eds.)

Multimedia/Hypermedia
in Open Distributed Environments

Proceedings of the Eurographics Symposium
in Graz, Austria, June 6–9, 1994

1994. 105 figures. VIII, 330 pages. ISBN 3-211-82587-8
Soft cover DM 118,–, öS 826,–. (Eurographics)

This book represents the results from the Eurographics symposium on "Multimedia/Hypermedia in Open Distributed Environments", June 6–9, 1994, Graz, Austria. Its six sessions "Standards and Standards Exploitation", "Demonstrations", "Tools", "Hypermedia and Authoring", "Architectures", and "CSCW and Information Services" give a comprehensive overview about current research and development, including the future mm/hm standards MHEG and PREMO. The reader will profit in getting up-to-date information about the current trends in (the development of) mm/hm services and applications in open, distributed environments.

Prices are subject to change without notice

Springer-Verlag Wien New York

Sachsenplatz 4–6, P.O.Box 89, A-1201 Wien · 175 Fifth Avenue, New York, NY 10010, USA
Heidelberger Platz 3, D-14197 Berlin · 3-13, Hongo 3-chome, Bunkyo-ku, Tokyo 113, Japan

Springer-Verlag
and the Environment

WE AT SPRINGER-VERLAG FIRMLY BELIEVE THAT AN international science publisher has a special obligation to the environment, and our corporate policies consistently reflect this conviction.

WE ALSO EXPECT OUR BUSINESS PARTNERS – PRINTERS, paper mills, packaging manufacturers, etc. – to commit themselves to using environmentally friendly materials and production processes.

THE PAPER IN THIS BOOK IS MADE FROM NO-CHLORINE pulp and is acid free, in conformance with international standards for paper permanency.